QP
301
F77   Frontiers of
1983   exercise biology

$31.95   72504

Frontiers of Exercise Biology

**Big Ten Body of Knowledge
Symposium Series, Volume 13**

Editors:

Katarina T. Borer, Ph.D.
D.W. Edington, Ph.D.
Timothy P. White, Ph.D.

University of Michigan

Human Kinetics Publishers, Inc.
Champaign, Illinois 61820

Publications Director
Richard Howell

Production Directors
Margery Brandfon
Kathryn Gollin Marshak

Editorial Staff
Dana Finney
Peg Goyette

Typesetters
Sandra Meier
Carol McCarty

Text Layout
Lezli Harris

Cover Design
Jack Davis

Library of Congress Catalog Number: 83-81601

ISBN: 0-931250-49-8

Human Kinetics Publishers, Inc.
Box 5076, Champaign, IL 61820

Contents

Big Ten body of knowledge symposia series

In 1972 The University of Michigan hosted the sixth in the then-new series of "Body of Knowledge Symposia" sponsored by the Big Ten Physical Education Directors. Today marks the beginning of the thirteenth in the series, once again hosted by The University of Michigan.

This symposium series began in 1968 as a project of the Big Ten Physical Education Directors (originally known as the Western Conference Association). The primary purpose of these symposia is to encourage the development and dissemination of knowledge considered basic to a "discipline" of physical education. The symposia provide a forum for the exploration of new concepts and ideas at the "cutting edge" of knowledge in an effort to accelerate the quest for excellence in the profession and provide direction for developing the potential of physical education in the service of humankind.

There is no doubt that these symposia have had significant effect on people and programs in the Big Ten Conference and throughout the profession at large. With so many conferences, conventions, symposia, and seminars available today, it seems unbelievable that only 14 years ago few opportunities existed for specialists in the physical education subdisciplines to share their research with colleagues in an open forum.

The formally authorized symposium series was an outgrowth of several years of discussion and planning led by King McCristal of the University of Illinois and the late Arthur A. Daniels of Indiana University. Seed money for the project was obtained from the Big Ten Committee on Institutional Cooperation, a consortium of all Big Ten Universities and the University of Chicago. The original format made provision for symposia to be held on topics including the Sociology of Sport, Motor Learning, Biomechanics, History of Sport and Physical Education, Exercise Physiology, and Administrative Theory in Physical Education. Subsequently, special symposia were approved for the examination of other topics including Physical Education for the Handicapped, Measurement and Evaluation, Neural Processing and Motor Control, and Motor Development.

Table 1 presents a summary of each symposium topic and the host university for the entire series.

The proceedings of the first six symposia were published by and are still available from The Athletic Institute, 200 Castlewood Drive, North Palm Beach, Florida 33408. The seventh and eighth symposia proceedings were printed by the Indiana State Board of Health, 1330 West Michigan, Indianapolis, Indiana; the ninth by Academic Press, and the

Table 1

1968	Sociology of Sport	University of Wisconsin
1969	Motor Learning	University of Iowa
1970	Biomechanics	Indiana University
1971	History of Sport	Ohio State University
1972	Physiology of Fitness and Exercise	University of Minnesota
1973	Administrative Theory	University of Michigan
1974	Physical Education for the Handicapped	University of Iowa
1975	Measurement and Evaluation	Indiana University
1976	Motor Control and Learning	University of Wisconsin
1978	Sport Sociology	University of Minnesota
1979	Motor Skill Development	University of Iowa
1980	Biomechanics	Indiana University

tenth are available from Leisure Press, West Point, New York. The papers from the eleventh symposium were published in book form by John Wiley & Sons, Baffins Lane, Chichester Sussex PO19 1UD, England. The proceedings of last year's biomechanics symposium were published by the Indiana State Board of Health and are available through the School of Health, Physical Education, and Recreation of Indiana University.

A great many people and several organizations have made extremely valuable contributions to the development and support of this project. For the first six years or so the Athletic Institute made substantial contributions in support of the symposium series in addition to publishing and distributing the proceedings. The Indiana State Board of Health has been a faithful supporter of these symposia, publishing the 1974, 1975, and 1980 proceedings. All of the host universities have been generous in underwriting the symposia held on their respective campuses. In many cases several departments within institutions have made separate contributions supporting specific symposia.

As official representatives of the Big Ten Physical Education Body of Knowledge Symposium Committee, we would like to express our gratitude to all individuals on The University of Michigan campus whose generous contributions of time, talent, and financial support have made it possible to present this symposium. Of course, we are grateful to all of the Big Ten institutions whose annual contributions provide the financial foundation of this project.

SYMPOSIUM STEERING COMMITTEE
Mary Beyrer
Dee Edington
Dale Hanson
Margaret J. Safrit
Wynn F. Updyke, Chair

Preface

The study of Exercise Biology at the cellular level is less than 25 years old. In this short period of time interest in this area has spread to several continents and continues to expand. Both experienced and newly trained scientists have kept pace with the leading edge of science through the use of sophisticated analytical techniques.

At The University of Michigan we felt a need to provide a forum for the expression of current views and current perspectives related to Exercise Biology. We invited selected leaders who are actively involved in research on current and controversial topics of significant interest. The scope of the book is limited to muscle physiology, microvasculature, endocrine physiology, neural function, and the interactions between these disciplines. Professor V.R. Edgerton was chosen as the keynote speaker in honor of his accomplishments in the field, his ability to synthesize knowledge from the various areas, and his thought-stimulating projections for the future.

With the continued growing interest in exercise and healthy lifestyles, we have an urgent need for a broader and deeper base of scientific knowledge in Exercise Biology. The results of this symposium have "applied" as well as "basic" implications, which is inherent to the nature of Exercise Biology. These proceedings should be of interest to scholars and graduate students seeking the forefront of knowledge and to those professionals who desire a scientific basis for their work.

We thank the speakers and participants for their enthusiastic interaction. Financial support was provided by the Department of Physical Education at Michigan, the CIC Body of Knowledge series, Applied Electrochemistry, Inc., and Cybex Division of Lumex, Inc. We thank Janet Larson and Kay Wilkinson who provided supportive assistance, without which the organization of the symposium and the preparation of manuscripts would have been impossible. Finally, thanks is extended to Human Kinetics Publishers for their editorial and production professionalism. The order of editors was established alphabetically.

K.T.B.
D.W.E.
T.P.W.

Section 1
Skeletal muscle

Skeletal muscle is a tissue providing force generation, usually across a joint or series of joints, thereby enabling movement. This movement allows the organism to maintain vegetative and homeostatic functions and provides the basis to do work, participate in sports, and interact socially. In short, skeletal muscle is a tissue that allows function in a manner consistent with survival in an environment.

Skeletal muscle fibers display morphological and functional adaptations to a chronic change in use. Of particular interest to many exercise biologists have been the responses of skeletal muscle fibers to acute and chronic changes in functional demands induced by exercise stress or surgical removal of synergistic muscles. Some exercise biologists are interested in these data from a practical performance-oriented framework, whereas others are intrigued by the basic science questions. The primarily descriptive studies of these changes are now starting to be directed toward an understanding of the mechanisms underlying these adaptations. Future studies on the mechanisms by which exercise alters structure and function of skeletal muscle will benefit in part by a focus on several of the disease states facing society. Integrating comprehensive analyses of skeletal muscle together with synergistic systems, such as cardiovascular and neuroendocrine function, seems requisite for continued progress in exercise biology.

The introductory chapter by John Faulkner directs the reader to the fundamental question of what constitutes the stimulus inducing adaptation. Motor unit adaptations to increased or decreased activity levels need to be evaluated in light of the frequency, intensity, and duration of the change in functional load. It is likely that as the adaptation proceeds, the magnitude of the steady exercise stimulus as perceived by the motor unit will diminish and the degree of adaptation will be attenuated.

The chapter by Bill Gonyea reviews many of the issues of adult muscle growth, especially as it pertains to resistance exercise. He discusses the evidence indicating that hypertrophic and longitudinally divided fibers are found in control muscles of cats and with increased frequency following prolonged resistance exercise. Phil Gollnick and co-workers evaluate experimental techniques and review potential mechanisms underlying changes in muscle size in response to selected exercise and surgical interventions. They address the uncertainty about whether the number of fibers can be altered as a result of changes in the state of physical activity.

The contractile characteristics of skeletal muscle fibers have interested exercise biologists for decades, with numerous reports describing contractile properties of muscle isolated in situ or in vitro. An expanding number of research laboratories are making progress in understanding the neuromuscular regulation of force and shortening velocity characteristics of muscle fibers in vivo during well defined activities. Others are correlating the functional dimensions with the myoelectric signals from skeletal muscle. Reggie Edgerton and colleagues describe some of the architectural factors that determine force and velocity of contracting skeletal muscle and the adaptability of the neuromuscular system to perturbations. In addition, these authors emphasize the need to increase our understanding of the adaptive-inducing agents or events that occur in those models.

One contemporary approach to studying the mechanism of muscle cell hypertrophy is exemplified by the experiments of Herman Vandenberg and Seymour Kaufman. These investigators have examined membrane transport of amino acids in muscle fiber cells stretched in culture. Their data indicate that stretching increases membrane transport of amino acids, activates sodium pumps, and may contribute to muscle fiber hypertrophy in tissue culture.

Bob Beyer has integrated extensive literature on the regulation of connective tissue proteins during aging. Future directions for research on the effects of exercise in reversing and delaying the connective tissue changes that accompany aging are suggested.

The contributions of microvascular function to muscle performance has long been at issue in exercise biology. Brian Duling reviews the idealized model of microcirculation which is the basis for much of the thought regarding tissue oxygen transport. Based on his elegant experiments using intravital microscopy at the level of a single muscle fiber and the microvasculature, he reveals the more realistic complexities of striated muscle microcirculation and enhances our understanding of the limits to tissue oxygenation during exercise.

Over 100 years ago William Gaskell documented that skeletal muscle blood flow increased concomitant with exercise. With his rudimentary techniques by today's standards, he demonstrated the exercise hyperemic response, but stated the mechanism by which this increase in blood flow occurred was not understood. Harvey Sparks has been at the forefront in exploring the neural, humoral, and myogenic mechanisms controlling blood flow during exercise. His studies reveal that the relative importance of each of the several vasodilators depends on the exercise pattern, duration and intensity of exercise, and the muscle fiber type. He also describes the lines of evidence regarding adenosine as the mediator of sustained exercise hyperemia in skeletal muscle.

The nature of the stimulus
for adaptation

John A. Faulkner
University of Michigan

Charles Darwin's evolutionary concept of adaptation focusing on the role of adaptation in the survival of species was not helpful to physiologists. Physiologists deal with adaptations that occur during the lifespan of an organism and rarely do they have evidence for the survival value of adaptations. Claude Bernard and Walter B. Cannon modified the concept of physiological adaptation during their work on homeostasis of the internal environment and Joseph Barcroft applied the concept to adaptations in response to the external environment. Historical uses of the term adaptation (24) have culminated in the current views expressed by Prosser (32), Selye (35), and Hochochka and Somers (19). For exercise biologists, adaptation is defined in terms of altered structure or function in response to endurance conditioning, strength conditioning, stretch, or immobilization. The emphasis is on adaptations that result in an essential constancy of the internal environment and improved function in response to changing environmental demands.

Levels of organization

Many exercise biologists study adaptation by measuring oxygen consumption ($\dot{V}O_2$), minute ventilation ($\dot{V}_E$), and cardiac output ($\dot{Q}$) of sub-

LEVELS OF ORGANIZATION

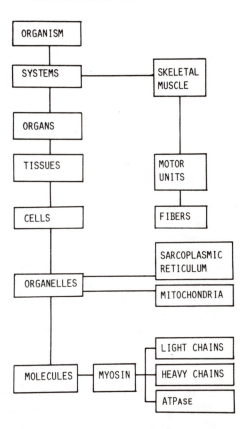

Figure 1—The levels of organization of the total organism at which an adaptive response can occur. Skeletal muscle is presented as an example: Architectural changes can occur at the system level and modulation of light or heavy chains can occur at the submolecular level.

jects exercising on a treadmill or bicycle ergometer (34). These variables are measurements of the metabolism of the total organism, the volume of gas moved out of the lungs by the respiratory system, and the volume of blood pumped by an organ—the heart. As such they represent three different levels of organization at which adaptation may be studied. However, even though a change may occur in one of these variables it does not imply that the adaptation has occurred at that level. The change actually reflects adaptations at the level of cells, organelles, or molecules (Figure 1). Physiological systems have multiple mechanisms by which they adapt to environmental influences. Since adaptations occur at the cellular and subcellular levels, those measured at the level of the total organism are difficult to interpret (1).

An example of a total organism adaptation is the 5-25% increase that occurs in $\dot{V}O_2$max with endurance conditioning (6,17,28,36). Increased $\dot{V}O_2$max reflects an adaptation of oxidative enzymes in all of the fibers of specific motor units in the skeletal muscles that contract during the

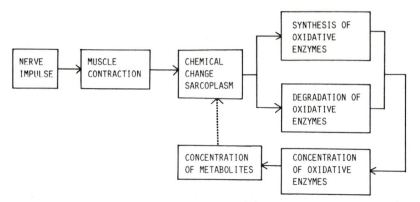

Figure 2 — **Biological feedback control systems. (A) Classical flow diagram for stimulus-response with negative feedback; (B) flow diagram for the localized stimulus-response to increased muscle contractions resulting in an increased concentration of oxidative enzymes.**

conditioning activity (2). The response is an increase in the concentrations of oxidative enzymes (20). The increased concentration of oxidative enzymes provides each conditioned fiber with a higher maximal rate of cellular respiration. The summation of the higher maximal rates of respiration for individual fibers results in a higher rate for total body $\dot{V}O_2$max.

Control of the adaptive response

The mechanisms by which an adaptive response occurs are best approached by using flow diagrams (Figure 2). A stimulus — the impulses in a motor nerve — activates the receptors — the muscle fibers of a motor unit — resulting in contractions at a given intensity, duration, and frequency. The contractions cause a change in the chemical environment of fiber sarcoplasm. This chemical change acts as the transmitter of the stimulus to the oxidative enzymes (21). The output is an increase in mitochondrial enzymes, and this greater concentration of oxidative enzymes increases the maximal respiratory rate of a given fiber. Since all of the fibers in a motor unit receive the same stimulus, adaptations occur homogeneously throughout the fibers of a motor unit (23,29).

The adaptive response, in this case oxidative enzymes, is then regulated by negative feedback about the degree of chemical change (the transmitter). As the oxidative enzyme concentration increases, more adenosine triphosphate (ATP) is produced by oxidative phosphorylation and less by glycolysis. An alternative explanation is that the rates of energy flow through the two pathways remain the same but the increased oxidative capacity results in oxidation of a greater proportion of pyruvate. Each of these interpretations results in a lower concentration of muscle metabolites after, compared to before, a conditioning program. Under these circumstances fiber homeostasis is disrupted less by a given pattern of contraction. Consequently, synthesis and degradation of oxidative enzymes equilibrate at a new concentration.

In addition to oxidative enzymes, similar feedback-control flow diagrams can be constructed for adaptations in glycolytic enzymes, protein turnover, substrates, myosin subfragments, sarcoplasmic reticulum function, capillary density, and vascular bed vasodilator capacity. For each of these adaptations much more is known of the output or response than of the mechanisms by which the response is mediated.

Nature of the conditioning stimulus

The size principle for the recruitment of motor units (7,13,18) relates the order of recruitment to the size of the motor unit and consequently to the size of the cell body in the anterior horn of the spinal column. Small anterior horn cells are depolarized easily and are recruited first during low-frequency, low-intensity stimulation. Large anterior horn cells require high-intensity stimulation for depolarization and are recruited infrequently. Intermediate motor units are intermediate as to both size and use. Small motor units are composed of fibers with slow myosin and high oxidative capacity, intermediate motor units are of fast myosin and high oxidative capacity, and large motor units are of fast myosin and low oxidative capacity (5,7,18).

Observations of these nerve-muscle interactions led investigators to test the hypothesis that the characteristics of the fibers of motor units were dependent on the impulse pattern they habitually received. The habitual impulse pattern was subsequently modulated by total organism conditioning programs (6,17,28,36), cross-innervation (4), cross-transplantation (16), and long-term, low-frequency stimulation (31,33).

Each of these experimental interventions resulted in adaptations in skeletal muscle fibers consistent with the hypothesis that the natural neurotransmitter released with each impulse was the primary stimulus. If trophic materials other than the natural neurotransmitter were involved, they appeared to be related to the impulse pattern. The exact role of the trophic materials on skeletal muscle remains obscure (8). There is evidence that the motoneuron provides axonal transport of materials and release at the nerve terminals (30). Trophic materials appear to exert control over postsynaptic sensory cells (14). In denervated muscle, loss of trophic materials initiates the depolarization of the membrane and the decline in junctional acetylcholine activity (15).

The nature of the impulse (action potential)

Nerve impulses in motoneurons can be described according to their frequency, duration, and pattern (Figure 3). In mammals, the frequency

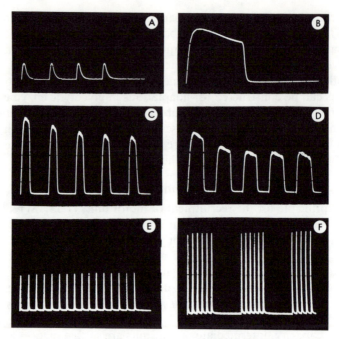

Figure 3 — Protocols for muscle contractions. (A) Isometric twitches; (B) maximal isometric tetanus; (C) a duty-rest ratio of 1:3 and cycle rate of 1/sec; (D) a duty-rest ratio of 1:1 and a cycle rate of 1/sec; (E) a continuous cycle rate at 30% of maximal tension; and (F) a discontinuous cycle rate at 80% of maximal tension. For discontinuous exercise, the activity:recovery periods must be described.

may vary from 1 to approximately 250 Hz to provide a frequency:force relation from twitch to maximal tension. A mouse extensor digitorum longus (EDL) muscle, which is fast, will have the largest range of stimulation frequencies and a human soleus muscle, which is slow, the smallest (Figure 4). Within human muscles, the same stimulation of frequency produces a higher proportion of maximal tension in slow than in fast skeletal muscle fibers. During endurance activities, including walking and long-distance running, the frequency seldom exceeds 30 Hz. Higher frequencies are associated with the powerful contractions required for explosive efforts in shot putting and high jumping (39). A single impulse is approximately 0.1 msec duration. Physiologically, impulses usually occur at frequencies at which there is summation and for durations from a few msec to minutes or hours. Throwing a baseball requires brief, vigorous, isotonic contractions of muscles in the arms and shoulders, whereas carrying a parcel might require sustained, isometric contractions for minutes or hours.

A given frequency of impulse may vary with the duty-rest cycle and with the length of time a duty-rest cycle is performed. The pattern of

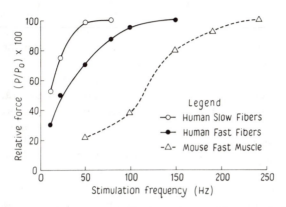

Figure 4—Frequency-force curves for human slow and fast muscle fibers and for a mouse fast muscle (extensor digitorum longus). Other slow and fast muscles from different species would have curves between the two extremes.

duty-rest cycles may be either repetitive or highly variable. The frequency of the impulse results in a given tension developed by a motor unit during the activity cycle, whereas the rest cycle allows a period of recovery from periods of muscle activity. The complexity of different duty-rest cycles may make it difficult to perform a definitive experiment regarding the interactions of the intensity of contraction, duration of contraction, and the duration of the rest period. Exercise biologists are well advised to keep exercise protocols as simple as possible to facilitate the interpretation of the response to a specific stimulus.

Applications

Interpreting adaptive responses in terms of the stimulus that induced them provides insight into some of the controversies in exercise biology. Within a month, long-term, low-frequency stimulation resulted in a significant conversion of fast to slow myosin in many fibers of rabbit EDL muscle (31,33), yet for rats, a year of rigorous running for 1 hr/day produced no significant conversion (40). Long-term, low-frequency stimulation consisted of 10 Hz stimulation of almost all motor units continuously for 24 hr/day (33), whereas during a running program the low tension activity was rarely for more than 1 hr/day. Even then, running involved only 30% of the motor units.

Programs designed to overload specific muscle groups result in significant muscle enlargement (11,12). Following weight-training, Gonyea et al. (12) attributed the 7% enlargement of the flexor carpi radialis muscle of cats to fiber splitting. Gollnick et al. (11) found that ablation of synergistic muscles resulted in 10-100% increases in the muscle mass of the remaining muscles. A rigorous fiber counting technique indicated that no significant change in fiber number had occurred. Therefore, hypertrophy, rather than hyperplasia, was cited as the mechanism responsible for the increase in muscle mass. Even though each of these two models results in muscle enlargement, the stimulus for adaptation differs markedly in intensity, duration, and pattern.

An increase in resting muscle length is a stimulus for adaptation that is receiving increasing attention because of its applications in orthognathic and orthopedic surgery and because of its role in pulmonary dysfunctions. Stretching an immobilized chicken wing with a spring-loaded device produces significant muscle enlargement (22). Conversely, a bite-opening device increases fiber length of the temporalis (26) and modifies the contractile properties of the masseter (9) but makes no significant change in muscle mass. Even though the basic stimulus in each case is one of an increased resting length, other aspects of the two models result in different adaptive stimuli. Differences include the degree of stretch and the activity permitted during stretch.

Hypertrophy may occur in denervated skeletal muscle fibers, as evident from the in vitro skeletal muscle experiments of Vandenburgh and Kaufman (37,38). Increased protein synthesis of the myotubes, in response to constant passive stretch, was associated with activation of the sodium pump (38). Conversely, during weight-lifting, stretch was induced by active muscle contractions. Under these circumstances the stretch is intermittent and of variable intensities. The stretched chicken wing model appears to be closer to the extreme of passive stretch, whereas the bite-opening appliance has elements of both passive and active stretch.

Removal or diminution of the adaptive stimulus results in regression back toward control values (10). When control muscles are immobilized by casting (3), pinning (25) or nonweight-bearing suspension (27), muscle atrophy occurs. Each of these conditions allows for some measure of muscle contraction. Contractions are more isometric in the casted or pinned limbs and are isotonic but unweighted in the suspended limb. Denervation results in even more complicated adaptations because of the elimination of trophic factors as well as the inactivity (15).

Controversy stimulates research in a field, but exercise biology is a complex field with many inherent problems. In such a field, integrative concepts are more productive than divisive concepts. If there is controversy in exercise biology, the controversy should focus on valid comparisons between comparable results.

The classical flow diagram for biological feedback systems is proposed as a means to encourage comparisons between comparable results in studies of physiological adaptations. The flow diagram can be modified to accommodate the pathways involved in adaptation at any level of organization from that of the total organism to the submolecular level. Traditionally, adaptation has been investigated more intensively in terms of the response. Considerable insight into adaptation may be gained through a shift from the traditional emphasis to a broader perspective that includes interpretation of the nature of the adaptive stimulus and the intervening mechanisms involved.

Acknowledgments

My studies of the skeletal muscle adaptation have been enhanced by long-term collaborations with many colleagues: David S. Carlson, Leo C. Maxwell, Kevin K. McCully, James A. McNamara, and Timothy P. White. The research was supported in part by United States Public Health Service grant DE 04857 from the National Institute of Dental Research and NS 17017 from the National Institute of Neurology, Communicable Diseases and Stroke.

References

1. Adolph, E.F. Some general and specific characteristics of physiological adaptations. *Am. J. Physiol.* **184**:18-28, 1956.

2. Armstrong, R.B., Marcum, P., Saubert, C.W. IV, Seeherman, H.J., and Taylor, C.R. Muscle fiber activity as a function of speed and gait. *J. Appl. Physiol.* **43**:672-677, 1977.

3. Booth, F.W., and Kelso, J.R. Effect of hind-limb immobilization on contractile and histochemical properties of skeletal muscle. *Pflugers Arch.* **342**:231-238, 1973.

4. Buller, A.J., Eccles, J.C., and Eccles, R.M. Interactions between motoneuron and muscles in respect of the characteristic speeds of their response. *J. Physiol. London* **150**:417-439, 1960.

5. Burke, R.E., and Edgerton, V.R. Motor unit properties and selective involvement in movement. In: *Exercise and sports sciences reviews*, vol. 3. Academic, New York, 1975, pp. 31-81.

6. Davies, C.T.M., and Knibbs, A.V. The training stimulus, the effects of intensity, duration and frequency of effort on maximum aerobic power output. *Int. Z. Angew. Physiol.* **29**:299-305, 1971.

7. Desmedt, J.E. (ed). *Motor unit types, recruitment and plasticity in health and disease.* S. Kargar AG, Basel, 1981.

8. Drachman, D.B. The role of acetylcholine as a neurotrophic transmitter. In: D.B. Drachman (ed.), *Trophic functions of the neuron.* New York Academy of Sciences, New York, 1974, pp. 160-175.

9. Faulkner, J.A., Maxwell, L.C., and Lieberman, D.A. Histochemical characteristics of muscle fibers from trained and detrained guinea pigs. *Am. J. Physiol.* **222**:836-840, 1972.

10. Faulkner, J.A., McCully, K.K., Carlson, D.S., and McNamara, J.A., Jr. Contractile properties of the muscles of mastication of monkeys following an increase in muscle length. *Arch. Oral Biol.* **27**:841-845, 1982.

11. Gollnick, P.D., Timson, B.F., Moore, R.L., and Riedy, M. Muscular enlargement and number of fibers in skeletal muscles of rats. *Am. J. Physiol.* **50**:936-943, 1981.

12. Gonyea, W., Ericson, G.C., and Bonde-Petersen, F. Skeletal muscle fiber splitting induced by weight-lifting exercise in cats. *Acta Physiol. Scand.* **99**:105-109, 1977.

13. Granit, R., Phillips, C.G., Skoglund, S., and Steg, G. Differentiation of tonic from phasic ventral horn cells by stretch, pinna, and crossed extensor reflexes. *J. Neurophysiol.* **20**:470-481, 1957.

14. Guth, L. Effect of immobilization of sole-plate and background cholinesterase of rat skeletal muscle. *Exp. Neurol.* **24**:508-513, 1969.

15. Guth, L., Kemerer, V.F., Samaras, T.A., Warnick, J.E., and Albuquerque, E.X. The roles of disuse and loss of neurotrophic function in denervation atrophy of skeletal muscle. *Exp. Neurol.* **73**:20-36, 1981.

16. Gutmann, E., and Carlson, B.M. Contractile and histochemical properties of regenerating cross-transplanted fast and slow muscles in the rat. *Pflügers Arch.* **353**:227-239, 1975.

17. Hartley, L.H., Grimby, G., Kilbom, A., Nilsson, N.J., Astrand, I., Bjure, J., Ekblom, B., and Saltin, B. Physical training in sedentary middle-aged and older men. *Scand. J. Clin. Lab. Invest.* **24**:335-344, 1969.

18. Henneman, E., and Olson, C.B. Relations between structure and function in the design of skeletal muscles. *J. Neurophysiol.* **28**:581, 1965.

19. Hochochka, P.W., and Somers, G.N. *Strategies of biochemical adaptation.* W.B. Saunders, Philadelphia, 1973.

20. Holloszy, J.O., and Booth, F.W. Biochemical adaptations to endurance exercise in muscle. *Ann. Rev. Physiol.* **38**:273-291, 1976.

21. Holloszy, J.O., and Winder, W.W. Induction of γ-aminolevulinic acid synthetase in muscle by exercise or thyroxine. Am. J. Physiol. **236**:R180-R183, 1979.

22. Holly, R.G., Barnett, G.J., Ashmore, C.R., Taylor, R.G., and Molé, P.A. Stretch-induced growth in chicken wing muscles: A new model of stretch hypertrophy. *Am. J. Physiol.* **7**:C62-C71, 1980.

23. Kugelberg, E., and Edström, L. Differential histochemical effects of muscle contractions on phosphorylase and glycogen in various types of fibres: Relation to fatigue. *J. Neurol. Neurosurg. Psych.* **31**:415-423, 1968.

24. Leake, C.D. Perspectives of adaptation: Historical backgrounds. In: D.B. Dill, E.F. Adolph and C.G. Wilber (eds.), *Handbook of physiology, section 4: Adaptation to the environment*. American Physiological Society, Washington, DC, 1964, pp. 1-10.

25. Maier, A., Crockett, J.L., Simpson, D.R., Saubert, C.W., and Edgerton, V.R. Properties of immobilized guinea pig hind limb muscles. *Am. J. Physiol.* **231**:1520-1527, 1976.

26. Maxwell, L.C., Carlson, D.S., McNamara, J.A., and Faulkner, J.A. Adaptation of the masseter and temporalis muscles following alteration in length, with or without surgical detachment. *Anat. Rec.* **200**:127-137, 1981.

27. Musacchia, W.J., Deavers, D.R., Meininger, G.A., and Davis, R.P. A model for hypokinesia: Effects on muscle atrophy in the rat. *J. Appl. Physiol. Respirat. Environ. Exercise Physiol.* **48**:479-486, 1980.

28. Naughton, J., and Nagle, F. Peak oxygen intake during physical fitness program for middle-aged men. *J. Am. Med. Assoc.* **191**:899-901, 1965.

29. Nemeth, P.M., Pette, D., and Vrbova, G. Comparison of enzyme activities among single muscle fibres within defined motor units. *J. Physiol.* **331**:489-495, 1981.

30. Ochs, S. Systems of material transport in nerve fibers (axoplasmic transport) related to nerve function and trophic control. In: D.B. Drachman (ed.), *Trophic functions of the neuron*. New York Academy of Sciences, New York, 1974, pp. 202-223.

31. Pette, D., and Schnez, U. Coexistence of fast and slow type myosin light chains in single muscle fibres during transformation as induced by long term stimulation. *FEBS Lett.* **83**:128-130, 1977.

32. Prosser, C.L. Perspectives of adaptation: Theoretical aspects. In: D.B. Dill, E.F. Adolph and C.G. Wilber (eds.), *Handbook of physiology, section 4: Adaptation to the environment*. American Physiological Society, Washington, DC, 1964, pp. 11-26.

33. Salmons, S., and Vrbova, G. The influence of activity on some contractile characteristics of mammalian fast and slow muscles. *J. Physiol. London* **201**:535-549, 1969.

34. Saltin, B., Blomqvist, G., Mitchell, J., Johnson, R.L., Wildenthal, K., and Chapman, C.B. Response to exercise after bed rest and after training. *Circulation* **37** and **38** (Suppl. 7):1-78, 1968.

35. Selye, H. The story of the adaptation syndrome. *Montreal Acta*, 1952, **252**.

36. Skinner, J., Holloszy, J., and Cureton, T. Effects of a program of endurance exercise on physical work capacity and anthropometric measurements of fifteen middle-aged men. *Am. J. Cardiol.* **14**:747-752, 1964.

37. Vandenburgh, H., and Kaufman, S. In vitro model for stretch-induced hypertrophy skeletal muscle. *Science* **23**:265-268, 1979.

38. Vandenburgh, H., and Kaufman, S. Stretch-induced growth of skeletal myo-

tubes correlates with activation of the sodium pump. *J. Cell. Physiol.* **109**:205-214, 1981.

39. Walmsley, G., Hodgson, J.A., and Burke, R.E. Forces produced by medial gastrocnemius and soleus muscles during locomotion in freely moving cats. *J. Neurophysiol.* **41**:1203-1216, 1978.

40. White, T.P., Faulkner, J.A., and Villanacci, J.V. Contractile properties of rat soleus and plantaris following prolonged running. *Physiologist* **23**:96, 1980.

Skeletal muscle growth induced by strength training

William J. Gonyea
The University of Texas Health Science Center
at Dallas

Adult skeletal muscle can achieve tremendous increases in size and strength in response to prolonged weight-lifting exercise. Traditionally, the growth process has been shown to be a result of increased girth (cross-sectional area) of individual fibers without increasing the total number of muscle fibers. Recent reports, however, of greater fiber numbers in hypertrophied muscles after prolonged strength training have challenged the traditional concept that fiber number is not altered by exercise. The purpose of this report is to review our knowledge of adult muscle growth, especially as it pertains to exercise.

Postnatal growth

It has been demonstrated that the number of fibers in a muscle increases considerably during fetal development, with little or no increases in fiber number occurring during early postnatal development. Hence, the postnatal growth in muscle mass occurs nearly exclusively by increases in the length and girth of individual fibers with no change in number (18). However, muscle fibers contain a considerable number of nuclei and as each fiber continues to grow the number of nuclei found in each continues to increase. The increase in the number of myonuclei is associated with an increase in the girth and length of muscle fibers. The postnatal increase in the number of fiber nuclei does not appear to result from mitotic division of the existing nuclei. Indeed, certain cells known as satellite cells fuse with muscle fibers and thus donate nuclei to the growing fibers (39,40,42,49).

It would seem that there would be physiological limits to the girth that a muscle fiber could achieve before metabolic efficiency becomes compromised. With the capillary bed located outside the muscle fiber, increased cross-sectional area increases the diffusion distance. Also, it is known that the time necessary for the radial spread of depolarization down the t-tubules and the release of calcium from the sarcoplasmic reticulum are related to the cross-sectional area of the muscle fiber. Hence, it is possible that increasing size would result in too great a distance for the transmission of the impulse down the t-tubule system to the centermost myofibrils (1). It appears that in larger animals, fiber number is increased rather than fiber size. It seems, then, that there may be a size beyond which increases in the cross-sectional area of the muscle fibers become less efficient, either in terms of metabolic transport or contractile properties. If in fact, increasing the size of muscle fibers ultimately decreases their metabolic or physiological efficiency, then this could have profound implications in understanding the growth process of muscle that is undergoing exercise-induced hypertrophy. Hence, although speculative at this point, there may be size limitations beyond which function is so impaired that additional gains in cross-sectional area of muscle fibers become counterproductive.

Muscle regeneration

Adult skeletal muscle potentially can undergo alternative growth processes that bring about simple increases in cross-sectional area. We can gain insight into this occurrence by studying muscle regeneration after injury resulting in substantial loss of muscle tissue. The experimental evidence collected over the last 2 decades overwhelmingly demonstrates that the damaged muscle fiber is the primary source of myogenic cells. Within the muscle fiber are two possible sources of nuclei, myonuclei which form more than 95% of the total nuclear population in mature fibers, and satellite cells which constitute the remainder of the total nuclear population. The myonuclei are postmitotic nuclei that are incapable of DNA synthesis, mitosis, or of providing a source for new myogenic cells (8,45). Instead, this new nuclear population is provided by satellite cells that are in close association with the muscle fiber (2,42). Since Mauro's (39) initial description, most investigators have considered the evidence to overwhelmingly favor the satellite cell as the stem cell necessary for muscle regeneration.

The regeneration following muscle damage produces excellent functional and histological results (3). Nevertheless, regenerated muscle fibers are often small in diameter, increased in number compared to control tissue, split longitudinally (fiber splitting), and surrounded by a thicker endomysium than that of intact muscle. Hence, in many cases fiber splitting is commonly observed (9). This has been interpreted as possibly reflecting two processes: A large fiber may literally separate into several smaller ones in one segment of its length, and within a single endomysial tube; or alternatively, small-diameter fibers may regenerate and, in segments of their length, undergo partial side-to-side fusion. Sprouting from the cut end of a single fiber may also result in multiple small-diameter fibers (32). Also unknown is whether any of these possibilities result in new, independent daughter fibers. Considerably more information must be accumulated about the mechanisms involved in fiber splitting before a reasonable assessment can be made about the significance of this process in muscle regeneration and growth.

Specificity of exercise training

Maximal overloading of muscle can be accomplished using a wide range of contraction force and duration. For example, a weight may be lifted which permits only one or as many as 50 repetitions. It is obvious that almost all of the 50 repetitions would be performed at a submaximal level of muscle force. However, as the muscle fatigues, more and more motor units would have to be recruited to produce the force necessary to lift the weight. As would be expected, these two forms of maximally overloading muscle cause different adaptive processes to be stimulated. Some evidence suggests that the stimulus for muscle growth is the tension developed within the muscle during exercise (17). It is possible that the greater the tension, the greater the stimulus. Hence, exercises involving a few repetitions with high resistance should favor maximal muscle growth.

Since the work of Morpurgo (41), exercise-induced muscle growth has been thought to be exclusively related to an increase in cross-sectional area of individual muscle fibers, with the total number of fibers remaining unaffected by training. In Morpurgo's studies, dogs were exercised on a treadmill. This form of exercise is considered endurance training, which is not equivalent to strength training in inducing muscle growth. The specificity of training is very important because skeletal muscle adapts quite differently to dissimilar forms of training (13). It has been demonstrated that endurance exercise usually induces little if any muscle hypertrophy, whereas high-resistance exercise, such as weight training does increase muscle strength and size (13,24). Although Morpurgo's studies did show a significant increase in gross weight of exercised muscles, more recent studies have not been successful in causing muscle hypertrophy in treadmill-exercised animals (5,6,14,15).

Goldspink and Howells (19) used an exercise regimen in which a counterweighted food basket had to be pulled down so the animals could obtain a food reward. As in Morpurgo's study, mean fiber area showed a significant increase. However, most of the hypertrophy was to the small fibers, whereas the area of the large fibers remained essentially unchanged from control values. Although histochemical fiber typing was not performed, the small fibers probably were slow-twitch oxidative (SO) fibers. Accordingly, it is possible that the exercise intensity was insufficient to induce hypertrophy to the fast-twitch fibers.

Surgically-induced growth

Compensatory muscle hypertrophy has been used frequently as a model for work-induced hypertrophy (7,12,16,27-30,33,37,52). This method consists of eliminating a number of muscles in a synergistic group by tenotomy or surgical excision. This procedure functionally overloads the remaining intact muscles of the group which then undergo rapid hypertrophy to compensate for the lost tension; hence the name compensatory hypertrophy.

It is obvious that compensatory hypertrophy differs in several fundamental aspects from exercised-induced hypertrophy. Surgical alteration of synergistic muscles places a continuous workload on the muscle, whereas high-resistance exercise is intermittent, with the muscle in a nonwork phase most of the day. In addition, the work performed by surgically overloaded muscle is not under volitional control, which differs from an exercise program.

Using the compensatory model, the overworked muscle rapidly increases in weight, and a number of studies have demonstrated that growth of the muscle primarily resulted from an enlargement of muscle fibers without an increase in their number (7,16,29,51). Others using the surgically induced hypertrophy model have observed fibers that appeared to be undergoing longitudinal division (fiber splitting), which in some cases was thought to increase the number of fibers in the muscle. Determining the number of fibers in a given muscle usually was accomplished by counting all fibers in a section taken through the greatest girth of the muscle belly. Both hypertrophy and hyperplasia (assumed to be caused by fiber splitting) occurred in muscles that had undergone training after the removal or denervation of synergistic muscles or had undergone continued surgically induced overload for prolonged periods (31,35,36,46,47,50,52). Because branched fibers appeared, it was assumed that one of the mechanisms involved in increasing fiber number was fiber splitting.

In many cases the histological profile of the overworked muscles exhibited degenerative changes such as fiber necrosis, hyaline degeneration, karyopknosis, and monocyte infiltration (46). The initial increase in muscle weight in the hypertrophic response of muscle to the removal of synergistic muscles has been demonstrated to be caused by an inflammatory reaction (4).

Recently Gollnick and colleagues (20) have restudied muscular enlargement produced by surgical ablation and exercise on the number of fibers in several rat hindlimb muscles using a different counting technique. The number of fibers per muscle was determined by direct counts of individual fibers dissected from HNO_3-treated muscles. This technique was chosen over direct counts of all the muscle fibers located in the section taken through the greatest girth of the muscle belly because it was thought that differences in muscle architecture may influence this count. It was argued that a significant number of muscle fibers would not be represented in the cross-section taken through the greatest girth in a complexly pennated muscle. Also, a change in fiber angle due to a hypertrophic response could result in more fibers being represented in cross-section without an actual increase in total fiber number (20).

Even after inducing substantial muscle hypertrophy, Gollnick's study revealed no increase in fiber number in any of the muscles studied (20). Also, fibers exhibiting a longitudinal branching were observed in equal numbers between control and surgically overloaded muscles. Additional increases could be induced in the surgically overloaded muscles of animals with additional treadmill exercise. In some cases these weight gains exceeded 100% of control values in as little as 12 wk. Such dramatic gains in muscle mass as observed with the surgical ablation technique in animals would require several years of intensive high-resistance exercise in the human athlete. Hence, one has to view ablation experiments with some caution as to their applicability in elucidating exercise growth processes that would be analogous to either human or animal exercise regimens.

The possibility exists that the very rapid muscle weight gains achieved using the surgical-ablation overload technique exceeds the muscle's "normal" growth capacity to respond to increased work, representing an abnormal response to pathological stress such as surgically induced muscle overload. The dramatic differences in the growth response time observed in muscle certainly argues in favor of the possibility of fundamentally different processes being stimulated in response to surgically induced overload when compared to high-resistance exercise.

Exercise-induced growth

Few studies are available that have assessed the adaptive changes occurring in skeletal muscle after intensive weight training. This gap is mainly attributed to the lack of animal models which use high-resistance exercise of sufficient intensity and duration to induce consistent muscle hypertrophy comparable to human strength-training programs. Such models have been available only recently for experimental use (13,21,34). For example, Gonyea and Ericson (21) have demonstrated that cats can be operantly conditioned to lift weights with their right forelimbs to receive a food reward. It was assumed in developing this model that the left unexercised limb could be used for comparative purposes, providing an intra-animal control. However, our observations have shown that the left limb, used as a brace during exercise, undergoes a considerable training effect even though it is not directly performing the exercise. This has been shown by comparing the left and right limbs of the exercised cats with those from weight- and sex-matched control animals. It has been demonstrated, though, that weight-lifting exercise in cats can induce significant increases in both weight and fiber diameters in the muscles from the exercised limb (22-24). In addition, there was a significant increase in the total number of muscle fibers observed in the total cross-sectional area of the exercised flexor carpi radialis muscle (FCR) from the cat. The cross-section was made through the greatest girth of the muscle belly and at right angles to the long axis of the muscle.

Gollnick and colleagues (20) have demonstrated that an increased representation of muscle fibers could be achieved in hypertrophic muscle simply by altering the angle of pennation and maintaining the section taken at right angles to the fiber direction in order to cut the fibers in cross-section. However, in our studies all sections were taken at right angles to the longitudinal axis of the muscle, which should eliminate this problem. Nevertheless, many fibers in the cat FCR were still cut in cross-section, and the pennation pattern in this muscle was complex. Thus, we cannot rule out the possibility that simple muscle fiber hypertrophy was altering fiber pennation patterns to the point of inducing an artificial increase in fibers from a section taken through the muscle belly. This point certainly warrants future clarification.

In the cat, the onset of increased fiber number found in the cross-section through the muscle belly of hypertrophied muscles was correlated with the intensity of exercise (25). However, increases in fiber number in the palmaris longus muscle (PLM) lagged behind that observed in the FCR. It was demonstrated that these synergistic muscles responded somewhat differently to work-induced stress (23). Hence, caution should be used in extrapolating the results of the adaptive process of one muscle to all skeletal muscles. A more appropriate approach to investigating muscle adaptation is to study all muscles in a synergistic (functional) group (10).

In response to strength training, all three fiber types undergo hypertrophy in the cat FCR (24). The onset of increased fiber number in the exercised FCR of the cat appears to be associated with exercise intensity. When exercise intensity is sufficient to induce fast-twitch glycolytic fiber (FG) hypertrophy, then and only then does fiber number increase and correlated with this is an onset of fiber splitting (26). Below an intensity level sufficient to induce FG hypertrophy there is no increase in fiber number. Since all three fiber types have been observed to undergo increases in fiber number, their representation in the cross-sectional area of the FCR remains proportional to control values, and no shift in fiber type distribution occurs in this muscle (25). Accordingly, a plot of muscle fiber cross-sectional area for the cat's exercised FCR demonstrates increases in both smaller and larger fibers than those observed in weight-matched control animals (26). It should be noted that if fiber hypertrophy were the only growth mechanism occurring in the cat FCR muscle, then there should only be an increase in the number of fibers with a larger cross-sectional area than control values, instead of both larger and smaller fibers being present after prolonged strength training. Hence it is appropriate, based on this type of observation, to assume that other mechanisms may be involved in the exercise-induced growth process in addition to muscle fiber hypertrophy.

Studies have demonstrated increases in muscle fiber area in humans who have undergone strength-training programs (11,44). Such studies rely on a muscle biopsy in order to assess the effect of training on muscle. Thus, because a limited fiber sample size is available for biopsy material, it is extremely difficult to determine whether the exercised muscle's growth is limited to increases in muscle fiber area. Several studies, however, have questioned whether the growth observed in trained skeletal muscle of athletes resulted from fiber hypertrophy exclusively. In this regard, several studies have analyzed muscle biopsy samples from elite athletes, whereas most earlier studies relied on a brief training regimen involving nonathletes. For example, elite female swimmers were shown to have significantly smaller fibers in their bulky deltoid muscles compared to nonswimmer control women (48). The finding of a large number of small fibers in these athletes' trained muscles may be consistent with the idea of new fiber development induced by the prolonged training program. Certainly it is difficult to propose another process to explain the small size of the muscle fibers observed in this study.

In another study, biopsies were taken from the triceps muscle of national class Canadian body builders. When the muscle fiber area from these athletes was compared to that from large control subjects there was no difference in fiber area between the two groups, even though the athletes' arm girth was significantly greater than the control subjects' (38). These data also suggest that there is a possible ceiling size for the cross-sectional area of muscle fibers undergoing hypertrophy, and that possibly the body builders had a greater total number of muscle fibers than did the control subjects as a result of prolonged, high-resistance training.

It remains to be determined definitively whether the muscle fiber number increases after prolonged weight-lifting exercise. The only acceptable method now available to answer this question is direct counting following HNO_3 digestion. Since total fiber numbers can only be determined using experimental animals, we felt that our cat exercise model would be suitable to use. To date we have weighed FCR muscles from 53 control cats with a mean body weight of 3.2 ± 0.10 kg and a mean FCR weight of 1.10 ± 0.04 g. The correlation between body and muscle weights was highly significant with $r = 0.83$. These data indicate that body weight and muscle weight, at least for the FCR, are tightly coupled during growth. We have weighed the FCR from 18 trained cats that had an average body weight of 3.4 ± 0.12 kg, which was not significantly different from the control animals. The average weight of the trained FCR was 1.40 ± 0.10 g, representing a highly significant increase of 27% over control values. The difference in muscle weight between exercised and size-matched control animals ranged upward to 65%. The trained cats performed a one-armed lift with an average maximal weight of 1.43 kg, which was an average of 42% of their body weight. The maximal lift for this group was 2.19 kg—over 60% of their body weight.

The average weight of 17 control muscles was 1.04 g. The average number of muscle fibers in the cat FCR was found to be 36,695; this figure represents more than a four-fold increase in the number of fibers we observed in counting the total fibers found in a section taken through the greatest girth of the FCR (25). If muscle fiber hypertrophy altered the number of fibers represented in the cross-section through the greatest girth of the FCR, this method of counting obviously could give extremely misleading results (20). Hence, the fiber-counting technique should provide an accurate method of counting the total number of muscle fibers in the exercised FCR. The correlation between muscle weight and fiber number was highly significant, $r = 0.89$. These parameters apparently had far less variation than was observed in the rat hindlimb muscles (20). This finding may result from the unusual growth pattern in the rat, for this species continues to grow throughout its lifespan. Such a pattern is certainly unlike that of humans or cats, who spend most of their lifespan in the nongrowth adult phase.

Two exercised FCR muscles from the cat have been counted; the first had an approximate 16% increase in fiber number over size-matched control values. However, there was only a 4% increase over the left FCR, possibly again indicating that the left muscle makes a poor control. The possibility cannot be ruled out that this cat simply was born with an exceedingly high number of muscle fibers in both limbs. The second cat had 3% fewer fibers in the trained FCR compared to size-matched control values, whereas the trained right FCR contained 17% more fibers than the left FCR. The results from these two exercised animals are certainly inconclusive and a larger sample must be processed in order to determine if weight training increases fiber number in the cat FCR. As stated previously, the left limb is used as a brace during training and does undergo a training effect, although the limb is not directly exercised (25). As Gollnick has pointed out, there is a need for an intra-animal control to be absolutely certain about alterations in fiber number due to training (20). To accomplish this we are currently removing the left FCR before the onset of training. In this way the left FCR fiber counts will be free from any training effect and should provide a more useful intra-animal control to directly assess the effects of weight-lifting exercise on fiber number.

References

1. Adrian, R.H., Constantin, L.L., and Peachy, L.D. Radial spread of contraction in frog muscle fibers. *J. Physiol.* **204**:231-257, 1969.

2. Allbrook, D.B., and Han, M.F. Population of muscle satellite cells in relation to age and mitotic activity. *Pathology* 3:233-243, 1971.

3. Allbrook, D.B. Skeletal muscle regeneration. *Muscle and Nerve* **4**:234-245, 1981.

4. Armstrong, R.B., Marum, P., Tullson, P., and Saubert, C.W. IV. Acute hypertrophic response of skeletal muscle to removal of synergists. *J. Appl. Physiol.* **46**:835-842, 1979.

5. Barnard, R.J., Edgerton, V.R., and Peter, J.B. Effect of exercise on skeletal muscle. I. Biochemical and histochemical properties. *J. Appl. Physiol.* **28**:762-766, 1970a.

6. Barnard, R.J., Edgerton, V.R., and Peter, J.B. Effect of exercise on skeletal muscle. II. Contractile properties. *J. Appl. Physiol.* **28**:767-770, 1970b.

7. Bass, A., Macková, E., and Vítek, V. Activity of some enzymes of the energy-supplying metabolism in the rat soleus after tenotomy of synergistic muscles and in the contralateral control muscle. *Physiolog. Bohem. Praha* **22**:613-621, 1973.

8. Bischoff, R. Tissue culture studies on the origin of myogenic cells during muscle regeneration in the rat. In: A. Mauro (ed.), *Muscle regeneration.* Raven Press, New York, 1979, pp. 13-30.

9. Bradley, W.G. Muscle fiber splitting. In: A. Mauro (ed.), *Muscle regeneration.* Raven Press, New York, 1979, pp. 215-231.

10. Collatos, T.C., Edgerton, V.R., Smith, J.L., and Botterman, B.R. Contractile properties and fiber type compositions of flexors and extensors of the elbow joint in cat: Implications for motor control. *J. Neurophysiol.* **40**:1292-1300, 1977.

11. Costill, D.L., Coyle, E.F., Fink, W.F., Lesmes, G.R., and Witzman, F.A. Adaptations in skeletal muscle following strength training. *J. Appl. Physiol.* **46**:96-99, 1979.

12. Denny-Brown, D. Experimental studies pertaining to hypertrophy, regeneration and degeneration. In: R.D. Adams, L.M. Eaton, and A.M. Shy (eds.), *Proceedings for the Association of Research on Nervous Mental Disorders*, chap. 4. Williams and Wilkins, Baltimore, 1980.

13. Edgerton, V.R. Neuromuscular adaptation to power and endurance work. *Can. J. Appl. Sport Sci.* **1**:49-58, 1976.

14. Edgerton, V.R., Gerchman, L., and Carrow, R. Histochemical changes in rat skeletal muscle fibers after exercise. *Exp. Neurol.* **24**:110-123, 1969.

15. Edgerton, V.R., Barnard, R.J., Peter, J.B., Gillespie, C.A., and Simpson, D.R. Overloaded skeletal muscles of a nonhuman primate *(Galago senegalensis)*. *Exp. Neurol.* **37**:322-339, 1972.

16. Goldberg, A.L. Muscle hypertrophy in hypophysectomized rats. *Physiologist* **8**:173, 1965.

17. Goldberg, A.L., Etlinger, J.D., Goldspink, D.F., and Jablecki, C. Mechanism of work-induced hypertrophy of skeletal muscle. *Med. Sci. Sports* **7**:248-261, 1975.

18. Goldspink, G. Morphological adaptation to growth and activity. In: E.J. Brisky, R.G. Cassens, and B.B. Marsh (eds.), *The physiology and biochemistry of muscles as a food*. University of Wisconsin, Madison, 1970.

19. Goldspink, G., and Howells, K.F. Work-induced hypertrophy in exercised normal muscles of different ages and the reversibility of hypertrophy after cessation of exercise. *J. Physiol.* **239**:179-193, 1974.

20. Gollnick, P.D., Timson, B.F., Moore, R.L., and Riedy, M. Muscular enlargement and number of fibers in skeletal muscles of rats. *J. Appl. Physiol.* **50**:936-943, 1981.

21. Gonyea, W., and Ericson, G.C. An experimental model for the study of exercise-induced skeletal muscle hypertrophy. *J. Appl. Physiol.* **40**:630-633, 1976.

22. Gonyea, W., Ericson, G.C., and Bonde-Petersen, F. Skeletal muscle fiber splitting induced by weight-lifting exercise in cats. *Acta Physiol. Scand.* **99**:105-209, 1977.

23. Gonyea, W., and Bonde-Petersen, F. Electromyographic analysis of two wrist flexor muscles studied during weight-lifting exercise in the cat. *Biomechanics* **6a**:207-212, 1978a.

24. Gonyea, W., and Bonde-Petersen, F. Alterations in muscle contractile prop-

erties and fiber composition after weight-lifting exercise in cats. *Exp. Neurol.* **59**:75-84, 1978b.

25. Gonyea, W.J. The role of exercise in inducing increases in skeletal muscle fiber number. *J. Appl. Physiol.* **48**:421-426, 1980.

26. Gonyea, W.J. Muscle fiber splitting in trained and untrained animals. *Ex. Sport Sci. Rev.* **8**:19-39, 1980.

27. Guth, L., Brown, W.C., and Ziemnowicz, J.D. Changes in cholinesterase activity of rat muscle during growth and hypertrophy. *Am. J. Physiol.* **211**:1113-1116, 1966.

28. Gutmann, E., Hájeck, I., and Horsky, P. Effect of excessive use on contraction and metabolic properties of cross-striated muscle. *J. Physiol.* **203**:46P-47P, 1969.

29. Gutmann, E., Hájeck, I., and Víteck, V. Compensatory hypertrophy of the latissimus dorsi posterior muscle induced by elimination of the latissimus dorsi anterior muscle of the chicken. *Physiol. Bohem. Praha* **19**:483, 1970.

30. Gutmann, E., Schiaffino, S., and Hanzliková, V. Mechanism of compensatory hypertrophy in skeletal muscle of the rat. *Neurology* **31**:451-464, 1971.

31. Hall-Craggs, E.C.B. The longitudinal division of fibers in overloaded rat skeletal muscle. *J. Appl. Anat. London* **107**:459-470, 1970.

32. Hall-Craggs, E.C.B. The regeneration of skeletal muscle fibers per continuum. *J. Anat.* **117**:171-178, 1974.

33. Hamosh, M., Lesch, M., Braon, J., and Kaufman, S. Enhanced protein synthesis in a cell-free system from hypertrophied muscle. *Science* **157**:935-937, 1967.

34. Ho, K.W., Roy, R.R., Tweedle, C., Heusner, W.W., Van Huss, W.D., and Carrow, R.E. Skeletal muscle fiber splitting with weightlifting exercise in rats. *Am. J. Anat.* **157**:433-440, 1980.

35. Inauzzo, C.D., Gollnick, P.D., and Armstrong, R.B. Compensatory adaptations of skeletal muscle fiber types to a long-term functional overload. *Life Sci.* **19**:1517-1724, 1976.

36. James, N.I. Compensatory hypertrophy in the extensor digitorum longus muscle of the rat. *J. Anat.* **116**:57-65, 1973.

37. Lesch, M., Parmley, W.W., Hamosh, M., Kaufman, S., and Sonneblick, H. Effect of acute hypertrophy on the contractile properties of skeletal muscle. *Am. J. Physiol.* **214**:685-690, 1968.

38. MacDougall, J.D., Sale, D.G., Sulton, J.R., Elder, G., and Moroz, J.R. Muscle ultrastructural characteristics of elite powerlifters and bodybuilders. *Eur. J. Appl. Physiol.* **48**:117-126, 1982.

39. Mauro, A. Satellite cell of skeletal muscle fibers. *J. Biophys. Biochem. Cytol.* **9**:493, 1961.

40. Mauro, A. *Muscle and myogenesis.* Excerpta Medica, Amsterdam, 1973. The Netherlands, 1973.

41. Morpurgo, B. Uber Aktivitat-Hypertrophie der willkürlichen Muskeln. *Virch. Arch. Pathol. Anat.* **150**:522-554, 1897.

42. Moss, F.P., and Leblond, C.P. Satellite cells as the source of nuclei in muscles of growing rats. *Anat. Rec.* **170**:421-436, 1971.

43. Peter, J.B. Histochemical, biochemical and physiological studies of skeletal muscle and its adaptation to exercise. In: *Contractility of muscle cells and related processes.* Symposium of the Society of General Physiologists, Prentice-Hall, Englewood Cliffs, NJ, 1971.

44. Prince, F.G., Hikida, R.S., and Hagerman, F.C. Human muscle fiber types in power lifters, distance runners and untrained subjects. *Pfluegers Arch.* **363**:19-26, 1976.

45. Pullman, W.E., and Yeoh, G.C.T. The role of myonuclei in muscle regeneration: An in vitro study. *J. Cell. Physiol.* **96**:245-251, 1978.

46. Reitsma, W. Skeletal muscle hypertrophy after heavy exercise in rats with surgically reduced muscle function. *Am. J. Phys. Med.* **48**:237-257, 1969.

47. Reitsma, W. Some structural changes in skeletal muscles of the rat after intensive training. *Acta Morphol. Neerl. Scand. Utrecht* **7**:229-246, 1970.

48. Saltin, B., Henriksson, J., Jensen, E., and Anderson, P. Fiber types and metabolic potentials of skeletal muscles in sedentary man and endurance runners. *Ann. N.Y. Acad. Sci.* **301**:3-29, 1977.

49. Shafiq, S.A. Satellite cells and fiber nuclei in muscle regeneration. In: A. Mauro, S.A. Shafiq, and A.T. Milhorat (eds.), *Regeneration of striated muscle and myogenesis.* Excerpta Medica, Amsterdam, 1970, pp. 122-132.

50. Sola, O.M., Christensen, D.L., and Martin, A.W. Hypertrophy and hyperplasia of adult chicken anterior latissimus dorsi muscles following stretch with and without denervation. *Exp. Neurol.* **41**:76-100, 1973.

51. Tomanek, R.J., and Woo, K. Compensatory hypertrophy of the plantaris muscle in relation to age. *J. Gerontol.* **25**:23-29, 1970.

52. Van Linge, B. The response of muscle to strenuous exercise. *J. Bone Jt. Surg.* **44b**:711-721, 1962.

An evaluation of mechanisms modulating muscle size in response to varying perturbations

Philip D. Gollnick, Dorabeth Parsons, Mark Riedy,
Russell L. Moore, and Benjamin F. Timson
Washington State University

Following conception, mammalian development is characterized by intrauterine (prenatal) and extrauterine (postnatal) growth leading to the adult animal. For skeletal muscle, prenatal growth is considered the primary period for cellular proliferation with total fiber number being determined either before or shortly after birth. This conclusion comes from studies of the total fiber number of skeletal muscle of fetuses and fully mature animals, including man. Therefore, it follows that most postnatal growth is the result of circumferential and longitudinal growth of the fibers in skeletal muscles.

An example of the growth and development of rabbit skeletal muscle from birth to maturity was published by Meara (54). In these experiments changes in the weight and length of rabbit gastrocnemius and psoas muscles were measured. In addition, fiber length, diameter, the number of fibers per bundle, and the angle of the fibers in the muscle (gastrocnemius) were followed with body growth (Table 1). The psoas is

Table 1
Body and Muscle Growth of the Rabbit[a]

			Gastrocnemius				Psoas		
BW	MW	D	ML	BL	A	MW	D	ML	BL
Birth	0.048	10.91	0.99			0.109	8.32	2.72	2.53
100 g	0.056		1.08			0.156		3.58	3.25
220 g	0.226		2.04	0.73	12.8	0.431		5.16	4.78
480 g	0.727		3.00	1.01	14.8	1.564		8.04	7.41
600 g	1.000	39.57	3.37	0.93	19.4	1.950	19.16	8.85	8.12
1200 g	1.900	51.18	4.12	0.90	22.9	4.600	27.69	10.17	9.51
1800 g	2.950	67.78	5.00	1.00	23.6	8.600	37.04	12.44	11.13
2400 g	3.710	74.44	5.48	0.99	25.9	11.550	42.25	14.50	12.75
3000 g	4.640	81.55	5.93	0.94	28.1	14.790	44.76	15.82	13.83

[a]BW body weight in grams, MW muscle weight in grams, D average fiber diameter in μm, ML length of the muscle in cm, BL length of the muscle bundles in cm, and A the angle of the fibers in the gastrocnemius muscle. The number of fibers per bundle of fibers was 48 and 92 at birth and 51 and 94 at a body weight of 3,000 g for the gastrocnemius and psoas muscles, respectively. These data have been compiled from Meara (54).

a muscle with a relatively parallel fiber architecture and the gastrocnemius has a bipennate fiber arrangement (Figure 1). Of particular interest in these two muscles was the change in the length and diameter of the fibers in relation to the whole muscle from birth to maturity. Meara reported no change in the number of fibers per bundle.

The potential for growth of human skeletal muscles is illustrated by the fact that, at birth, the biceps brachii muscle weighs about 2.0 g as compared to 110-150 g in the average adult (Saltin, Nygaard, and Colling-Saltin, personal communication). There are also increases in fiber diameter that parallel overall growth of skeletal muscles (1,8,9,13, 63). For the laboratory rat, muscles can increase 30- to 40-fold in weight from birth to maturity (11,17,18,48), whereas chicken skeletal muscle weight can increase more than 300-fold from hatching to maturity (59,78). This article asks whether postnatal development in skeletal muscle is produced exclusively by hypertrophy (increased cellular mass) or whether there is also an increase in muscle fiber number (hyperplasia).

The question of how increases in muscle bulk occur with heavy manual labor or weightlifting and body building programs has vexed man for more than a century. Similarly, the mechanism(s) producing the loss of muscle mass with disuse, whether volitional or the result of muscular denervation or skeletal immobilization, has been contemplated. In addition to satisfying a curiosity about the adaptability of muscle to varying patterns of physical activity, there are commercial, physical perfor-

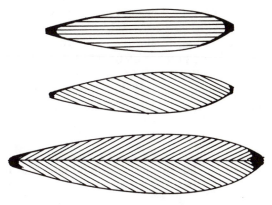

Figure 1 — A schematic drawing illustrating the different types of fiber arrangements that exist in skeletal muscle. The upper panel depicts a parallel fiber arrangement, the middle panel is of a single penniform fiber arrangement, and the lower panel is that of a bipenniform fiber arrangement. Muscles also exist that possess more than two pennations. These are identified as multipenniform muscles.

mance, and medical reasons for continued research in this area. The commercial interest comes from a need to increase meat production (54,66,78,81), which may be related to the number of fibers contained in a given muscle for a given animal strain. The interest from a physical performance standpoint is related to the potential for increasing muscular strength (primarily a function of the muscle's cross-sectional area) because success in many sports is related to strength. Increasing fiber number within a muscle would be one way of increasing total cross-sectional area without excessive enlargement of the individual fibers. Finally, many medical conditions exist in which muscle fibers are lost through nutritional deficiencies, disease, neural injury, or physical damage (19,39). If the potential exists for a postnatal fiber proliferation, a muscle could be restored, at least partially, and its function greatly improved.

Historical aspects

The question of hyperplasia versus hypertrophy in the enlargement of skeletal muscle is not new as evidenced by the frequent citing of Morpurgo's studies (57). This early work is the cornerstone for the concept that fiber number after birth is fixed and that increases in bulk result from hypertrophy rather than hyperplasia. In these studies the sartorius muscle was removed from one hindlimb of dogs and fiber size and number were determined on cross-sectional segments from the muscle. The dogs were subsequently exercised with a running program, after which the sartorius muscle of the contralateral leg was removed for similar measurements.

The results indicated that though the total cross-sectional area of the muscle had increased, the number of fibers contained in a cross-section taken from the muscle belly was unchanged. Total cross-sectional area of the muscle fibers paralleled that of the overall increase in muscle size. This finding was contrary to earlier reports of an increase in fiber number in the intestinal wall where muscular enlargement was induced by stenosis (57). A number of subsequent studies, in which enlargement of skeletal muscle was induced by a variety of experimental manipulations, supported the conclusion that postnatal increases in muscle bulk occurred from an increase in fiber size and not by hyperplasia (53,64,76,77,83).

Results of studies concerning the number of fibers in the muscle of fetuses and at various stages of postnatal development are equivocal. For example, there are reports that myogenesis ceases before birth (52) and that it extends into the postnatal period (5,11,48,55,56,68), with the period for postnatal muscle fiber proliferation reported as being short. One reason for the disparity in these results may lie with the type of muscles studied and the stage of fiber development. In many muscles the fiber arrangement is such that not all of the fibers are included in a single cross-sectional cut across the belly of the muscle (as discussed later), making it difficult to determine total muscle fiber number. Even in parallel fibered muscles a period of growth may be required before the fibers traverse the entire muscle or extend through the midpoint of the muscle (64), and in some parallel fibered muscles the fibers do not extend the entire length of the muscle. Most evidence from the studies of fetuses and postnatal man suggests that muscle fiber proliferation ceases either before or shortly after birth (10,11,13,39,48).

Some studies have reported declines in the number of fibers, presumably from a loss of motor units, with age (21,22,34,43,68). However, methodological considerations make these data equivocal.

A recent impetus for determining the total fiber number of muscle has come from attempts to establish the number of fibers per motor unit. In such studies the number of alpha-motoneurons has been determined in attempts to estimate the average number of fibers based on total fiber number in the muscle. Some recent studies have demonstrated that the muscle fibers of the newborn rat are polyinnervated and are contained in more than one motor unit (5,10). One of these studies has suggested that fiber number in skeletal muscles increases during the immediate postnatal period (5). Estimation of total fiber number in the chicken from hatching to full maturity leads to the conclusion that skeletal muscle fiber number was unchanged in this animal species during a 300-fold increase in muscle size (59,78).

Though most experimental evidence suggests that the fiber number of skeletal muscle is determined early in life, there are reports to the contrary. Thus, it has also been reported that a major increase in the number of fibers occurs in skeletal muscles of marsupials during postnatal development (7). This seems reasonable since intrauterine development ceases in these animals while they are relatively immature. Thus, birth may not represent a uniform state of development for all animals.

Early nutrition has been reported to influence total fiber number of skeletal muscles (39,53). Notable here is a report that 3 days of fasting reduced fiber number in rat skeletal muscle by about 30% (39). Refeeding with a return to original body weight restored the original number of muscle fibers.

Some muscle fibers have branch points or central cleavages, which has led to the suggestion that the fiber number of skeletal muscle can increase (14,19,29,32,33,35-37,39,40,45,46,69,71,73,74,80,84-86). Such fibers were first observed before the turn of the century (19,86). Their existence also has led to the suggestion that muscle fibers reproduce by a longitudinal division frequently referred to as "fiber splitting." This suggestion comes primarily from the studies of van Linge (84) and Reitsma (69) in which such fibers were observed in rat muscle that had enlargement induced by a combination of removing a synergistic muscle and exercise. These branched fibers were considered as evidence for an increase in total fiber number.

Numerous reports have appeared suggesting that total fiber number does increase in response to a variety of experimental perturbations that produce muscular growth (14,32,33,40,42,69,71,73,74,79,84,85). In some cases attempts were made to quantify the number of fibers contained in the muscles whereas in other instances the mere existence of such "split" fibers was assumed to constitute evidence for an increased fiber number. Unfortunately, the incidence of the "split" fibers was not determined in studies where its existence has been evoked as the mechanism for an increase in total fiber number.

Methodological considerations

Part of the disagreement over the effects of varying experimental manipulations on the fiber number in skeletal muscle probably lies in the methods used. This controversy stems both from the types of muscles, that is, the fiber arrangements, that have been studied and the methods for counting the fibers.

Muscle structure

Figure 1 illustrates three types (there are more) of fiber arrangements in skeletal muscles. The upper portion of the figure illustrates an arrangement in which fibers are parallel to the long axis of the muscle and traverse the entire muscle. The second fiber orientation is a single pennation with the fibers arising not only from the origin on the skeleton, but also from an aponeurosis along the long axis of the muscle. The fibers insert into another aponeurosis that merges into a tendon that inserts onto the bone. A third organization pattern is a bipennate muscle in which fibers run from two outer aspects of the muscle and insert into a central tendon. Some muscles have more than two pennations (multipennate muscles). Figure 1 illustrates the difficulties encountered in determining total fiber number from cross-sections made at the midpoint of a muscle, or at the point of greatest girth as done frequently.

Fiber number

Several methods have been used for estimating the total fiber number of muscle, including (a) making a cross-sectional cut through the muscle and counting, either manually or with computers (72), the number of fibers in histological cross-sections; (b) cutting a cross-sectional segment from the muscle and preparing the fibers in the section into segments that are suspended in fluid for counting with an electronic device (80); (c) using the DNA concentration to estimate total fiber number (18,51); and (d) manually dissecting fibers and counting them individually (29). Perhaps the most frequently used method for determining fiber number is based on method a. Modifications of this method include counting all fibers in a cross-section either with a light microscope or from micrographs prepared from the cross-sections, or by counting the number of fibers contained in a given area and extrapolating this to the total muscle area (47). This method is valid only for muscles having all fibers included in a cross-sectional cut. This means that either the muscle must be the type in the upper part of the figure, or that multiple cuts must be made through the muscle such that all fibers can ultimately be included. If multiple cross-sectional segments are taken, each fiber must be transected only once or at least counted only once.

The limitations in this method for determining total fiber number in penniform muscle was discussed by Clark in 1931 (12). However, the proper methods have been rarely used for penniform muscles. The method breaks down completely when applied to multipenniform muscle. Here the problem of making multiple histological preparations that will ultimately include all fibers is evident. The problem is not one of being able to count all the fibers from a histological section but of including all fibers in the section.

Procedure b is a modification of procedure a with the fibers being counted electronically. The method was developed for use with a Coulter counting device. The limitations are all those applicable to procedure a, and the segments must be uniform enough in size so that they will all be sensed by the counter. The use of DNA to estimate fiber number makes the assumption that the DNA content of the fibers is constant. The proliferation of DNA in the extrafiber component of muscle during growth makes this an unreliable indicator of total fiber number (39,60). Thus, the method of isolating and counting all of the fibers manually appears to be the most valid. It has, however, been assumed to be too tedious for routine use with muscles containing large numbers of fibers.

Fiber weight cross-sectional area and length

During muscular enlargement in the mature animal the cross-sectional area of the muscle increases. The weight of a muscle must be a function of fiber number and the average weight per fiber. Expressed mathematically, this is simply

$$MW = Fn \cdot F\bar{w},$$

where MW is the total muscle weight, Fn is fiber number and $F\bar{w}$ is mean weight per fiber. This simplistic formula must be corrected for 15% total extrafiber material in muscle (23,49). To further fractionate the muscle weight into its component parts it is clear that fiber weight is a function of volume ($F\bar{v}$) times the density (D) of muscle. For a muscle, $F\bar{v}$ can be calculated from the mean cross-sectional area ($Fx\bar{a}$) and mean fiber length ($F\bar{l}$). This relationship is expressed as

$$F\bar{v} = Fx\bar{a} \cdot F\bar{l}.$$

Average weight per fiber is then

$$F\bar{w} = Fx\bar{a} \cdot F\bar{l} \cdot D.$$

A number of methods have been used to determine the cross-sectional area of muscle fibers, including planimetry of the fibers from micrographs or projections of the fibers, measurements of fiber diameters, preparing micrographs of the fibers and cutting out areas of paper and weighing them, and estimation from electronic sizing devices (15,72,80, 82). Direct planimetry of the fibers from micrographs is tedious and time-consuming. It is, however, very accurate and generally recognized as the best for determining the cross-sectional area of the fibers. Newly developed electronic devices, including computer programs, are making this method practical and fast.

The measurement of fiber diameters is a popular way of assessing changes in fiber size with growth or atrophy. This method suffers the main disadvantage that fibers are not cylinders and thus a number of diameters can be measured. The usual choices are either the longest or shortest diameters. The question is how these diameters should be interpreted. If the fibers were cylinders their cross-sectional areas could be calculated according to the equation

$$F\bar{x}a = \pi r^2.$$

Since most fibers are not cylinders a choice must be made of the diameter used. The longest diameter will overestimate and the shortest diameter will underestimate fiber area. Fiber diameter may be useful for estimating relative changes in muscle fiber area but it cannot be used in a quantitative manner to account for gains or losses of muscle mass in response to experimental perturbations or disease states since the percentage error may exceed the change in muscle mass.

The Coulter method also has been used to determine fibers' cross-sectional area. However, it makes the incorrect assumption that all fibers are cylinders.

We may ask why we should be concerned with estimating total fiber weight and subsequently estimating MW from Fw and Fn. It appears to us that any suggestion of a change in total fiber number must withstand the test of whether the total muscle weight is equal to the sum of its parts. This implies that the $F\bar{x}a$ and $F\bar{l}$ of the muscle are known or can be estimated with reasonable accuracy. In most experiments for which cross-sectional cuts were used to assess the total Fn, these quantities have not been determined directly. However, if all components of the equation for estimating muscle weight except fiber length are available, this characteristic can be estimated. This estimation is useful because when total muscle weight, fiber cross-sectional area, and average fiber length are known, they can be substituted into the general formula for the muscle weight and total fiber number can be estimated. It represents a check on the validity of estimating total fiber number by any method.

Fiber proliferation

A common observation used to support fiber hyperplasia during muscular enlargement is the presence of fibers with branching points (14,32,33,40,67,71,72,79,82,85). Such fibers have been observed in a number of species after a variety of experimental treatments designed to increase muscle mass. They are identified in histological cross-sections as one fiber that in adjacent cross-sections becomes two fibers. The limitation here is that it is a random accident when such fibers are encountered. Examples of branched fibers are presented in Figure 2. These fibers were teased from muscle digested in 15% nitric acid (29). This figure illustrates the multiplicity of branched patterns that exist in fibers from skeletal muscle. It also exemplifies the problem of finding all such fibers in a muscle with histological methods and of quantifying their importance in muscular growth.

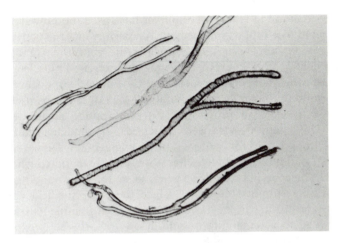

Figure 2 — Examples of muscle fibers with varying branched structures. These are fibers that were dissected from nitric acid digested muscle. As illustrated, the point of branching can occur anywhere along the longitudinal axis of the fiber resulting in appendages of varying lengths. The sum of the diameters of the appendages does not necessarily equal that of the stem, being greater in most instances.

At present no studies have been published in which such techniques were applied to establish the extent of "fiber splitting" during muscular enlargement. Moreover, the term "fiber splitting" implies a dynamic process which has not been verified. The existence of branched fibers as viewed under the light (14,25,26,32,33,69,72,84) and electron microscope (35-37,40,41,63,64,73,74,76) cannot be considered as evidence that these fibers are dividing. They could be fibers in the process of fusing (51,63,64,74,76). It has not been established whether the branched fibers found in skeletal muscle are anything but an occasional anomalous structure present in all muscles. Thus, the observation that fibers with branch points exist in normal muscles suggests that they are not unique to enlarging muscles.

Functional overload

The experimental methods for producing muscular enlargement include the surgical removal of part or all of a synergistic muscle, endurance exercise, heavy resistance exercise, chronic stretch, or combinations of these regimens. Though endurance exercise has been used to produce muscular enlargement, it is generally accepted that it is not an effective method for increasing muscle mass. Swimming has been used in the study of muscle growth (14,87) but it has not been conspicuous for its ability to produce skeletal muscle enlargement. Weightlifting is well known for its potential to increase muscle mass in humans. Attempts to extend this method to laboratory animals have used food rewards (31-33) or pain avoidance (40) as inducement for performing the activity. Such programs have not been overly successful from the standpoint of muscular enlargement in exercised versus nonexercised muscles. Surgical ablation of synergistic muscles or portions of mucles produces an extensive and rapid muscular enlargement (3,29,42,43). It can be used in conjunction with exercise programs (29) to produce greater muscular growth. This method has been criticized for inducing pathological changes in muscle and for being nonphysiological (32). However, the occurrence of pathological changes has not been substantiated when care is taken with the experiments (29). The criticism that it is nonphysiological is not entirely supportable either, since there are medical conditions where loss of all or part of a muscle or surgical treatments transfer an enlarged load to a remaining muscle. Moreover, the early experiments that are frequently cited (69,84) as having demonstrated an increase in fiber number as a result of "fiber splitting" used some variation of the surgical removal or inactivation of a synergistic muscle either alone or in combination with exercise. Chronic stretch or overload produced by hanging weights on limbs or by placing a spring-like device across a joint (4,41,79) has produced large increases in muscle weight without surgical intervention.

There are reports of the effects of exercise on the area of muscle fibers (16,20,28,67). Gollnick and co-workers (28) observed that the cross-sectional area of fibers in the muscles from weight lifters were larger than those of sedentary individuals or of athletes who did not practice heavy resistance exercise. Edström and Ekblom (16) and Prince et al. (67) subsequently reported that weight lifters possessed fast twitch fibers with average diameters greater than those of other individuals.

Muscular enlargement and hyperplasia

From Morpurgo's experiments (57) the general conclusion has been that fiber number in the skeletal muscles of mature animals is unchanged during growth induced by exercise and that increases in muscular bulk result from changes in the size of individual muscle fibers (hypertrophy). This conclusion was supported by numerous studies showing increases in muscle weight after birth to be the result of hypertrophy rather than hyperplasia. These supporting data were derived from studies during growth in man (52,75) and in a variety of animals whose growth was induced in response to exercise (76,87).

van Linge (84) and Reitsma (69) were perhaps the first to suggest fiber hyperplasia via "fiber splitting" in response to extirpation of a synergistic muscle and exercise. van Linge (84) examined the plantaris of rats in which a 22-150% enlargement had been induced by combining denervation of synergistic muscles with treadmill exercise. This exercise involved walking on a treadmill up a $+27°$ grade for from one 4.5-hr exercise bout to 31 days, when the walk covered 9 hr. Unfortunately, insufficient data are included in the paper, such as muscle weight, total fiber number, cross-sectional area, or fiber length to permit a complete evaluation of the response that occurred. Reitsma (69) did state that van Linge observed 34 fibers with branches in the plantaris muscle of 3,400 total fibers. However, 3,400 fibers is only a fraction of the total number of fibers in the plantaris muscle (29). The existence of small fibers was interpreted as evidence for fiber proliferation. It was stated that changes in the angle of the fibers in the muscle during enlargement made it impossible to make a transverse section that would be comparable in the control and enlarged muscles.

Reitsma (69) induced muscular enlargement via inactivation of synergistic muscles and exercise. Analysis included standard histological sections along with dissecting fibers from nitric acid digested muscles. Branched fibers were observed in the enlarged muscles but there was no quantitative assessment of total fiber number or frequency of fiber "splitting." Rowe and Goldspink (71) induced average weight increases of 60 and 83%, respectively, in the soleus muscle of male and female mice by removing synergistic muscles. Though frequently cited as evidence for fiber proliferation in response to functional overload, this conclusion is unwarranted because there was no change in fiber number for the male mice whereas that of the females averaged 15% more in experimental compared to control groups. As comparisons were made between animals and not within animals, it cannot be unequivocally stated that the difference in fiber number is not a result of normal biological variation.

Edgerton (14) examined the effect of swim training on rat skeletal muscle. Histological sections were made of the plantaris, soleus, and gastrocnemius muscles. The differences in the muscle weights between groups were not reported nor was total fiber number determined. It was stated that soleus muscles from the exercised groups contained more fibers with necrotic lesions and "splits" than did those from sedentary animals. No mention was made of the effect of the experimental treatments on the plantaris or gastrocnemius muscles. Results of these experiments are not sufficiently quantitative to support the contention that the exercise produced fiber proliferation. Walker (87) observed no increase in the mean fiber diameter of mice following training by swimming that could be used to suggest any muscular enlargement had occurred or that it was necessary to increase fiber number.

It has been reported that fiber number in the plantaris muscle of the guinea pig declines with age (21,22) and that this fiber loss could be prevented by exercise. However, it was subsequently demonstrated that errors had been made in enumerating the fibers and that there probably was no change in total fiber number as a result of the exercise (53).

Ianuzzo et al. (42) observed 103 and 46% enlargements, respectively, of rat plantaris and soleus muscles in response to surgical ablation of the gastrocnemius muscle. In these experiments there were 29% more fibers in a cross-sectional segment taken from the point of greatest girth of the enlarged plantaris but the soleus muscle showed no change. This difference can be attributed to the different fiber architecture of the two muscles. The single penniform fiber arrangement of the plantaris muscle would necessitate a change in fiber angle to accommodate their enlargement without a change in muscle length and would thereby change the number of fibers in a cross-section made perpendicular to the long axis of the fibers (6,29).

Schiaffino et al. (74) reported a 26% increase in the number of fibers in extensor digitorum longus muscles in which bulk increased an average of 32% in 1- to 165-day-old rats 4-76 wk after surgical extirpation of the tibialis anterior muscle. These investigators suggested that the number of fibers in the enlarged muscle had been underestimated and exceeded that which was reported. Branched fibers teased from nitric acid digested muscles was cited as evidence for fiber proliferation via "splitting." Gollnick et al. (29) determined fiber number in the rat extensor digitorum longus muscle after enlargement produced by ablation of the tibialis anterior muscle. Direct count following nitric acid digestion of this single penniform muscle revealed a total fiber number of about 5,200 (29) fibers in normal and enlarged muscles. This was 50-20% more fibers than found by the histological method (74). This finding further illustrates the difficulty of including all fibers in cross-sectional cuts of muscles in which fiber arrangement is not parallel to the long axis of the muscle.

The effect of overloading chicken muscle on the length and cross-sectional area of the fibers has been studied (4,41,79). Sola and co-workers (79) observed a continual increase in the number of fibers of the anterior latissimus dorsi muscle as it enlarged up to 200% in 8 wk in response to hanging weights on the wing. Fiber number in five chickens, counted from histological cross-sections 1.5 cm from the muscle's insertion, averaged 32% (range 27-38%) more fibers in the enlarged than control muscle. The rate of "new fiber appearance" was estimated at about 70 per wk. This increase was attributed to "fiber splitting" which was supported by the existence of small fibers interspersed among normal fibers.

Gollnick et al. (30) examined control and enlarged anterior latissimus dorsi muscles from chickens in which growth was induced using the method of Sola et al. (79). There was no evidence of an increase in fiber number in this parallel, fibered muscle with enlargement for which fiber number was determined by nitric acid-direct count method. The increase in muscle weight could be accounted for by an increase in the length and cross-sectional area of the fibers.

Holly and associates (41) also observed increases in the length and cross-sectional area of the fibers of several enlarged shoulder muscles of the chicken that were closely correlated with the increase in wet weight of the various muscles. In subsequent studies (4) Ashmore and Summers demonstrated that the increase in muscle weight was due to both longitudinal and circumferential growth of the individual fibers with the circumferential growth resulting from a division of myofibrils. The increased number of myofibrils in the skeletal muscle agrees with the observation of Richter and Kellner (70) of a greater number in the enlarged myocardium. Goldspink (24-26) has suggested that myofibril splitting occurs due to a change in the angle of pull on the myofibril as a result of their increased size.

Gonyea and co-workers (31-33) used a model of weightlifting for cats in which a lever was moved against graded resistance for a food reward. Total fiber number in the multipennate flexor carpi radialis muscle was estimated from cross-sections made at the point of its greatest girth. Weightlifting increased muscle weight 6-16%, fiber number 20%, and fiber diameter about 10%. The problem here is that the total does not equal the sum of the parts. A 20% increase in fiber number should produce a 20% increase in muscle weight unless the fibers are all smaller. However, average fiber diameter was increased by about 10%. The combination of a 20% increase in fiber number and a 10% increase in fiber diameter (a 20% increase in cross-sectional area) should translate to a 44% increase in total muscle weight.

Ho et al. (40) trained rats with a weightlifting program that involved placing a belt-like device with weights attached around the rats' midsections. The rats were conditioned to lift the weight by standing erect on their hindlegs to avoid an electrical shock. Muscles examined included the adductor longus and the rectus femoris. Changes in muscle weight, fiber area, and fiber number were evaluated on the basis of differences between sedentary control animals and the weightlifting group. The effectiveness of the weightlifting can be judged from the results presented in Table 2. The adductor longus muscle increased in weight by about 14%. Fiber numbers and cross-sectional areas, made from histological sections of the muscle, were reported to have increased 12% and decreased about 22%, respectively. The increase in fiber number was attributed to longitudinal splitting based on the existence of branched fibers in the muscles. Quantitative evidence for a splitting was not presented nor were data presented to substantiate the fact that the branched fibers were restricted to the enlarged muscles.

Gollnick and associates (29) approached the problem of whether

Table 2

Analysis of the Changes in Fiber Characteristics of Muscle Reported to Have Undergone Fiber Splitting (40)

Comparison	Control	Experimental	% Change
Muscle weight (mg)	108	123	+ 13.8
Weight of muscle fibers (mg)[a]	91.8	104.6	+ 13.8
Total fiber number	2204	2477	+ 12.4
SO[b]	1939	2180	+ 12.4
FOG[b]	265	297	+ 12.0
Total cross sec. area (mm^2)	10.6	10.8	+ 1.9
Fiber cross sec. area (μm^2)			
SO	3248.2	2638.6	− 18.8
FOG	2909.5	2204.0	− 24.2
Area of fibers (mm^2)			
SO	6.298	5.752	− 8.7
FOG	0.770	0.655	− 14.9
Area SO + FOG fibers	7.068	6.407	− 9.4
Percent of total area			
SO	88.7	89.8	+ 1.2
FOG	11.3	10.2	− 9.7
Weight/fiber type (mg)			
SO	81.4	93.9	+ 15.1
FOG	10.4	10.7	+ 2.9
Weight/fiber (μg)			
SO	41.9	43.1	+ 2.8
FOG	39.2	36.0	− 8.2
Fiber length (mm)			
SO	129.0	163.3	+ 26.6
FOG	134.7	163.3	+ 21.2

[a]Based on 15% of the weight of the muscle being nonfiber material.
[b]Estimated from Ariano et al. (2).

hyperplasia occurred in skeletal muscle with the dissection-direct counting method for determining total fiber number and the frequency of branched fibers. The variability of the number of fibers in the same muscle from both limbs of the same rat and for the same muscle between rats was examined. Muscles examined included the parallel fibered soleus and the penniform plantaris and extensor digitorum longus muscles of the rat. A high degree of congruity existed for the number of fibers in the muscles from the right and left limbs of the same animals. However, inter-animal variation was about 50 and 65% for the soleus and plantaris muscles, respectively. Muscular enlargement (10 to over 100%) was produced either by the ablation of synergistic muscles or by the combination of synergistic ablation and treadmill running up a + 25% grade for 20 min/day at 38 m/min. Animals were allowed a minimum of 4 wk to recover from the surgery before being studied in order to avoid complications from inflammation, edema, or pathological damage (3,43). The exercise was for 6-8 wk and resulted in muscular enlargements that were about 50% greater than that which occurred in response to only the extirpation of the synergistic muscle. There were no differences in fiber number between control muscles (nonoperated) and enlarged muscles regardless of the degree of difference in muscle weight, the age of the rats at the time overload was imposed, or the duration of the functional overload. Comparison of the two legs of the same animal, despite the fact that the operated leg may have been favored and used less for both the sedentary and exercised groups, was mandated by the results from control animals demonstrating the large inter-animal but small intra-animal variation between muscles that were examined (29).

Branched fibers existed in all muscles but the total number was not different for the enlarged compared to the control muscles. The dry weight of the individual fibers increased proportionately to total wet weight ($r = 0.87$ between the percentage difference in dry fiber weight of the control and enlarged muscles versus the percentage difference in wet weights of the two muscles). These data support the concept that muscular growth resulted from an increase in the mass of the individual fibers and not from an increase in fiber number. Fiber length in these groups was essentially unchanged as a result of the increase in muscle bulk. Estimation of fiber length from the fiber number, muscle weight, and fiber diameter resulted in a value similar to the measured length.

Attempts were made to calculate fiber length from the data published by Gonyea and co-workers (32) and Ho et al. (40). Since Gonyea et al. (32) published only fiber diameters, it was necessary to consider the fibers as cylinders in the estimation of cross-sectional area. This procedure is obviously incorrect, but should produce a reasonable estimate of fiber length. On this basis it was estimated that the fibers were between 7 and 14 cm long, depending on the fiber type, to account for the muscle weight as given. This is a fiber length that would exceed that of the total muscle and of the cat forelimb. Thus, fiber number must have been grossly underestimated. Direct counts of the fibers in the cat flexor carpi radialis revealed approximately 28,000 fibers per muscle (29) rather than the 7,500-9,000 contained in the cross-sectional segment taken from the point of greatest muscle girth (32). To accommodate the change in the muscle as described by Ho et al. the length of the fibers would have had to increase 21-27% as a result of the training. Such changes in fiber length are unlikely modes of adaptation. The increase in fiber number reported during muscular enlargement can be accounted for by a change in fiber angle, depending on how the cross-sectional cut was made. If the cut is made perpendicular to the long axis of the muscle, the section will contain fewer fibers due to a change in the fiber angle. Conversely, the cross-sectional area will be overestimated as the "cylinders" are cut tangentially. If the sample is cut at a right angle to the fibers there will be more fibers in the cross-section.

The question remains as to what is the meaning or importance of the branched fibers found in skeletal muscles. Clearly, it has not been demonstrated that their incidence increases during massive muscular enlargement. The existence of such fibers in the enlarged muscle cannot be evoked as evidence for producing fiber proliferation on the basis of currently existing evidence. Moreover, the frequently cited studies of Hall-Craggs and colleagues (35-37) and James (45,46) do not contain evidence that overloads produce an increase in fiber number via a longitudinal division of fibers. Hall-Craggs concluded that the longitudinal cleavages in muscle fibers could be caused by a degeneration of portions of the fibers (35) and that "fibre division does not seem to add to the cross-sectional area of a muscle undergoing hypertrophy . . . but is evidence of trauma to a number of its fibres" (37). Similarly, James (45) stated, "Clearly it is not possible to establish directly in tissue sections whether the satellite structures arise by muscle fibre *splitting* as previously described, whether they arise independently, or whether they may even be in the process of *fusing* with muscle fibres." James (46) concluded on the basis of a conservation of matter (measurements of total muscle weight and fiber cross-sectional area) in studies where enlargement of the extensor digitorum longus muscle was induced by surgical removal of its synergist that there may in fact have been a loss of fibers (hypoplasia). Thus, fiber cross-sectional area increased to a greater extent than did total muscle weight.

Maturation, aging, and nutrition

Maturation
Changes have been reported in the number of fibers in skeletal muscle of animals during the period immediately after birth (5,7,9,11,53-56,64). Morpurgo (58) reported the existence of 25% more fibers in the radialis muscle of the rat 15 days after birth compared to the fibers at birth. Chiakulas and Pauly (11) also reported that the number of fibers in the soleus, plantaris, and extensor carpi radialis longus muscles increased from birth to 6 wk of age. Betz et al. (5) reported a 40% increase in the number of fibers in the lumbrical muscle of the rat during the first weeks after birth. A close scrutiny of these data reveals that errors were made in determining total fiber number. For example, Chiakulas and Pauly (11) reported that 1 wk after birth there were 5,801, 2,389, and 3,320 fibers in the rat extensor carpi radialis longus, soleus, and plantaris muscles, respectively. At 6 wk of age these muscles reportedly contained 8,587, 3,475, and 6,750 fibers, respectively.

Using the fiber dissection methods, Gollnick et al. (29) observed considerable inter-animal variability in the number of fibers contained in the soleus and plantaris muscles. They also found no difference with growth (29,65). For the soleus muscle, fiber number ranged from about 2,200 to 3,300 fibers whereas for the plantaris, a penniform muscle, this range was from about 8,500 to 13,000 fibers. These data illustrate that though the number of fibers as reported for the soleus by Chiakulas and Pauly (11) appears to have increased during early growth, the values are all within the normal variation between animals. Thus, the change is not necessarily the result of a change in fiber number.

The fiber number in the plantaris muscle was grossly underestimated due to its penniform nature and therefore these data cannot be interpreted as evidence of a change in total fiber number. In these studies the cross-sectional segments were cut perpendicular to the long axis of the muscle. Since the angle of fibers changes in penniform muscle with growth (54), an increasing number of fibers appears in the section (29). Many studies with meat-producing animals support the concept that most postnatal growth is via hypertrophy rather than hyperplasia (59,66,78,81). Montgomery (55,56) reported that the number of fibers in human sartorius muscle increased during the first 4 months of postnatal life. Whether this represents the longitudinal growth of fibers such that they appear in the histological sections is unknown but possible.

Considerable variation also exists in the number of fibers in human skeletal muscle. Nygaard (61,62) estimated the total number of fibers in human biceps to range from 280,000 to 500,000. In these studies males had slightly more fibers than females but there was no difference between trained and sedentary individuals. The general pattern from reports of growth in man has been an increase in fiber diameter (1,8,9,13,52).

Aging

Decreases in the total number of fibers has also been reported to occur with age (34,44,68). This decrease has been reported to be as much as a 31-32% loss of fibers in the dog between 2 and 12 months of age (44). Though the fibers in this muscle were purported to run parallel to the long axis of the muscle and to traverse the entire length of the muscle, this somewhat large loss of muscle fibers over a rather short period needs verification. Gutmann and Hanzlíková (34) observed a decline in the number of fibers in the soleus muscle of young adult (4 months) and old (2 years) rats. Work by Kugelberg (50) and Parsons and co-workers (65) did not support these findings.

In humans, Montgomery (55,56) observed a decrease in the number of fibers in the sartorius muscle of from 134,000 at 4 months of age to 114,000 in a 74-year-old. Based on the normal variation between individuals these data do not support the concept of a major reduction in fiber number with age.

Nutrition

Nutritional status has been reported to influence the growth and total fiber number of skeletal muscle. The general conclusion from these investigations is that fiber diameter is smaller in malnourished animals, including humans (23,27,38,39,55). This condition is reversed by a return to a well nourished state (27,38,55). Short periods of food deprivation have been reported to lower the wet weight of rats by about 25% when compared with muscles from normal animals (39). Associated with these lower muscle weights were reductions in fiber number of about 30%. These data fail to pass the test of being usable in calculating reasonable fiber weights and lengths from the values of muscle weight, fiber diameters, and fiber numbers that were published. In all cases major shifts in fiber lengths were necessary to accommodate the total change in muscle weight, with the fibers becoming longer when the muscle lost weight and shorter when it became heavier. This adaptive response to altered nutritional state was not observed by Parsons et al. (65).

Montgomery (55) has also reported that malnutrition early in life can result in the development of fewer than normal muscle fibers in man. These studies also produced the result that there was a proliferation of muscle fibers during the first 4 months of postnatal life.

Summary

It is clear that considerable disagreement exists concerning the relative importance of hypertrophy and hyperplasia in the increase in total mass of skeletal muscle. Few papers have been published that accomplish an exact evaluation of the total number of muscle fibers. Moreover, the claim of increased fiber number resulting from longitudinal cleavage of single fibers into one or more "daughter cells" has not been confirmed as anything but the existence of a few fibers in muscle that have a normal branched structure. Where it has been possible to carefully examine total fiber number in the "control" and enlarged states in muscles derived from the same gene pool, there has been no evidence of an increase in fiber number. The total increase in muscle mass can be explained by the increase in diameter and length of the preexisting fibers.

References

1. Ahrene, W., Ayyar, D.R., Clarke, P.A., and Walton, J.N. Muscle fibre size in normal infants, children and adolescents. An autopsy study. *J. Neurol. Sci.* **14:**171-182, 1971.

2. Ariano, M.A., Armstrong, R.B., and Edgerton, V.R. Hindlimb muscle fiber populations of five mammals. *J. Histochem. Cytochem.* **21**:51-55, 1973.

3. Armstrong, R.B., Marum, P., Tullson, P., and Saubert, C.W. IV. Acute hypertrophic response of skeletal muscle to removal of synergists. *J. Appl. Physiol: Respirat. Environ. Exercise Physiol.* **46**:835-842, 1979.

4. Ashmore, C.R., and Summers, P.J. Stretch-induced growth in chicken wing muscles: Myofibrillar proliferation. *Am. J. Physiol.* **241**:C93-C97, 1981.

5. Betz, W.J., Caldwell, J.H., and Ribchester, R.R. The size of motor units during postnatal development in the rat lumbrical muscle. *J. Physiol.* **297**:463-478, 1979.

6. Binkhorst, R.A., and van't Hof, M.A. Force-velocity relationship and contraction time of the rat fast plantaris muscle due to compensatory hypertrophy. *Pfluegers Arch.* **342**:145-158, 1973.

7. Bridge, D.T., and Allbrook, D. Growth of striated muscle in an Australian marsupial *(Setonix brachyurus). J. Anat.* **106**:285-295, 1970.

8. Brooke, M.H., and Engel, W.K. The histographic analysis of human muscle biopsies with regard to fiber types. I. Adult male and female. *Neurology* **19**:221-223, 1969.

9. Brooke, M.H., and Engel, W.K. The histographic analysis of human muscle biopsies with regard to fiber types. IV. Children. *Neurology* **19**:591-605, 1969.

10. Brown, M.D., Jansen, J.K.S., and Van Essen, D. Polyneuronal innervation of skeletal muscle in new-born rats and its elimination during maturation. *J. Physiol.* **261**:387-422, 1976.

11. Chiakulas, J.J., and Pauly, J.E. A study of postnatal growth of skeletal muscle in the rat. *Anat. Rec.* **152**:55-62. 1965.

12. Clark, D.A. Muscle counts of motor units: A study in innervation ratios. *Am. J. Physiol.* **96**:296-304, 1931.

13. Colling-Saltin, A.-S. Skeletal muscle development in the human foetus and during childhood. In: K. Berg and B. Eriksson (eds.), *Children and exercise IX*. University Park Press, Baltimore, 1980, pp. 193-207.

14. Edgerton, V.R. Morphology and histochemistry of the soleus muscle from normal and exercised rats. *Am. J. Anat.* **127**:81-88, 1970.

15. Edström, L., and Torlegard, K. Area estimation of transversely sectioned muscle fibres. *Z. Wiss. Mikroscop.* **69**:166-178, 1969.

16. Edström, L., and Ekblom, B. Differences in sizes of red and white muscle fibres in vastus lateralis of muscularies quadriceps femoris of normal individuals and athletes. Relations to physical performance. *Scand. J. Clin. Lab. Invest.* **30**:175-181, 1972.

17. Enesco, M., and Puddy, D. Increase in the number of nuclei and weight in skeletal muscle of rats of various ages. *Am. J. Anat.* **111**:235-244, 1964.

18. Enesco, M., and LeBlond, C.P. Increase in cell number as a factor in the

growth of the organs and tissues of the young male rat. *J. Embryol. Exp. Morph.* **10**:530-562, 1962.

19. Erb, W.H. Dystrophia muscularis progressiva. Klinische und pathologische Studien. *Dtsch. Z. Nervenheilk.* **1**:227-261, 1891.

20. Etemadi, A.A., and Hosseini, L.F. Frequency and size of muscle fibers in athletic body build. *Anat. J.* **162**:269-274, 1968.

21. Faulkner, J.A., Maxwell, L.C., Brook, D.A., and Lieberman, D.A. Adaptation of guinea pig plantaris muscle fibers to endurance training. *Am. J. Physiol.* **221**:291-297, 1971.

22. Faulkner, J.A., Maxwell, L.C., and Lieberman, D.A. Histochemical characteristics of muscle fibers from trained and untrained guinea pigs. *Am. J. Physiol.* **222**:836-840, 1972.

23. Flear, C.T.G., Crampton, R.F., and Matthews, D.M. An in vitro method for the determination of the inulin space of skeletal muscle with observations on the composition of human muscle. *Clin. Sci.* **19**:483-493, 1960.

24. Goldspink, G. The combined effects of exercise and reduced food intake on skeletal muscle fibers. *J. Cell Comp. Physiol.* **63**:209-216, 1964.

25. Goldspink, G. The proliferation of myofibrils during muscle fibre growth. *J. Cell Sci.* **6**:593-602, 1970.

26. Goldspink, G. Changes in striated muscle fibres during contraction and growth with particular reference to myofibril splitting. *J. Cell Sci.* **9**:123-137, 1971.

27. Goldspink, G. Cytological basis of decrease in muscle strength during starvation. *Am. J. Physiol.* **209**:100-104, 1965.

28. Gollnick, P.D., Armstrong, R.B., Saubert, C.W. IV, Piehl, K., and Saltin, B. Enzyme activity and fiber composition in skeletal muscle of untrained and trained men. *J. Appl. Physiol.* **33**:312-319, 1972.

29. Gollnick, P.D., Timson, B.F., Moore, R.L., and Riedy, M. Muscular enlargement and number of fibers in skeletal muscles of rats. *J. Appl. Physiol: Respirat. Environ. Exercise Physiol.* **50**:936-943, 1981.

30. Gollnick, P.D., Parsons, D., Riedy, M., and Moore, R.L. Fiber number and size in overloaded chicken anterior latissimus dorsi muscle. *J. Appl. Physiol: Respirat. Environ. Exercise Physiol.* **54**:1292-1297, 1983.

31. Gonyea, W.J., and Ericson, G.C. An experimental model for the study of exercise-induced skeletal muscle hypertrophy. *J. Appl. Physiol.* **40**:630-633, 1976.

32. Gonyea, W., Ericson, G.C., and Bonde-Petersen, F. Skeletal muscle fiber splitting induced by weight-lifting exercise in cats. *Acta Physiol. Scand.* **99**:105-109, 1977.

33. Gonyea, W.J. Role of exercise in inducing increases in skeletal muscle fiber number. *J. Appl. Physiol: Respirat. Environ. Exercise Physiol.* **48**:421-426, 1980.

34. Gutmann, E., and Hanzlìkovà, V. Motor units in old age. *Nature* **209**:921-922, 1966.

35. Hall-Craggs, E.C.B. The longitudinal division of fibres in overloaded rat skeletal muscle. *J. Anat.* **107**:459-470, 1970.

36. Hall-Craggs, E.C.B., and Lawrence, C.A. Longitudinal fibre division in skeletal muscles: A light- and electronmicroscopic study. *Z. Zellforsch.* **109**:481-494, 1970.

37. Hall-Craggs, E.C.B. The significance of longitudinal fibre division in skeletal muscle. *J. Neurol. Sci.* **15**:27-33, 1972.

38. Hansen-Smith, F.M., Picou, D., and Golden, M.H. Growth of muscle fibres during recovery from severe malnutrition in Jamaican infants. *Br. J. Nutr.* **41**:275-282, 1979.

39. Hegarty, P.V.J., and Kim, K.O. Changes in skeletal muscle cellularity in starved and refed young rats. *Br. J. Nutr.* **44**:123-127, 1980.

40. Ho, K.W., Roy, R.R., Tweedle, C.D., Heusner, W.W., Van Huss, W.D., and Carrow, R. Skeletal muscle fiber splitting with weight-lifting exercise in rats. *Am. J. Anat.* **157**:433-440, 1980.

41. Holly, R.G., Barnett, J.G., Ashmore, C.R., Taylor, R.G., and Molé, P.A. Stretch-induced growth in chicken wing muscles: A new model of stretch hypertrophy. *Am. J. Physiol.* **238**:C62-C71, 1980.

42. Ianuzzo, C.D., Gollnick, P.D., and Armstrong, R.B. Compensatory adaptations of skeletal muscle fiber types to a long-term functional overload. *Life Sci.* **19**:1517-1524, 1976.

43. Ianuzzo, C.D., and Chen, V. Metabolic character of hypertrophied rat muscle. *J. Appl. Physiol: Respirat. Environ. Exercise Physiol.* **46**:738-742, 1979.

44. Ihemelandu, E.C. Decrease in fibre numbers of dog pectineus muscle with age. *J. Anat.* **130**:69-73, 1980.

45. James, N.T. Compensatory hypertrophy in the extensor digitorum longus muscle of the rat. *J. Anat.* **116**:57-65, 1973.

46. James, N.T. Compensatory muscular hypertrophy in the extensor digitorum longus muscle of the mouse. *J. Anat.* **122**:121-131, 1976.

47. Jimmenez, A.S., Cardinet, G.H. III, Smith, J.E., and Fedde, M.R. Evaluation of an indirect method for estimating myofiber number in transverse sections of skeletal muscle. *Am. J. Vet. Res.* **36**:375-378, 1978.

48. Katsuta, S. Light and electron microscopic studies on the postnatal development of skeletal muscle fibers in rats. *Jpn. J. Phys. Educ.* **24**:201-208, 1979.

49. Kobayashi, N., and Yonemura, K. The extracellular space in red and white muscles of the rat. *Jpn. J. Physiol.* **17**:698-707, 1967.

50. Kugelberg, E. Adaptive transformation of rat soleus motor units during growth. Histochemistry and contraction speed. *J. Neurol. Sci.* **27**:269-289, 1976.

51. Layman,. D.K., Hegarty, P.V.J., and Swan, P.B. Comparison of morphological and biochemical parameters of growth in rat skeletal muscle. *J. Anat.* **130**:159-171, 1980.

52. MacCallum, J.B. On the histogenesis of the striated muscle fiber and the growth of the human sartorius muscle. *Johns Hopkins Hosp. Bull.* **9**:208-215, 1898.

53. Maxwell, L.C., Faulkner, J.A., and Hyatt, G.C. Estimation of number of fibers in guinea pig skeletal muscle. *J. Appl. Physiol.* **37**:259-264, 1974.

54. Meara, P.J. Post-natal growth and development of muscle, as exemplified by the gastrocnemius and psoas muscles of the rabbit. *Onderstepoort J. Vet. Sci. Anim. Indust.* **21**:329-466, 1947.

55. Montgomery, R.D. Muscle morphology in infantile protein malnutrition. *J. Clin. Pathol.* **15**:511-521, 1962.

56. Montgomery, R.D. Growth of human striated muscle. *Nature* **195**:194-195, 1962.

57. Morpurgo, B. Ueber Aktivatats-Hypertrophie der willkuerlichen Muskeln. *Virch. Arch. Pathol. Anat. Physiol.* **150**:522-554, 1897.

58. Morpurgo, B. Ueber die postembryonale Entwickelung der quergestreiften Muskeln von weissen Ratten. *Anat. Anz.* **15**:200-206, 1898.

59. Moss, F.P. The relationship between the dimensions of the fibres and the number of nuclei during normal growth of skeletal muscle in the domestic fowl. *Am. J. Anat.* **122**:555-564, 1968.

60. Moss, F.P., and LeBlond, C.P. Nature of dividing nuclei in skeletal muscle of growing rats. *J. Cell Biol.* **44**:459-462, 1970.

61. Nygaard, E. Number of fibers in skeletal muscle of man. *Muscle Nerve* **3**:268, 1980.

62. Nygaard, E. Skeletal muscle fibre characteristics in young women. *Acta Physiol. Scand.* **112**:299-304, 1982.

63. Ontell, M. Muscle satellite cells: A validated technique for light microscopic identification and a quantitative study of changes in their population following denervation. *Anat. Rec.* **178**:211-228, 1973.

64. Ontell, M. Neonatal muscle growth: A quantitative study. *Am. J. Anat.* **152**:539-556, 1978.

65. Parsons, D., Riedy, M., Moore, R.L., and Gollnick, P.D. Acute fasting and fiber number in rat soleus muscle. *J. Appl. Physiol: Respirat. Environ. Exercise Physiol.* **53**:1234-1238, 1982.

66. Powell, S.E., and Aberle, E.D. Cellular growth of skeletal muscle in swine differing in muscularity. *J. Anim. Sci.* **40**:476-485, 1975.

67. Prince, F.P., Hikida, R.S., and Hagerman, F.C. Human muscle fiber types in power lifters, distance runners and untrained subjects. *Pfluegers Arch.* **363**:19-23, 1976.

68. Rayne, J., and Crawford, G.N.C. Increase in fibre numbers of the rat pterygoid muscles during postnatal growth. *J. Anat.* **119**:347-357, 1975.

69. Reitsma, W. Skeletal muscle hypertrophy after heavy exercise in rats with surgically reduced muscle function. *Am. J. Phys. Med.* **48**:237-258, 1969.

70 Richter, G.W., and Kellner, A. Hypertrophy of the human heart at the level of fine structure. *J. Cell Biol.* **18**:195-206, 1963.

71. Rowe, R.W.D., and Goldspink, G. Surgically induced hypertrophy in skeletal muscles of the laboratory mouse. *Anat. Rec.* **161**:69-76, 1968.

72. Rowe, R.W.D., and Pisansarakit, P. Skeletal muscle tissue preparation for image analysis systems. *Stain Tech.* **35**:59-65, 1980.

73. Salleo, A., Anastasi, G., La Spada, G., Falzea, G., and Denaro, M.G. New muscle fiber production during compensatory hypertrophy. *Med. Sci. Sports Exercise* **12**:268-273, 1980.

74. Schiaffino, S., Pierobon Bormioli, S., and Aloisi, M. Fiber branching and formation of new fibers during compensatory muscle hypertrophy. In: A. Mauro et al. (eds.), *Muscle regeneration.* Raven Press, New York, 1979, pp. 177-188.

75. Schiefferdecker, P. Untersuchung einer Anzahl von Kaumuskelm des Menschen und Saugetiere in Bezug auf ihren und ihre Kernverhaltnisse nebst einer korrrektur meiner Herzarbeit. *Pfluegers Arch.* **173**:265-384, 1919.

76. Schmalburch, H. The morphology of regeneration of skeletal muscles in the rat. *Tissue Cell* **8**:673-692, 1976.

77. Siebert, W.W. Untersuchungen ueber Hypertrophie des skelettmuskels. *Z. Klin. Med.* **109**:350-360, 1929.

78. Smith, J.H. Relation of body size to muscle cell size and number in the chicken. *Poult. Sci.* **12**:283-290, 1963.

79. Sola, O.M., Christensen, D.L., and Martin, A.W. Hypertrophy and hyperplasia of adult chicken anterior latissimus dorsi muscles following stretch with and without denervation. *Exp. Neurol.* **41**:76-100, 1973.

80. Song, S.K., Shimada, N., and Anderson, P.J. Orthogonal diameters in the analysis of muscle fibre size and form. *Nature* **200**:1220-1221, 1963.

81. Staun, H. Various factors affecting number and size of muscle fibers in the pig. *Acta Agric. Scand.* **13**:293-322, 1963.

82. Thompson, E.H., Levine, A.S., Hegarty, P.V.J., and Allen, C.E. An automated technique for simultaneous determination of muscle number fiber and diameter. *J. Anim. Sci.* **48**:328-337, 1979.

83. Thorner, W. Trainingsversuche an Hunden. 3. Histologische Beobachtungern an Herz- und Skelettmuskel. *Arbeitsphysiol.* **8**:359-370, 1934.

84. van Linge, B. The response of muscle to strenuous exercise. An experimental study in the rat. *J. Bone Jt. Surg.* **44B**:711-721, 1962.

85. Vaughan, H.S., and Goldspink, G. Fibre number and fibre size in a surgically overloaded muscle. *J. Anat.* **129**:293-303, 1979.

86. Von Eulenberg, A., and Cohnheim, R. Ergebnisse der anatomischen Untersuchung eines Falles von sogenannter Muskelhypertrophie. *Verh. Ber. Med. Ges.* **1**:191-210, 1866.

87. Walker, M.G. The effect of exercise on skeletal muscle fibres. *Comp. Biochem. Physiol.* **19**:791-797, 1966.

The matching of neuronal and muscular physiology

V.R. Edgerton, R.R. Roy, S.C. Bodine,
and R.D. Sacks
University of California at Los Angeles

Within the design of any skeletal muscle exists some relative priority for producing force versus displacement and velocity. This priority is reflected in the length of the fibers relative to the length and weight of the whole muscle. The number of sarcomeres in series (fiber length), the angle of pinnation, and the biochemical properties of a muscle will dictate the velocity at the muscle's tendon. Assuming a consistent biochemical profile, the longer the fiber and the smaller the amount of pinnation the higher the potential maximal velocity of shortening. The muscle with the longer fibers can produce nearly twice the displacement than the muscle with shorter fibers, but will produce less force. The greater force production in the muscle with the shorter fibers results from a greater cross-sectional area (sarcomeres in parallel).

The cat semitendinosus muscle can be used to illustrate the relationship between muscle architecture and physiology. Anatomically, the semitendinosus actually consists of two muscles attached in series by a connective tissue band with each end having separate innervation (3).

The proximal and distal ends are almost identical in their histochemical properties and have similar cross-sectional areas. The proximal end has fibers that extend about one-third the distance of the whole muscle whereas the distal component has fibers that extend the remaining two-thirds of the muscle's length. Physiologically, the shortening velocities of the two ends are proportional to the fiber lengths. When both ends are stimulated simultaneously the velocity of shortening is equivalent to the sum of the velocities of the two ends when stimulated independently. The maximal tetanic force is identical when either end is stimulated independently or when both are stimulated simultaneously. This is true because both ends have similar numbers of sarcomeres in parallel, and the net number of sarcomeres in parallel largely determines the force that can be generated by a muscle when it is activated maximally.

The concept that there is an orderly and predictable recruitment of motor units in almost all types of physical efforts has become increasingly clear since the initial series of papers was published in the mid-1960s by Henneman and his co-workers (17). The order in which motor units are recruited in a single muscle during a voluntary effort is extremely constant over a wide variety of efforts (7). There are some exceptions, however, to this relatively constant order (8,13). For example, occasionally in rapid efforts some reversal in the appearance order of action potentials in two motor units can occur (9,37). In most cases the force thresholds of these units are similar and the functional significance of the force threshold changes would appear to be minimal. Rather marked changes in the force threshold of motor units is possible in rapidly oscillating, low-amplitude efforts exerted up to 15 sec. But, it should be stressed that the accomplishment of this threshold modification requires considerable concentration and practice. It is probably safe to generalize that for all practical purposes there is no significant alteration in recruitment order regardless of the type of athletic effort required.

This orderly recruitment is most often explained in terms of the "size principle," that is, the order of recruitment is a function of motoneuron size. The smaller the motoneuron the greater the input resistance to current and the lower its excitation threshold (17). Others prefer to consider the critical factor in determining order to be a net effect of motoneuron cell size and number of synaptic inputs which collectively determine synaptic density (5). However, since it appears that the quantity and kind of synaptic input is generally similar for all motoneurons, cell size seems to be the variable that determines, for the most part, synaptic density.

This orderly recruitment of motor units within a muscle results in a predictable production of force when a given proportion of the motoneuronal pool is activated. If all motor units produced the same tension when tetanically stimulated, there would be a linear relationship between the number of motor units activated and the total tension from those

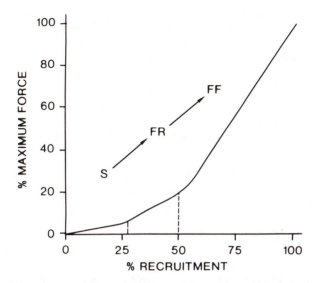

Figure 1 — **Percentage recruitment of motor units of the cat medial gastrocnemius muscle is plotted against percentage maximal force production. This graph illustrates the logarithmic relationship between cumulative tension and the number of motor units recruited. As the tension requirements of the muscle increase, the larger, faster motor units which have greater tension production capabilities are recruited in an orderly manner. S = slow, FR = fast fatigue-resistant, FF = fast fatigable or SO, FOG, and FG according to reference 7.**

units. However, this is not the case, at least in the cat gastrocnemius (6) and human first dorsal interosseus (23) muscles. For example, Figure 1 illustrates the logarithmic relationship of cumulative tension with the number of units activated in the cat gastrocnemius. This graph assumes that motor units are recruited in ascending order according to their tension production and presumably their "size." Given the "size principle" and that apparently the largest tension units have the highest threshold for activation, it seems likely that during essentially all efforts the controlling variable under voluntary control is the proportion of the motoneuronal pool activated in a given muscle.

It seems appropriate to attempt to integrate the factors noted above into some generalized concepts which may provide further insight into "exercise" as a stimulus that can induce adaptation. For example, in their classic work Buller et al. (4) severed the nerves to a slow and a fast muscle and reunited the proximal end of the nerve to the distal end of the nerve projecting to the foreign muscle. This procedure several months later resulted in the contraction time of the slow muscle becoming shorter and that of the fast muscle becoming longer. This experiment, and many of those that have followed, are consistent with the hypothesis that the motoneuron controls at least some of the properties associated with the "slowness" and "fastness" of a muscle as measured by contraction time. Buller et al. (4) proposed that the motoneuron could be controlling the muscle properties by the quality of activation (frequency pattern), the quantity of impulses, or via some neurotrophic factor not related to the action potential per se. Each of these hypotheses, as well as others, remain today as possible means of muscle protein control. To evaluate through which means exercise exerts a stimulus that can modify protein synthesis, it will be useful to examine several "use-disuse" models.

Selected experimental models that result in the interconversion of muscle fiber types

Cross-reinnervation

A fundamental assumption of this experimental model is that motoneurons use the same means of controlling muscle fiber properties after denervation and cross-reuniting as before the manipulation. For example, if a "fast" motoneuron does indeed generate action potentials at a high frequency, but within rarely occurring bursts of impulses, does the motoneuron continue to function that way following surgery and after reinnervation of a foreign muscle? If we accept this assumption, then this model can be used to demonstrate which properties are controlled and to what degree they are controlled by the motoneuron.

If the underlying assumption just noted is appropriate, it is clear that the fatigue properties of slow-twitch fibers are not controlled by the motoneuron. When slow-twitch, fatigue-resistant muscle fibers were reinnervated by fast-twitch fatigable units the cross-reinnervated fibers had a significantly shorter contraction time as expected. However, these units had maintained their resistance to fatigue some 14 months after the cross-uniting surgery (10). This failure to convert its fatigue properties was not a function of the denervation-reinnervation process, as shown by the observation that self-reinnervated motor units had properties identical to motor units in a normal fast-fatigable muscle. These results were supported by the histochemical profiles of the cross-reinnervated soleus muscle showing slow-oxidative (SO) and fast-oxidative-glycolytic (FOG) types but no fast-glycolytic (FG) fibers (10,25). These results are also consistent with the earlier work of Prewitt and Salafsky (28), who found that the malate dehydrogenase activity did not change in the cross-reinnervated soleus even though myosin ATPase did decrease as would be expected if this enzyme is controlled by the motoneuron.

It is not certain that the myosin ATPase staining property of a muscle fiber is totally determined by the type of motoneuron which innervates it. Although a relationship between contraction time (CT) and ATPase has been demonstrated for a few motor units in normal muscle, it is unknown if this relationship exists following any model in which muscle fiber types, as identified histochemically, are "interconverted." It is usually assumed that all motor units in a cat having a CT < 45 msec will stain darkly for ATPase after alkaline pH preincubation whereas this stain will be light if CT > 45 msec. However, there is little relationship after cross-reinnervation between the proportion of motor units in the soleus that have a short ("fast") CT (< 45 msec) and the proportion of histochemically identified "fast" fibers (dark ATPase stain). In the cross-reinnervated soleus muscles the proportion of histochemically converted fibers (SO to FOG) were around 14% consistently, which was unrelated to the percentage of twitch tension produced by the original and foreign nerves (10).

Complete low thoracic spinalization

Following complete transection of the cat spinal cord at about T_{12} a variety of changes occur in the hindlimb skeletal muscle, including atrophy and conversion of muscle fibers toward a fast-twitch profile. This finding immediately presents the question of what variables are imposed by transection that induce these effects. Within the all-too-broad concept enveloping many models, spinal transection might be considered one of "disuse" (11). However, a brief review of recent research on chronically spinalized cats questions the validity of cord transection as a disuse model.

It is now clear that the lumbar spinal cord is capable of executing locomotor patterns in the hindlimbs that are near normal in spite of the absence of any supraspinal input (34). In fact, if low thoracic spinalized cats are housed with litter mates, there is extensive spontaneous electromyographic activity in slow (soleus) and fast (medial gastrocnemius) muscles (1). In order to investigate this effect of muscular activity on atrophy and fiber type conversion, cats were spinalized at 2 or 12 wk of age. One-half of these cats were exercised 20-30 min/day on a motor-driven treadmill 5 days/wk for about 3 months. During this 3-month period a detailed analysis of the locomotor capability of each cat was studied (34). To summarize briefly, it was found that all cats, regardless of experimental treatment, could generate alternating flexion and extension of the legs when held suspended in a vertical position and when their hindlimbs were placed on the treadmill belt. However, the exercised animals were able to execute a locomotor pattern, including weight support, that was closer to normal than the nonexercised ones.

When the contractile properties of single motor units and whole muscles were studied 3-4 months after transection, it was found that the CT of the slow soleus tended to be shortened more in the exercised than the nonexercised transected cats (Figure 2) (21,35). Also, the fatigue

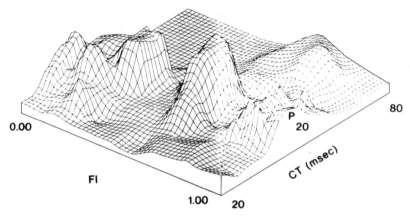

Figure 2 — Contractile properties of single motor units from the cat medial gastrocnemius and soleus muscles after 3-4 months spinal transection. The contraction time (CT), expressed in msec, is plotted against the fatigue index (FI), and tension produced at a frequency of 20 Hz (P_{20}). The fatigue index represents the tension developed after 2 min of stimulation relative to the maximal tension developed. Four populations of motor units are apparent in this diagram. The population in the region next to the P_{20} symbol are the motor units of soleus which have a decreased CT and unchanged FI compared to normal soleus motor units.

properties of the soleus and medial gastrocnemius of the transected cats were the same as in normal cats, regardless of whether they were exercised. These findings are inconsistent with the hypothesis that the quantity of activity is the controlling variable of either CT or fatigue. In addition, the lack of change in the fatigue properties is consistent with the cross-reinnervation results described earlier (Figure 2) which suggested an independence of fatigue properties and neuromuscular activity.

What variable(s) control the CT and fatigue properties if it is not the quantity of activity (the number of action potentials)? Excitation frequency certainly remains a possible means of control in light of reports that a fast muscle can be converted to a slow muscle by chronically stimulating it at 10-20 Hz and that a slow muscle reinnervated by a "fast" nerve, but also stimulated at 10 Hz during the reinnervating period, does not convert to a fast muscle (31). Evidence on the in vivo firing frequency of motor units in the cat or in any species is severely limited in that almost all data are on low-threshold units under rather restricted experimental conditions.

What do these results on spinally transected cats imply with regard to a neurotrophic controlling hypothesis? In this spinalized model the transection is sufficiently cephalic to avoid transecting dendrites of the motoneurons innervating the soleus and medial gastrocnemius. The motoneurons of spinalized animals can remain near the normal state, at least morphologically (39). If a motoneuron does exert its effects in this spinalized preparation via a neurotrophic factor, then it could just be assumed that the "slow" neurotrophic factor in some slow motoneurons is converted to a "fast" neurotrophic factor.

Compensatory hypertrophy

Compensatory hypertrophy is an experimental preparation used as early as the 1890s by Morpurgo (24). Its purpose is to induce muscle enlargement by removing synergistic muscles, thereby necessitating the intact muscle to perform the function that all of the synergists normally do. This technique is also commonly called compensatory overload. The muscular changes it induces can be as dramatic as any other model discussed in this paper in regard to fiber type conversions and functional adaptations.

Baldwin et al. (2) and Roy et al. (30) recently described the biochemical-, speed-, and force-related properties of the rat plantaris muscle about 3 months after removal of its synergists, the gastrocnemius and soleus muscles. Briefly, only a 10% increase was found in contraction time whereas the maximal velocity of shortening was about one-half the normal velocity for the plantaris. The maximal tetanic tension was about 50% larger in the hypertrophied muscle, reflecting the increase in total cross-sectional area. Some of the suspected biochemical correlates of these physiological results were somewhat surprising (Figure 3). For example, the change in myosin ATPase activity as demonstrated histochemically (percentage of fibers having an SO profile) and biochemically (as assayed standardly and after preincubation at varying pH values to test for pH sensitive inhibition-activation of slow and fast myosin ATPase) was consistent in direction but not in magnitude with the maximal velocity of shortening. Only about a 10% decrease in the Ca^{2+} uptake capacity of the fragmented sarcoplasmic reticulum was found. In general, compensatory overload produces effects opposite in direction to those of spinal transection, that is, "conversion" from fast- toward slow-twitch properties.

In spite of detailed knowledge about the effects of compensatory hypertrophy (2,14,19,30) little is known about the variables that are modified which are responsible for the specific adaptations observed. Some evidence suggests that compensatory "overload" is a model of stretch-induced hypertrophy (32). For example, a transient hypertrophy can be induced in denervated, overloaded muscles. However, after several weeks atrophy persists (38). One week after surgery, compensatory hypertrophy in normally innervated muscles, which are deafferented, is as great as if the muscles were not deafferented (32). This finding is consistent with the hypothesis that stretch induces transient hyper-

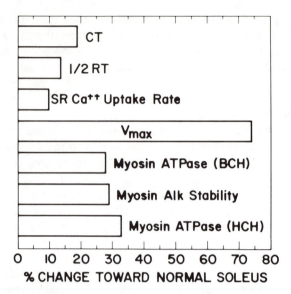

Figure 3—Percentage conversion of selected biochemical and physiological parameters in the overloaded plantaris toward normal soleus values. Conversion values were calculated as:

$$\frac{\text{Normal plantaris} - \text{overload plantaris}}{\text{Normal plantaris} - \text{normal soleus}} \times 100.$$

trophy directly and not via a reflex activation of its afferents. However, these results have little significance to the hypertrophy which exists after 3-4 months because the initial increase in muscle weight results from a proliferation of nonmuscle fiber cells such as phagocytes and endothelial cells (20). Functionally the 1-wk hypertrophied muscle can produce no more tension than a normal muscle (16). So again, with the compensatory hypertrophy model as with the others we have detailed information on specific responses of muscle to a treatment, but we are almost totally uninformed about the stimulus inducing the effect.

Hypertrophy as we are using the term in this paper refers to muscle enlargement as determined by that muscle's weight. Muscle hypertrophy should be evaluated with respect to the dimensions of the enlargement. For example, a muscle's weight may increase rather rapidly (within a week) by increasing its length. Thus, when a muscle "hypertrophies" in response to chronic stretch, how much of the additional weight is accountable in its length compared to its cross-sectional area? In the compensatory hypertrophy model just described it is evident that most sarcomeres were added in parallel which accounted for the increased force production (30). The changes in velocity of shortening were related to changes in the intrinsic biochemical properties (myosin ATPase) of the muscle.

Analysis of events characterizing models
in which fiber type interconversions occur

In order to understand how "exercise" can induce an adaptation the exercise event must be dissected into its adaptive-inducing components, the nature of which are largely unknown and, for the most part, largely unexplored. This general concept certainly is not a new one, for it essentially is an extension of the principle more commonly called "specificity of exercise." Although it is generally recognized that specific adaptations result from specific types of exercise, little progress has been made in finding the nature of the stimuli that occur in vivo which can be identified as adaptive-inducing agents for a specific exercise.

Some potential adaptive-inducing agents or events produced in varying degrees during different types of exercise are shown in Figure 4. For example, the messenger responsible for the modulation of a protein, such as myosin, may be related to electrical-ionic events of the membranes. Examples of these events are the small membrane fluctuations caused by random release of acetylcholine to inititiate an action potential that will propagate the full length of the muscle fiber. Each action potential produced in a motoneuron is presumed to propagate to the neuromuscular junction of all terminals extending from that one motoneuron, and the sarcolemma of each fiber receiving that neural signal is presumed to respond in the form of a propagated action potential along the sarcolemma. In regard to identifying adaptive-inducing events related to exercise, the possibility should be explored that electrical-ionic events could be important messengers, whether or not excitation-contraction coupling occurs.

The next event that could play a role in modulating an adaptive response in muscle is the contraction process itself. Although the specific event could occur within the tremendously complex chain of events that provide the tension-displacement by muscle fibers, it is possible that the critical adaptive-inducing event simply could be the tension or the displacement that results from the excitation. Alternatively, the contractile response may be an insignificant factor, in which case there are other chemical modulators to consider, such as calcium. In fact, based on our current understanding of calcium-modulated proteins and the cell responses predicted by cytosolic calcium (22), this ion is an excellent candidate for an adaptive-inducing agent in muscle.

The next sequence of events that follows excitation-contraction coupling is the response of the immediate [ATP, creatine phosphate (CP)] and secondary (glycolysis, glycogenolysis, and oxidative phosphorylation) metabolic events (Figure 4). In addition, the fallout from these biochemical aberrations such as reduced pH and elevated temperature may be important adaptive-inducing events.

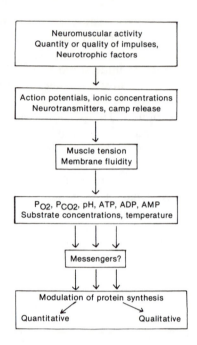

Figure 4—Flow diagram of various agents and events which are produced in varying degrees during different types of exercise and which may potentially induce adaptations.

It is clear from our consideration of a single excitation-contraction event that the number of potential adaptive-inducing events is enormous. In addition, specific combinations of events may be capable of or necessary for inducing an adaptation. If one considers the additional complexities incurred by humans when performing a sprint compared to those of a marathon, it is obvious that the current concept of exercise specificity is grossly inadequate.

In our laboratory a series of studies has been initiated which represents a beginning effort of what is certain to be a long search for adaptive-inducing events. Motoneurons provide a detailed signal to which muscle fibers respond predictably and precisely in the form of force and displacement. When this excitation occurs repetitively, specific energy-support mechanisms are brought into play to maintain the activity. Our approach has been to identify the sequence, the timing, and the amplitude of forces of single muscles with respect to the timing and the amplitude of tendon displacements and to identify as quantitatively as possible the electrical signal that reaches the muscle. In order to accomplish this task, the in vivo force-velocity relationships of single muscles are being determined in unrestrained movements of the cat with simultaneous recording of electromyographic signals from the same muscle.

An example of the force-velocity-EMG events in the medial gastrocnemius of a single step by a cat running on a treadmill at a rate of 1.13

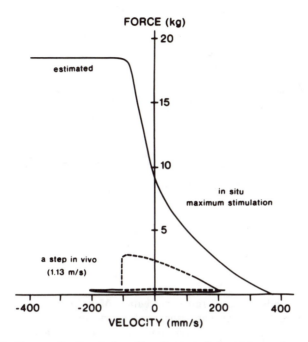

Figure 5 — Force-velocity relationship of cat medial gastrocnemius as measured in situ with maximal stimulation and in vivo during locomotion at 1.13 m/sec. Dashed portions of the in vivo force-velocity curve represent periods when EMG occurred in the muscle. Forces produced in situ at negative velocities are estimations based on Hill's data (18). Figure from unpublished observations (R. Gregor, R.R. Roy, C.L. Hager and V.R. Edgerton).

m/sec is shown in Figure 5 (15). Several points about this figure are notable. The uppermost line represents the force-velocity relationship of a cat's medial gastrocnemius as determined in a terminal experiment when the muscle was stimulated maximally (200 Hz) in an in situ preparation. The force at negative velocities is estimated based on the data of Hill (18) and this may be as much as twice the force that can be produced at zero velocity (isometric conditions). Note that the peak force in the step cycle occurs during a time when the muscle is lengthening. Following this peak the force drops precipitously.

In order to determine the reason for this drop in force during the weight-supporting and ankle-extending phases of the step (E_3 according to Philippson, ref. 27), the EMG and velocity of shortening data are required. The dashed portion of the line in Figure 5 represents the period when EMG occurred in the muscle. It is apparent that fluctuations in the force-velocity relationship are a function of factors other than the presence of EMG. For example, the drop in force as the velocity increases during E_3 can be explained by the fundamental property of all

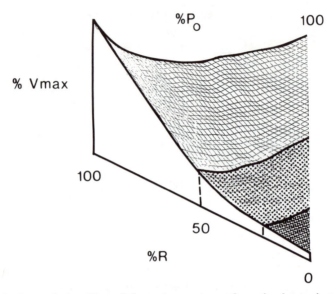

Figure 6—Interrelationships of force (percentage of maximal tetanic tension), velocity (percentage of maximal velocity of shortening), and activation of motoneuronal pool (percentage of recruitment). This diagram demonstrates that the basic force-velocity relationship is maintained at various submaximal levels of activation. The first shaded area represents a force-velocity relationship at approximately 20% recruitment whereas the second area represents 50% recruitment.

skeletal muscle as described by several investigators, the most notable being Hill (18). If the level of activation is held at a constant submaximal level (by reducing the current applied to the nerve or by reducing the frequency of activation) and the load is varied, then the curve will still follow the one described mathematically by Hill. The constants will vary slightly but the basic force-velocity relationship is consistent (Figure 6) (26). Consequently, a drop in the force produced by a muscle can be a function of absence (or decrease) of activation (EMG) or an increase in velocity.

Since most muscles work as synergistic groups that often have a common attachment, the architecture and function of all the synergists must be known (36,40). The mean maximal force-velocity relationship of the medial gastrocnemius and the soleus for a group of adult cats is shown in Figure 7. Velocity is expressed in mm/sec, which is the unit of importance at the point of common attachment. This figure illustrates the maximal force the two muscles can produce at any velocity. For example, at the peak velocity of shortening that occurs in E_3 at 1.13 m/sec the force that the medial gastrocnemius could produce is less than 5-10% of its peak isometric force. With the increasing velocities that occur in rapid

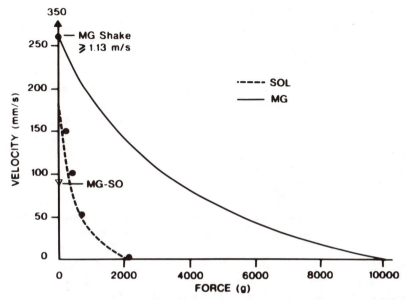

Figure 7 — **Force-velocity relationships of cat medial gastrocnemius (MG) and soleus (SOL) muscles. Velocity is expressed as mm/sec and force is expressed in g. Note that during the most rapid phase of a paw shake the soleus would not be contributing any significant amount of force. Also note that MG slow-oxidative units (MG-SO) produce velocities that are one-half of the SOL units.**

oscillating events such as a paw shake, which can be induced by placing tape or water on the paw, no force can be produced by the soleus muscle at the higher velocities (33). In addition, it should be obvious that the slower soleus muscle could not be contributing any significant force during the rapid shortening phase of a paw shake. These slow fibers of the medial gastrocnemius are only one-half as long as the slow fibers in the soleus, so they are one-half as fast assuming they have the same intrinsic properties. Thus, the slow units in the medial gastrocnemius, which are almost certainly activated if the fast units are recruited, probably contribute little to the forces produced by the medial gastrocnemius in any situation other than lengthening or near-zero velocity conditions.

Understanding the interrelationships between force-velocity and recruitment of individual muscles for a specific exercise should reveal more meaningful parameters rather than simply addressing the speed, distance, or grade at which animals, including humans, move. For example, how does the force produced by a muscle relate to the speed of running? It may be of some surprise that the peak forces tend to remain relatively constant at least in slow muscle over a three-fold change in the speed of running. Forces during E_3 may even be reduced as the running speed increases. So, how does one run faster?

As noted in Figures 5 and 7, the force-velocity curve as described by Hill for a given level of activation varies such that force can be maximal at zero velocity, or vice-versa with the same level of activation but under varying load conditions. Therefore, the third variable is the percentage of motoneurons activated in a given motoneuronal pool. The inter-relationships of these three variables are illustrated in Figure 6. One can speculate where a particular movement falls within the three-dimensional structure. Also, one can postulate the type of motor units required to perform any given movement. Since the order of recruitment is fixed, one need only know the percentage of the motoneuronal pool required to function at a specific point on the force-velocity curve. For example, if the combination of force and velocity for a movement requires 60% of the motoneuronal pool and the person has 50% slow-twitch fibers, no fast-twitch motor units need be recruited. Remember that to produce half of the maximal force, as many as 75% of the motoneurons may be needed (but at least 50% of the muscle mass). One major and unproven assumption in this calculation is that the lower threshold slow-twitch units produce less tension than the higher threshold fast units. This appears to be true in the first dorsal interrosseus in humans (37). Also unknown is whether slow-twitch units produce less tension per cross-sectional area than fast-twitch units as appears to happen in mixed, but predominantly fast, muscles in cats and rats.

Another variable often ignored in comparing the effects of training at varying speeds is the relative time of muscle activation as shown by EMG. If one assumes the conditioning stimulus has a time constant such that the controlling modulators change over a period of minutes as opposed to a single step, then the activation time should be studied over a period of minutes. When one runs faster, the length of time a muscle is activated during each step is reduced but the number of steps increases. These two variables tend to counteract each other. Consequently, total EMG increases less than might be expected as the running speed increases. There is, however, a slightly greater amount of EMG as running speed increases because in order to obtain higher speeds a greater proportion of the motoneuronal pool must be recruited.

The relationship of running speed, grade, and total integrated EMG (IEMG) per minute for the soleus and lateral gastrocnemius of guinea pigs is shown in Figure 8. Note that at any given grade, running speed (m/min) has a relatively moderate effect on the IEMG, particularly compared to the effect of a grade increase at any given speed. Gardiner et al. (12) also found that as grade was increased with speed held constant the step duration and frequency remained unchanged. Therefore, the marked increase in IEMG/min can be explained almost totally by a greater percentage of the motoneuronal pool being recruited and by a greater activation (higher frequency) of those motoneurons.

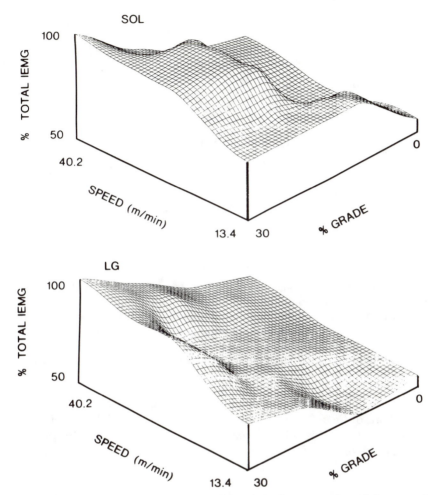

Figure 8 – Relationship of speed (m/min), grade (percentage), and integrated EMG (percentage of total integrated EMG) in the soleus (SOL) and lateral gastrocnemius (LG) of the guinea pig. Note that at any given grade, running speed has little effect on the total IEMG compared to the increase in IEMG caused by an increase in running speed at any given grade (12).

A final dimension to be discussed in our analysis of exercise is fatigue. This variable is not independent of percentage recruitment or force-velocity properties of a movement. The interdependence of these four variables (time-to-exhaustion, force, velocity, and percentage recruitment) is illustrated in Figure 9. The validity of assuming a logarithmic relationship between force and time-to-exhaustion is suggested by the finding of Reigel (29), in which he demonstrated a log-log relationship between the average speed maintained by world record holders (in events

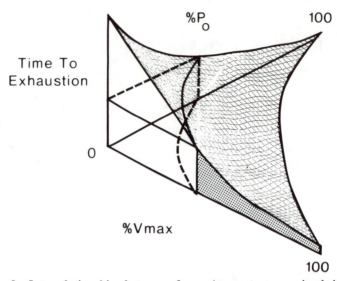

Figure 9—Interrelationship between force (percentage maximal isometric tension), velocity (percentage maximal shortening velocity), and time to exhaustion. This diagram illustrates the interdependence of these three variables. Two force-velocity curves are drawn on this diagram. The first curve represents 100% recruitment of the motor unit pool whereas the second curve represents recruitment of approximately 60% of the motor unit pool. The vertical lines extended from the force-velocity curves represent the relative time-to-exhaustion.

lasting 3.5-230 min) and the distance of the event. By taking the logarithms of time vs distance for a variety of sports and determining the lines of best-fit using a least squares technique, an endurance equation was formulated:

$$t = ax^b,$$

where t = time (min), x = distance (km), and a and b are constants unique to each activity.

In running events for men under 40 years old, a = 2.299 and b = 1.07732 for distances ranging 1.5-42.2 km and within a time range of 3.5-129 min. Algebraic manipulation of the endurance equation describing the relationship of velocity vs time and distance is:

$$V = \frac{x}{t} = \frac{t^{(1-b)/b}}{a^{1/b}} = \frac{x^{(1-b)}}{a}.$$

This equation describes for any distance the fastest time of covering that distance. It also should be recognized that the velocities discussed are averages for that distance.

One of the assumptions made in Figure 9 is that when an individual has completed a race in which a world record is attained, the individual is exhausted at the end of the race. Accepting the underlying assumptions, Figure 9 at least provides a conceptual basis for studying the interrelationships of force, velocity, recruitment, and time-to-exhaustion. Note that two force-velocity curves are drawn in the figure; each curve represents a different proportion of the motoneurons recruited to achieve a combined force-velocity effect. If a vertical line is extended from any point on one of those force-velocity curves, the relative time-to-exhaustion will be represented by the height of that vertical line.

Summary

Muscles execute lengthening and shortening as well as isometric contractions. These features are well known, but they usually are considered casually when testing physiological adaptations in response to exercise-related models. Also well known is the relationship of a muscle's architecture and its physiology. However, many adaptation models commonly omit this feature in integrating and interpreting the results.

Results of experiments involving several exercise-related models were presented in which "conversion" of fiber types from fast to slow or slow to fast occurs. Although these models provide clear examples of muscle adaptation they provide little insight into the adaptive-inducing agents or events that occur in those models. It is suggested that in order to define how these models may induce the adaptations a detailed analysis of the forces, velocities, and percentage recruitment of a motoneuronal pool for the muscle being studied must be known. Knowledge of these variables, in turn, may provide further understanding of the secondary and tertiary adapting modulators that may be produced in a given exercise.

References

1. Alaimo, M.A., Smith, L.A., and Smith, J.L. Chronic spinal kitten: 24 hour EMG profile of fast and slow ankle extensors. *Soc. Neurosci. Abstr.* **7**:897, 1981.

2. Baldwin, K.M., Valdez, V., Herrick, R.E., MacIntosh, A.M., and Roy, R.R. Biochemical properties of overloaded fast-twitch skeletal muscle. *J. Appl. Physiol. Respirat. Environ. Exercise Physiol.* **52**:467-472, 1982.

3. Bodine, S.C., Roy, R.R., Meadows, D.A., Zernicke, R.F., Sacks, R.D., Fournier, M., and Edgerton, V.R. Architectural, histochemical, and contractile characteristics of a unique biarticular muscle: The cat semitendinosis. *J. Neurophysiol.* **48**:192-201, 1982.

4. Buller, A.J., Eccles, J.C., and Eccles, R.M. Interactions between moto-neurons and muscles in respect of the characteristic speeds of their responses. *J. Physiol.* **150**:417-439, 1960.

5. Burke, R.E. On the central nervous system control of fast and slow twitch motor units. In: J.E. Desmedt (ed.), *New developments in electromyography and clinical neurophysiology*, vol. 3. Karger, Basel, 1973, pp. 69-94.

6. Burke, R.E. Motor unit types: Functional specialization in motor control. *Trends Neurosci.* **3**:255-258, 1980.

7. Burke, R.E., and Edgerton, V.R. Motor unit properties and selective involve-ment in movement. In: J. Wilmore and J. Keogh (eds.), *Exercise and sport science reviews*, vol. 3. Academic Press, New York, 1975, pp. 31-81.

8. Cremer, S.A., Gregor, R.J., Mirsky, M., and Edgerton, V.R. Voluntarily in-duced differential alteration in force threshold of single motor units of the human vastus lateralis. *Soc. Neurosci. Abstr.* **6**:463, 1980.

9. Desmedt, J.E., and Godaux, E. Ballistic contractions in man: Characteristic recruitment pattern of single motor units of the tibialis anterior muscle. *J. Physiol. London* **264**:673-693, 1977.

10. Edgerton, V.R., Goslow, G.E., Rasmussen, S.A., and Spector, S.A. Is resis-tance of a muscle to fatigue controlled by its motoneurons? *Nature* **285**:584-590, 1980.

11. Gallego, R., Huizan, P., Kudo, N., and Kuno, M. Disparity of motoneuron and muscle differentiation following spinal transection in kitten. *J. Physiol. London* **281**:253-265, 1978.

12. Gardiner, K.R., Gardiner, P.F., and Edgerton, V.R. Guinea pig soleus and gastrocnemius electromyograms at varying speeds, grades and loads. *J. Appl. Physiol. Respirat. Environ. Exercise Physiol.* **52**:451-457, 1982.

13. Garnett, R., and Stephens, J.A. Changes in the recruitment threshold of motor unit produced cutaneous stimulation in man. *J. Physiol.* London **311**:463-473, 1981.

14. Gollnick, P.D. Muscular growth in response to functional overload — Hyper-trophy or hyperplasia? *Symposium on Future Issues in Exercise Biology*, 1981.

15. Gregor, R.J., Hager, C.L., Roy, R.R., and Whiting, W.C. In vivo force-velocity characteristics of fast ankle extensors in the cat hindlimb. *Med. Sci. Sports Exercise* **13**:128, 1981.

16. Hamosh, M., Lesch, M., Barton, J., and Kaufman, S. Enhanced protein syn-thesis in a cell-free system from hypertrophied skeletal muscle. *Science* **157**:935-937, 1967.

17. Henneman, E., Somjen, G., and Carpenter, D.O. Excitability and inhibitibil-ity of motoneurons of different sizes. *J. Neurophysiol.* **28**:599-620, 1965.

18. Hill, A.V. The heat of shortening and the dynamic constants of muscle. *Proc. Royal Soc. London Ser. B.* **126**:136-195, 1938.

19. Iannuzzo, C.D., Gollnick, P.D., and Armstrong, R.B. Compensatory adaptations of skeletal muscle fiber types to a long term functional overload. *Life Sci.* **19**:1517-1524, 1976.

20. Jablecki, C.K., Heuser, J.E., and Kaufman, S. Autoradiographic localization of new RNA synthesis in hypertrophying skeletal muscle. *J. Cell. Biol.* **57**:743-759, 1973.

21. Johnson, D.J., Smith, L.A., Eldred, E., and Edgerton, V.R. Exercise-induced changes of biochemical, histochemical and contractile properties of muscle in cordotomized kittens. *Exp. Neurol.* **76**:414-427, 1982.

22. Kretsinger, R.H. Mechanisms of selective signalling by calcium. *Neurosci. Res. Prog. Bull.* **19**:213-328, 1981.

23. Milner-Brown, H.S., Stein, R.B., and Lee, R.G. Synchronization of human motor units: Possible roles of exercise and supraspinal reflexes. *Electroenceph. Clin. Neurophysiol.* **38**:245-254, 1975.

24. Morpurgo, B. Ueber Activtats-Hypertrophie der Willkurlichen Muskecn. *Virch. Arch. Pathol. Anat.* **150**:522-554, 1897.

25. Peter, J.B., Barnard, R.J., Edgerton, V.R., Gillespie, C.A., and Stemple, K.E. Metabolic profiles on three fiber types of skeletal muscle in guinea pigs and rabbits. *Biochemistry* **11**:2627-2633, 1972.

26. Petrofsky, J.S., and Phillips, C.A. The influence of temperature, initial length and electrical activity on the force-velocity relationships of the medial gastrocnemius muscle of the cat. *J. Biomech.* **14**:297-306, 1981.

27. Philippson, M. L'Autonomie et la centralisation dans le systeme nerveux des animaux. *Trav. Lab. Physiol. Inst. Solvay Bruxelles* **7**:1-208, 1905.

28. Prewitt, M.A., and Salafsky, B. Enzymic and histochemical changes in fast and slow muscles after cross-innervation. *Am. J. Physiol.* **218**:69-74, 1970.

29. Reigel, P.S. Athletic records and human endurance. *Am. Sci.* **69**:285-290, 1981.

30. Roy, R.R., Meadows, I.D., Baldwin, K.M., and Edgerton, V.R. Functional significance of compensatory overloaded rat fast muscle. *J. Appl. Physiol. Respirat. Environ. Exercise Physiol.* **52**:473-478, 1982.

31. Salmons, S., and Sreter, F.A. Significance of impulse activity in the transformation of skeletal muscle type. *Nature* **263**:30-34, 1976.

32. Schiaffino, S., and Hanzlikova, V. On the mechanism of compensatory hypertrophy in skeletal muscles. *Experientia* **26**:152-153, 1970.

33. Smith, J.L., Edgerton, V.R., Betts, B., and Collatos, T.C. EMG of slow and fast ankle extensors of cat during posture, locomotion and jumping. *J. Neurophysiol.* **40**:503-513, 1977.

34. Smith, J.L., Edgerton, V.R., Eldred, E., and Zernicke, R.F. The chronic spinalized cat: A model for neuromuscular plasticity. *Int. Symp. on Nervous System Regeneration*, Int. Soc. Neurochem. Cantania. A.R. Liss, Italy, 1982.

35. Smith, L.A., Edgerton, V.R., and Eldred, E. Fatigue properties of single motor units in exercised chronic spinal cats. *Soc. Neurosci. Abstr.* **7**:683, 1981.

36. Spector, S.A., Gardiner, P.F., Zernicke, R.F., Roy, R.R., and Edgerton, V.R. Muscle architecture and the force velocity characteristics of the cat soleus and medial gastrocnemius: Implications for motor control. *J. Neurophysiol.* **44**:951-960, 1980.

37. Stephens, J.A., and Usherwood, T.P. The mechanical properties of human motor units with special reference to their fatigability and recruitment threshold. *Brain Res.* **125**:91-97, 1977.

38. Stewart, D.M., Sola, O.M., and Martin, A.W. Hypertrophy as a response to denervation in skeletal muscle. *Z. Vergl. Physiol.* **76**:146-167, 1972.

39. Tarlov, I.M. Rigidity and primary motoneuron damage in tetanus. *Exp. Neurol.* **44**:246-254, 1974.

40. Walmsley, B., Hodgson, J.A., and Burke, R.E. Forces produced by medial gastrocnemius and soleus muscles during locomotion in freely moving cats. *J. Neurophysiol.* **41**:1203-1216, 1978.

Stretch and skeletal myotube growth: What is the physical to biochemical linkage?

Herman H. Vandenburgh
Brown University

Seymour Kaufman
National Institute of Mental Health

Exercise has a multitude of effects on the interacting organ systems of the human body — its metabolic rate, endocrine responses, salt and water balance, temperature regulation, and psychological state, to name only a few. It also has a profound effect on the most active tissue during exercise, the skeletal muscle cells which perform the mechanical work of exercise. The muscle's steady-state metabolic and protein-turnover rates are altered both acutely and chronically by exercise, with the type of exercise important in determining the type of alteration. Thus, protein turnover rates in long distance runners and weightlifters respond in a manner such that protein accumulation increases substantially in individuals who engage in weightlifting, but not in those who run for exercise.

The mechanism by which physical activity alters muscle protein turnover rates is unknown, but both the rate of protein synthesis and protein degradation are affected. Because of the complicated response of the whole animal to exercise, a number of model systems have been used to simplify analysis of this coupling of muscle activity with alterations in skeletal muscle growth. These systems include the in vivo tenotomy model for skeletal muscle hypertrophy developed by Denny-Brown (8), which has been used extensively (reviewed in 17). In this model system, the tendons of synergistic leg muscles are cut, requiring increased work of the remaining intact muscles for normal animal movement. This model for stimulating muscle cell growth is of a more direct nature than whole body exercise because the tenotomy operation places the remaining intact leg muscles under direct stress without substantially altering other organ systems of the animal. Mechanical stretch of the muscle fibers appears to be an essential component for growth stimulation in this model (31).

A second model system involves the use of direct electrical stimulation of skeletal muscle cells to alter muscle protein turnover rates in the whole animal and in isolated organ-cultured adult muscles (16) as well as in embryonic skeletal muscle cells grown in tissue culture (4). These model systems mimic the muscle activity induced by the nervous system and produce many of the characteristics associated with innervation of skeletal muscle cells (21).

A third type of model used has been direct mechanical stretch of muscle cells, which has been known for many years to stimulate the tissue's metabolic rate (Feng effect) (10). In vivo stretch studies using plaster casts (18,34) and immobilization of adult muscle in organ culture (16,17) have been used to show that passive stretch of adult muscle stimulates muscle cell growth and partially inhibits many of the atrophic changes that occur upon denervation. Several years ago we developed a tissue culture system in which we could passively stretch embryonic muscle cells grown and differentiated in a tissue culture system (36). We felt that an in vitro tissue culture model system would offer additional advantages over other model systems available, including the ability to grow relatively pure skeletal myotube cultures which are spontaneously contractile. The differentiation and development of embryonic chick muscle cells in tissue culture is a well studied field. In addition, most contaminating fibroblasts can be removed from the cultures using inhibitors of cell proliferation after the myoblasts have fused to form skeletal myotubes and are no longer undergoing DNA synthesis. Additional advantages of an in vitro tissue culture system are the ease in altering the extracellular environment of the cells and the possibility that the cells would respond to growth-related stimuli more rapidly than in the other in vivo models. These advantages have been substantiated by our subsequent studies. We chose mechanical stretch of the skeletal myotubes as our growth-promoting stimulus for several reasons: It is a physiological stimulus that all muscle cells undergo during their activity and has been shown to be an important element in both the tenotomy model and in the electrical stimulation model.

Isolation of the embryonic skeletal muscle cells from 11-day-old embryonic chick pectoralis muscle and their growth in tissue culture follows standard procedures outlined previously (35). The myoblasts under our growth conditions proliferate for 24-48 hr after isolation and then fuse to form branched, multinucleated myotubes that become spontaneously contractile after 3-4 days in culture. Mechanical stretch of the myotubes involves growing the cells on a collagen-coated, elastic substratum and subjecting the differentiated myotubes to various degrees of stretch for extended periods of time. Using this system, we have shown that embryonic skeletal myotubes respond in a manner similar to the growth-related alterations that occur in the tenotomy model system for skeletal muscle hypertrophy, in the electrical stimulation model systems, and in the mechanical stretch of adult muscle fiber systems. These growth-promoting changes include the stimulation of Na^+-dependent amino acid transport rates (40), the stimulation of protein synthesis rates (40), and the inhibition of protein degradation rates (39) which lead to the accumulation of muscle cell proteins, including myosin heavy chains (36) — that is, to skeletal muscle hypertrophy.

Subjecting the elastic tissue culture substratum to a stretch of 10.8% resulted in a longitudinal myotube stretch of 10.8% and was found to give optimal stimulation of these growth-related changes within 2 hr of stretching the myotubes and maintaining them in a stretched position. We have reviewed our results with this system recently (38,39) and a more complete description of the system can be found in these papers. We will briefly describe some of our recent results with this system in an attempt to dissect out the biochemical and molecular bases for muscle cell growth stimulation by mechanical stretch. We believe this stystem has potential for contributing to an understanding of the mechanism by which exercise regulates the rate of skeletal muscle growth.

Insulin and stretch: Similarities in muscle response

Passive stretch of skeletal myotubes grown in culture has been found to have many of the growth-promoting characteristics of insulin on adult muscle (Table 1). Several of these changes also occur when adult, organ-cultured skeletal muscle is passively stretched (17). Our early experiments with the tissue culture system were performed with myotubes stretched 10.8% in serum-containing medium that contains a number of growth-factors, including insulin.

One possible mechanism by which passive stretch of the myotubes could mimic the action of insulin might be by increasing the cell's sen-

Table 1

Summary of the Growth-stimulating Effects
of Insulin or Passive Stretch on Skeletal Muscle[a]

---

1. Stimulation of Na$^+$-dependent amino acid transport
2. Stimulation of protein synthesis
3. Inhibition of protein degradation
4. Stimulation of Na pump activity

---

[a]Insulin effects are those on adult muscle fibers whereas stretch effects are those on skeletal myofibers grown in tissue culture. The myotubes were stretched 10.8%, which gives optimal stimulation of these changes. See references 36-39 for experimental details.

sitivity to insulin or other medium growth factors. The increase in Na$^+$-dependent amino acid transport was chosen to test this model using the amino acid analog α-aminoisobutyric acid (AIB)[1]. This assay was chosen for several reasons. AIB in the cultured myotubes is transported in a manner similar to its transport in adult muscle fibers (19) and its rate of uptake is stimulated in the tenotomy model for skeletal muscle hypertrophy (14), on electrical stimulation of muscle cells (24), and on passive stretch of adult myofibers in organ-culture (16). Muscle atrophy upon denervation is associated with a decreased rate of AIB uptake (15). Insulin is well known to stimulate amino acid uptake in skeletal muscle (24,28); thus, an increased rate of AIB uptake is associated with muscle cell growth under most conditions. The possibility that passive stretch of the muscle fibers increases muscle growth rates by increasing their sensitivity to insulin was additionally attractive (if the in vitro stretch model system is applicable to understanding how exercise influences muscle growth rates) because increased insulin sensitivity of skeletal muscle has been found in exercising muscles (3). The mechanism by which exercise increases skeletal muscle responsiveness to insulin is unknown.

Basal rates of AIB uptake were stimulated two-fold by 15% (v/v) serum when the spontaneously contractile skeletal myotubes in culture were preincubated for several hours in serum-free medium (41). The myotubes' response to serum was dose-dependent, with a concentration of 15% giving maximal stimulation. This stimulatory effect of serum on the myotube's amino acid transport rate apparently is not caused by insulin as the embryonic myotubes developed in culture are insensitive to insulin levels present in serum (Figure 1). Uptake of 3-0 methyl glucose by cultured myotubes was similarly insensitive to insulin (data not shown).

---

[1]Abbreviations: AIB, α-aminoisobutyric acid; MSA, multiplication stimulating activity; colc, colchicine; vinc, vincristine; str, stretch; amil, amiloride; ouab, ouabain; TTX, tetrodotoxin.

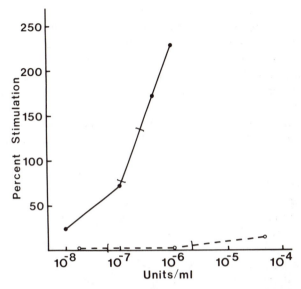

Figure 1—Stimulation of AIB uptake by various concentrations of insulin or Multiplication Stimulating Activity (MSA) factor. Cultured myotubes were preincubated in serum-free basal medium (Eagle's) for 2 hr prior to the addition of insulin (Actrapid, Novo Laboratories) or MSA (Collaborative Research) for 90 min. ^{3}H-AIB was then added for a 30-min uptake period. Control experiments indicate that myotubes take up ^{3}H-AIB at a linear rate under these conditions for at least 1 hr (see ref. 36-39 for experimental details of the culturing and assay techniques). Bracketed sections of the lines represent the physiological range of these compounds. Results are expressed as percentage stimulation over untreated control cultures. Each point is the mean value of triplicate dishes. ●——● , MSA (1 unit = 1 g); ○----○ , insulin (1 unit = 10^2 IU).

In contrast, the cells are quite responsive to other serum growth factors, such as the somatomedin-like Multiplication Stimulating Activity (MSA) of Pierson and Temin (25) (Figure 1). Similar skeletal muscle insensitivity to insulin has been reported for cultured myotubes (22) and for neonatal muscle (9). If stretch in our in vitro system stimulates amino acid transport by increasing the myotube's sensitivity to serum growth factors, it must be attributed to growth factors other than insulin.

In order to test this idea, myotube stretch experiments were performed in either serum-free medium or in medium containing various concentrations of serum. These experiments and all subsequent ones were performed as follows. The myotubes were preincubated at 37°C for 2 hr in serum-free medium (basal medium [Eagle's] with 0.05% [w/v] polyvinyl-proprylidole 40,000 and 0.02% bovine serum albumin, RIA-grade), stretched 10.8%, and held in a stretched position. Fresh medium was added immediately after the stretching procedure, either serum-free or medium containing various concentrations of serum (up to 15%); the myotubes were then incubated for a further 90 min at 37°C. ^{3}H-AIB and ^{14}C-urea were then added for a 30-min uptake period. ^{14}C-urea exchanges rapidly across the myotube's plasma membrane and was used to calculate intracellular volumes. The results could then be expressed as a distribution ratio of AIB concentration inside the cells compared to that in the medium.

Under these experimental conditions, ^{3}H-AIB was taken up by the myotubes at a linear rate for at least 1 hr and was concentrated from two to six times above the concentration found in the medium. A 10.8% stretch of the myotubes under our previous standard assay conditions (5% serum, 5% chicken embryo extract) increased AIB uptake by 20-40% over unstretched control myotubes by 30 min after the stretch and this stimulated rate of uptake was maintained by the stretched myotubes for at least 8 hr (40).

The results of a typical stretch experiment, in the presence or absence of serum, are shown in Figure 2. Two important results were found in experiments of this type: (a) In serum-free medium, stretch of the myotubes stimulated AIB uptake, even after up to 12 hr of preincubation in serum-free medium; and (b) at a serum concentration that maximally stimulated basal AIB uptake (15% serum), stretch had no effect, that is, maximal stimulation of AIB uptake by serum and stretch were not additive. These results indicate that myotube stretch does not stimulate amino acid transport by increasing the cell's sensitivity to hormones or growth factors found in serum but rather that stimulation of AIB uptake by serum and stretch occur by a common underlying mechanism, as the two are not additive. These results are consistent with those of Goldberg on the lack of a requirement for insulin or other growth factors in the in vivo tenotomy model for skeletal muscle hypertrophy (13,17).

Microtubules and amino acid transport

The coupling mechanism by which insulin or other growth factors stimulate amino acid transport rates is unknown at present. The results presented in the previous section indicated that myotube stretch does not require exogenous hormones or growth factors to stimulate AIB uptake, but that stretch may act directly on one of the secondary, transducing mechanisms beyond the initial hormone-receptor binding step. The possible involvement of microtubules as a component of this transducing mechanism was of particular interest for several reasons. These cytoskeletal elements have been shown to play a role in hormonally induced cell shape changes (26), in amino acid transport regulation (11) and in insulin stimulation of amino acid transport (27). Their possible involvement in our system where a physically induced change in cell shape leads

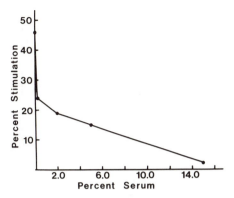

Figure 2 — Effect of myotube stretch on AIB uptake in various concentrations of serum. This experiment was performed as described in the legend to Figure 1, with the myotubes exposed to various serum concentrations for 90 min after 2 hr of preincubation in serum-free medium. The myotubes were also stretched 10.8% at the start of the 90-min incubation period and held in a stretched position for the 90 min and also for the subsequent 30 min when AIB uptake was measured. Results are expressed as the percentage stimulation of ^{3}H-AIB uptake by 10.8% stretch over unstretched controls in different concentrations of serum (v/v). AIB uptake in unstretched control myotubes was increased 134% by the addition of 15% serum in this experiment. Each point is the mean difference between seven control and seven stretched dishes. Stretch stimulation of AIB uptake was statistically significant at the p < .001 level for serum concentrations of 5% or less (Student's t-test for paired values).

to an increase in AIB uptake seemed attractive and was therefore studied. In control, unstretched skeletal myotubes, 10-30% of the basal and serum-stimulated AIB uptake was found to be sensitive to inhibitors of microtubule function, colchicine or vincristine. But neither inhibitor was found to prevent stretch-induced AIB uptake in serum-free medium (Figure 3). Thus, microtubules do not appear to be involved in the coupling of muscle stretch and the stimulation of AIB uptake. These results indicate, therefore, that this is not the common mechanism by which serum growth factors and stretch stimulate amino acid transport.

Membrane potential and amino acid transport

Another mechanism by which myotube stretch could be coupled with a stimulation of AIB uptake would involve a stretch-induced change in the membrane potential of the muscle cells. A mechanism of this type was attractive for the following reasons. We have previously found that myotube stretch in serum-containing medium is associated with the long-term activation of the myotube's Na pump (Na⁺K⁺ATPase) and that inhibition of this activation with ouabain, a specific inhibitor of Na pump activity,

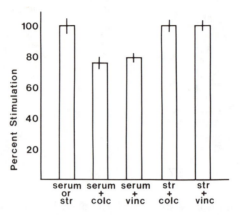

Figure 3 — Effect of inhibitors of microtubular function, colchicine (colc) and vincristine (vinc), on serum-stimulated and stretch-stimulated AIB uptake in skeletal myotubes. Results are expressed as percentage stimulation of basal AIB uptake by either 15% serum (v/v) or 10.8% stretch in serum-free medium (str) in the presence or absence of the inhibitor. One hundred percent stimulation equaled 92 and 35% increases for serum and stretch, respectively. Experimental protocol was as described in the legends to Figures 1 and 2. Colchicine and vincristine were used at 1×10^{-5} M and 5×10^{-6} M, respectively, which gave maximal inhibition of basal AIB uptake. Each bar is the mean ± SE of three to seven dishes.

inhibits many of the growth-stimulating actions of stretch, including increased AIB uptake (40). Stretch-induced activation of the Na pump occurs as well in serum-free medium. This Na pump activation is the result of an increase in the V_{max} of the pumps already present in the plasma membrane and is not due to the appearance of new Na pump sites; new pump sites are measured with the ^{3}H-ouabain-binding technique (40). Because the Na pump probably is electrogenic in cultured skeletal myotubes (30), this activation would tend to hyperpolarize the membrane potential. Insulin also stimulates the Na pump (5) and many of the growth-promoting characteristics of insulin have been attributed to its hyperpolarizing effects (12). In addition, the amino acid-stimulating activity of serum on cells in culture is coupled with its ability to hyperpolarize these cells (42). For these reasons, we studied the relationship of changes in membrane potential to stretch-induced AIB uptake. Figure 4 shows a diagrammatic representation of some of the processes involved.

A number of methods are available for altering a muscle cell's membrane potential. Ouabain, a direct inhibitor of the Na pump, depolarizes adult muscle fibers and was found in culture to completely inhibit both serum-stimulated AIB uptake and stretch-induced AIB uptake in serum-free medium (Figure 5). Elevated extracellular potassium also is an effective depolarizer of muscle cells in culture (33), and as can be seen in

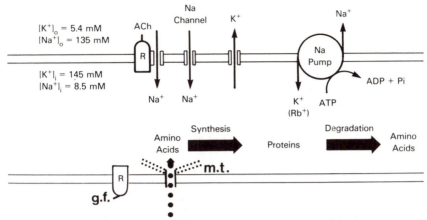

Figure 4 — Diagrammatic representation of a muscle fiber and some of the inter-acting systems involved in regulating growth of the cells. $[K^+]_o$, $[Na^+]_o$, $[K^+]_i$, $[Na^+]_i$, sodium and potassium ion concentrations outside and inside an adult myofiber, respectively; AChR, acetylcholine and its receptor; Na channel, voltage-sensitive Na channel, blocked by tetrodotoxin; Na pump, $Na^+ K^+ATPase$ activity; g•f – R, growth factors and their receptors; m.t., microtubules and their coupling to amino acid transport. Modified from reference 39.

Figure 5, 105 mM extracellular potassium prevented any significant stretch-induced stimulation of AIB uptake. Interestingly, TTX, which binds to and inhibits the activity of the membrane voltage-sensitive Na channels of electrically excitable cells, also completely inhibited the stretch-induced uptake of AIB. This effect was specific for TTX because the drug amiloride, which inhibits nonelectrogenic passive Na fluxes, had no effect on stretch-induced AIB uptake (Figure 5).

In contrast, TTX and amiloride were equally effective in inhibiting serum-stimulated AIB uptake 30-50%. Thus, only a portion of serum stimulation of AIB uptake occurs via an electrogenic mechanism, where-as stretch-induced AIB uptake occurs exclusively via an electrogenic mechanism. Although TTX would not be expected to depolarize directly the membrane potential of a skeletal muscle fiber, it would prevent the spontaneous action potentials that occur in these cells in culture (6). Mechanically induced action potentials have been shown to be present in cultured myotubes and TTX-sensitive, mechanically induced hyper-polarization has been shown to occur in other electrically excitable tissues (1,2,23,29).

These results indicate that stretch-induced increases in AIB uptake in the absence of serum in cultured myotubes requires alterations in mem-brane potential that involve the activity of the voltage-sensitive Na chan-nels. This alteration is most likely the hyperpolarization of the mem-brane potential caused by long-term activation of the Na pump, which

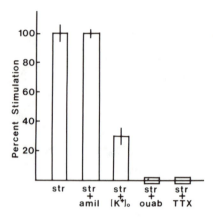

Figure 5—Effect of changes in membrane potential on stretch-induced AIB uptake. Experimental protocol was as described in the legends to Figures 1 and 2. Results are expressed relative to stretch-induced AIB uptake in serum-free medium equaling 100%. Results are the mean ± SE of the stimulation that was observed in five to eight dishes. The drug concentrations were as follows: amiloride (amil), 5×10^{-5} M; extracellular potassium, $[K^+]_o$, 105 mM, ouabain (ouab), 5×10^{-4} M; tetrodotoxin (TTX), 0.5 μg/ml.

increases the Na gradient across the cell membrane, a known energy source for Na-dependent transport (7,42). Thus, the similarity in the response of muscle cells to insulin and passive stretch, at least in regard to stimulation of amino acid transport, may result from their ability to hyperpolarize the cell's membrane potential.

Summary and conclusions

We have reviewed some of our recent results on the use of a tissue-culture model system for studying the regulation of growth-related biochemical alterations in skeletal muscle cells. Our intention was to indicate the advantages of this system for studying the basic processes possibly associated with exercise-induced skeletal muscle growth at the biochemical and molecular levels. As with all model systems our tissue culture system has advantages and disadvantages.

One of the advantages of the in vitro stretch model is that one is able to work with a relatively pure population of skeletal myofibers. Skeletal muscle hypertrophy in most other model systems, such as the in vivo tenotomy model, is associated not only with growth of the myofibers, but also with proliferation of the interstitial fibroblast (20,32). Proliferation of interstitial fibroblasts complicates interpretation of the biochemical mechanisms responsible for myofiber hypertrophy. Using a relatively pure preparation of skeletal myotubes, where greater than 90% of the fibroblasts have been eliminated, simplifies interpretation of the biochemical results. Also along this line, the myotubes in culture are spontaneously contractile but are uninnervated and the complicating influence of the nervous system is eliminated. A third advantage of the tissue culture system is that the myotubes are grown on a monolayer where diffusion of small molecules such as oxygen is not a problem and the environment of the cells can be quickly and easily manipulated. Finally, the cells respond quite rapidly to the stretch stimulus and changes in transport rates can be measured within minutes whereas changes in protein synthesis and degradation rates occur within a matter of hours.

The disadvantages of the in vitro model system are intertwined with the advantages. The myotubes are embryonic cells grown under artificial conditions in an unnatural environment. Probably all that is true of the characteristics of stretch-induced muscle growth in vitro will not hold for exercise-induced muscle growth in vivo. Differences may result from either the immature, embryonic nature of the cells, or the artificial environment in which the cells develop. The inability of the in vitro myotubes to respond to physiological concentrations of porcine insulin is a good example of differences that exist between embryonic and adult muscle cells. We hope our results with this in vitro model system will lead to a better understanding of exercise-related changes in skeletal muscle growth and will act as a stimulus for other investigators to develop new in vitro model systems so that in the future, exercise biology can be studied at both molecular and whole-animal levels.

An integration of the results from a number of different in vitro model systems should increase their applicability to what happens in the whole animal. The present finding that the growth-related increase in amino acid transport caused by passive stretch of skeletal myotubes is dependent on activation of the voltage-sensitive Na channel responsible for propagation of action potentials along a muscle fiber, and which probably result in the hyperpolarization of these cells, is but a first step in understanding how muscle activity, membrane-associated ionic fluxes and skeletal muscle growth rates are interrelated.

Acknowledgments

We thank Betty Edwards Smith, Rosanna Bailey, Humi Lamer, and Juan Rosales for technical assistance, Gabrial de la Haba for reading the manuscript, and Kathleen King for preparing the manuscript. This work was supported in part by National Institutes of Health Grant NS 16753 (to H. Vandenburgh).

References

1. Albuquerque, E.X., and Grampp, W. Effects of tetrodotoxin on the slowly adapting stretch receptor neuron of lobster. *J. Physiol. London* **195**:141-156, 1968.

2. Baylor, D.A., and Nicholls, J.G. After effects of nerve impulses on signalling in the central nervous system of the leech. *J. Physiol. London* **203**:571-589, 1969.

3. Berger, M., Hagg, S., and Ruderman, N.B. Glucose metabolism in perfused skeletal muscle. Interaction of insulin and exercise on glucose uptake. *Biochem. J.* **146**:231-238, 1975.

4. Brevet, A., Pinto, E., Peacock, J., and Stockdale, F.E. Myosin synthesis increased by electrical stimulation of skeletal muscle cell cultures. *Science* **193**:1152-1154, 1976.

5. Brodal, B.P., Jebens, E., Öy, V., and Iversen, O.J. Effects of insulin on (Na^+, K^+)-activated adenosine triphosphatase activity in rat muscle sarcolemma. *Nature* **249**:41-43, 1974.

6. Cohen, S.A., and Fischbach, G.D. Regulation of muscle acetylcholine sensitivity by muscle activity in cell cultures. *Science* **181**:76-78, 1973.

7. Crane, R.K. Interstitial absorption of sugars. *Physiol. Res.* **40**:789-825, 1960.

8. Denny-Brown, D. Experimental studies pertaining to hypertrophy, regeneration and degeneration. *Neuromusc. Disorders* **38**:147-196, 1961.

9. Elsas, L.J., MacDonnel, R.C., Jr., and Rosenberg, L.E. Influence of age on insulin stimulation of amino acid uptake in rat diaphragm. *J. Biol.* **246**:6452-6459, 1971.

10. Feng, T.P. The effect of length on the resting metabolism of muscle. *J. Physiol. London* **74**:441-454, 1932.

11. Fyfe, M.J., Loftfield, S., and Goldman, I.D. A reduction in energy-dependent amino acid transport by microtubular inhibitors in Ehrlich ascites tumor cells. *J. Cell. Physiol.* **86**:201-212, 1975.

12. Gavryck, W.A., Moore, R.D., and Thompson, R.C. Effect of insulin upon membrane-bound (Na^+, K^+)-ATPase extracted from frog skeletal muscle. *J. Physiol. London* **252**:43-58, 1975.

13. Goldberg, A.L. Role of insulin in work-induced growth of skeletal muscle. *Endocrinology* **83**:1071-1073, 1968.

14. Goldberg, A.L., and Goodman, H.M. Amino acid transport during work-induced growth of skeletal muscle. *Am. J. Physiol.* **216**:1111-1115, 1969.

15. Goldberg, A.L., and Goodman, H.M. Effects of disuse and denervation on amino acid transport by skeletal muscle. *Am. J. Physiol.* **216**:1116-1119, 1969.

16. Goldberg, A.L., Jablecki, C., and Li, J.B. Effects of use and disuse on amino acid transport and protein turnover in muscle. *Ann. N.Y. Acad. Sci.* **228**:190-201, 1974.

17. Goldberg, A.L., Etlinger, J.D., Goldspink, D.F., and Jablecki, C. Mechanism of work-induced hypertrophy of skeletal muscle. *Med. Sci. Sports* **7**:248-261, 1975.

18. Goldspink, D.F. The influence of immobilization and stretch on protein turnover of rat skeletal muscle. *J. Physiol. London* **264**:267-282, 1977.

19. Grove, B.K., and Stockdale, F.E. Membrane function in differentiating skeletal muscle cells. I. Kinetic analysis of amino acid transport. *Devel. Biol.* **66**:142-150, 1978.

20. Jablecki, C.K., Heuser, J.E., and Kaufman, S. Autoradiographic localization of new RNA synthesis in hypertrophying skeletal muscle. *J. Cell. Biol.* **57**:743-759, 1973.

21. Lømo, T., Westgaard, R.H., and Engebretsen, L. In: *Plasticity of muscle.* Walter de Gruyter, Berlin, 1980, pp. 297-309.

22. Merrill, G.F., Florini, J.R., and Dulak, N.C. Effects of multiplication stimulating activity (MSA) on AIB transport into myoblast and myotube cultures. *J. Cell. Physiol.* **93**:173-182, 1977.

23. Nakajima, S., and Takahashi, K. Post-tetanic hyperpolarization and electrogenic Na pump in stretch receptor neurons of crayfish. *J. Physiol. London* **197**:105-127, 1965.

24. Narahara, H.T., and Holloszy, J.O. The actions of insulin, trypsin and electrical stimulation on amino acid transport in muscle. *J. Biol. Chem.* **249**:5435-5439, 1974.

25. Pierson, R.W., Jr., and Temin, H.M. The partial purification from calf serum of a fraction with multiplication-stimulating activity for chicken fibroblasts in cell culture and with non-suppressible insulin-like activity. *J. Cell. Physiol.* **79**:319-330, 1972.

26. Porter, K.R., Puck, T.T., Hsie, A.W., and Kelley, D. An electron microscope study of the effects of dibutyryl cyclic AMP on Chinese hamster ovary cells. *Cell* **2**:145-162, 1974.

27. Prentiki, M., Crettaz, M., and Jeanrenaud, B. Role of microtubules in insulin and glucagon stimulation of amino acid transport in isolated rat hepatocytes. *J. Biol. Chem.* **256**:4336-4340, 1981.

28. Riggs, T.R., and McKirahan, J. Action of insulin on transport of L-alanine into rat diaphragm in vitro. *J. Biol. Chem.* **248**:6450-6455, 1973.

29. Ritchie, J.M., and Staub, R.W. The hyperpolarization which follows activity in mammalian non-medullated fibers. *J. Physiol.* **136**:80-97, 1957.

30. Sampson, S.R., and Bannett, R.R. Effects of thyroxine on membrane potentials of developing rat skeletal muscle cells in culture. *Soc. Neurosci. Abstr.* **7**:597a, 1981.

31. Schiaffino, S., and Hanzlikova, V. On the mechanism of compensatory hypertrophy in skeletal muscle. *Experientia* **26**:152-153, 1970.

32. Schiaffino, S., Bormioli, S.P., and Aliosi, N. Cell proliferation in rat skeletal muscle during stages of compensatory hypertrophy. *Virch. Arch. Abt. B. Zellpath* **II**:268-273, 1972.

33. Steinbach, J.H. Role of muscle activity in nerve-muscle interactions in vitro. *Nature* **248**:70-71, 1974.

34. Thomsen, P., and Luco, J.V. Changes of weight and neuromuscular transmission in muscles of immobilized joints. *J. Neurophysiol.* **7**:245-251, 1944.

35. Vandenburgh, H.H. Separation of plasma membrane markers by glycerol-induced blistering of muscle cells. *Biochim. Biophys. Acta.* **466**:302-314, 1977.

36. Vandenburgh, H.H., and Kaufman, S. In vitro model for stretch-induced hypertrophy of skeletal muscle. *Science* **203**:265-268, 1979.

37. Vandenburgh, H.H., and Kaufman, S. Protein degradation in embryonic skeletal muscle. Effect of medium, cell type, inhibitors and passive stretch. *J. Biol. Chem.* **255**:5826-5833, 1980.

38. Vandenburgh, H.H., and Kaufman, S. In: *Plasticity of muscle.* Walter de Gruyter, Berlin, 1980, pp. 493-506.

39. Vandenburgh, H.H., and Kaufman, S. In: *Mechanism of muscle adaptation to functional requirements.* Akademiai Kiado, Budapest, 1981, pp. 291-304.

40. Vandenburgh, H.H., and Kaufman, S. Stretch-induced growth of skeletal myotubes correlates with activation of the sodium pump. *J. Cell. Physiol.* **109**:205-214, 1981.

41. Vandenburgh, H.H., and Kaufman, S. Coupling of voltage-sensitive sodium channel activity to stretch-induced amino acid transport in skeletal muscle in vitro. *J. Biol. Chem.* **257**:13448-13454, 1982.

42. Villereal, M.L., and Cook, J.S. Regulation of active amino acid transport by growth-related changes in membrane potential in a human fibroblast. *J. Biol. Chem.* **253**:8257-8262, 1978.

Regulation of connective tissue metabolism in aging and exercise: A review

Robert E. Beyer
The University of Michigan

A rich literature exists on the biochemical changes that accompany the aging of mammalian organisms, including humans. A very large amount of information also has appeared describing biochemical changes accompanying and forming the basis of adaptation to endurance types of exercise. Until recently, most endurance-trained athletes of our species were in their twenties or thirties; in addition, the social and psychological emphasis has focused on that early, relatively immature portion of the lifespan, so that the effect of endurance exercise in the elderly has received scant attention at the biochemical level.

Despite this scarcity of biochemical information on the metabolic and chemical changes that parallel endurance exercise in the elderly, organizers and participants of "exercise for seniors" group programs generally acknowledge that benefits accrue in terms of improved physical and psychological well-being. What is unclear, however, is whether these effects are due to a general biochemical response to exercise or to being a part of group activity with its emotional rewards (c.f. 36). What does appear to be clear is that when one examines either the factors limiting progressive improvement in physical conditioning of such individuals, or injuries interrupting that process, a failure of some aspect of connective tissue function is usually to blame. The purpose of this article is to examine and report on (a) the literature describing changes in connective tissue proteins which accompany aging, (b) differences between connective tissue proteins of sedentary and endurance-trained individuals, and (c) the effects of exercise on the connective tissue metabolism of aged animals, including humans.

Connective tissue biochemistry and nomenclature

The tensile strength of our tissues is derived from the unique structure of the connective tissue proteins comprising that particular tissue. These proteins are collagen, elastin, connectin, and the proteoglycans. Most of the attention in this article will focus on the collagen class of proteins, although some aspects of elastin function and metabolism will be included. However, because of the enormous literature on the subject of collagen, about 1,500 new papers each year (55), this discussion must necessarily omit many authors and aspects of the subject. I have thus been very discriminating in my selection of the literature cited and discussed.

Collagen, the most abundant protein in mammals, consists of about 25% of the total and is the major structural element of bone, tendon, cartilage, skin, blood vessels, and teeth. In addition, collagen exists in nearly all organs and its presence in the basement membrane allows cells to exist as discrete units. Table 1 contains a list of the types of collagen and their distributions in mammalian tissues. Collagen types differ in the kinds and extent of cross-linking within and between their triple-chain tropocollagens, in the extent of their glucosyl and galactosyl residues, and in the composition and sequence of the peptides making up the triple-stranded tropocollagen molecule. Although the classification of collagen types in Table 1 appears to be fairly general, collagen biochem-

Table 1

Collagen Type Distribution

Type	Distribution
I	Skin, tendon, bone
II	Cartilage, intervertebral disc
III	Cardiovascular system, fetal skin
IV	Basement membranes, placenta
V	Amnion and chorion: placenta

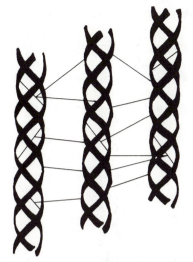

Figure 1— Intra- and intermolecular cross-linking bonds of collagen.

istry is under vigorous investigation and the nomenclature will probably change with time and discoveries.

The present complex state of the structurally distinct types of collagen has been the subject of recent review (8) and lucid discussion (20). Collagen is distinctive in its ability to form long, insoluble fibers of great tensile strength and metabolic stability, and in its rather unique amino acid sequence and composition. It contains a remarkably high proportion of glycine (about 30% of the amino acid composition), more proline than most other proteins, and is unique in its content of posttranslationally modified hydroxylysine and hydroxyproline. The basic structural unit of type I collagen is tropocollagen, which is a very long (3,000 Å) and narrow (15 Å) unit consisting of three peptide chains in extended *trans* helices wound around each other in a superhelical cable stabilized by hydrogen bonding and van der Waals interactions. In addition, collagen and elastin fibers are further strengthened by covalent cross-linking between lysine residues within the tropocollagen triple helix and between these cross-links and amino acid residues of adjacent tropocollagen molecules (Figure 1). This type of covalent, cross-linked bonding results in fibers of amazing strength, enabling a fiber of 1-mm diameter to hold a 10-kg weight without rupture. The chemical groups involved in, and the chemistry of the formation of, collagen cross-links have been reviewed (45).

The intramolecular cross-links between peptide chains within the triple helix are formed between two lysyl residues as an aldol cross-link (Figure 2). The intermolecular cross-links involve interaction of a histidyl residue which can react with a $C = C$ bond in the intramolecular aldol cross-link to form a histidine aldol cross-link (Figure 3). In addition, the aldehyde group of the aldol-histidine cross-link may react with and bond to a

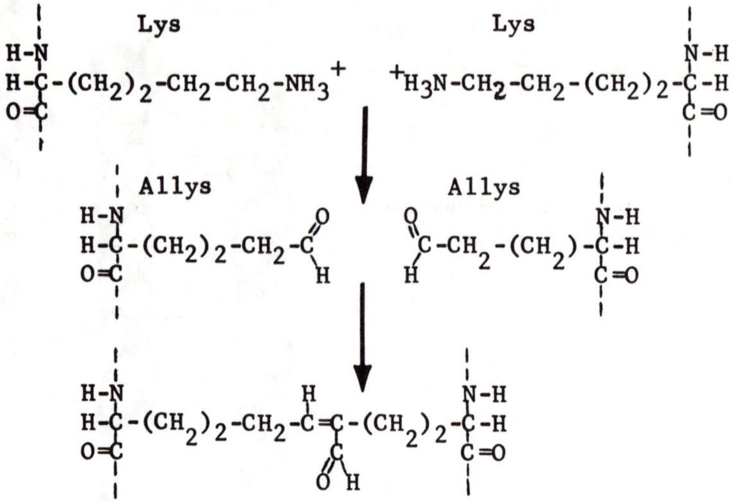

Figure 2—Interaction between lysyl residues of collagen to form an aldol cross-link.

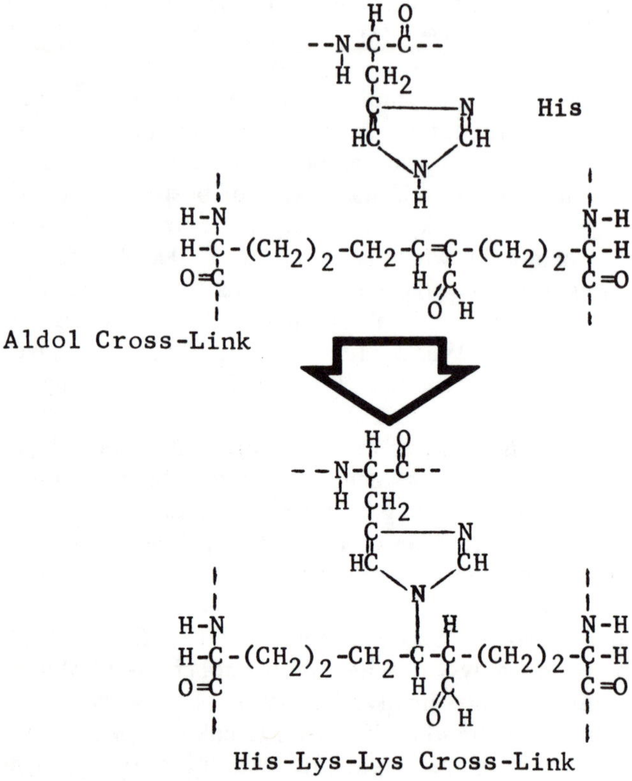

Figure 3—Formation of histidine-aldol cross-link.

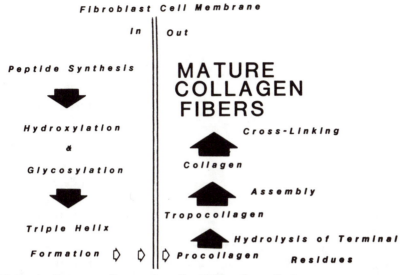

Figure 4—Sequence of events in collagen fiber formation.

hydroxylysyl residue on another peptide chain. A combination of cross-links can covalently link four separate residues, forming a large part of the basis for the structural strength of collagen. These types of interactions appear to be used in two kinds of proteins, collagen and elastin. The sequence of events in the formation of the final, mature collagen fiber is depicted in Figure 4.

Elastin, which is responsible for the plasticity of elastic tissues, is composed mainly of hydrophobic amino acid residues, is highly cross-linked and, consequently, very insoluble and difficult to analyze. In addition to the kinds of cross-links found in collagen, elastin contains desmosine, a cross-link involving four lysyl side groups (Figure 5). The molecular and supramolecular structure of elastin have been reviewed recently (44). Elastin appears to be one of the most metabolically inert proteins; its biological half-life in rodent lung is expressed in terms of years (17).

Native collagen and elastin are not susceptible to attack by the usual intracellular proteolytic enzymes. However, collagenase and elastase are enzymes that nick their respective substrates, opening them up to attack by other proteolytic enzymes.

Connective tissue changes with age

As the mammalian organism ages, so does its connective tissue. This topic has been the subject of an excellent book by Hall (23) and a chapter in a volume by Kanungo (29). The initial observations in this field were made by Verzar and Huber who noted that the striation frequency of the rat's tail tendon increased with age (53). In addition, Brocas and Verzar

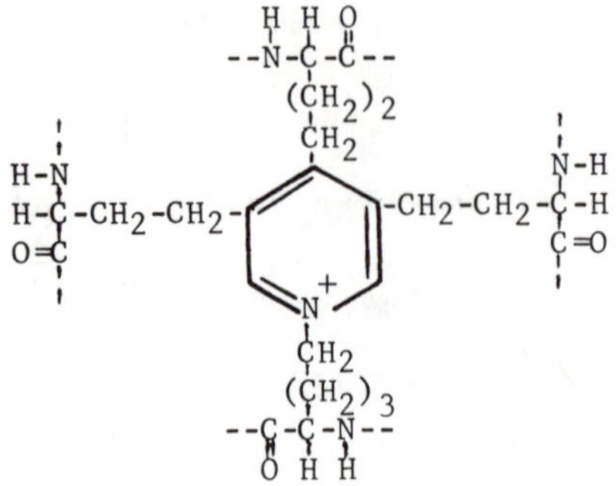

Figure 5 — The unique cross-link of elastin, desmosine.

noted that the extractability (i.e., solubility) of collagen decreased with age and, upon further investigation, found that the force exerted by the contraction of isolated collagen upon heating (thermocontraction) increased with age (10). These observations suggested the possibility that collagen molecules become more heavily cross-linked with age and led Verzar to propose (52) a theory of aging based on collagen cross-linking. Later work has confirmed the change in solubility of collagen with age (19) and has provided data supporting an increased cross-linking with age (15,24). The cross-linking of rat tail tendon collagen has been reported to increase by a factor of 10 between 3 and 100 weeks of age (54).

Subsequent, more detailed analyses (4), however, suggest that all of the cross-links are present upon the early formation of collagen fibers and that the reducible cross-links become more stable with time. These authors (4) also suggest that stabilization of the intermolecular bonds is due to spontaneous events and not enzymatic action and that "it is not necessary to propose a continuous increase in the number of cross-links, with all the attendant difficulties of enzyme reactions within the fiber: rather a spontaneous conversion of the reducible intermediates to the stable mature form would account for the observed facts" (4).

Tanzer and Mechanic have reported (46) that progressive changes occur during maturation in the chemical nature of the aldehydes (links) in collagen. Davison (14) has reported no change in the number of cross-links when measured in 3- and 12-year-old cattle. In addition, the change in the number of cross-links with age appears to depend on the species studied. Moriguchi and Fumimoto have reported (35) that the number of cross-links in tendon and cartilage in humans decreases after the age of 30 years whereas they increase in the laboratory rat following maturity. When the two principal types of cross-links, hydroxylysinonorleucine and dihydroxylysinonorleucine, were measured, they did not change with age (51).

An interesting aspect of collagen and age is the question of whether the molecule is different when synthesized at different ages. The stability of newly formed collagen as measured by extraction with weak acetic acid appears to be identical when obtained from young and old donors (27). However, the report (28) that newly synthesized collagen in sponge implants from young and old rats showed differential susceptibility to digestion by collagenase suggests molecular differences between collagen synthesized by young and old animals. Also of interest is the finding that parabiosis diminishes this difference (28).

We are thus forced to conclude that an increase in the number of cross-links is not the ultimate aging mechanism. The physical changes observed between young and old connective tissue may be just one of many changes that accompany the passage of biological time for each species and may represent a stabilization of labile cross-links, the potential for which is present when the molecules originally are synthesized, associated, and secreted from the cell. This area is very unsettled at present. Incisive research will have to be accomplished on the numbers and types of cross-links in the various types of collagen and other connective tissue proteins from a variety of tissues. This information will allow a correlation between observed changes with age and the biochemical and physiological functions of the tissues.

Some progress has been made in this direction. For example, Epstein (18) has reported that type III collagen predominates in the skin of human fetuses. By term, type I is three times as plentiful, a ratio which remains fairly constant to age 78.

Cultured chondrocytes normally make type II collagen but respond to the addition of bromodeoxyuridine, an analog of thymidine, by switching their synthesis to type I collagen and another type of collagen not native to the tissue (33). Chondrocytes normally shift the type of collagen from II to I as they age. In addition, the same or similar shifts between types of collagen synthesized occur in various disease states involving cartilage in humans (37). One self-imposed environmental disease, tobacco smoking, results in both qualitative and quantitative changes in the connective tissue of human lungs (38).

For reasons detailed later, the connective tissue changes occurring with age in the lung are of interest. Surprisingly little is known about the biochemical changes in lung tissue during aging, whereas a considerable amount of information is available on changes in lung mechanics. This subject has been discussed by Thurlbeck (47). The lung contains elastin in addition to collagen, as do other distensible tissues. Elastin, because of its unique molecular architecture and cross-linking, is highly distensible, in contrast to collagen. One of the effects of age on lung is a decrease in the elasticity of alveolar tissue (41). The content of connective tissue in lung at various ages appears to depend on the species studied and those studying the problem. It is fairly clear, however, that with the rabbit as a model the rate of connective tissue synthesis in lung is high in the fetus, decreases until weaning, and thereafter remains quite low, but not zero

(9). In human lung, the acid-soluble collagen (new collagen) content decreases with age, a rate of loss which is more rapid in tobacco smokers (38).

Connective tissue changes with exercise

As an animal progresses from the sedentary to the endurance-trained state, many changes accompany, and would appear to form a biochemical basis for, this transformation. Some of the biochemical adaptations to endurance exercise in skeletal muscle have been reviewed (26) and an enormous literature has grown documenting the remarkable increase in aerobic capacity for those muscles involved in the particular type of endurance exercise used. One would expect any change in the capacity of a muscle to catalyze energy-releasing reactions to also be accompanied by a change in the supportive structure of that muscle, that is, in the associated connective tissue. If one hypothesizes that connective tissue changes will occur in supportive structures of tissues adapting to endurance exercise, one might also expect changes in the opposite direction in the same tissues upon detraining, immobilization, or denervation of the part involved. A number of studies support these contentions and have been the subject of an excellent review (7).

One of the most active groups in research on connective tissue changes with exercise is led by Charles Tipton at the University of Iowa. This group has studied, among other aspects of this problem, the influence of physical activity on ligaments and tendons and their attachments to bone (49). The junctional strength, a function of bonding between these connective tissues, is increased by endurance training and decreased by immobilization. In addition, the amount of collagen in both soleus and gastrocnemius muscles, as estimated by hydroxyproline content, increases with time after denervation (22). A parallel increase also occurs in the first two enzymes of the pentose phosphate pathway, glucose-6-phosphate dehydrogenase and 6-phosphogluconate dehydrogenase, both of which produce a molecule of NADPH required for reductive synthesis; subsequent reactions of the pathway produce pentose precursors for polynucleotide synthesis, a prelude to protein synthesis (21). This parallel increase in the connective tissue proteins and these two enzymes is of interest because of (a) the role played by connective tissue in removing cellular debris after injury and as a supporting matrix, and (b) the potential uses for measuring the activity of these enzymes, simple and straightforward compared to analyzing connective tissue protein, to follow the level of connective tissue metabolism.

Additional evidence belying the view of connective tissue as a metabolically inert tissue comes from studies indicating that immobilized periarticular connective tissue from the rabbit knee shows an increase in reducible dihydroxylysinonorleucine cross-links (1) and the presence of only type I collagen (2). Further research by this group has shown that immobilization leads to an increase in the rate of knee tendon and ligament collagen turnover (3).

Because immobilization affects the metabolism of connective tissue protein, one might assume that endurance training would also affect this function. The rate of turnover of ligament collagen appears to be higher in trained dogs (48) and mice (55), but not in rats or rabbits (49). Experimental results on the effect of endurance training on skeletal muscle metabolism appear to be more consistent. The rate of collagen synthesis is accelerated in skeletal muscle as a result of endurance training in rats (30), humans (42), and cows (31).

Under conditions of increased collagen metabolism in muscle in response to endurance training, one might expect to observe, in addition to an increased synthesis, an increase in the rate of old collagen removal. In order to prepare collagen for attack by cellular proteolytic enzymes to which the native molecule is not susceptible, the molecule must first be nicked by specific collagenases. Preliminary experiments in my laboratory on the ability of gastrocnemius muscle homogenates to attack DNP-Pro-Gln-Gly-Ile-Ala-Gly-Gln-D-Arg-OH, an octapeptide containing a sequence similar to that at the cleavage site of the collagen molecule by vertebrate collagenase (32), suggest that collagenase activity is increased by endurance training and ascorbic acid in middle-aged rats (V.A. Vaughn, M.P. Chang, and R.E. Beyer, unpublished observations). In these experiments, four groups of 12-month-old Sprague-Dawley rats were used. Two groups were trained to run on a mechanical treadmill 5 days per week for a period of 19 weeks. One of the trained groups received ascorbic acid in their drinking water at a level of 0.125 g of ascorbate per kg body weight. Two sedentary groups, one receiving ascorbate, also were maintained. The gastrocnemius collagenase activity is greater in all animals receiving ascorbic acid than in those not, and greater in all runners than in sedentary animals.

Although it is beyond the scope of this article, I should mention the contributions to the field of regulation of connective tissue metabolism and the discovery of connective tissue activating peptides (CTAP) by Castor (11).

Connective tissue changes with exercise in the aged

The increasing number of elderly participating in endurance events and the increase in the number of publications (almost autocatalytic in nature) devoted to the consequences of exercise for those of us in advancing years attest to the growing awareness of the benefits of exercise among the elderly, although whether exercise affects longevity is unclear.

Nevertheless, on the basis of a number of studies it is reasonable to conclude that the response of elderly animals, including our own species, to exercise is quantitatively similar to that of young and middle-aged individuals when expressed in percentage increases of capacity (16,43). The results of experiments in my laboratory suggest that the percentage increase in oxidative capacity of gastrocnemius muscle of two-year-old, endurance-trained rats over sedentary controls is greater than the percentage increment in younger animals similarly trained (5,6). The initial baseline is considerably lower in the older sedentary muscle, however.

Because the aged animal's biochemistry is capable of responding and adapting to endurance exercise programs in a manner similar to that of younger animals, we should expect that some replacement of heavily cross-linked connective tissue protein might also occur in the elderly trained animal. An early study on the relationship between age, chronic exercise, and connective tissue of the heart in rats (50) reported an increase with age in cardiac connective tissue, measured as hydroxyproline content. Small decreases in cardiac hydroxyproline were observed with training in both young and old rats. Suominen and Heikkinen (42) have reported increased muscle collagen biosynthetic activity, measured as prolylhydroxylase activity, in leg muscles of habitually trained, middle-aged, and old endurance athletes, but did not observe such changes in 69-year-old humans after 8 weeks of physical training (43). Heikkinen and Vuori have noted (25) an increased rate of collagen degradation in the Achilles tendons of 1-year-old, endurance-trained mice, suggesting a greater rate of collagen turnover induced by hyperkinesis.

The connective tissue that appears to be the most responsive to exercise in the elderly animal is that of bone. In bone, calcium and collagen are deposited and turn over in relation to one another. In humans, bones decline in mineral mass (osteoporosis) and strength by 15-30% by age 70. Similar changes happen with hypodynamic states resulting from bedrest during illness, immobilization, or weightlessness. Greater bone size, density, and strength are seen in certain types of athletes such as baseball pitchers, tennis players, etc. Both the decline of bone mass and strength with age and the influence of exercise on bone in the aged have been reviewed recently (39). Dalen and Olsson (13) have reported that distance runners betwen 50 and 59 years of age had 20% greater femur and humerus mineral content than did appropriate controls. A study of the bone mineral and dimensions of dominant and nondominant limbs of world class tennis players of average age 64 years, playing this sport for an average of 40 years, has revealed an increase in all dimensions of the dominant limb (34). In a study of women of average age 81 years, exercise over a period of 3 years has been shown (40) to slow the rate of bone loss and/or increase bone mineral content. In this context, preliminary experiments in my laboratory (J.C. Huang and R.E. Beyer, unpublished observations) suggest that 16 weeks of endurance training of 26-month-old male rats increases the fat-free density of the femurs and tibia-fibulas in comparison to 26-month-old sedentary controls and to the level of 9-month-old sedentary animals. Both the calcium and collagen densities of these bones also are increased as a result of the 16 weeks of endurance training. Thus, the development of osteoporosis, which occurs during aging in both females and males, may be reversed by an appropriate exercise program.

The influence of endurance exercise, which we might expect to affect changes in lung connective tissue of aged animals, does not appear to have received attention. This problem also is under investigation in my laboratory (A. Aggarwal and R.E. Beyer, unpublished observations).

Conclusions and recommendations

Despite the earlier belief that connective tissue, once synthesized, is relatively inert, becoming even more refractory to regulation due to increased or more stable cross-linking of its constituent proteins with age, the ability of a lifelong program of exercise to delay some of the changes in connective tissue accumulating with age is well documented. With the exception of bone, the ability of exercise to reverse these changes is not so clear and remains an area desperately requiring research. More information is needed on the regulation of synthesis and catabolism of the several kinds of collagen in various tissues, as well as elastin of blood vessels and lung tissue in disease, under normal conditions, and during endurance and other types of exercise. Modern techniques of analyses must be applied to the regulation of the breakdown and replacement of "stiff" collagen and elastin of the skeletomuscular, circulatory, and respiratory systems of mature animals in response to nutritional and hormonal treatments and various types and intensities of exercise. Exercise biologists might also give serious consideration to determining the influence of graded exercise programs over the entire lifespan on the longevity of a standardized laboratory model in order to gain insight into this controversial subject. The role of connective tissue activating factors (CTAF) in response to normal maintenance turnover of collagen is beginning to receive attention (12). The possible role of CTAF in the response of connective tissue to exercise could well be an extremely fruitful avenue of exploration.

Because the real number, as well as the percentage of elderly in our population, will increase over the next decades due to improvements in health care delivery, it is incumbent upon us as investigators to discover the basis for maintenance of vitality which results from exercise at all ages. In addition, we must inquire into the possibility of limitations and dangers in such activities in the very elderly. I hope to be able to contribute to this "frontier in exercise biology."

Acknowledgments

Some of the research reported herein received generous financial support from the Cutcheon Fund of The University of Michigan Honors Program. I thank Margaret A. Madouse for her help in preparation of the manuscript and Kathleen D. Timberlake for her critical reading of this review.

Dedication

This brief review on aspects of aging and exercise is dedicated to Professor Dee W. Edington who, despite his advanced physiological age, participates in vigorous exercise regularly with his wife, Marilyn. He serves as an outstanding example to all of us who know him with regard to the physical accomplishments that can be achieved in our later years.

References

(Because of the vast literature related to subjects discussed herein, this list of references is intended to be minimally representative rather than inclusive.)

1. Akeson, W.H., Amiel, D., Mechanic, F.L., Woo, S.L-Y., Harwood, F.L., and Hamer, M.L. Collagen cross-linking alterations in joint contractures: Changes in the reducible cross-links in periarticular connective tissue collagen after nine weeks of immobilization. *Conn. Tissue Res.* **5**:15-19, 1977.

2. Amiel, D., Akeson, W.H., Harwood, F.L., and Mechanic, G.L. The effect of immobilization on the types of collagen synthesized in periarticular connective tissue. *Conn. Tissue Res.* **8**:27-32, 1980.

3. Amiel, D., Woo, S.L-Y., Harwood, F.L., Winters, J., and Akeson, W.H. The effect of immobilization on collagen turnover in connective tissue. Presented at the 27th Annual ORS, Las Vegas, NV, Feb. 24-26, 1981.

4. Bailey, A.J., Robins, S.P., and Balian, G. Biological significance of the intermolecular crosslinks of collagen. *Nature* **251**:105-109, 1974.

5. Beyer, R.E., Compton, R.T., Edington, D.W., Kwasman, M.A., Lipton, R.J., Ponte, L.D., and Starnes, J.W. Age-associated decline of skeletal muscle exergonic pathways: Reversal with exercise. *Age* **4**:138, 1981.

6. Beyer, R.E., Edington, D.W., Starnes, J.W., Kwasman, M., and Lipton, R.J. Biochemical evidence for a training effect in aged animals. *Med. Sci. Sports Exer.* **13**:81, 1981.

7. Booth, F.W., and Gould, E.W. Effects of training and disuse on connective tissue. *Exer. Sport Sci. Rev.* **3**:83-112, 1975.

8. Bornstein, P., and Sage, H. Structurally distinct collagen types. *Ann. Rev. Biochem.* **49**:957-1003, 1980.

9. Bradley, K.H., McConnell, S.D., and Crystal, R.G. Lung collagen composi-

tion in synthesis: Characterization and changes with age. *J. Biol. Chem.* **249**:2674-2683, 1974.

10. Brocas, J., and Verzar, F. The aging of *Xenopus laevis*, a South African frog. *Gerontologia* **5**:228-240, 1961.

11. Castor, C.W., Jr. Regulation of connective tissue metabolism. In: D.J. McCarty (ed.), *Arthritis and allied conditions*, 9th Edition, chapt. 12, Lea & Febiger, Philadelphia, 1979, pp. 201-213.

12. Castor, C.W., Jr. Autacoid regulation of wound healing. In: L.E. Glynn (ed.), *Handbook of inflammation*, Vol. 3, Elsevier, Amsterdam, 1981, pp. 177-209.

13. Dalen, N., and Olsson, K.E. Bone mineral content and physical activity. *Acta Orthop. Scand.* **45**:170-174, 1974.

14. Davison, P.F. Bovine tendons: Aging and collagen cross-linking. *J. Biol. Chem.* **253**:5635-5641, 1978.

15. Delbridge, L., and Everitt, A.V. Age changes in polymer composition of collagen by molecular-sieve chromatography. *Gerontologia* **18**:169-175, 1972.

16. deVries, H.A. Physiological effects of an exercise training regimen upon men aged 52-88. *J. Gerontol.* **25**:325-336, 1970.

17. Dubick, M.A., Rucker, R.B., Cross, C.E., and Last, J.A. Elastin metabolism in rodent lung. *Biochim. Biophys. Acta* **672**:303-306, 1981.

18. Epstein, E.H. [1(III)]$_3$ human skin collagen: Release by pepsin digestion and preponderance in fetal life. *J. Biol. Chem.* **249**:3225-3231, 1974.

19. Everitt, A.V., and Delbridge, L. Two phases of collagen aging in tail tendon of hypophysectomized rats. *Exp. Gerontol.* **7**:45-51, 1972.

20. Eyre, D.R. Collagen: Molecular diversity in the body's protein scaffold. *Science* **207**:1315-1322, 1980.

21. Garcia-Bunuel, L., and Garcia-Bunuel, V.M. Connective tissue and the pentose phosphate pathway in normal and denervated muscle. *Nature* **213**:913-914, 1967.

22. Garcia-Bunuel, L., and Garcia-Bunuel, V.M. Connective tissue metabolism in normal and atrophic skeletal muscle. *J. Neurol. Sci.* **47**:69-77, 1980.

23. Hall, D.A. *The aging of connective tissue*. Academic, London, 1976.

24. Heikkinen, E., and Kulonen, E. Age factor in the maturation of collagen: Intramolecular linkages in mildly denatured collagen. *Experientia* **20**:310, 1964.

25. Heikkinen, E., and Vuori, I. Effect of physical activity on the metabolism of collagen in aged mice. *Acta Physiol. Scand.* **84**:543-549, 1972.

26. Holloszy, J.O., and Booth, F.W. Biochemical adaptations to endurance exercise in muscle. *Ann. Rev. Physiol.* **38**:273-291, 1976.

27. Hruza, Z., and Hlavackova, V. The characteristics of newly formed collagen during aging. *Gerontologia* **7**:221-232, 1963.

28. Jolma, V.H., and Hruza, Z. Differences in properties of newly formed collagen during aging and parabiosis. *J. Gerontol.* **27**:178-182, 1972.

29. Kanungo, M.S. *Biochemistry of aging.* Academic, London, 1980, pp. 129-154.

30. Kovanen, V., Suominen, H., and Heikkinen, E. Connective tissue of "fast" and "slow" skeletal muscle in rats: Effects of endurance training. *Acta Physiol. Scand.* **108**:173-180, 1980.

31. Krueggel, W.G., and Field, R.A. Cross-linking of collagen in active and quiescent bovine muscle. *Growth* **38**:495-499, 1974.

32. Masui, Y., Takemoto, T., Sakakibara, S., Hori, H., and Nagai, Y. Synthetic substrates for vertebrate collagenase. *Biochem. Med.* **17**:215-221, 1977.

33. Mayne, R., Vail, M.S., and Miller, E.J. Analysis of changes in collagen biosynthesis that occur when chick chondrocytes are grown in 5-bromo-2'-deoxyuridine. *Proc. Natl. Acad. Sci.* **72**:4511-4515, 1975.

34. Montoye, H.J., Smith, E.L., Fardon, D.F., and Howley, E.T. Bone mineral in senior tennis players. *Scand. J. Sports Sci.* **2**:26-32, 1980.

35. Moriguchi, T., and Fumimoto, D. Age-related changes in the content of the collagen crosslink, pyridinoline. *J. Biochem.* **84**:933-935, 1978.

36. Nickoley-Colquitt, S. Preventive group interventions for elderly clients: Are they effective? In: T. Wells, (ed.), *Aging and Health Promotion*, Aspen, Rockville, MD, 1981, pp. 167-186.

37. Nimni, M., and Deshmukh, K. Differences in collagen metabolism between normal and osteoarthritic human articular cartilage. *Science* **181**:751-752, 1973.

38. Rickert, W.S., and Forbes, W.F. Changes in collagen with age. II. Age and smoking related changes in human lung connective tissue. *Exp. Gerontol.* **11**:89-101, 1976.

39. Smith, E.L. Bone changes in the exercising older adult. In: E.L. Smith and R.C. Serfass (eds.), *Exercise and aging: The scientific basis*, Enslow, Hillside, NJ, 1981, pp. 179-186.

40. Smith, E.L., Reddan, W., and Smith, P.E. Physical activity and calcium modalities for bone mineral increase in old women. *Med. Sci. Sports Exercise* **13**:60-64, 1981.

41. Sugihara, J., Martin, C.J., and Hildebrandt, J. Length-tension properties of alveolar wall in man. *J. Appl. Physiol.* **30**:874-878, 1971.

42. Suominen, H., and Heikkinen, E. Enzyme activities in muscle and connective tissue of m. vastus lateralis in habitually trained and sedentary 33 to 77 year old men. *Eur. J. Appl. Physiol.* **34**:249-254, 1975.

43. Suominen, H., Heikkinen, E., and Parkatti, T. Effect of eight weeks' physical training on muscle and connective tissue of the m. vastus lateralis in 69-year-old men and women. *J. Gerontol.* **32**:33-37, 1977.

44. Tamburro, A.M. Elastin: Molecular and supramolecular structure. In: Z. Deyl and M. Adam (eds.), *Connective tissue research: Chemistry, biology, and physiology*, Alan Liss, New York, 1981, pp. 45-62.

45. Tanzer, M.L. Cross-linking of collagen. *Science* **180**:561-566, 1973.

46. Tanzer, M.L., and Mechanic, G. Collagen reduction by sodium borohydride: Effect of reconstitution, maturation and lathyrism. *Biochem. Biophys. Res. Commun.* **32**:885-892, 1968.

47. Thurlbeck, W.M. The effect of age on the lung. In: A.A. Dietz (ed.), *Aging: Its chemistry*, Am. Assn. Clin. Chem., Washington, DC, 1980, pp. 114-131.

48. Tipton, C.M., James, S.L., Mergner, W., and Tcheng, T.K. Influence of exercise on the strength of the medial callateral knee ligament of dogs. *Am. J. Physiol.* **218**:894-902, 1970.

49. Tipton, C.M., Matthes, R.D., Maynard, J.A., and Cary, R.A. The influence of physical activity on ligaments and tendons. *Med. Sci. Sports* **7**:165-175, 1975.

50. Tomanek, R.J., Taunton, C.A., and Liskop, K.S. Relationship between age, chronic exercise, and connective tissue of the heart. *J. Gerontol.* **27**:33-38, 1972.

51. Torres, A.R. Cross-linking of collagen depending on age. *Gerontology* **24**:337-342, 1978.

52. Verzar, F. Aging of the collagen fiber. *Int. Rev. Conn. Tissue Res.* **2**:243-300, 1964.

53. Verzar, F., and Huber, K. Die Structure der Sehnen-Faser. *Acta Anat.* **33**:215-229, 1958.

54. Vihersaari, T., and Heikkinen, E. Enzyme activities of glycolysis, pentose phosphate cycle, and Krebs cycle of a new connective tissue in young and aged rats. *Scand. J. Clin. Lab. Invest.* **27**(Suppl. 116):30, 1971.

55. Viidik, A. The effect of training on the tensile strength of isolated rabbit tendons. *Scand. J. Plastic Reconst. Surg.* **1**:141-147, 1967.

Relationships of microvascular and tissue heterogeneities to oxygenation of skeletal muscle

Brian R. Duling
University of Virginia

The magnitude of the contribution of microvascular function to muscle performance has long been at issue in the field of exercise biology. It has been proposed that the state of the microcirculation is a major determinant of muscle fatigue, endurance, and oxygen consumption (11,46,48). It is known that endurance training induces microvascular alterations and raises tissue PO_2 (51), presumably with a resultant improvement in performance, but specific relationships between such parameters as capillary oxygen transport and performance changes remain in doubt (11,23,46). The purpose of this chapter is two-fold: first, to review the rather idealized model of microcirculation which is the basis for much of the thought regarding tissue oxygen transport; and second, to consider certain more realistic complexities of the microcirculation of striated muscle — important elements in understanding the limits to tissue oxygenation.

It might be asked what remains to be learned about a subject investigated so extensively in the past. However, examination of the literature shows that a variety of apparently simple questions are as yet unanswered regarding relations between microvessel function and muscle performance. For example, it is not definitely established if the resting metabolic rate of striated muscle is limited by the availability of oxygen (flow-limited oxygen consumption). Certainly, oxygen supply to a tissue can become limiting if the flow and/or arterial oxygen content are sufficiently reduced relative to the metabolic rate (28), but the status of tissue oxygenation under free flow conditions with normal oxygen content in the blood remains in doubt despite years of investigation (4,15,26,40, 53,58).

The reason for the continuing inability to resolve what should be a straightforward question remains unclear. However, the problem may reflect difficulty in preparing striated muscles for measurement of blood flow and oxygen consumption. For example, Duran and Renkin (15) report that in a single series of measurements, some preparations are found in which oxygen consumption appears to be flow-limited, and others, indistinguishable on other grounds, are found in which the oxygen consumption is quite flow-independent. Which aspects of microcirculatory function might be sufficiently sensitive to manipulation to be altered during preparation of the tissue are unknown. However, since the uniformity of tissue perfusion is related to the vasomotor state of the microcirculation, and since it is likely that regulatory mechanisms serve to maintain uniform distribution of flow within the tissues, disruption of normal regulatory processes may compromise the transport capacity of the microcirculation (43). It has been claimed that supply-dependent oxygen consumption is related to a loss of autoregulation (53) but there does not appear to be a consistent association between flow limitation of oxygen consumption and the absence of autoregulation (15). Other factors contributing to the appearance of flow limitation in some preparations but not in others remain to be established.

Honig has proposed that much of the confusion regarding this point comes from a scaling problem in the microcirculation design (26). Both capillary density and oxygen consumption are related to the size of the animal (32,49). Honig et al. (26) have observed that flow limitation of oxygen consumption is most commonly observed in smaller animals. They attribute this to a capillary density that is low relative to the exaggerated metabolic rate of small animals. Their findings suggest that the relative scaling of capillary bed and mitochondrial density is such that, in the dog, oxygen consumption is never flow-limited; in the cat, it is marginally limited; and, in the rat, it is substantially limited (26). Again, this reasoning cannot entirely explain the observed data, because flow dependence and flow independence are observed in different preparations of the dog gracilis (15).

If consumption of oxygen is supply-limited, then vasodilation should cause an increase in the metabolic rate of skeletal muscle. This is not the case, however. The relationships between bulk flow of blood into a tissue and the distribution of capillary flow within the tissue are quite complex, and it appears that bulk perfusion can increase at the same time that local perfusion of some regions of the tissue is reduced. Vetterlein and Schmidt (57) observed that vasodilator infusion, which causes the anticipated increase in blood flow, may cause a paradoxical reduction in capillary red cell velocity in some vessels. This "perfusion heterogeneity," in which some microvessel elements steal from others within the tissue, may also be manifested as a decrease in the transport capacity or permeability-surface area product of the capillary bed (1,43).

Vasodilation also need not be correlated with a rise in tissue PO_2. In fact, the relationship between vasomotor state and tissue oxygenation appears to be quite dependent on the type of agonist used, not just on vasodilation. Schroeder and Rathscheck (50) found that epinephrine and isoproterenol caused vasoconstriction and vasodilation, respectively, with the expected change in tissue PO_2. Acetylcholine, on the other hand, caused the anticipated increase in blood flow but, surprisingly, caused a reduction in the mean tissue PO_2. Tissue PO_2 also behaves in an unexpected way when arterial blood gases are altered. Lund et al. (38) have observed that elevating arterial PO_2 produces only an insignificant rise in tissue PO_2 and causes a marked spreading of the range of PO_2s measured in human skeletal muscle.

The unpredictable changes in capillary perfusion and tissue PO_2 have their counterpart in the behavior of the tissue as a whole. Both the metabolic rate (7,56) and muscle performance (24) may be reduced by vasodilation. Again, this finding presumably is the result of the vasodilators causing a maldistribution of flow among the capillaries, but direct measurement of perfusion heterogeneity during a period in which oxygen consumption diminishes in the face of elevated flow remains to be made.

The foregoing observations would suggest that tissue perfusion is more complex than is sometimes appreciated. Furthermore, it seems that oxygen supply to tissues certainly is not in great excess, and that perhaps tissue oxygen supply plays a major role in determining oxygen consumption and even muscle performance. Therefore, it is of interest to examine in detail factors determining the capacity of microcirculation to oxygenate tissues.

Elements governing capillary oxygen supply to tissues

The utimate expression of the balance between the rate of oxygen use by a tissue and the rate of oxygen supply by its microcirculation is the PO_2 within the tissue. No single tissue PO_2 exists, however. Rather, the ox-

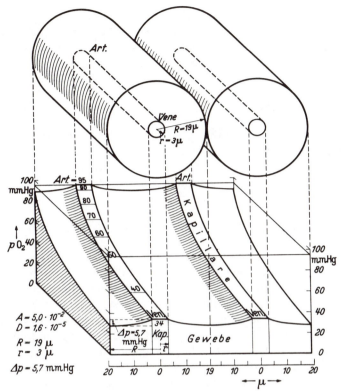

Figure 1 — The Krogh cylinder model. Radial and longitudinal gradients determine the range of tissue PO$_2$s. (Reprinted with permission of Springer-Verlag, New York.)

ygen tension varies spatially and is related to a number of factors, including the cell types within the muscle, the distribution of capillaries, the distribution of flow among the capillaries, and the location of a particular tissue site relative to a capillary. The complexities of tissue oxygenation are most easily viewed starting with the simplified model shown in Figure 1, taken from the work of Opitz and Schneider (39). The figure shows the idealized distribution of PO$_2$ around capillaries within a striated muscle. The significant feature is that the oxygen tension varies in a complex fashion both radially and longitudinally.

Radial gradients

Krogh modeled the basic elements contributing to the radial gradient in oxygen tension around the capillary, and his conceptual model was expressed mathematically by Ehrlanger. Their work remains most useful for describing qualitatively the flux of oxygen from capillary to tissue (35). The striated muscle is approximated as a rectangular array of

capillaries with radius r, separated by a distance 2R. Each capillary therefore supplies a tissue cylinder of radius R. The diffusion coefficient for
oxygen through the tissue is D, and the cells consume oxygen at a rate A.
The oxygen tension at any point x in the tissue, when the capillary oxygen
tension is PO_{2_c}, is:

$$PO_{2_t} = PO_{2_c} - A/2D \, [1/2 \; R^2 \ln (x/r) - (x^2 - r^2)/4] \qquad (1)$$

Interest often focuses on the case in which the oxygen supply is small
enough to limit tissue metabolism, meaning the equation is analyzed at
the point in the tissue most distant from the capillary, that is, x = R,
since this is the point where the minimal tissue PO_2 would be observed.
The Krogh equation then reduces to:

$$PO_{2_R} = PO_{2_c} - A/2D \, [1/2 \; R^2 \ln (R/r) - (R^2 - r^2)/4] \qquad (2)$$

Figure 2 illustrates the utility of the Krogh equation in analyzing the
nature of the radial oxygen gradient around the capillary. The predicted
radial distribution of tissue PO_2 is shown under three different circumstances. In one, it is assumed that the ratio of the metabolic rate to
twice the diffusion coefficient (A/2D) is low and that the intercapillary
distance is large (low A/2D – long ICD). In the second case, metabolic
rate is assumed to be high with a large intercapillary distance (high A/2D
– long ICD). In the third case, it is assumed that the metabolic rate is
high but that the intercapillary distance is reduced (high A/2D – short
ICD). When metabolic rate is increased, the tissue PO_2 gradient is
steepened and the minimal value of the tissue PO_2 is reduced. The increased requirement for oxygen delivery at the higher metabolic rate may
be met by reducing the tissue PO_2, thereby steepening the gradient for
oxygen diffusion.

Augmentation of oxygen delivery by tissue PO_2 reduction is possible
only as long as the tissue PO_2 remains in excess of the minimal value
necessary for oxidative phosphorylation to continue, that is, the "critical
PO_2." If oxygen tension falls below the critical level, the tissue metabolic
rate becomes supply-limited. This eventuality may be forestalled in
skeletal muscle, however, by perfusing additional capillaries as the
metabolic rate is increased. This process of "capillary recruitment" serves
to reduce the diffusion distance and raise the PO_2 everywhere within the
tissue, as shown by the line labeled "high A/2D – short ICD."

A secondary effect of increasing the number of perfused capillaries
should be noted. Since tissue PO_2 is elevated by diminishing the diffusion
distance, the radial gradient is smaller and capillary PO_2 can reach a
lower value and still maintain the tissue PO_2 above the limiting value. In
other words, more oxygen can be extracted from the capillary blood and
the efficiency of the capillary oxygen supply can be increased.

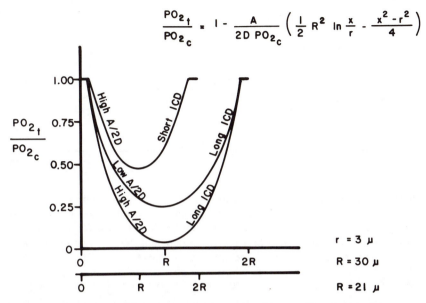

$$\frac{PO_{2_t}}{PO_{2_c}} = 1 - \frac{A}{2D\,PO_{2_c}}\left(\frac{1}{2}\,R^2\,\ln\frac{x}{r} - \frac{x^2 - r^2}{4}\right)$$

Figure 2 — **Radial gradients in tissue PO_2 predicted by the Krogh equation.**

In this context we see that as long as capillary blood flow and blood oxygen content do not change, oxygen extraction can be increased by only two means: either by a reduction in tissue PO_2 or by reduced intercapillary distance. If striated muscle is stimulated to contract at low frequencies, the oxygen consumption increases without an increase in flow (5); this is accomplished by increasing oxygen extraction. Based on the observations made relative to Figure 2, one can conclude that increased capillary extraction of oxygen can come about only as a result of reduced tissue PO_2 or as a result of increased capillary density. It follows that tissue PO_2 at the time of stimulus sets a limit on the increase in extraction that can occur without an increase in capillary density.

Longitudinal gradient

Both longitudinal and radial gradients are shown in Figure 1. The roughly cylindrical mass of tissue assumed to be supplied by a single capillary has come to be known as a "Krogh cylinder." Factors determining the shape of the longitudinal gradient are complex and not fully understood. However, the general nature of the gradient and the salient features controlling its magnitude and shape have been addressed by a number of workers (17,31,39,55). Figure 3A depicts a synthesis of their ideas and a simple qualitative analysis of the relevant variables.

If the tissue surrounding the capillary is uniform in size and metabolic activity and if the capillary blood velocity is constant, the oxygen content

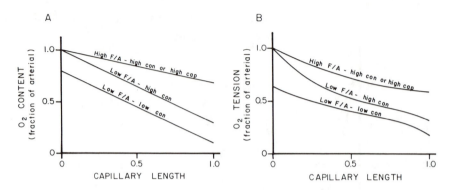

Figure 3 — Longitudinal gradients within a capillary. The assumption of homogeneous blood velocity within the capillary and homogeneous oxygen consumption in the tissue space leads to the prediction of a linear fall in capillary O_2 content (panel A). The transformation between O_2 content and PO_2 is based on the shape of the human O_2-hemoglobin dissociation curve (panel B).

(con) of capillary blood must decrease linearly as blood flows along the vessel (see Figure 1). The slope of the line relating longitudinal position and oxygen content is determined by the flow-to-metabolic rate ratio of the surrounding tissue (F/A) and by the oxygen capacity of the blood (cap). Blood enters the capillary with a content determined by the quantity of oxygen in the arterial blood and by any losses that may occur in the precapillary vasculature (12,13).

Figure 3A shows three different cases. If the oxygen content of blood entering the capillary is decreased without a reduction in oxygen capacity, for example, by reducing arterial PO_2, the content is reduced all along the length of the capillary without a change in slope (low F/A − low con vs low F/A − high con). On the other hand, if either the flow or the oxygen capacity is raised (high F/A − high con or high cap), the slope of the line is reduced.

Variations in capillary oxygen content, considered in Figure 3A, do not per se determine the rate of oxygen diffusion. Rather, it is the capillary PO_2 that determines the rate of diffusion to the tissue. Capillary PO_2 is related to capillary oxygen content by the oxygen-hemoglobin dissociation curve. In Figure 3B the changes in content shown in Figure 3A are translated into changes in capillary PO_2 using the shape of the human oxygen dissociation curve. It is apparent that the presence of hemoglobin in the capillary serves to buffer the longitudinal decrement in capillary PO_2, so that the driving force for oxygen diffusion remains high along the capillary length. The fundamental relationships among the curves shown in Figure 3A remain unchanged, however. When flow or oxygen content is elevated, part or all of the capillary PO_2 is raised and the gradient driving oxygen diffusion is increased at all points along the capillary.

The Krogh equation has been used extensively in analyzing the adequacy of microcirculatory oxygen transport. For example, if one knows the capillary PO_2 as well as the appropriate values for the metabolic rate, the tissue diffusion coefficient, and the diffusion distance (intercapillary distance), it is possible to predict whether the tissue PO_2 will fall to values limiting oxidative phosphorylation. Essentially no experimental data are available on capillary PO_2, so it is usually assumed that venous PO_2 is an adequate estimate of the PO_2 at the end of the capillary. Several investigators have made such calculations with somewhat mixed results but, in general, the findings suggest that the resting skeletal muscle should be well oxygenated and that blood flow should not limit oxygen consumption to a major extent (17,26,35,36,53). Even the working muscle appears to be adequately oxygenated. In fact, arterial PO_2 can fall to lower levels in the working muscle than in the resting muscle before O_2 consumption is reduced due to the existence of a population of unperfused capillaries that can be recruited in proportion to the tissue metabolic activity.

Because a number of experimental observations, as cited above, suggest that the tissue O_2 supply is barely adequate when the results of the Krogh calculation suggest that the tissue should be well oxygenated, the use of both the Krogh equation and the experimental data is questionable. However, there is no reason to believe that the transport of oxygen depends on any process other than passive diffusion and it thus seems reasonable to look more carefully at how well the Krogh cylinder fits with modern knowledge of microcirculation.

Tissue and vessel heterogeneities

Derivation of the Krogh equation and analysis of the longitudinal gradient in capillary oxygen content are both based on the assumption that the capillary bed and surrounding tissues are relatively homogeneous. As already illustrated, such an assumption is, to a first approximation, valid and serves the most useful purpose of conveying an understanding of the important elements in oxygen diffusion between a capillary and a site in the tissue. However, our current understanding of heterogeneities in the construction of striated muscle and the angioarchitectonics of the microcirculation make the classical Krogh cylinder an inadequate representation for a realistic description of oxygen transport. Several heterogeneities are likely to be important determinants of tissue oxygenation, and these are discussed in the remainder of the text.

Fiber type

Striated muscles are composed of fibers with quite different contractile properties and metabolic activities. This fact has received little attention in the form of experimental measurements made by those interested in tissue oxygenation, but several general statements may be made. In a mixed muscle composed of both oxidative and glycolytic fibers (the most common case), the various fiber types are mixed throughout the body of the muscle, with oxidative fibers frequently lying immediately adjacent to glycolytic fibers and the two sharing capillaries (19). Obviously, a radially symmetrical model, such as that shown in Figure 1, is likely to be inadequate in describing the oxygen tension distribution if the oxygen consumption rates of the two fibers differ. Analysis of the effects of such fiber type distribution on oxygen supply to tissue is complicated by the fact that there is little agreement as to the relative resting metabolic rates in the two fiber types or to the augmentation of oxygen consumption with work (6,16).

Tissue heterogeneity extends beyond the existence of different cell types within the muscle to the level of the placement of the mitochondria within the individual fibers. The mitochondria are not distributed uniformly either among fibers of different types or within fibers of a given type. Highly oxidative fibers have more mitochondria and, within fibers of this type, the mitochondria tend to be clustered at the edges of the fiber and diminish toward the interior (27,29,44). Thus, the fundamental assumption of the Krogh equation—that the rate of oxygen consumption is relatively homogeneous spatially—is invalid. In fact, the work of James and Meek (29) suggests that the density of mitochondria to some extent mirrors the PO_2 profiles predicted for the homogeneous case shown in Figure 2. This would tend to steepen the PO_2 gradient at the edges of the cells and to flatten the gradient toward the center of the cells.

A related complication in our understanding of tissue oxygenation is the report by Hoppeler and co-workers (27) that peripheral and central mitochondria in a muscle fiber respond differently to training. These investigators reported that, during endurance training, proliferation of mitochondria is exaggerated in a peripheral mitochondrial population compared to a central population. If this report is substantiated it may mean that the degree of mitochondrial heterogeneity is dependent on the level of training.

The presence of complex mixtures of cell types within a striated muscle also implies a nonuniform distribution of myoglobin within the tissue (42). Myoglobin is thought capable of acting either as an oxygen store or as a facilitator of oxygen diffusion (59) and, since myoglobin is distributed differentially within red and white fibers, the diffusion coefficients and solubility for oxygen may vary spatially with the fiber type. The importance of this heterogeneity remains to be established because the role of myoglobin in facilitating oxygen diffusion is still somewhat controversial.

Vessel distribution

Fiber type influences the density and location of the mitochondria and the amount of myoglobin present as well as capillary distribution. Although subject to many variables, in general, the size of a muscle fiber can be correlated with the fiber type; highly oxidative fibers tend to be smaller (3). Since capillaries exist only on the periphery of the fiber, the presence of a mixture of fiber types within a muscle implies a nonuniform distribution of capillaries and intercapillary distances. In Figure 2, the sensitivity of tissue PO_2 distribution to intercapillary distance is apparent, and it can therefore be anticipated that fiber type heterogeneity can confer a correspondingly large heterogeneity on tissue PO_2.

Even muscles of relatively homogeneous composition have a wide distribution in capillary spacing. It follows that heterogeneity in spacing must be considered in tissue oxygenation analysis, but this kind of study has been attempted only rarely. Henquell et al. (22) have emphasized the fact that the extremes in capillary spacing limit oxygen consumption and perhaps performance of a muscle. An analysis based on mean PO_2 values is, for this reason, likely to underestimate the sensitivity of tissue metabolism to capillary oxygen supply. When the largest values of intercapillary distance are used in computing PO_2 distributions according to the Krogh equation, much lower tissue PO_2s are predicted which may limit metabolism in resting and/or working muscle. The obvious conclusion is that future work in the field will require more accurate statistical analysis of capillary spacing distribution in a muscle before the contribution of intercapillary distance to tissue oxygenation can be fully appreciated.

The length of the exchange vessels is another element subject to spatial heterogeneity that may make important contributions to tissue oxygenation. If red cells flow through a capillary at constant velocity, as the length of a microvessel is increased the oxygen tension at the distal end of the vessel declines, and ultimately the PO_2 in the tissue surrounding the vessel is reduced to a level too low to support continued tissue oxidative phosphorylation. Measurements of vessel length show a substantial range and the lengths measured depend on the particular muscle studied (25,47). There are no corresponding measurements of tissue oxygenation that might show how length contributes to heterogeneities in tissue PO_2.

A further complication imposed by the nature of longitudinal gradients on tissue oxygenation derives from the fact that in many muscles the parallel array assumed typical of striated muscle often is absent (2,10,47). Capillaries show many cross-connections and loops that run transversely to the long axis of the muscle fibers rather than longitudinally. The capillary patterns are highly variable among muscles and, as yet, it is unknown whether the more complex networks are correlated with a particular fiber type within an individual muscle, although this is certain-

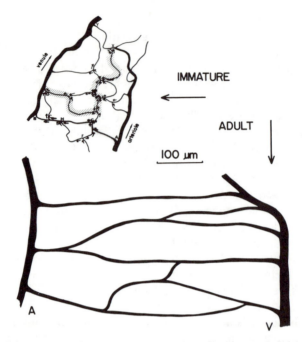

Figure 4 — Comparison of capillary patterns in striated muscle of juvenile and mature hamsters. The juvenile animal was 35 days old and the mature animal was 132 days old. The arrows superimposed on the drawing from the immature animal represent flow directions observed over a period of approximately 30 min. The shaded pathways represent the shortest and the longest pathways a red cell might have taken (47).

ly true when comparing red and white muscle types (44).

Network complexity is definitely related to the age of the animal, however (2,47). Figure 4 shows tracings of two capillary networks, one from the cremaster of a 35-day-old (immature) animal and one from a 132-day-old (adult) animal. During maturation of hamsters there is a gradual transition from a very complex pattern to a relatively simple, almost linear, pattern. Interestingly, this pattern is not correlated with changes in the fiber type, as the hamster cremaster is predominantly composed of fast oxidative fibers throughout the age range studied (Sarelius, Maxwell, Gray, and Duling, unpublished observations).

Recently we have observed the microcirculation of a variety of striated muscles in the hamster using an epifluorescence microscope and serum albumin labeled with fluorescein. With this approach, it is possible to visualize the capillaries from the surface of a muscle to a depth of about 200 microns, enabling us to extend our observations to many muscles other than the sheet type normally observed in microcirculatory studies. Using this methodology we have found striking differences in capillary patterns in different muscle fibers. Muscles seem to fall into two groups: The spinotrapezius, tibialis anterior, vastus medialis, vastus lateralis, and gastrocnemius all have very complex networks with tortuous capillaries and many cross-connections; on the other hand, the gracilis, gluteus maximus, and sartorius muscles have long capillaries organized in quite regular, parallel arrays with fewer cross-connections.

The complex geometry that exists in the microcirculation of some striated muscles even makes the actual definition of capillary length a problem. Cross-connections such as those shown in Figure 4 provide multiple pathways for a red cell to take in passing from an arteriole to a venule. Therefore, a simple anatomical definition of capillary length is not necessarily consistent with the flow path actually taken by the red cells; the flow path could be substantially larger.

Flow patterns

The microcirculation most often is viewed as a simple model in which blood flows in a rather monotonic pattern out of arterioles into capillaries and back into the venules. The actual flow path need not be confined to a straight run through a single capillary, however, as shown by the arrows in Figure 4. The arrows on the tracing from the young animal were drawn during the course of a period of observation lasting about 30 min and show the actual flow patterns observed at branch points in one network. The figure makes it clear that in the young animal the capillary flow pattern is far more complex than the Krogh cylinder and that the anatomical path and the actual flow path taken by a red cell may be quite different. The two shaded pathways illustrate two different flow paths a red cell might have taken.

Other measurements of this type suggest that, even in those capillaries appearing to be relatively straight, the adjacent muscle planes often are cross-connected so that the potential three-dimensional flow pattern may be quite complex (8,47).

Not only are capillary flow patterns complex, but the flow directions need not be concurrent (8,21,54; Damon and Duling, unpublished observations). Theoretical studies show that, should significant countercurrent flow exist, substantial alteration in the tissue oxygen distribution would be observed (20). There is as yet insufficient systematic study of the presence or absence of countercurrent flow in capillary distribution within striated muscle to permit a conclusion about its importance.

Gas exchange also occurs across larger vessels of the microcirculation lying parallel to one another in which the flow is countercurrent. Therefore, these vessels may provide an opportunity for diffusional shunting of oxygen between arteriole and venule (30,41,45,52). This shunting will cause the oxygen to be unavailable for tissue oxygenation; arterial PO_2 will underestimate the early capillary PO_2 and venous PO_2 will overestimate the level of end-capillary blood PO_2. As a result, computations using the Krogh equation and the assumption that end-capillary PO_2 equals venous PO_2 will tend to overestimate the availability of oxygen to the tissue.

Capillary oxygen capacity

Figure 3 (A and B) emphasizes the importance of the oxygen content and/or oxygen capacity in determining capillary PO_2 and therefore tissue oxygenation. In general, it is implicitly assumed that the oxygen content of capillary blood is determined by arterial oxygen tension and oxygen capacity. However, the distribution of red cells among the various possible capillary flow paths need not be homogeneous and therefore all capillaries need not have the same hematocrit and oxygen capacity. Thus, the capillary hematocrit must be viewed as a potential variable in the analysis of capillary oxygen transport.

In theory, the potential exists for capillary oxygen capacity ranging from that of pure plasma (hematocrit = 0%) to that of pure red cells (hematocrit = 100%); plus, there is reason to believe that differences in velocity among various capillaries may automatically lead to inhomogeneous red cell distribution and therefore to differences in capillary oxygen content (9,18,34). Relatively few measurements have been made of the statistical distribution of capillary hematocrits but it would appear that, whereas the capillary hematocrits do vary, the range is not great (34,47) and essentially no capillaries filled with plasma alone are seen (10).

An examination of published values for capillary hematocrit discloses a remarkable fact, however. The absolute values of capillary hematocrits are very much less than the arterial hematocrit. Mean capillary hematocrits average 15-25%, whereas arterial hematocrits are in the range of 50%; in other words, a 50-80% dilution of red cells occurs between arterial and capillary blood. Such a low capillary hematocrit is potentially of enormous importance in understanding tissue oxygenation because it implies that the capillary blood oxygen content may be as little as one-fifth the systemic value. At this time we have no widely accepted explanation for the low hematocrits observed.

Very low capillary hematocrits could be most simply explained by the existence of some population of "shunt" vessels that permits red cells to move from arteriole to venule without passing through capillaries (37). Duling et al. (14) examined the quantitative relationships that would be necessary to explain the observed capillary hematocrits by a shunt process. The computations showed that in order to lower capillary hematocrit from 50% to the values actually observed in capillaries, as much as 50% of the total red cell mass would have to pass through shunt vessels.

Clearly, a shunt of this magnitude would fundamentally alter our perceptions of tissue oxygenation.

No anatomical shunts of this magnitude have been observed in skeletal muscle. The absence of anatomical shunts does not exclude the presence of some form of physiological shunt, however, and therefore, in an effort to reveal the presence of a noncapillary pathway for red cells, Klitzman and Duling (33) made direct counts of red cell passage through capillaries and compared these with bulk flow of red cells into the hamster cremaster muscle. Capillary hematocrits averaged on the order of 14%. The capillary red cell flow in individual capillaries was estimated from the product of red cell flux (no./tube), and the mean corpuscular volume. Total red cell flow was then estimated from the product of capillary flow and the number of capillaries per 100 g of tissue. The actual bulk flow of red cells into the cremaster muscle was measured using the arterial hematocrit and actual blood flow measured with microspheres. The two estimates of capillary red cell flow, one based on direct count of capillary red cell flux and one based on total flow entering the tissue, were not different, thus suggesting that all red cells traversed the microcirculation via the capillaries. Further refutation of the idea that significant shunting occurs in this muscle was provided by the observation that the venous effluent from the cremaster contained less than 1% of the injected microspheres, thus suggesting that no large bore shunts existed.

A variety of explanations for the low hematocrit have been advanced but none have been experimentally validated and there are objections to all of them (9,14,18,34). Despite the lack of understanding for the source of the low capillary hematocrit, the phenomenon cannot be ignored in any discussion aimed at understanding tissue oxygenation. The importance of the phenomenon is enhanced by the fact that the capillary hematocrit is not only low but it varies with the vasomotor state of the vascular bed. Vasodilation induced either by the application of dilators or by stimulation of striated muscle causes capillary hematocrit to rise. Maximal vasodilation raises the capillary hematocrit as high as 37% (33). Therefore, the possibility exists that the blood oxygen content of the capillary blood is a variable and is subject to control by the working muscle.

Summary

The transport of oxygen from blood to mitochondria is a diffusive process and, thus, is ultimately dependent on relatively simple physical laws. The Krogh cylinder model is a useful tool for developing a qualitative understanding of the relationships between the various components which determine tissue oxygenation. However, it fails to predict a variety of responses of the striated muscle to altered oxygen supply. It is likely that this failure reflects the lack of consideration of the true complexity of the microcirculation of skeletal muscle. In particular, the lack of uniformity of the various tissue and microvessel elements is ignored. Heterogeneities in vessel geometry, flow patterns, red cell distribution, and tissue type all exist and must contribute to the overall level of tissue oxygenation. A more complete description of the role of microcirculation in tissue oxygenation will require the use of models that incorporate the statistics of these heterogeneities into the computations.

References

1. Appelgren, L. Perfusion and diffusion in shock. *Acta Physiol. Scand. Suppl.* **378**:72, 1972.

2. Aquin, L., and Banchero, N. The cytoarchitecture and capillary supply in the skeletal muscle of growing dogs. *J. Anat.* **132**:341-356, 1981.

3. Aquin, L., Sillau, A.H., Lechner, A.J., and Banchero, N. Growth and skeletal muscle microvascularity in the guinea pig. *Microvasc. Res.* **20**:41-50, 1980.

4. Bacaner, M.B., Lioy, F., and Visscher, M.B. Coronary blood flow, oxygen delivery rate and cardiac performance. *J. Physiol. London* **216**:111-128, 1971.

5. Belloni, F.L., Phair, R.D., and Sparks, H.V. The role of adenosine in prolonged vasodilation following flow-restricted exercise of canine skeletal muscle. *Circulation Res.* **44**:759-766, 1979.

6. Bockman, E.L., McKenzie, J.E., and Ferguson, J.L. Resting blood flow and oxygen consumption in soleus and gracilis muscles of cats. *Am. J. Physiol.* **239**:H516-H524, 1980.

7. Bolme, P., and Gagnon, D.J. The effects of vasodilating drugs and vasoconstrictor nerve stimulation on oxygen uptake in skeletal muscle. *Eur. J. Pharmacol.* **20**:300-307, 1972.

8. Chang, B.-L., Yamakawa, T., Nuccio, J., Pace, R., and Bing, R.J. Microcirculation of left atrial muscle, cerebral cortex, and mesentery of the cat: A comparative analysis. *Circulation Res.* **50**:240-249, 1982.

9. Cokelet, G.R. Speculation on a cause of low vessel hematocrits in the microcirculation. *Microcirculation* **2**:1-18, 1982.

10. Damon, D.H., and Duling, B.R. Comparison of epifluorescence (EPI) and transillumination (TRANS) microscopy in the evaluation of capillary flow. *Microvasc. Res.* **23**:247, 1982.

11. Davies, K.J.A., Maguire, J.J., Brooks, G.A., Dallman, P.R., and Packer, L. Muscle mitochondrial bioenergetics, oxygen supply and work capacity during dietary iron deficiency and repletion. *Am. J. Physiol.* **242**:E418-E427, 1982.

12. Duling, B.R. Microvascular responses to alterations in oxygen tension. *Circulation Res.* **31**:481-489, 1972.

13. Duling, B.R., Kuschinsky, W., and Wahl, M. Measurements of the perivascular PO_2 in the vicinity of the pial vessels of the cat. *Pflügers Arch.* **383**:29-34, 1979.

14. Duling, B.R., Sarelius, I.H., and Jackson, W.F. A comparison of microvascular estimates of capillary blood flow with direct measurements of total striated muscle flow. *Int. J. Microcirc. Clin. & Exp.* **1**:409-424, 1982.

15. Duran, W.N., and Renkin, E.M. Oxygen consumption and blood flow in resting mammalian skeletal muscle. *Am. J. Physiol.* **226**:173-177, 1974.

16. Folkow, B., and Halicka, H.D. A comparison between "red" and "white" muscle with respect to blood supply, capillary surface area and oxygen uptake during rest and exercise. *Microvasc. Res.* **1**:1-14, 1968.

17. Forster, R.E. Factors affecting the rate of exchange of O_2 between blood and tissues. In: F. Dickens and E. Neil (eds.), *Oxygen in the animal organism*. International Union of Biochemistry Symposium Series, Vol. 31, Pergamon Press, Oxford, 1964, pp. 393-407.

18. Gaehtgens, P. Flow of blood through narrow capillaries: Rheological mechanisms determining capillary hematocrit and apparent viscosity. *Biorheology* **17**:183-189, 1980.

19. Gray, S.D., and Renkin, E.M. Microvascular supply in relation to fiber metabolic type in mixed skeletal muscles of rabbits. *Microvasc. Res.* **16**:406-425, 1978.

20. Grunewald, W.A., and Sowa, W. Capillary structures and O_2 supply to tissue. An analysis with a digital diffusion model as applied to skeletal muscle. *Rev. Physiol. Biochem. Pharmacol.* **77**:149-209, 1977.

21. Grunewald, W.A., and Sowa, W. Distribution of the myocardial tissue PO_2 in the rat and the inhomogeneity of the coronary bed. *Pflügers Arch.* **374**:57-66, 1978.

22. Henquell, L., Odoroff, C.L., and Honig, C.R. Coronary intercapillary distance during growth: Relation to PtO_2 and aerobic capacity. *Am. J. Physiol.* **231**:1852-1859, 1976.

23. Hermansen, L., and Wachtlova, M. Capillary density of skeletal muscle in well-trained and untrained men. *J. Appl. Physiol.* **30**:860-863, 1971.

24. Hirvonen, L., and Sonnenschein, R.R. Relation between blood flow and contraction force in active skeletal muscle. *Circulation Res.* **10**:94-104, 1962.

25. Honig, C.R., Feldstein, M.L., and Frierson, J.L. Capillary lengths, anastomoses, and estimated capillary transit times in skeletal muscle. *Am. J. Physiol.* **233**:H122-H129, 1977.

26. Honig, C.R., Frierson, J.L., and Nelson, C.N. O_2 transport and VO_2 in resting muscle: Significance for tissue-capillary exchange. *Am. J. Physiol.* **220**:357-363, 1971.

27. Hoppeler, H., Luthi, P., Claassen, H., Weibel, E.R., and Howald, H. The ultrastructure of the normal human skeletal muscle. A morphometric analysis

on untrained men, women and well-trained orienteers. *Pflügers Arch.* **344**:217-232, 1973.

28. Horstman, D.H., Gleser, M., and Delehunt, J. Effects of altering O_2 delivery on VO_2 of isolated, working muscle. *Am. J. Physiol.* **230**:327-334, 1976.

29. James, N.T., and Meek, G.A. Stereological analysis of the structure of mitochondria in pigeon skeletal muscle. *Cell Tissue Res.* **202**:493-503, 1979.

30. Kampp, M., Lundgren, O., and Nilsson, N.J. Extravascular shunting of oxygen in the small intestine of the cat. *Acta Physiol. Scand.* **72**:396-403, 1968.

31. Kety, S.S. Determinants of tissue oxygen tension. *Fed. Proc.* **16**:666-670, 1969.

32. Kleiber, M. *The fire of life.* Wiley and Sons, New York, 1961, pp. 454.

33. Klitzman, B., and Duling, B.R. Microvascular hematocrit and red cell flow in resting and contracting striated muscle. *Am. J. Physiol.* **237**:H481-H490, 1979.

34. Klitzman, B., and Johnson, P.C. Capillary network geometry and red cell distribution in hamster cremaster muscle. *Amer. J. Physiol.* **242**:H211-H219, 1982.

35. Krogh, A. The supply of oxygen to the tissues and the regulation of the capillary circulation. *J. Physiol. London* **52**:457-474, 1919.

36. Landis, E.M., and Pappenheimer, J.R. Exchange of substances through the capillary walls. In: W.F. Hamilton and P. Dow (eds.), *Handbook of physiology, section II, circulation*, vol. II. American Physiological Society, Washington, DC, 1963, chapt. 29, pp. 961-1034.

37. Lipowsky, H.H., Usami, S., and Chien, S. In vivo measurements of "apparent viscosity" and microvessel hematocrit in the mesentery of the cat. *Microvasc. Res.* **19**:297-319, 1980.

38. Lund, N., Jorfeldt, L., and Lewis, D.H. Skeletal muscle oxygen pressure fields in healthy human volunteers. A study of the normal state and the effects of different arterial oxygen pressures. *Acta Anaesthesiol. Scand.* **24**:272-278, 1980.

39. Opitz, E., and Schneider, M. Uber die Sauerstoffversorgung des Gehirns und den Mechanismus von Mangelwirkungen. *Ergeb. Physiol. Biol. Chem. Exp. Pharmakol.* **46**:126-260, 1950.

40. Pappenheimer, J.R. Blood flow, arterial oxygen saturation, and oxygen consumption in the isolated perfused hindlimb of the dog. *J. Physiol. London* **99**:282-303, 1941.

41. Pittman, R.N., and Duling, B.R. The determination of oxygen availability in the microcirculation. In: F.F. Jobsis (ed.), *Oxygen and physiological function*. Professional Information Library, Dallas, TX, 1977, pp. 133-147.

42. Reis, D.J., and Wooten, G.F. The relationship of blood flow to myoglobin, capillary density, and twitch characteristics in red and white skeletal muscle in cat. *J. Physiol. London* **210**:121-136, 1970.

43. Renkin, E.M. Exchange of substances through capillary walls. In: G.E.W. Wolstenholme and J. Knight (eds.), *CIBA Foundation symposium on circulatory and respiratory mass transport*. J. & A. Churchill, London, 1969.

44. Romanul, F.C.A. Capillary supply and metabolism of muscle fibers. *Arch. Neurol.* **12**:497-509, 1965.

45. Roth, A.C., and Feigl, E.O. Diffusional shunting in the canine myocardium. *Circulation Res.* **48**:470-480, 1981.

46. Saltin, B., and Rowell, L.B. Functional adaptations to physical activity and inactiviy. *Fed. Proc.* **39**:1506-1513, 1980.

47. Sarelius, I.H., Damon, D.N., and Duling, B.R. Microvascular adaptations during maturation of striated muscle. *Am. J. Physiol.* **241**:H317-H324, 1981.

48. Scheuer, J., and Tipton, C.M. Cardiovascular adaptations to physical training. *Ann. Rev. Physiol.* **39**:221-252, 1977.

49. Schmidt-Nielsen, K., and Pennycuik, P. Capillary density in mammals in relation to body size and oxygen consumption. *Am. J. Physiol.* **200**:746-750, 1961.

50. Schroeder, W., and Rathscheck, W. Investigation of the influence of acetylcholine on the distribution of capillary flow in the skeletal muscle of the guinea pig by recording of the PO_2 in the muscle tissue. *Pflügers Arch.* **345**:335-346, 1973.

51. Schroeder, W., Treumann, F., Rathscheck, W., and Muller, R. Muscle PO_2 in trained and untrained nonanesthetized guinea pigs and in men. *Eur. J. Appl. Physiol.* **35**:215-221, 1976.

52. Sejrsen, P., and Tonnesen, K.H. Shunting by diffusion of inert gas in skeletal muscle. *Acta Physiol. Scand.* **86**:82-91, 1972.

53. Stainsby, W.N., and Otis, A.B. Blood flow, blood oxygen tension, oxygen uptake, and oxygen transport in skeletal muscle. *Am. J. Physiol.* **206**:858-866, 1964.

54. Steinhausen, M., Tillmanns, H., and Thederan, H. Microcirculation of the epimyocardial layer of the heart: I. A method for in vivo observation of the microcirculation on superficial ventricular myocardium of the heart and capillary flow pattern under normal and hypoxic conditions. *Pflügers Arch.* **378**:9-14, 1978.

55. Thews, G. Uber die mathematische bahandlung physiologischer diffusionsprozesse in zylinderformigen objekten. *Acta Biotheor. Leiden* **10**:105-138, 1957.

56. Vetterlein, F., and Schmidt, G. Changes in oxygen consumption in the hindlimb of the cat during various forms of vasodilation. *Naunyn-Schmiedeberg's Arch. Pharmacol.* **275**:263-275, 1972.

57. Vetterlein, F., and Schmidt, G. Effects of vasodilating agents on the microcirculation in marginal parts of the skeletal muscle. *Arch. Int. Pharmacodyn.* **213**:4-16, 1975.

58. Whalen, W.J., Buerk, D., and Thuning, C.A. Blood flow-limited oxygen consumption in resting cat skeletal muscle. *Am. J. Physiol.* **224**:763-768, 1973.

59. Wittenberg, J.B. Myoglobin-facilitated oxygen diffusion: Role of myoglobin in oxygen entry into muscle. *Physiol. Rev.* **50**:559-636, 1970.

Adenosine as a mediator of sustained exercise hyperemia

Harvey V. Sparks, Jr., and Barry D. Fuchs
Michigan State University

The mechanisms responsible for the increase in skeletal muscle blood flow associated with exercise have been under study since Gaskell first proposed in 1880 that vasodilator metabolites may be the responsible agents (6). Studies over the past few years have identified several mechanisms and have begun to delineate the situations in which each of the mechanisms may predominate. There is now good evidence that the relative importance of each of several vasodilators depends on: (a) the exercise pattern, that is, twitch vs. tetanic contractions; (b) the duration of the exercise bout; (c) the relationship between O_2 supply and consumption; and (d) muscle fiber type.

The vasodilation in response to *short, tetanic contractions* appears to have a time course that is more rapid than that of oxidative metabolism. Therefore, this type of vasodilation cannot be caused by factors closely related to oxidative metabolism (e.g., vessel wall PO_2) (17). The mechanisms responsible for the hyperemia following a brief tetanic burst include K^+ release (18) and a myogenic response to the compressive force generated by the tetanic contraction (19).

When sustained twitch exercise is performed under conditions which restrict flow to the extent that marked fatigue occurs, sequential mechanisms seem to be involved (27). Initiation of vasodilation at the beginning of the exercise bout is at least partly the result of increased K^+ release (10), and tissue osmolarity (21). Vessel wall PO_2 also must drop rapidly because the increase in oxygen consumption is not matched by increased flow delivery of O_2 (28). Another factor that may be important in the initiation of exercise vasodilation is the local neurogenic vasodilator response proposed by Honig (12). As exercise continues, the relative importance of K^+ and osmolarity decreases because (a) the increases in both of these factors wane with time (11,21) and (b) their vascular effects are transient (7,8). The effects of increased osmolarity may be more sustained in glycolytic than in oxidative skeletal muscle (discussed later). If restricted flow exercise continues for 10 min or longer, tissue adenosine begins to rise (3), probably reflecting an increase in interstitial adenosine, although this has not been proven. Thus, during sustained exercise in the presence of restricted flow, the sustained vasodilation may be the result of (a) reduced arteriolar wall PO_2, and/or (b) increased interstitial adenosine. If flow is restricted during the exercise bout, a prolonged period of vasodilation follows cessation of exercise (21,27). The mediators of the prolonged vasodilation appear to be adenosine and vasodilator prostaglandins (1,32). Histamine also may contribute to this response (22). Tabaie et al. (30) presented evidence that a concentration of theophylline, which blocks exogenous adenosine, reduces the magnitude and duration of the period of vasodilation following exercise with restricted flow. This finding supports a role for adenosine in the presence of restricted flow. Unfortunately, this group had to use norepinephrine to counteract the vasodilation observed during theophylline infusion. Honig and Frierson (13) have suggested that the reduced vasodilation during and following exercise was due to the norepinephrine, not the theophylline. They were unable to reduce the vasodilation associated with exercise of a milder intensity, and sustained for a shorter time, using aminophylline.

The most common pattern of exercise (in the laboratory) is a sustained train of twitch contractions. Such exercise patterns can be maintained for hours in high-oxidative muscles and the increase in flow also is sustained. The mechanism of the sustained increase in flow over many minutes to hours is the subject of the rest of this review. The initiation of the vasodilation associated with this type of exercise bout may be caused by the same factors responsible for the vasodilation occurring with restricted flow exercise: K^+, increased osmolarity, and a local neurogenic mechanism. The sustained response is another matter. In cats, whose muscles are primarily of the low-oxidative type, increased osmolarity may play a more sustained role than in high oxidative muscle (15). In high-oxidative muscle the major mechanism has not been identified although studies of the dynamics of oxidative metabolism and vascular resistance suggest that these two events are closely linked (20). The potential candidates include adenosine (3), acetate (29), ATP (4), and a local neurogenic mechanism (13). The data supporting each of these candidates are no better than fragmentary under conditions of *sustained, free flow* exercise. The remainder of this review will be devoted to an evaluation of the current status of the adenosine hypothesis as it pertains to this particular situation.

Four criteria must be met before a substance can be accepted as a mediator of metabolic vasodilation. First it must be vasoactive. Second, its concentration in the vicinity of vascular smooth muscle must be sufficient to cause the vasodilation observed during increased metabolic activity. Third, agents capable of blocking the action of the substance must block the metabolic vasodilation. Fourth, agents capable of raising or lowering the interstitial levels of the substance must cause appropriate changes in the observed metabolic vasodilation.

Adenosine definitely meets the first criterion. It is a good dilator of skeletal muscle resistance vessels. It appears to work by antagonizing the inward flux of Ca^{++} across the vascular smooth muscle plasma membrane (9).

The question of whether adenosine is present in a sufficiently high concentration in the interstitial space cannot be fully answered at this time, although both tissue content and adenosine release into capillary blood have been used as an estimate of $[ADO]_{ISF}$. Our first test of whether $[ADO]_{ISF}$ increases during sustained free flow exercise was measurement of tissue adenosine during rest and exercise (23). We failed to observe a statistically significant increase in tissue adenosine content during exercise. We then calculated how much of an increase in tissue adenosine would be expected if adenosine were solely responsible for the increased flow. We did this by infusing adenosine and finding the blood concentration of adenosine, which was needed to cause an increase in flow equivalent to that observed during exercise. In this calculation we assumed that the concentration of ADO established in the blood was also established in the interstitium (more comments on this assumption later). From this calculation we concluded that if this concentration (3.7×10^{-5} M) of adenosine were established in as little as 10% of the interstitium, we could have observed the increase by measuring total tissue adenosine.

This led us to conclude it was unlikely that adenosine mediated free-flow exercise vasodilation. However, the interpretation of these tissue content measurements has potential problems. Measurement of tissue adenosine content would be an accurate reflection of $[ADO]_{ISF}$ if all of the measured adenosine were in the interstitial space. Although there were reasons to accept this "extracellular assumption" at one time (see 23 for a discussion of this subject), it now appears that a large portion (perhaps as much as 90%) of measured tissue adenosine is not free in the interstitial space; it is possible that much of tissue adenosine is intracellular. One finding supporting this possibility is the discrepancy between plasma adenosine concentration and tissue adenosine content. The concentration of adenosine in venous plasma draining resting skeletal muscle is .06 $\pm$ .02 μM. We might assume that the interstitial concentration equals the venous plasma concentration because there is no net uptake or release. If this is so, and if interstitial fluid volume is 15 ml/100 g, we would expect a tissue content of .009 nM/g. Yet we observe a much higher concentration of 1.1 $\pm$ 0.11 nM/g (23). This discrepancy could be explained (a) by metabolism of adenosine by capillary endothelium so that the plasma adenosine concentration does not serve as an accurate indication of interstitial adenosine, or (b) if most of the adenosine measured in tissue is not free in the interstitial space. A possible site of that adenosine which is not free in the interstitium is an intracellular protein known to bind adenosine: S-adenosyl homocysteine hydrolase (31).

A second argument against the "extracellular assumption" is the sensitivity of vascular smooth muscle to adenosine (24). A tissue content of 1 nM/g would correspond to an interstitial concentration of 7 μM. This concentration is more than sufficient to dilate resistance vessels when adenosine is directly applied in microcirculatory experiments (B.R. Duling, personal communication). Thus, if all of the adenosine found in skeletal muscle were in the interstitium, we would expect resting resistance to be much lower than is actually found. Finally, a cellular pool of adenosine is not destroyed by extracellular adenosine deaminase (2), also suggesting intracellular compartmentation. Although these lines of evidence do not demonstrate conclusively that the "extracellular assumption" concerning adenosine is incorrect, they introduce a strong element of uncertainty which causes the data interpretation on tissue levels to be equally uncertain.

Measurement of the rate of release of adenosine into venous plasma can be done by measuring the arterial and venous plasma [ADO] and plasma flow. A change in release rate reflects a change in interstitial adenosine if (a) there is no change in the diffusional barrier offered by the capillary endothelium (no change in capillary PS), (b) the rate of uptake of adenosine by endothelium is unchanged, (c) adenosine or a precurser is not released from a formed element in blood or from endothelium, or (d) destruction of adenosine by blood is slow enough to allow its collection before a significant amount is destroyed. We have evaluated the last of these criteria by observing the disappearance of tracer adenosine from dog plasma. Its rate of disappearance is slow enough to indicate that this factor can be safely ignored if care is taken to stop adenosine degradation as soon as blood samples are collected (16). Although we will not consider the other three assumptions here, because of a lack of experimental data, they represent potentially serious problems.

When we observed adenosine release under the same conditions used for studying tissue adenosine (5), we found a large increase in adenosine release into venous plasma (Table 1). We tested two alternatives to the possibility that the release we observed during exercise resulted from an increase in $[ADO]_{ISF}$. The first possibility is that increased flow washes adenosine out of the interstitium but that no increase in $[ADO]_{ISF}$ occurs. We evaluated this possibility by infusing enough isoproterenol to raise flow as much as exercise did. This procedure did not result in any release of adenosine. A second possibility is that the increase in venous adenosine concentration resulted from the release of nucleotides from formed elements (e.g., platelets) in blood and their subsequent degradation to adenosine via ecto 5′ nucleotidase. We tested this possibility by infusing an inhibitor of ecto 5′ nucleotidase, adenosine 5′-methylene diphosphonate (AOPCP), in a concentration (50 μM) capable of blocking the action of this enzyme (26). This test resulted in a 33% decrease in adenosine release during exercise. Further studies showed that we could cause an equivalent reduction in release by simply placing AOPCP in the tubes used to collect the blood samples. This finding suggests that exercise causes formed elements in venous blood to release an adenine nucleotide during the blood collection procedure. The nucleotide is then degraded to adenosine. These experiments also suggest, but do not prove, that adenosine itself is released during exercise.

If we assume that the adenosine released into the venous blood in the presence of AOPCP results from an increase in $[ADO]_{ISF}$, we have the paradox that no change in tissue adenosine occurred under conditions

Table 1

Adenosine Release During Steady-state Exercise (6 twitches/sec) of Canine Calf Muscles

	Flow (ml/min·100 g)	Oxygen consumption (ml/min·100 g)	Adenosine release (nM/min·100 g)
Control (5)	9.5 ± 3.0	0.26 ± 0.1	− 0.1 ± 0.1
Exercise (5)	129 ± 25*	14.5 ± 0.9*	6.1 ± 4.2*
Isoproterenol (3)	144 ± 31*	0.55 ± 0.7	− 0.7 ± 2.4
Exercise & AOPCP (4)	122 ± 16*	17.3 ± 0.9*	4.0 ± 2.5*

Control values (means ± SD) consist of averages of observation taken before and after exercise runs. *Indicates different from control value ($p < 0.05$).

that result in increased $[ADO]_{ISF}$. One possible explanation is that the increase in $[ADO]_{ISF}$ established during exercise is sufficiently small to be lost in the background noise of the tissue measurement. In order to test this possibility we must have a quantitative estimate of $[ADO]_{ISF}$. $[ADO]_{ISF}$ can be calculated using the Sheehan and Renkin capillary model (25):

$$[ADO]_{ISF} = \frac{Ca\ e^{-PS/F} - Cv}{e^{-PS/F} - 1},$$

where Ca = arterial plasma concentration of adenosine; Cv = venous plasma concentration of adenosine; F = plasma flow; and PS = permeability-surface area product for adenosine.

This calculation is subject to all of the assumptions outlined by Sheehan and Renkin when the model was put forward (25). We have measures of each of the variables in the equation except PS, and we can assume a PS for adenosine based on the PS measured for substances having a similar size (e.g., sucrose). Using a value of 6.5 ml/min/100 g for PS, .07 μM for Ca, .13 μM for Cv, and 122 ml/min/100 g for F, we calculate that $[ADO]_{ISF}$ during exercise would be 1.23 μM. We can calculate what fraction of the total tissue adenosine is present in the interstitium by assuming that the interstitium represents approximately 15% of tissue weight. This gives us a tissue content of 0.18 nM/g which is only about 18% of the values observed (3,23). This result suggests that any increase in $[ADO]_{ISF}$ that occurs during exercise would be lost in the noise of a total tissue content measurement. This set of calculations also supports the recent view that interstitial adenosine may only represent a small fraction of total tissue adenosine. Obviously our ignorance of the endothelial barrier's action on the relationship between plasma and ISF adenosine makes these calculations suspect. They are only meant to demonstrate that the observation of increased release of adenosine with exercise is not necessarily in conflict with the previous observation of no increase in tissue content.

Assuming we are correct in concluding that $[ADO]_{ISF}$ goes up during exercise, we need to know whether its concentration is sufficient to result in the vasodilation that occurs during exercise. Dose-response curves from intraarterial infusion suggest that an arterial plasma concentration of greater than 10 μM adenosine is necessary to produce the vasodilation observed during exercise (23). This is much higher than the ISF concentration of adenosine we have calculated (1.23 μM). However, the infusion data probably underestimate the potency of adenosine because (a) infused adenosine must diffuse down its concentration gradient across the endothelial barrier to reach the ISF and vascular smooth muscle; (b) much of the infused adenosine does not remain in the interstitial space, but instead it is taken up by skeletal muscle cells; and (c) adenosine may be taken up by capillary endothelial cells before reaching the ISF and vascular smooth muscle. So little is known about these processes that it is very difficult to extrapolate from arterial plasma concentration to the concentration in the vicinity of the vascular smooth muscle. It would be desirable to have a better knowledge of the $[ADO]_{ISF}$ established during exercise and adenosine infusions, but that will require us to learn much more about the capillary barrier to adenosine transport.

The final two criteria for evaluating the role of adenosine in exercise hyperemia involve the use of blocking drugs. The methylxanthines are capable of blocking exogenous adenosine's vasodilator effect. Unfortunately, no studies have been done on the effects of methylxanthines on free-flow, sustained exercise vasodilation. Because of the relatively low affinity of methylxanthines for the adenosine receptor, such studies will only be meaningful when they are accompanied by adenosine release data; that is, any change in $[ADO]_{ISF}$ in the presence of methylxanthines could alter the expected result. For example, if $[ADO]_{ISF}$ were increased in the presence of a methylxanthine, a lack of an effect on exercise vasodilation would not mean that adenosine should be ruled out. In fact, McKenzie et al. (14) have shown that the heart releases more adenosine in the presence of theophylline and that this may explain the relatively weak effect of theophylline in metabolic vasodilation in that tissue.

In summary, it may be that adenosine is responsible for sustained functional hyperemia in skeletal muscle, but much work must be done before this can be firmly established. In addition to quantitative studies of tissue adenosine content and release of adenosine during exercise, we need studies evaluating the nature of the endothelial barrier to adenosine, the compartmentation of tissue adenosine, and the effect of agents such as methylxanthines and adenosine deaminase on exercise vasodilation as well as tissue level and release rates of adenosine.

Acknowledgment

This research was supported by USPHS Grant HL 25779.

References

1. Belloni, F.L., Phair, R.D., and Sparks, H.V. The role of adenosine in prolonged vasodilation following flow-restricted exercise of canine skeletal muscle. *Circ. Res.* **44**:759-766, 1979.

2. Belloni, F.L., Rubio, R., and Berne, R.M. Location of adenosine produced by hypoxic liver cells. *Fed. Proc.* **39**:270, 1980.

3. Bockman, E.L., Berne, R.M., and Rubio, R. Adenosine and active hyperemia in dog skeletal muscle. *Am. J. Physiol.* **230**:1531-1537, 1976.

4. Forrester, T. Adenosine or adenosine triphosphate? In: P.M. Vanhoulte and J. Leusen (eds.), *Vasodilation*, Raven, New York, 1981.

5. Fuchs, B.D., Gorman, M.W., and Sparks, H.V. Adenosine release from skeletal muscle during free flow exercise (abstract). *The Physiologist* **24**:76, 1981.

6. Gaskell, W.H. On the changes of the blood stream in muscle through stimulation of their nerves. *J. Anat. London* **11**:360-402, 1877.

7. Gellai, M., and Detar, R. Evidence in support of hypoxia but against high potassium and hyperosmolarity as possible mediators of sustained vasodilation in rabbit cardiac and skeletal muscle. *Circ. Res.* **35**:681-691, 1974.

8. Haddy, F.J., and Scott, J.B. Metabolic factors in peripheral circulatory regulation. *Fed. Proc.* **34**:2006-2011, 1975.

9. Harden, D.R., Belardinelli, L., Sperelakis, N., Rabio, R., and Berne, R.M. Differential effects of adenosine and nitroglycerin on the action potentials of large and small coronary arteries. *Circ. Res.* **44**:176-181, 1979.

10. Hazeyama, Y., and Sparks, H.V. Exercise hyperemia in potassium depleted dogs. *Am. J. Physiol.* **236**:H480-H486, 1979, or *Am. J. Physiol. Heart Circ. Physiol.* **5**:H480-H486, 1979.

11. Hazeyama, Y., and Sparks, H.V. A model of potassium ion efflux during exercise of skeletal muscle. *Am. J. Physiol.* **236**:R83-R90, 1979, or *Am. J. Physiol. Reg. Integr. Compr. Physiol.* **5**:R83-R90, 1979.

12. Honig, C.R. Contributions of nerves and metabolites to exercise vasodilation: A unifying hypothesis. *Am. J. Physiol.* **236**:H705-H719, 1979.

13. Honig, C.R., and Frierson, J.L. Role of adenosine in exercise vasodilation in dog gracilis muscle. *Am. J. Physiol.* **238**:H703-H715, 1980.

14. McKenzie, J.E., Steffen, R.P., Price, R.B., and Haddy, F.J. Effects of theophylline on adenosine and coronary vascular resistance during increased cardiac work. *The Physiologist* **24**:26, 1981.

15. Mellander, S. Differentiation of fiber composition, circulation and metabolism in limb muscles of dog, cat and man. In: P.M. Vanhoutte and J. Leusen (eds.), *Vasodilation*, Raven, New York, 1981.

16. Manfredi, J.P., and Sparks, H.V. Lack of evidence for involvement of adenosine (ADO) in the hyperemia induced by pacing (abstract). *The Physiologist* **23**:5, 1980.

17. Mohrman, D.E., Cant, J.R., and Sparks, H.V. Time course of vascular resistance and venous oxygen changes following brief tetanus of dog skeletal muscle. *Circ. Res.* **33**:323-336, 1973.

18. Mohrman, D.E., and Sparks, H.V. Role of potassium ions in the vascular response to a brief tetanus. *Circ. Res.* **35**:384-390, 1974.

19. Mohrman, D.E., and Sparks, H.V. Myogenic hyperemia following brief tetanus of canine skeletal muscle. *Am. J. Physiol.* **227**:531-535, 1974.

20. Mohrman, D.E., and Sparks, H.V. Resistance and venous oxygen dynamics during sinusoidal exercise of dog skeletal muscle. *Circ. Res.* **33**:337-345, 1973.

21. Morganroth, M.L., Mohrman, D.E., and Sparks, H.V. Prolonged vasodilation following fatiguing exercise of dog skeletal muscle. *Am. J. Physiol.* **229**:38-43, 1975.

22. Morganroth, M.L., Young, E.W., and Sparks, H.V. Prostaglandin and histaminergic mediation of prolonged vasodilation after exercise. *Am. J. Physiol.* **233**:H27-H33, 1977.

23. Phair, R.D., and Sparks, H.V. Adenosine content of skeletal muscle during active hyperemia and ischemic contraction. *Am. J. Physiol.* **237**:H1-H9, 1979.

24. Schrader, J., and Gerlach, E. Compartmentation of cardiac adenine nucleotides and formation of adenosine. *Pflüegers Arch.* **367**:129-135, 1976.

25. Sheehan, R.M., and Renkin, E.M. Capillary interstitial and cell membrane barriers to blood-tissue transport of potassium and rubidium in mammalian skeletal muscle. *Circ. Res.* **30**:588-607, 1972.

26. Shutz, W., Schrader, J., and Gerlach, E. Different sites of adenosine formation in the heart. *Am. J. Physiol.* **240**:H963-H970, 1981.

27. Sparks, H.V. Mechanism of vasodilation during and after ischemic exercise. *Fed. Proc.* **39**:1487-1490, 1980.

28. Sparks, H.V., Effect of local metabolic factors on vascular smooth muscle: Vessel pO_2, K^+ and osmolarity. In: D.F. Bohr, A.P. Somlzo, and H.V. Sparks (eds.), *Handbook of physiology — The cardiovascular system: Vascular smooth muscle*. Am. Physiol. Soc., Washington, DC, 1980.

29. Steffen, R.P., McKenzie, J.E., Yachnis, A.T., and Haddy, F.J. Correlation between skeletal muscle acetate content and vascular resistance (abstract). *The Physiologist* **24**:76, 1981.

30. Tabaie, H.M.A., Scott, J.B., and Haddy, F.J. Reduction of exercise vasodilation by theophylline. *Proc. Soc. Exp. Biol. Med.* **154**:93-97, 1977.

31. Ueland, P.M., and Saebo, J. Sequestration of adenosine in crude extract from mouse liver and other organs. *Biochim. Biophys. Acta* **587**:341-352, 1979.

32. Young, E.W., and Sparks, H.V. Prostaglandin E release from dog skeletal muscle during restricted flow exercise. *Am. J. Physiol.* **236**:H596-H599, 1979.

Section 2
Endocrinology and neuroscience in the eyes of exercise scientists

Exercise scientists recently have shifted their endocrine interests from a focus on physical performance and its impact on disease states to exercise-induced endocrine changes influencing biological functions unrelated to physical performance. Examples of this shift in interest are recent reports of physical activity's influence on reproductive function in women athletes (see Bonen and Frisch chapters for review), on skeletal growth in animals (2,24) and man (16), and on release of endogenous opiates (4).

Within the remaining two decades of the 20th Century we foresee a growing engagement of exercise scientists in three areas of endocrine research. First, we anticipate heightened interest in the effects of exercise on pulsatile patterns of hormone release. Appreciation has been growing for the importance of hormone release patterns in mammalian fertility (11), and in the control of tissue sensitivity to hormones (5). Animal studies have demonstrated that physical activity is a rhythmical, biological phenomenon as well (19,20). Some evidence suggests that rhythms of physical activity are strongly correlated with certain endocrine rhythms (22). A closer understanding of the interrelationship between the rhythms of physical activity and of hormone secretion may help explain exercise-induced infertility in women athletes, facilitation of growth in mammals, and changes in tissue sensitivity to hormones.

Second, we foresee rapid developments on the research front dealing with subcellular mechanisms of hormone action during exercise and training. Contemporary immunobiological and cytochemical techniques have yet to be applied to questions of how exercise and training influence hormone-receptor binding and hormonal activation of metabolic pathways beyond the receptor level.

The third area of rapid development will encompass the role of exercise in the release of brain and gut peptides. This emerging field of endocrinology has revealed a collection of biologically active peptides, many of which appear to be affected by exercise or to have cardiovascular actions (see Vinik chapter for review).

We anticipate that the next 20 years of research will be marked by the realization that physical activity represents one of the most powerful natural stimuli for hormone release, and that this insight will catalyze fruitful collaboration among exercise scientists, endocrinologists, and chronobiologists.

Interest in neuroscience has grown among exercise scientists. It is manifest in studies documenting changes in central neurotransmitter release during physical activity (1,3,12) and in the realization that such alterations in neural functioning may be of fundamental therapeutic importance in alleviating psychomotor and depressive illness or in retarding psychomotor impairment that accompanies aging (see Spirduso chapter for review).

Despite the exercise scientists' inactivity, a large body of knowledge on the role of the nervous system in movement has been collected by neuroscientists and pharmacologists. Progress has been made in two broad areas. First, different types of complex movements have been characterized in terms of discharge patterns for the neurons in the central nervous system (see Evarts chapter for review).

Second, pharmacological studies of depressive illness, utilizing general locomotor activity or wheel-running activity as indicators of psychomotor activation, have identified brain circuits that contribute to spontaneous psychomotor activation or quiescence. Thus, it has been shown that among the principal neurotransmitter systems, stimulation of brain circuits using norepinephrine (27), epinephrine (15), and dopamine (8,18) is associated with increased physical activity, whereas activation of cholinergic (21), gabaergic (17,25), and serotonergic circuits (13,26,28) suppresses spontaneous physical activity. A complex picture emerges of integrated cortical and limbic circuits subserving volitional and motivated movement. Its sites of action are neocortex where dopamine, norepinephrine, and acetylcholine influence movement; the globus pallidus, nucleus accumbens and ventral tegmental area where GABA and dopamine interact; and it involves adrenergic, noradrenergic, dopaminergic, and cholinergic fiber systems that interconnect these areas.

Third, the relationship between specific types of movement or subunits of discrete movement have been subjected to neurological and pharmacological analyses and related to motivated motor patterns, motor development, and movement disorders (6,7,9,10,14,19,23). This last area thus bridges knowledge of movement as recognized by physiologists and kinesiologists and studied by classical neurophysiologists with study of movement as a manifestation of internal motivations or altered mental states as studied by physiological psychologists, pharmacologists, and psychiatrists.

Thus, exercise science is on the threshold of an exciting era that promises to shift the research focus from applied issues tied to improvement of physical performance to basic issues on how movement influences brain and endocrine function. We anticipate active collaboration among exercise scientists, psychiatrists, and physiological psychologists in studies focusing on the biological basis of mood changes in long-distance runners or on the role of obesity in psychomotor activation. We expect an involvement of exercise scientists in experiments exploring the effects of physical activity in treatment of depressive illness and various psychomotor diseases. Given that physical activity has powerful influence over both of these body systems, the time has come to bring the contemporary research approaches of endocrinology and neuroscience within the scope of exercise science.

References

1. Barchas, J.D., and Freedman, D.X. Brain amines: Response to physiological stress. *Biochem. Pharmacol.* **12**:1232-1235, 1963.

2. Borer, K.T., and Kuhns, L.R. Radiographic evidence for acceleration of skeletal growth in adult hamsters by exercise. *Growth* **41**:1-13, 1977.

3. Brown, B.S., Payne, T., Kim, C., Moore, G., Krebs, P., and Martin, W. Chronic response of rat brain norepinephrine and serotonin levels to endurance training. *J. Appl. Physiol.* **46**:19-23, 1979.

4. Carr, D.B., Bullen, B.A., Shrinar, G.S., Arnold, M.A., Rosenblant, M., Beitins, I.Z., Martin, J.B., and McArthur, J.W. Physical conditioning facilitates the exercise-induced secretion of beta-endorphine and beta-lipotropin in women. *New Engl. J. Med.* **305**:560-562, 1981.

5. Catt, K.J., Harwood, J.P., Aguilera, G., and DuFau, M.L. Hormonal regulation of peptide receptor and target cell responses. *Nature* **280**:109-116, 1979.

6. Cheng, J.T., Schallert, T., DeRyck, M., and Teitelbaum, P. Galloping induced by pontine tegmentum damage in rats: A form of "Parkinsonian festination" not blocked by haloperidol. *Proc. Natl. Acad. Sci.* **78**:3279-3283, 1981.

7. DeRyck, M., Schallert, T., and Teitelbaum, P. Morphine versus haloperidol catalepsy in the rat: A behavioral analysis of postural support mechanisms. *Brain Res.* **201**:143-172, 1980.

8. Fink, J.S., and Smith, G.P. Mesolimbicocortical dopamine terminal fields are necessary for normal locomotor and investigatory exploration in rats. *Brain Res.* **199**:359-384, 1980.

9. Golani, I., Wolgin, D.L., and Teitelbaum, P. A proposed natural geometry of recovery from akinesia in the lateral hypothalamic rat. *Brain Res.* **164**:237-267, 1979.

10. Golani, I., Bronchti, G., Moualem, D., and Teitelbaum, P. "Warm-up" along dimensions of movement in the ontogeny of exploration in rats and other infant mammals. *Proc. Natl. Acad. Sci.* **78**:7226-7229, 1981.

11. Goodman, R.L., and Karsch, F.J. The hypothalamic pulse generator: A key determinant of reproductive cycles in sheep. In: B.K. Follett (ed.), *Biological blocks in seasonal reproductive cycles*, Colson Papers No. 32. John Wright and Sons, Bristol, 1981, pp. 223-236.

12. Gordon, J.H., and Schellenberger, M.K. Regional catecholamine content in the rat brain: Sex differences and correlation with motor activity. *Neuropharmacology* **13**:129-137, 1974.

13. Green, R.A., Gillin, J.C., and Wyatt, R.J. The inhibitory effect of intraventricular administration of serotonin on spontaneous motor activity of rats. *Psychopharmacology* **51**:81-84, 1976.

14. Hruska, R.E., and Silbergeld, E.K. Abnormal locomotion in rats after bilateral intrastriatal injection of kainic acid. *Life Sci.* **25**:181-194, 1979.

15. Katz, R.J., Turner, B.B., Roth, K., and Carroll, B.J. Adrenergic control of motor activity. Effects of PNMT inhibition upon open field behavior in the rat. *Pharmacol. Biochem. Behavior* **9**:417-420, 1978.

16. Malina, R.M. Exercise as influence upon growth. *Clin. Pediatr.* **8**:16-26, 1969.

17. Mogenson, G.J., Wu, M., and Jones, D.L. Locomotor activity elicited by injections of picrotoxin into the ventral tegmental area is attenuated by injections of GABA into the globus pallidus. *Brain Res.* **191**:569-571, 1980.

18. Pijnenburg, A.J.J., Honig, W.M.M., Van Der Heyden, J.A.M., and Van Rossum, V.M. Effect of chemical stimulation of the mesolimbic dopamine system upon locomotor activity. *Eur. J. Pharmacol.* **35**:49-58, 1976.

19. Pittendrigh, C.S., and Daan, S. A functional analysis of circadian pacemakers in nocturnal rodents. IV. Entrainment: Pacemaker as clock. *J. Compr. Physiol.* **106**:291-332, 1976.

20. Pittendrigh, C.S., and Daan, S. A functional analysis of circadian pacemakers in nocturnal rodents. V. Pacemaker structure: A clock for all seasons. *J. Compr. Physiol.* **106**:333-355, 1976.

21. Plech, A. The influence of microinjections of cholinomimetics into hypothalamus on the locomotor activity of rats. *Aggressologie.* **20**:279-282, 1979.

22. Rasmussen, D.D., and Malven, P.V. Relationship between rhythmic motor activity and plasma luteinizing hormone in ovariectomized sheep. *Neuroendocrinology* **32**:364-369, 1981.

23. Schallert, T., and Teitelbaum, P. Haloperidol catalepsy and equilibrating functions in the rat: Antagonistic interaction of clinging and labyrinthine righting reactions. *Physiol. Behavior* **27**:1077-1083, 1981.

24. Simon, M.R. The effect of dynamic loading on the growth of epiphyseal cartilage in the rat. *Acta Anat.* **102**:176-183, 1978.

25. Tanner, T. GABA induced locomotor activity in the rat, after bilateral injection into the ventral segmental area. *Neuropharmacology* **18**:441-446, 1979.

26. Waldbillig, R.J., Bartness, T.J., and Stanley, B.G. Disproportionate increases in locomotor activity in response to hormonal and photic stimuli following regional neurochemical depletion of serotonin. *Brain Res.* **217**:79-91, 1981.

27. Weiss, T.M., Bailey, W.H., Pohorecky, L.A., Korzeniowski, D., and Grillione, G. Stress induced depression of motor activity correlates with regional changes in brain norepinephrine but not dopamine. *Neurochem. Res.* **5**:9-22, 1980.

28. Williams, J.H., and Azmitia, E.C. Hippocampal serotonin reuptake and nocturnal locomotor activity after microinjections of 5, 7-DHT in the fornix-fimbria. *Brain Res.* **207**:95-107, 1981.

Endocrines and the adaptations associated with exercise training

Charles M. Tipton
The University of Iowa

Today's facts have evolved from concepts of the past. One belief from antiquity that has had profound influence on the scientific understanding of function is the humoral concept (2). This concept was based on the premise that the body contained four liquids, or humors — blood, phlegm, yellow bile (choler), and black bile (melancholy). In its most elementary form, the concept stated that health prevailed when the humors were in equilibrium whereas disease occurred when the equilibrium between the various humors had been displaced (2).

Although the humoral concept has been attributed to Hippocrates, similar ideas existed in India, China, Greece, and Egypt well in advance of the 4th Century BC. Its significance should not be minimized because it helped to separate health and disease from the sphere and influence of the "gods," providing impetus for the use of scientific methods to study health and disease, and because it exists today in terminology, explanations, and theories of endocrine function. An equally important consideration is that it provided the background for the studies of Claude Bernard (7) and Walter Cannon (12), which culminated in the naming and acceptance of the concept of "homeostasis" (12). It is of historical interest that Bernard used the term "internal secretions" to describe the release of glucose from the liver into the circulatory system. However, it was from Bayliss and Starling's research on secretin in 1902 that the word "hormone" was introduced into the scientific literature and because of their research, the concept of chemical messengers was accepted by scientific investigators (5).

In the 8 decades since that time, it has become clear that the maintenance of cellular homeostasis is a complex process facilitated by the integrative action of the nervous and endocrine systems. Consequently, hormones are circulating intercellular messengers capable of coordinating the functions of diverse tissues throughout the body. However, the mechanisms of their cellular and intercellular actions is beyond the scope of this manuscript. Of the many approaches available to study hormonal actions, ablation by chemical or surgical means is the oldest and the most frequently used. Since this approach will be emphasized here, it is important to recognize that the effects being evaluated could be indirect ones because hormones can act synergistically with other hormones. The magnitude of an endocrine effect is influenced by the amount of free hormone available to the receptor on the target cell, the number of receptors, the affinity of receptors for the hormone, the duration of the hormone-receptor interaction, and the number and function of other cell-surface and intracellular mediators of hormonal action.

As noted by Galbo et al. (18) and as summarized by Terjung (39), the concentrations of most hormones in the blood and urine are increased with strenuous exercise. The most notable exception is insulin (39). Hormonal concentrations, turnover rates, and effects are also influenced by training (3,4,9,13-16,21,22-25,29,30,35,36,39-44,46-52,54); therefore, it is essential to keep these points in perspective when the following questions are considered.

- How are the acute and chronic responses to exercise altered in hormonally deficient animals?
- How are the adaptations associated with chronic exercise dependent on the presence of circulating hormones?
- What are the mechanisms responsible for the adaptations associated with training?

Although it will be impossible to answer all of these questions, I am certain that other speakers will provide answers and insight concerning them. Before discussing aspects that pertain to this conference it is important to have reference definitions for exercise and for training adaptations. Exercise is considered to be a disruption of homeostasis by bodily movements whereas a training adaptation is either an anatomical, biochemical, biomechanical, or physiological change that improves perfor-

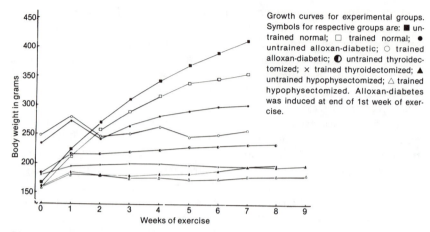

Figure 1—The influence of chronic exercise on the changes in body weight of hormone-deprived rats. These results are from the study of Gollnick and Ianuzzo (21). (Reprinted with permission of the American Physiological Society.)

mance as a result of chronic exercise—a change statistically different from the values obtained from nonexercised controls (37). For the purposes of this section, four topics will be discussed.

Section I: Body composition considerations

It is well documented that regular exercise is associated with lower body weights (37). Studies conducted by Gollnick and Ianuzzo (21) with normal, thyroidectomized, diabetic, and hypophysectomized rats clearly demonstrated that chronic exercise resulted in lower weights and slower body weight gains than exhibited by the control animals (Figure 1). Other training studies with thyroidectomized (49), hypophysectomized (13), adrenalectomized (46), and ovarianectomized rats (9) showed the same trends. When equal amounts of growth hormone were injected daily into nontrained and trained hypophysectomized rats for 8 wk, the trained animals had lower body weights (Figure 2). Careful studies on the food consumption patterns of hypophysectomized rats demonstrated that chronic exercise significantly reduced appetites by approximately 10% (13). Appetite suppression has also been found previously in studies with normal (50), thyroidectomized (49), and adrenalectomized groups (46). These results suggest that future training studies with hormonally deprived animals would be useful in elucidating the mechanisms involved.

Analysis of the fat percentage from trained and nontrained hypophysectomized rats revealed that the trained had lower values, although the differences noted were not statistically significant (13). In a related study, the size of adipocytes from nontrained and trained hypophysecto-

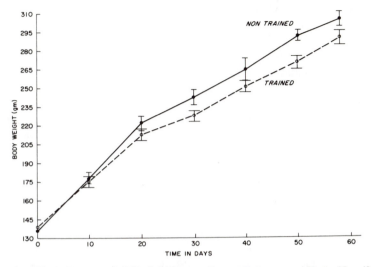

Figure 2 — The influence of daily injections of growth hormone (1 mg/day/200 g body weight) on body weight changes in nontrained and trained male hypophysectomized rats. Means and standard errors are listed. Ten rats comprised each group (C.M. Tipton, unpublished data).

mized rats was measured and the trained group had values significantly lower (35). An analysis of cell sizes revealed that training had shifted the distribution to the left (35).

Although there are numerous training studies with normal rats receiving exogenous hormones (11,15,16,25), a paucity of training studies exists concerning changes in skeletal muscle mass in hormonally deprived animals. Although Goldberg used the term "work-induced" hypertrophy in a short-term study to describe the increases in the mass of the soleus and plantaris muscle from hypophysectomized rats after surgical removal of the tendon to the gastrocnemius muscle, the work data were not quantified (20). This approach was used with normal, diabetic, and hypophysectomized rats receiving either insulin, growth hormone, or cortisone (19,20), and Goldberg concluded that contractile activity was primarily responsible for the 30-40% increase in muscle mass found in his animal model. Using the summarized findings of others, he concluded that neither testosterone nor thyroxine was essential for the effect being measured (20). One additional conclusion was that insulin was necessary to inhibit the proteolysis associated with inactivity (19).

Goldberg also demonstrated with his model that protein and DNA syntheses occurred in overloaded muscles from hypophysectomized rats (20). Compensatory hypertrophy studies by Ianuzzo and Armstrong (28) also showed that DNA synthesis can occur in diabetic animals. Unfortunately, trained animals from hormonally deprived groups have not been studied in perfused hemicorpus preparations. When nontrained hypophysectomized rats were studied, the removal of the hypophysis reduced the normal values for the rate of protein synthesis, the concentrations of RNA, and the efficiency of protein synthesis of the gastrocnemius muscle by 30-60% (17). The injection of growth hormone improved the efficiency of protein synthesis but had little influence on the rate of protein degradation. Hypophysectomy per se reduced protein degradation by approximately 50% (17). Perfusion of insulin into normal nontrained rats showed that the hormone did not alter the release of lysosomal enzymes which could modify muscle degradation events with activity or inactivity (31).

Although trained normal or hormonally deprived animals have not been used, such studies would be interesting in protein synthesis and tension investigations. Even so, it is clear that muscle tension will enhance protein synthesis with or without hormones present (20,34).

Tension either in the form of an afterload or a volume overload will produce cardiac enlargement in hypophysectomized rats that have been assigned to training, aortic constriction, or DOCA injection groups (47). Training by thyroidectomized rats was also associated with an increased cardiac mass (3). When anterior pituitary hormones were injected into nontrained and trained hypophysectomized rats (47), only the trained group receiving TSH exhibited significantly higher values. ICSH, on the other hand, was associated with smaller hearts in the trained group (47). Although growth hormone has been repeatedly advocated as being essential for cardiac enlargement (8), our published (47) and unpublished data do not confirm this concept.

One organ receiving minimal attention in hormonal studies is the spleen. More than a decade ago, we observed that trained hypophysectomized rats had significantly lighter spleens than their nontrained counterparts (50). Because spleen weight is responsive to graded dosages of growth hormone, spleen size is used as a sensitive indicator of the presence of this hormone. Collectively, these findings indicate that hormonally deprived rats will respond to exercise training in a manner similar to those experienced by normal animals.

Section II: Metabolic considerations

The influence of hormones on metabolic reactions is well documented (39). When in vitro comparisons were made between enzyme activity and oxygen consumption of tissues obtained from normal and hypophysectomized rats, the tissues from the hypophysectomized animals were generally lower (3) because of fewer mitochondria (51) (Figure 3).

In the late 1960s a new era in exercise physiology research was initiated with the publication of data demonstrating that chronic exercise was

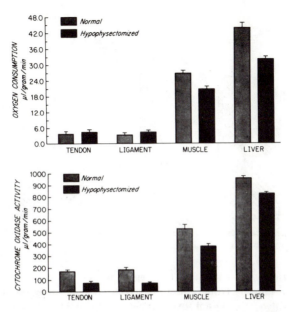

Figure 3 — Tissue oxygen consumption values and cytochrome oxidase enzyme activity of normal and hypophysectomized rats. These results are from the study by Vailas and associates (51). Means and SE are shown.

associated with changes in the number, size, and protein content of mitochondria as well as an increase in the activity of aerobic enzymes (22,26). The studies of Gollnick and Ianuzzo (21) provided insight on the importance of circulating hormones and training by demonstrating that enzyme activity was markedly reduced in thyroidectomized, diabetic, or hypophysectomized rats (Figure 4). One interesting finding was that enzyme activity and mitochondrial protein content were significantly increased by training in the hormonally deprived animals (21). Ianuzzo and associates extended these investigations with trained diabetic rats and observed that muscles from trained animals had significantly elevated SDH activity (29). Palmer and Tipton (35) as well as Edwards and associates (13) have also shown that trained hypophysectomized rats have significantly elevated muscle cytochrome oxidase activity. Baldwin and his co-workers reported that muscles from trained thyroidectomized rats had normal values for the oxidation of ^{14}C-pyruvate or ^{14}C-palmitate whereas the nontrained rats had means 40-50% lower than the controls (3). This same pattern occurred when Ianuzzo et al. (29) evaluated the oxidation of pyruvate and palmitate by muscles from nontrained diabetic rats. Studies of cytochrome c, a mitochondrial component, showed that trained thyroidectomized rats had significantly higher concentrations in a variety of different fiber types when compared to non-

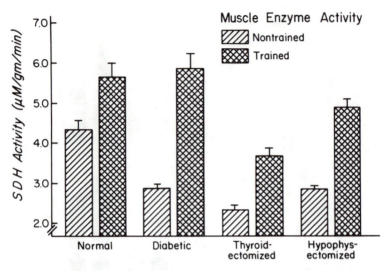

Figure 4 — **Influence of endurance training on muscle succinic dehydrogenase activity. These results are from Ianuzzo's PhD thesis at Washington State University (1971), entitled "Hormonal involvements in the metabolic adaptations in the succinic dehydrogenase activity and mitochondrial protein of rat muscle following training." Means and SE are shown. Between 8 and 10 animals were in each group.**

trained controls. Imaginative studies by Abraham and Terjung (1) and by Holloszy and Winder (27) on changes in δ-aminolevulinic acid synthetase activity with exercise training and thyroxine indicated that a specific mitochondrial enzyme responds to mechanical as well as to hormonal influences. It would be interesting to study changes in this enzyme with trained and nontrained hormonally deprived animals.

To exercise physiologists the single most important measure of performance capacity is the maximum oxygen consumption ($\dot{V}O_2$max) (6,10). Although this procedure is routine in human investigations, only in recent years have $\dot{V}O_2$ data been obtained from exercising animals (6,10). When this approach was used with nontrained diabetic rats (Figure 5), a significant reduction in $\dot{V}O_2$max was observed. Of interest is the finding that insulin injections returned the group oxygen consumption values to within "normal limits." Although insulin has myriad cellular effects, we have speculated that experimental diabetes will produce a condition of autonomic neuropathy that would be primarily responsible for the lower values. Data from Ernst et al. (14) provide experimental support for this possibility, as they have reported chemical sympathectomy in normal rats will reduce $\dot{V}O_2$max by 15%. Our preliminary results with sympathectomized hypertensive rats show that the temperature regulating system is greatly impaired with strenuous exercise (43). However, we

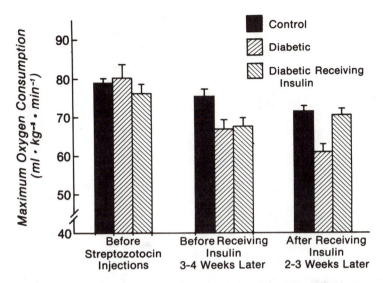

Figure 5 — Oxygen consumption changes in male rats made diabetic by strep-tozotocin injections. These results are from the study of Murphy et al. (33). Means and SE are shown. (Reprinted with permission of the American Physiological Society.)

were unable to demonstrate a training effect in $\dot{V}O_2$max values in these animals. Consequently, the influence of sympathectomy on $\dot{V}O_2$max may be more indirect than direct. Certainly, additional studies are needed on this subject.

Baldwin et al. (3) demonstrated that thyroidectomy lowers $\dot{V}O_2$max by 32% and that endurance training restored it to within normal nontrained values. This difference is somewhat unexpected, considering the data of Edwards et al. (13). Using hypophysectomized rats, they noted that removal of the hypophysis resulted in a decrease of approximately 40% when comparisons were made to sham-control values. After 14-17 wk of chronic exercise, the trained group exhibited an increase of approximately 10% when evaluated on a body weight or a fat-free weight basis (13).

The importance of the thyroid hormones for a change in $\dot{V}O_2$max was also investigated by our group (13). We found that 14 days of injections of T_4 into nontrained hypophysectomized rats restored $\dot{V}O_2$max values to within normal levels. With strenuous exercise by humans, plasma levels of testosterone will be increased (18). Interestingly, results from human training studies have suggested that the sex hormones were responsible for an increase in $\dot{V}O_2$max (36). Although the other possibilities were not measured, this explanation could account for the $\dot{V}O_2$ increase noted by Baldwin et al. (3) with their trained thyroidec-

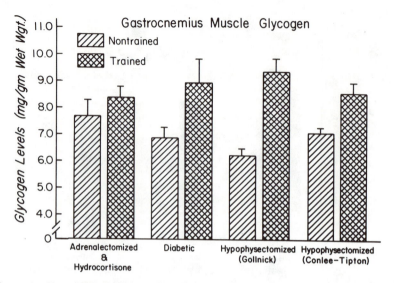

Figure 6 — Unpublished glycogen levels from different experimental groups. Data were compiled by P.D. Gollnick and C.M. Tipton. Means and SE are shown. Between 8 and 20 animals were in each group.

tomized group. Although the evidence suggests that $\dot{V}O_2$ increases occur in the absence of hormones, future studies with castrated, thyroidectomized, and/or sympathectomized animals would help elucidate the issue.

When careful attempts were made to measure resting metabolic rates in trained and nontrained normal, thyroidectomized, or hypophysectomized rats, training had no significant influence on the resting values (41). As one might surmise, the absolute values of the nontrained thyroidectomized and hypophysectomized rats were significantly lower than the means of the normal group.

The importance of muscle and liver glycogen levels for muscular performance is well established. The fact that glycogen sparing can occur with chronic exercise has provided new dimensions for dietary and training schedules. A variety of hormones (e.g., insulin, cortisol, and testosterone) are known to influence the chemical reactions associated with glycogen synthesis. Even so, the "supercompensation" that occurs with normal trained populations prevails when hormonally deprived animals are subjected to chronic exercise (Figure 6). Thus, it would appear that the metabolic adaptations associated with training can occur in the absence of many of the circulating hormones.

Section III: Circulatory considerations

Alterations in metabolic responses cannot be effectively isolated from the concomitant circulatory changes. This is particularly true when ef-

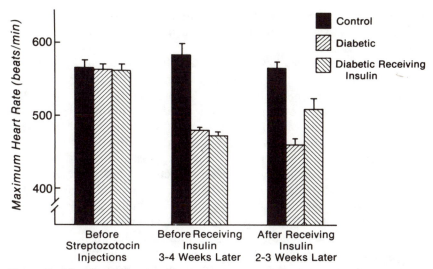

Figure 7 — **Maximal heart rates in rats made diabetic by streptozotocin injections. These results are from the study of Murphy et al. (33). Means and SE are shown. (Reprinted with permission of the American Physiological Society.)**

forts are made to resolve the long-standing debate on whether an increase in oxygen consumption is the result of a change in oxygen delivery or in oxygen use (37).

Interestingly, discussions on this topic have seldom included hormonal considerations. Of the limited data available from hormonally deprived rats, it is apparent that exercise heart rates are dramatically affected. For example, animals made diabetic by streptozotocin injections exhibited significantly lower maximal heart rates (33; Figure 7). Surprisingly, insulin replacement did not normalize heart rate although the same dosage restored $\dot{V}O_2$ to within normal limits (Figure 5). When animals were hypophysectomized, an even greater decrease in maximal heart rates occurred (13). In these experiments training had no influence on the values recorded. This was unexpected because trained populations generally have lower maximal heart rates (37). Unfortunately, with no stroke volume or cardiac output data, it is difficult to evaluate the significance of these results.

Baldwin's studies with trained and nontrained thyroidectomized rats are of interest because removal of the thyroid glands caused a 58% decline in myocardial ATPase activity (3). Their dp/dt measurements also revealed a significant reduction. Training had no appreciable influence on these parameters. The trained thyroidectomized rats had left ventricular pressures that were approximately 20% lower than the normal nontrained group but were 20% higher than the nontrained thyroidectomized group. Because of this difference and the presence of larger hearts, Baldwin et al. concluded that the trained group had sufficient reserve to compensate for the decrease in myofibrillar and myosin ATPase activity (3).

A resting bradycardia has been described as the hallmark of training (37). Experimental studies with thyroidectomized (49) and hypophysectomized rats (13,42) have shown that this adaptation can occur in the absence of pituitary hormones. Most trained populations exhibited less acceleration in heart rate after injections of atropine sulfate (37). This trend has also been observed in thyroidectomized and hypophysectomized groups (42,49). After neostigmine injections, normal and hypophysectomized trained rats showed greater reduction in heart rate than nontrained rats (37,42). Because these differences suggested changes in the parasympathetic nervous system, we measured choline acetyltransferase activity, the number of muscarinic receptors, and the binding affinity of the receptors (13; Figure 8). Our results indicated that the activity of the parasympathetic nervous system was increased, the number of receptors was reduced, and the binding affinity of the receptors was unchanged. Because others (32,52) have observed no differences between trained and nontrained rats with regard to the number of B_1 receptors, we believe the receptor data reflect an increased parasympathetic tone (13,37).

It is well demonstrated that trained populations will have lower exercise heart rates at submaximal work loads. Winder and associates (53) showed that the reduction in submaximal heart rates was associated with significant reductions in plasma catecholamine concentrations. When adrenalectomized rats were trained, the same submaximal heart rate trend occurred (46), indicating that the release of norepinephrine from the nerve endings was reduced by training in these animals. In conclusion, many of the cardiovascular changes observed in normal trained animals can occur in animals deprived of one or more hormones.

Section IV: Connective tissue considerations

It has been recognized for many decades that connective tissue is responsive to mechanical stimulation; in fact, some classical experiments have demonstrated this point (44). Our interest in this topic has been directed toward the influence of exercise training on the strength of the junctions between ligaments and bones. Because medial collateral ligaments are frequently injured in athletic events, we developed an instrument to test their junction strengths (45). Studies with normal rats, dogs, and primates demonstrated that junctions became stronger with training and weaker with inactivity or immobilization. In order to determine whether the same effect occurred with hypophysectomized rats, a series of studies was initiated (48,51). As shown in Figure 9, the same trend occurred in the absence of the pituitary gland. When replacement experiments were

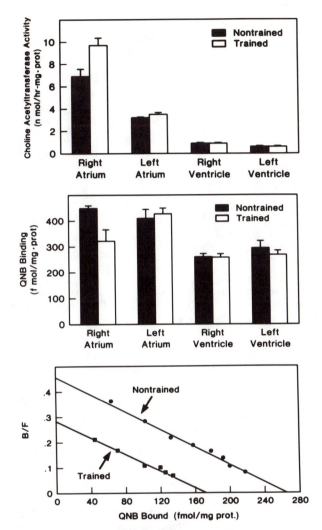

Figure 8—Influence of training by hypophysectomized rats on myocardial CAT and receptor number. (Top) Choline acetyltransferase activity from different regions of the heart. (Middle) Muscarinic receptor number determinations using ^{3}H-quinuclidynl benzilate (QNB) binding results. (Bottom) Scatchard analysis used to determine receptor density and affinity. Means and SE are shown. Eight animals were in each group. Results are from Edwards et al. (13). (Reprinted with permission of the American Physiological Society.)

conducted with the trophic hormones of the pituitary gland plus testosterone and thyroxine, higher strength values were associated with ICSH, TSH, and testosterone whereas ACTH and thyroxine injections resulted in lower means. These findings were explained by the known effects of

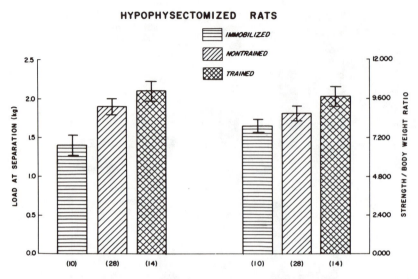

Figure 9 — Ligament-bone strength results from hypophysectomized rats. These results are from the study of Tipton et al. (48). Means and standard errors are shown. (Reprinted with permission of the American Physiological Society.)

TSH on glycoaminoglycan production — ICSH and testosterone influences on collagen formation and the inhibitory influences of ACTH and thyroxine on collagen synthesis (44).

These studies were extended to include the surgical repair of the medial collateral ligament. As anticipated, repaired ligaments were significantly weaker after being immobilized than when they were not immobilized. When progressive exercise was prescribed, the ligaments became stronger. In order to determine the influence of pituitary hormones on this response, investigations were conducted with hypophysectomized rats (48). In these investigations it was found that LH and testosterone were important in restoring the repair strength values to within normal limits. These findings were explained by the postulate that exercise was a beneficial process because it elevated the circulating level of androgens (36,38) and enhanced the volume and distribution of blood to the repair site. However, more studies are needed to prove this point. Finally, we have speculated that female athletes recovering from ligamentous repair will require a longer rehabilitation period because of their lower levels of circulating androgens.

For some time, we have been concerned about the effect of strenuous exercise on the growth of long bones. As shown in Figure 10, our results from normal, thyroidectomized, and hypophysectomized rats suggest that continuous mechanical compression will modify the processes at the growth plate. The specific role of the parathyroid gland in this process is

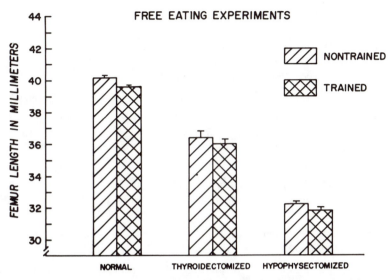

Figure 10 — Influence of endurance training on the length of bones. Means and SE are shown. Results were obtained from male animals used in a variety of studies. Ten or more animals were in each group.

unknown and merits investigation. However, the results did confirm earlier reports on the subject and indicated the need for more research on the topic. In conclusion, ligaments, tendons, and bones from hormonally deprived animals exhibit many of the adaptations observed in normal animal populations.

Summary

From the information presented on the topics selected, the following generalizations have been formulated.

- The magnitude and duration of an exercise response are markedly influenced by the presence of circulating hormones.
- Chronic exercise can be performed in the absence of circulating hormones and by adrenalectomized animals.
- Hormonally deprived animals will exhibit adaptations to chronic exercise. The available evidence suggests that the mechanical deformations of cells and the disruptions of homeostatic environments will initiate the events leading to an adaptation.
- The mechanisms responsible for the adaptations to training are obscure. Besides mechanical deformations, trophic factors from nerves, muscles, and other tissues, receptor modifications, substrate inductions, and cellular changes in metabolic function are other possibilities deserving attention and investigation.

References

1. Abraham, W.M., and Terjung, R.L. Increased δ-aminolevulinic acid synthetase activity in rat ventricle after acute exercise. *J. Appl. Physiol. Respirat. Environ. Exercise Physiol.* **44**:507-511, 1978.

2. Ackerman, L. *Health and hygiene.* Ronald Press, New York, 1943, pp. 47-63.

3. Baldwin, K.M., Ernst, S.B., Herrick, R.E., Hooker, A.M., and Mullin, W.J. Exercise capacity and cardiac function in trained and untrained thyroid-deficient rats. *J. Appl. Physiol. Respirat. Environ. Exercise Physiol.* **49**:1022-1026, 1980.

4. Barnard, R.J., Terjung, R.L., and Tipton, C.M. Hormonal involvement in the reduction of cholesterol associated with chronic exercise. *Int. Z. angew Physiol.* **25**:303-309, 1968.

5. Bayliss, W.M., and Starling, E.H. The mechanism of pancreatic secretion. *J. Physiol. London* **28**:325-353, 1902.

6. Bedford, T.G., Tipton, C.M., Wilson, N.C., Oppliger, R.A., and Gisolfi, C.V. Maximum oxygen consumption of rats and its change with various experimental procedures. *J. Appl. Physiol. Respirat. Environ. Exercise Physiol.* **47**:1278-1283, 1979.

7. Bernard, C. *Lecons de physiologie experimentale appliquee à medecine faites au college de France.* J.B. Baillere, Paris, 1855.

8. Beznak, M. The restoration of cardiac hypertrophy and blood pressure in hypophysectomized rats by large doses of lyophilized anterior pituitary and growth hormone. *J. Physiol. London* **124**:64-74, 1954.

9. Booth, F.W., and Tipton, C.M. Effects of training and 17-β-estradiol on the heart rates, organ weights and ligamenous strength of ovarianectomized rats. *Int. Z. angew Physiol.* **27**:187-197, 1969.

10. Brooks, G.A., and White, T.P. Determination of metabolic and heart rate responses of rats to treadmill exercise. *J. Appl. Physiol. Respirat. Environ. Exercise Physiol.* **45**:1009-1015, 1978.

11. Brown, B.S., and Pilch, A.H. The effects of exercise and Dianabol upon selected performances and physiological parameters in the male rat. *Med. Sci. Sports* **4**:159-165, 1972.

12. Cannon, W.B. *The wisdom of the body.* W.W. Norton, New York, 1939, p. 333.

13. Edwards, J.G., Lund, D.D., Bedford, T.G., Tipton, C.M., Matthes, R.D., and Schmid, P.G. Metabolic and cardiovascular adaptations in trained hypophysectomized rats. *J. Appl. Physiol. Respirat. Environ. Exercise Physiol.* **53**:448-454, 1982.

14. Ernst, S.B., Mullin, W.J., Herrick, R.E., and Baldwin, K.M. Exercise and cardiac performance capacity in rats with partial sympathectomy. *J. Appl. Physiol. Respirat. Environ. Exercise Physiol.* **53**:242-246, 1982.

15. Exner, C.V., Stuadte, H.W., and Pette, D. Isometric training of rats—Effects upon fast and slow muscle and modification by an anabolic hormone (nandrolone decanoate). I: Female rats. *Pflügers Arch.* **345**:1-14, 1973.

16. Exner, C.V., Stuadte, H.W., and Pette, D. Isometric training of rats—Effects upon fast and slow muscle and modification by an anabolic hormone (nandrolone decanoate). II: Male rats. *Pflügers Arch.* **345**:15-22, 1973.

17. Flaim, K.E., Li, J.B., and Jefferson, L.S. Protein turnover in rat skeletal muscle: Effects of hypophysectomy and growth hormone. *Am. J. Physiol.* **234**:E38-E43, 1978.

18. Galbo, H., Hummer, L., Petersen, I.B., Christensen, N.J., and Biel, N. Thyroid and testicular hormone responses to graded and prolonged exercise in man. *Eur. J. Appl. Physiol.* **36**:101-106, 1977.

19. Goldberg, A.L. Influence of insulin and contractile activity on muscle size and protein balance. *Diabetes Suppl.* **28**:18-24, 1979.

20. Goldberg, A.L., Etlinger, J.D., Goldspink, D.F., and Jablecki, C. Mechanism of work-induced hypertrophy of skeletal muscle. *Med. Sci. Sports* **7**:248-261, 1975.

21. Gollnick, P.D., and Ianuzzo, C.D. Hormonal deficiencies and the metabolic adaptations of rats to training. *Am. J. Physiol.* **223**:278-282, 1972.

22. Gollnick, P.D., and King, D.W. The immediate and chronic effect of exercise on the number and structure of skeletal muscle mitochondria. *Med. Sci. Sports* **3**:239-244, 1969.

23. Gyntelberg, F., Rennie, M.J., Hickson, R.C., and Holloszy, J.O. Effect of training on the response of plasma glucogen to exercise. *J. Appl. Physiol. Respirat. Environ. Exercise Physiol.* **43**:302-305, 1977.

24. Hickson, R.C., Hagberg, J.M., Conlee, R.K., Jones, D.A., Ehsani, A.A., and Winder, W.W. Effect of training on hormonal responses to exercise in competitive swimmers. *Eur. J. Physiol.* **41**:211-219, 1979.

25. Hickson, R.C., Huesner, W.W., Van Huss, W.D., Taylor, J.F., and Carrow, R.E. Effects of an anabolic steroid and sprint training on selected histochemical and morphological observations in rat skeletal muscle types. *Eur. J. Appl. Physiol.* **35**:251-259, 1976.

26. Holloszy, J.O. Effect of exercise on mitochondrial oxygen uptake and respiratory enzyme activity in skeletal muscle. *J. Biol. Chem.* **242**:2278-2282, 1967.

27. Holloszy, J.O., and Winder, W.W. Induction of δ-aminolevinic acid synthetase in muscle by exercise or thyroxine. *Am. J. Physiol.* **36**:R180-R183, 1979.

28. Ianuzzo, C.D., and Armstrong, R.B. DNA proliferation in normal and diabetic muscle during short-term compensatory growth. *J. Biochem.* **6**:889-892, 1975.

29. Ianuzzo, C.D., Lesser, M., and Battista, F. Metabolic adaptations in skeletal

muscle of streptozotocin-diabetic rats following exercise training. *Biochem. Biophys. Res. Commun.* **58**:107-111, 1974.

30. Irvine, C.H.G. Effect of exercise on thyroxine degradation in athletes and non-athletes. *J. Clin. Endocrinol. Metab.* **39**:313-320, 1967.

31. Jefferson, L.S., Li, J.B., and Rannels, S.R. Regulation by insulin of amino acid release and protein turnover in the perfused rat hemicorpus. *J. Biol. Chem.* **252**:1476-1483, 1977.

32. Moore, R.L., Riedy, M., and Gollnick, P.D. The effect of training on beta receptor number in rat heart. *J. Appl. Physiol. Respirat. Environ. Exercise Physiol.* **52**:1132-1137, 1982.

33. Murphy, R.D., Vailas, A.C., Tipton, C.M., Matthes, R.D., and Edwards, J.G. Influence of streptozotocin-induced diabetes and insulin on the functional capacity of rats. *J. Appl. Physiol. Respirat. Environ. Exercise Physiol.* **50**:482-486, 1981.

34. Palmer, R.M., Reeds, P.J., Lobley, G.E., and Smith, R.H. The effect of intermittent changes in tension on protein and collagen synthesis in isolated rat muscles. *Biochem. J.* **198**:491-498, 1981.

35. Palmer, W.K., and Tipton, C.M. Influence of hypophysectomy and training on size of isolated fat cells. *Am. J. Physiol.* **224**:1206-1209, 1973.

36. Remes, K., Kuoppasalmi, K., and Adlercreutz, H. Effect of long-term physical training on plasma testosterone, androstenedione, luteinizing hormone and sex-hormone-binding globulin capacity. *Scand. J. Clin. Lab. Invest.* **39**:743-749, 1979.

37. Scheuer, J., and Tipton, C.M. Cardiovascular adaptations to training. *Annu. Rev. Physiol.* **39**:221-231, 1977.

38. Sutton, J.R., Coleman, M.J., Casey, J., and Lazarus, L. Androgen responses during physical exercise. *Br. Med. J.* **1**:520-522, 1973.

39. Terjung, R.L. Endocrine systems. In: R.H. Strauss (ed.), *Sports medicine and physiology.* W.B. Saunders, Philadelphia, 1979, pp. 147-165.

40. Terjung, R.L., and Koerner, J.E. Biochemical adaptations in skeletal muscle of trained hypophysectomized muscle. *Am. J. Physiol.* **230**:1194-1197, 1976.

41. Terjung, R.L., and Tipton, C.M. Exercise training and resting oxygen consumption. *Int. Z. angew Physiol.* **28**:269-272, 1970.

42. Tipton, C.M., Barnard, R.J., and Tcheng, T.-K. Resting heart rate investigations with trained and nontrained hypophysectomized rats. *J. Appl. Physiol.* **26**:585-588, 1969.

43. Tipton, C.M., Matthes, R.D., Kershner, P.L., and Sturek, M.S. Influence of sympathectomy on the functioning capacity of spontaneously hypertensive rats. *Physiologist* **24**:35, 1981 (Abstract).

44. Tipton, C.M., Matthes, R.D., Maynard, J.A., and Carey, R.A. The influence of physical activity on ligaments and tendons. *Med. Sci. Sports* **7**:165-175, 1975.

45. Tipton, C.M., Matthes, R.D., and Sandage, D.S. In situ measurement of junction strength and ligament elongation in rats. *J. Appl. Physiol.* **37**:748-761, 1974.

46. Tipton, C.M., Struck, P.J., Baldwin, K.M., Matthes, R.D., and Dowell, R.T. Response of adrenalectomized rats to chronic exercise. *Endocrinology* **91**:573-579, 1972.

47. Tipton, C.M., and Tcheng, T.-K. Influence of physical training, aortic constriction and exogenous anterior pituitary hormones on the heart weights of hypophysectomized rats. *Pflügers Arch.* **325**:103-112, 1971.

48. Tipton, C.M., Tcheng, T.-K., and Mergner, W. Ligamentous strength measurement from hypophysectomized rats. *Am. J. Physiol.* **221**:1144-1150, 1971.

49. Tipton, C.M., Terjung, R.L., and Barnard, R.J. Response of thyroidectomized rats to training. *Am. J. Physiol.* **215**:1137-1142, 1968.

50. Tipton, C.M., Tharp, G.D., and Schild, R.J. Exercise, hypophysectomy and spleen weight. *J. Appl. Physiol.* **21**:1163-1167, 1966.

51. Vailas, A.C., Tipton, C.M., Laughlin, H.L., Tcheng, T.-K., and Matthes, R.D. Physical activity and hypophysectomy on the aerobic capacity of ligaments and tendons. *J. Appl. Physiol. Respirat. Environ. Exercise Physiol.* **44**:542-546, 1978.

52. Williams, R.S. Physical conditioning and membrane receptors for cardioregulatory hormones. *Cardiovasc. Res.* **14**:177-182, 1980.

53. Winder, W.W., Hagberg, J.M., Hickson, R.C., Ehsani, A.A., and McLane, J.A. Time course of sympathoadrenal adaptation to endurance exercise training in man. *J. Appl. Physiol. Respirat. Environ. Exercise Physiol.* **45**:370-374, 1978.

54. Winder, W.W., Hickson, R.C., Hagberg, J.M., Ehsani, A.A., and McLane, J.A. Training-induced changes in hormonal and metabolic responses to submaximal exercise. *J. Appl. Physiol. Respirat. Environ. Exercise Physiol.* **46**:766-771, 1979.

The sympathoadrenal system and exercise: Potential metabolic role in the trained and untrained states

James B. Young and Lewis Landsberg
Harvard Medical School and Beth Israel Hospital

The sympathoadrenal system is an important determinant of metabolic and cardiovascular function. The intention here is to review the metabolic effects of catecholamines as they relate to exercise and then to apply newer information in these areas as we consider the sympathoadrenal system's role in physiological adjustments occasioned by exercise.

Functional organization of the sympathoadrenal system

The sympathoadrenal system consists of the sympathetic nervous system and the adrenal medulla. The adrenal medulla principally secretes epinephrine (E), though on occasion it is the source of considerable quantities of norepinephrine (NE) as well. After E is released into the circulation it is distributed widely throughout the body, simultaneously producing effects in multiple tissues distant from its origin, thus meeting the classical definition of a hormone. The possibilities for discriminating responses to E in different tissues are provided by alterations in blood flow and in tissue sensitivity to catecholamines.

The sympathetic nervous system (postganglionic sympathetic neurons), on the other hand, releases NE, the adrenergic neurotransmitter which is under most, but not all, circumstances the major source of NE in plasma. Circulating levels of NE are of uncertain physiological importance. Because the NE actions are largely confined to the location of its release, the extent of its direct influence within the body in any given situation is determined by the distribution of sympathetic innervation in different tissues and by the pattern of sympathetic efferent impulses. The capacity for finely discriminating responses is considerably greater with the sympathetic nervous system than with the adrenal medulla; in experimental situations, not only has differential activation of sympathetic nerves in various tissues been noted (5,42), but also evidence of simultaneous stimulation and suppression of distinct sympathetic fibers in the same animal (60). These functional differences between sympathetic nerves and the adrenal medulla have acquired added significance with the recognition that the two branches of the sympathoadrenal system are regulated separately.

Both components of the sympathoadrenal system are governed by centers in the brainstem through descending neural pathways. The neurons of these brainstem centers have an intrinsic activity of their own, but they are also influenced by neural input from higher regions of the central nervous system (cortex, limbic lobes, and hypothalamus) and from visceral and somatic neural afferents. In addition, constituents of the blood such as glucose, oxygen, H^+, hormones, and electrolytes may alter the activity of these central neurons. Local mediators or metabolites, other neurotransmitters and even catecholamines themselves have been shown experimentally to alter the relationship between nerve impulse traffic and NE release by their actions on the presynaptic (or prejunctional) nerve cell (61).

The response of peripheral tissues to catecholamines released from sympathetic nerves and the adrenal medulla depends on the interaction of catecholamines with their receptors located on the surfaces of effector cells. With the exception of the β_2 receptor which mediates bronchodilation and vasodilation in muscle vascular beds and is more responsive to E than to NE, NE and E are approximately equally potent agonists for both α- and β-adrenergic receptors. β-adrenergic receptors may be more sensitive than α to low agonist concentrations whereas α receptor responses may predominate at higher agonist levels. As a consequence, the proximity of an adrenergic receptor to a sympathetic nerve terminal, rather than its designation as α or β, largely determines whether that receptor is influenced to a greater extent by sympathetic nerves or by the adrenal medulla.

Because both α- and β-adrenergic receptors are found on most if not all cells, the peripheral response to sympathoadrenal stimulation is the sum of α- and β-receptor-mediated events in a particular tissue. Several hormones (thyroid, glucocorticoids, insulin, estrogens, in particular), local mediators (such as prostaglandins), substrates (glucose, FFA, oxygen) and other factors (H^+, K^+, Ca^{++}, environmental temperature) may control the balance between α- and β-mediated events at the cellular level.

Assessment of sympathoadrenal activity

Various ablative or denervating procedures are insensitive and unsuitable for studying situations of reduced sympathetic nervous system or adrenal medullary activity. Tissue supersensitivity following sympathetic denervation may increase the regulatory contribution from catecholamines of adrenal medullary origin. The interpretation of effects consequent to the introduction of adrenergic blockade is confounded by potential actions of these agents distance from the site of interest, as for example within the central nervous system, and by uncertainty about the delivery of the administered compound to the tissues under study. A further complication of these approaches in the field of exercise biology is that many sympatholytic treatments adversely affect exercise performance.

Quantitation of urinary catecholamine excretion offers theoretical advantages compared to plasma measurements in assessing sympathoadrenal activity over time, but insensitivity and concerns about alterations in renal metabolism have limited the usefulness of urinary measurements.

Analytical methods of the requisite sensitivity and precision for plasma catecholamine determinations are available but several factors affecting plasma catecholamine levels argue for caution when interpreting data from many studies. First, NE may originate from either sympathetic nerves or adrenal medulla and should not be assumed to reflect sympathetic nervous system activity alone. Second, postganglionic sympathetic neurons participate in reuptake of catecholamines from plasma and alterations in their activity may be associated with corresponding changes in plasma clearance, as demonstrated in human subjects during fasting (43). Third, spurious elevations in plasma catecholamines occur if blood samples are not properly obtained (anesthesia, excessive phlebotomy, or decapitation), a problem of particular relevance to studies in small animals (32,48). Finally, plasma catecholamines have been measured in a number of exercise studies in the presence of adrenergic blockade, but the effects of blockade on the release of NE from sympathetic nerve endings (64) and the clearance of E and NE from plasma (13) make interpretation of such measurements difficult, if not impossible.

One application of plasma catecholamine determinations that has not been used sufficiently is the simultaneous measurement of arterial and venous NE levels. When coupled with an estimate of blood flow, the arterial-venous difference provides an indication of net NE release from a particular vascular bed. Such experimental design begins to approach the question of regional variations in sympathetic activity of which the system is clearly capable.

Two additional techniques for directly assessing sympathetic nervous system activity are available. Nerve impulse recordings can be obtained from sympathetic neurons in animals and in the extremities of human subjects. Because this invasive technique involves surgical implantation of electrodes on sectioned nerves, immobilization, and/or anesthesia, and measures sympathetic activity over a relatively short interval, it has not been used in exercise studies. The NE turnover technique is based on measurements of the NE disappearance rate from sympathetically inner-vated tissues of unanesthetized rats and mice following inhibition of NE biosynthesis or administration of tracer doses of radiolabeled NE. This method permits simultaneous comparisons of sympathetic activity in multiple organs of different treatment groups and has been applied suc-cessfully to the study of sympathetic activity during exercise in a limited number of reports.

Sympathoadrenal responses to exercise

The stimulatory effect of exercise on sympathoadrenal activity is well recognized and universally accepted (Figure 1). Numerous neural and cir-culatory inputs to the previously mentioned brainstem centers are likely to participate in the regulation of sympathoadrenal activity during exer-cise. Plasma NE levels rise in anticipation of physical exertion (38) in-dicating that cortical factors may initiate the sympathetic response. Baroreceptors from the region of the heart and great vessels and from the carotid sinus couple sympathoadrenal activity with venous return and arterial pressure, respectively, both of which may fall with peripheral vasodilation. Visceral neural afferents from liver (41) have been de-scribed that respond to changes in portal venous glucose levels, or perhaps to hepatic glucose content, and may link the sympathoadrenal system with changes in hepatic glucose metabolism.

From exercising muscles sensory fibers originating from stretch recep-tors or from metabolic sensors recently described in connection with dinitrophenol-induced cardioacceleration (36) may contribute to the regulation of sympathoadrenal activity. Thus, in both liver and muscle, neural afferents have been identified that may continuously relay metabolic information to central nervous system regions responsible for coordinating physiological responses during exercise. Finally, exercise-induced alterations in a variety of circulating factors such as glucose, K^+, P_{CO_2}, insulin, and even blood temperature may also modify the sym-pathoadrenal response to continuing exertion.

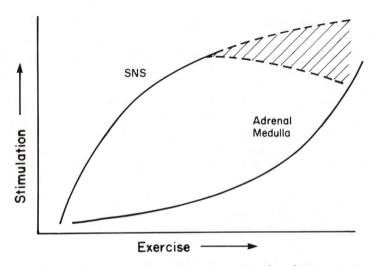

Figure 1—Schematic representation of the sympathoadrenal responses to exercise. Changes in exercise from left to right indicate increasing intensity or duration of physical activity. Activation of sympathetic nerves occurs at lower levels of exertion than adrenal medullary secretion and reaches a potential maximum while adrenal catecholamine release is still increasing. Changes in sympathetic nervous system activity as adrenal medullary stimulation develops are uncertain.

By whatever means used to assess sympathoadrenal function, exhaustive exercise has been shown to stimulate both sympathetic nervous system activity and adrenal medullary secretion (18,19,22,24,25,45). Similar patterns are obtained whether the study protocol involves short exercise periods of increasing intensity or prolonged periods of submaximal exercise. The great majority of such studies have used plasma catecholamine determinations as indices of sympathoadrenal activity, and the extent to which adrenal medullary secretion contributes to the plasma NE pool in this circumstance is unknown.

At mild-to-moderate levels of exertion, differences between sympathetic and adrenal medullary responses become apparent. Sympathetic activation occurs promptly and appears to approach a maximum at a lower exercise intensity than adrenal medullary secretion (18,19,24,25, 30,55). Changes in sympathetic activity between moderate and exhaustive exercise are uncertain because of potential alterations in NE clearance and in adrenal NE release. In the few studies in which arterial-venous differences have been measured, catecholamine levels in venous blood draining even nonexercising muscle may exceed arterial levels indicating net NE release from sympathetic nerves in that region (12,14,58). In contrast, the adrenal medulla probably is not much affected by moderate exercise.

Alterations in the content of inspired oxygen (10,26,59) and in environmental temperature (20) influence the levels of NE and E attained during exercise. Physical training decreases the plasma NE and E concentrations associated with any given workload (12,24,25,47). Antecedent diet also modifies the plasma catecholamine response to exercise. Fasting increases the exercise-induced plasma elevations of both NE and E (17,46), whereas 4 days of high fat feeding enhances only the plasma E response compared to that obtained after 4 days of high carbohydrate intake (19). Glucose administration to fat-fed subjects during exercise reduces the E rise (19), suggesting that relative glucose lack may have contributed to the adrenal medullary stimulation, because glucose levels with exercise after fat feeding are lower than those obtained after a carbohydrate diet. This hypothesis is not entirely satisfactory, however, because glucose infusions that diminish plasma E elevations during exercise are without appreciable effect on the blood glucose levels in these fat-feeding experiments.

Because patients with diabetes also manifest greater plasma NE and E responses to exercise than control subjects, a difference minimized by insulin treatment (8,57), insulin, rather than glucose, may exert a more important influence over the plasma catecholamine levels obtained during exercise. A role for insulin in this regard also is supported by studies demonstrating an effect of somatostatin on plasma catecholamine measurements during exercise (Figure 2). Without affecting blood glucose, somatostatin infusion lowers plasma NE levels during exercise (9); plasma E concentrations increase, but not to a statistically significant extent.[1] Although the link between somatostatin and diminished plasma NE levels during exercise is unknown, the data are consistent with diminished sympathetic activation secondary to somatostatin-induced suppression of insulin secretion, as discussed later.

In several other situations sympathetic nervous system activity dissociates from adrenal medullary secretion. Fasting suppresses sympathetic activity by inhibitory mechanisms within the central nervous system (33). When this suppressive influence is combined with a condition that normally stimulates sympathetic activity, such as cold exposure, adrenal medullary secretion is increased (66). In experiments in which rats housed in individual metabolic cages were both exposed to cold (4°C) and fasted, urinary NE excretion decreased with fasting in the cold whereas urinary E doubled. Subsequent experiments using NE turnover techniques demonstrated that the decrease in urinary NE excretion induced by fasting in cold-exposed animals was a reflection of diminished

---

[1]The authors of the original report, however, did not recognize the significance of the change in plasma NE with somatostatin, although when their data are subjected to three-way analysis of variance, the effect of somatostatin on plasma NE is significant at the 5% level.

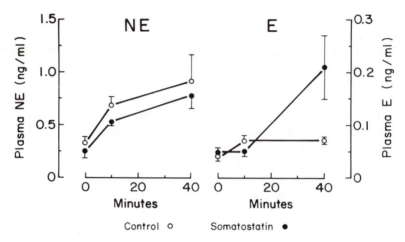

Figure 2— Effect of somatostatin on plasma catecholamine levels during exercise. Plasma NE and E concentrations were determined in four female subjects during bicycle exercise in the presence (closed circles) or absence (open circles) on a somatostatin infusion. Data are from Christensen et al. (9). When the data are examined by three-way analysis of variance (treatment, time, subjects) and the variance attributable to treatment is compared to the error variance (second-order interaction among all three factors), somatostatin infusion was associated with significantly lower NE levels ($F_{1,6} = 6.86$, $p < .05$). The differences in E levels were not significant ($F_{1,6} = 3.00$, $p > .10$).

sympathetic activity. Along similar lines, studies of several different models of hypoglycemia (fasting during third trimester rat pregnancy, fasting in combination with injections of phlorizin, a renal glycosuric agent, and oral or parenteral administration of 2-deoxyglucose, a non-metabolizable glucose analog) have each documented sympathetic nervous system suppression (decreased NE turnover) and adrenal medullary stimulation (increased urinary E excretion) (33,65). In hypoglycemic circumstances an elevation in urinary or plasma NE levels has been linked to the adrenal medulla since adrenal removal or denervation abolishes, or at least markedly diminishes, the NE response (21,56,65).

Insulin administration in the absence of hypoglycemia may selectively stimulate sympathetic nerves. In normal male subjects infused with insulin and sufficient glucose to maintain a stable glucose level, plasma levels of NE are progressively elevated over time in a pattern consistent with a dose-response relationship (51). These considerations, when applied to the previously described plasma catecholamine data, suggest the following hypothesis: Factors that restrain sympathetic nervous system activity augment the adrenal medullary response to exercise. Insulin is one such determinant of sympathetic activation. When insulin levels are low, therefore, as with fasting, diabetes, or somatostatin administration, sympathetic stimulation during exercise is reduced and adrenal medullary secretion is augmented; conversely, when insulin levels are increased by antecedent carbohydrate feeding or insulin administration, the opposite situation occurs. The relative balance between sympathetic and adrenal medullary responses to exercise may influence the metabolic changes that take place. Whether the decrease in insulin level that occurs during a given period of exercise exerts an immediate effect on the character of sympathoadrenal stimulation by exertion is unknown, but the acute suppression of the plasma NE response by somatostatin is consistent with this possibility.

Metabolic effects of catecholamines

Mounting evidence over the past 10 years has altered the traditional view that attributed mediation of lipolysis and glycogenolysis exclusively to β receptor stimulation of adenylate cyclase. As a consequence, the role of the α-adrenergic receptor in the regulation of intermediary metabolism has been gaining prominence (15). Moreover, the intracellular mechanisms through which α-adrenergic effects are mediated appear to be independent of changes in cyclic AMP and, perhaps, to be secondary to alterations in calcium availability within the cell.

The background of any discussion about metabolic effects of catecholamines includes the related changes in local blood flow induced by sympathoadrenal stimulation. α-adrenergic activation causes vasoconstriction whereas β (generally β_2) receptor stimulation leads to vasodilation. Thus, both adrenal epinephrine and sympathetic neuronal norepinephrine may produce vasoconstriction, although epinephrine may also, in selected vascular beds, promote vasodilation. The sympathetic nervous system may contain vasodilator neurons, but these appear to be cholinergic rather than noradrenergic.

Adipose tissue

In adipose tissue, catecholamines stimulate the breakdown of triglyceride into glycerol and FFA by a β-adrenergic mechanism (27). Although α receptors have been identified clearly on adipocytes and exert an antagonistic effect on lipolysis, their effect on this process in fed, euthyroid subjects is minor compared to β-mediated stimulation.

Catecholamines promote the reesterification of fatty acids into triglyceride; current thinking ascribes this effect to increased availability of FFA for triglyceride synthesis, although direct stimulation of the reesterification process may also occur. Both α and β receptor activation increase glycogenolysis (34), whereas glucose oxidation appears to be preferentially enhanced by the β receptor (53). Catecholamine stimulation of glucose uptake into adipocytes by an insulin-independent mechanism has been recognized for over 10 years (6) and has more recently been linked to the α receptor (37).

Removal of FFA from adipose tissue depends on their binding to albumin, and thus limitations in delivery of albumin via the circulation increase the quantity of FFA available for reesterification. The net result of catecholamine stimulation in adipose tissue then reflects changes in the rate of lipolysis and in local blood flow. Based on studies examining which adrenergic effects display denervation supersensitivity, the α-mediated vasoconstrictor response and β-mediated lipolysis in subcutaneous adipose tissue appear to be specifically related to sympathetic nerve activity (50).

Finally, there is regional heterogeneity in catecholamine-mediated lipolysis; for example, in dogs the lipolytic response to either catecholamine administration or sympathetic nerve stimulation is considerably less in mesenteric adipose tissue than in subcutaneous fat (3).

Liver

In liver, catecholamines antagonize the effects of insulin and act to promote hepatic glucose output (27). By independent mechanisms both α and β receptors stimulate glycogenolysis (15,16,27). Gluconeogenesis, on the other hand, is increased by α-adrenergic activation (15,29) which suppresses substrate flux through phosphofructokinase, a glycolytic enzyme, and enhances that through fructose diphosphatase, a gluconeogenic enzyme. Amino acid uptake into liver is augmented by α agonists (35); lactate entry may be similarly facilitated by catecholamines (16), although the receptor designation has not been determined. Vasoconstrictor action of E in the hepatic circulation has argued for a greater role of sympathetic nerves in the physiological effects of catecholamines in liver.

Muscle

In muscle, catecholamines stimulate glycogenolysis by a β receptor mechanism involving elevation of intracellular cyclic AMP and activation of phosphorylase (27). The influence of catecholamines on glucose uptake into muscle is a source of much confusion. Studies in vitro convincingly demonstrate both stimulatory and inhibitory effects (1,4,52); catecholamines via an α receptor mechanism increase glucose uptake, a response aided by the presence of FFA (52), whereas they inhibit insulin-mediated glucose transport through β-adrenergic receptor stimulation (1). Factors other than FFA and insulin, however, may also influence the relative balance between catecholamine-related stimulation and inhibition of glucose uptake. Both α and β receptors increase the rate of glycolysis in muscle, although only α receptors mediate activation of phosphofructokinase (11). Thus, lactate production increases as a consequence of either α or β receptor effects, but with α stimulation lactate derives from uptake of extracellular glucose, whereas with β it comes largely from glycogen breakdown. Catecholamines enhance FFA entry into muscle and mobilize triglyceride stored within muscle (27), but the receptor designations are unknown. Oxidative metabolism, in general, is stimulated by both α and β mechanisms. Preliminary data raise the possibility that NE from sympathetic nerves may be of particular importance for the fast-twitch fibers (both red and white) (39,49), and that adrenal E is important to red and intermediate muscle fibers (both fast-and slow-twitch) (23).

Substrate cycling

The breakdown of peripheral fuel stores increases delivery of metabolic substrates to the liver where they are converted into other forms, chiefly glucose, for return to peripheral tissues (Figure 3). This discussion will focus on glucose cycling.

Throughout the lactate-glucose (Cori) cycle, from gluconeogenesis to glucose uptake into muscle to glycolysis, catecholamine stimulation of cycle activity appears to occur exclusively via α-adrenergic mechanisms. Because glycogenolysis in liver and muscle and glucose use in muscle are responsive, solely or in part, to β-adrenergic influences, the possibility exists that the effect of catecholamines on the rate of substrate flux through the Cori cycle may be independent of glucose use (31). Moreover, catecholamine-induced glycogenolysis may be coupled to stimulation of glucose oxidation via a common β receptor mechanism. Thus, the activity of the Cori cycle may be determined by α receptor phenomena, whereas the entry and exit of glucose moieties from this metabolic transport system may be regulated by β-adrenergic stimulation.

Hormone secretion

Renin, insulin, glucagon, gastrin, thyroid hormones, PTH, calcitonin, erythropoietin, progesterone, testosterone, and perhaps even somatostatin are all known to be affected by sympathoadrenal activity (67). The plasma levels of nearly all of these hormones have been shown to change during exercise in a manner consistent with a catecholamine effect, but with the exception of suppressed insulin secretion and, perhaps, of enhanced glucagon release, none of the alterations has been causally connected with sympathoadrenal stimulation. The importance of the changes in these hormones for exercise physiology is unclear, but in all likelihood such changes provide indirect support for the direct metabolic effects of catecholamines.

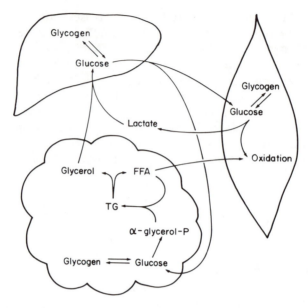

Figure 3 — **Effects of catecholamines on selected substrate cycles. As discussed in the text, catecholamines increase substrate flux through the Cori cycle, promote triglyceride breakdown and reesterification, and stimulate glycogenolysis in tissues throughout the body.**

Metabolic effects of catecholamines during exercise

In general, catecholamines interact synergistically with other metabolic regulators, both local and systemic, to coordinate the activity of one tissue with the needs of another. Thus, their influence may be most important under less-than-extreme conditions when the possibilities for metabolic regulation may be greatest. On the other hand, the preservation of a metabolic process in the face of some sympatholytic treatment does not preclude catecholamine involvement in the control of that process in an intact animal because other factors may be able to compensate for the absence of catecholamines.

In the discussion that follows, the contributions of catecholamines to metabolic regulation during exercise have been arbitrarily divided into three phases: an initial (or anticipatory) phase which may actually precede the start of an exercise period, a carbohydrate-predominant phase during which energy needs are met largely by glycogen reserves, and a fat-predominant phase when FFA supplants glucose as the principal substrate for oxidation. Depending on the duration and intensity of the exercise period, the effects of catecholamines at the conclusion of exercise will be assumed to continue into the recovery period.

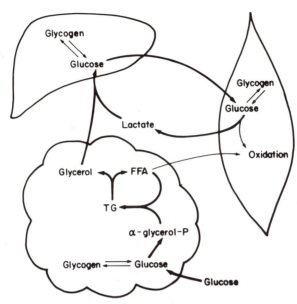

Figure 4—**Effects of catecholamines during initial phase of the response to exercise. Stimulation of Cori cycle activity and of triglyceride breakdown and reesterification may precede exercise period.**

Initial phase

The initial effects of catecholamines, mediated largely through activation of the sympathetic nervous system, involve stimulation of substrate cycling, both between organs and within individual tissue cells (Figure 4). Substrate flux through the Cori cycle increases immediately upon commencing physical activity although maximal rates of cycling are not reached until the second phase when measurable changes in tissue glycogen content occur (28,49). Lipolysis also begins, but the liberated fatty acids are preferentially reesterified into triglyceride as indicated by an abrupt fall in the ratio of FFA appearance to glycerol appearance when both are assessed simultaneously (i.e., the systemic appearance of FFA as measured by radioisotope techniques is less than that expected from the rate of appearance of glycerol) (54).

This effect may result from a sympathetically mediated reduction in blood flow (less removal of FFA and consequently more available for triglyceride resynthesis) in the regions of adipose tissue innervated by sympathetic fibers. Glucose clearance also increases acutely (28) which, as mentioned previously, may partly reflect the influence of catecholamines. Sympathetic stimulation of interorgan or of intracellular substrate cycling, as suggested recently (40), enhances the sensitivity of these biochemical reactions to subsequent metabolic control by catecholamines or other regulatory factors. In addition, the early acceleration in

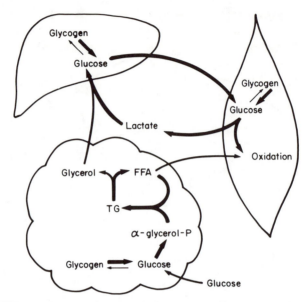

Figure 5 — Effects of catecholamines during carbohydrate phase of the response to exercise. During the phase of exercise in which carbohydrate serves as the predominant fuel, catecholamines contribute to Cori cycle activity by augmenting glucose uptake into muscle, glycogenolysis, glycolysis and lactate production, and hepatic gluconeogenesis.

the rates of substrate exchange, coupled with acute alterations in blood flow distribution, serve to prepare the organism to meet the energy demands imposed by exertion. Such anticipatory effects of sympathetic stimulation may be of particular importance for fast-twitch muscle fibers. Thus, in anticipation of exercise sympathetic stimulation of substrate cycling sensitizes metabolic processes to the influence of catecholamines and other controlling factors.

Carbohydrate phase

In the next phase, as energy demands increase, glycogen is mobilized from storage sites in liver, muscle, and adipose tissue (Figure 5). The catecholamine contribution to glycogenolysis is mediated through both α-and β-adrenergic mechanisms activated by sympathetic nervous system stimulation and adrenal E secretion. Although glycogen breakdown in muscle appears to be predominantly affected by adrenal E, glycogenolysis in liver may result from sympathetically mediated antagonism of insulin action by hepatic sympathetic nerves and from catecholamine-induced suppression of insulin and stimulation of glucagon secretion (49). Flux through the Cori cycle likewise increases, stimulated principally via α-adrenergic mechanisms.

Data in support of this postulated role for α-adrenergic mechanisms in the exercise-induced stimulation of peripheral glucose uptake have been obtained in several studies. In rats forced to swim for 1 hr, the decline in blood glucose observed in untreated animals is abolished by an α-adrenergic blockade (63); because mobilization of hepatic glycogen is actually impaired by drug administration, the effect of α-adrenergic blockade apparently is related to decreased peripheral glucose uptake. During treadmill exercise dogs given an α-adrenergic antagonist also display reduced glucose clearance (28). Although in this study the dogs' exercise tolerance decreased with drug treatment, the inference that diminished physical activity is primary and the reduction in glucose uptake secondary is not a unique interpretation of the data. Impaired Cori cycle activity could have contributed to the dogs' lack of tolerance for treadmill exercise. Thus, available data, though limited, are at least consistent with the idea that catecholamines contribute to the increase in glucose uptake by exercising muscle.

The systemic release of glycerol and FFA becomes more apparent during this phase, but depending on the intensity of exercise and of sympathetic activation, it occurs despite continued stimulation of reesterification. One consequence of a high local concentration of FFA might be to restrain β-adrenergic responses to catecholamines (7). The characteristic features of this phase of the response to exercise are prominent β-adrenergic effects in muscle, near-maximal sympathetic nervous system activation, and initial stimulation of adrenal medullary secretion. The duration of this phase is known to be affected by antecedent diet, by training and by the extent of tissue glycogen stores, but how these influences relate to changes in sympathoadrenal contribution is unknown.

Fat phase

Over the course of exercise period, predominant substrate oxidation shifts from carbohydrate to fat sources, a change associated with lessening of β-adrenergic responsiveness in skeletal muscle. That phase is characterized by diminished glycogenolysis and glucose use and by greater dependence on the mobilization and oxidation of fatty acids compared to the preceding period (Figure 6). Cori cycle activity continues unabated, but lactate production is now linked principally to glucose uptake.

Several factors related to catecholamines may be contributing to these changes. In adipose tissue, release of FFA into the circulation increases and may reflect a disappearance of local circulatory constraints. Vasodilation in adipose tissue may be the result of a local build-up of metabolites, an effect of circulating E, or a partial withdrawal of sympathetic activity. One effect of the increase in FFA delivery to skeletal muscle is to diminish β-adrenergic responsiveness in muscle. In a number

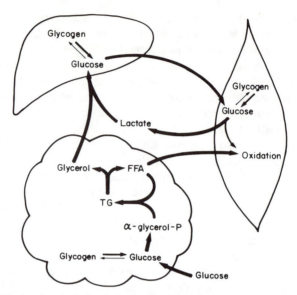

**Figure 6 – Effects of catecholamines during fat phase of the response to exercise.
During the phase of exercise in which fat serves as the chief source of fuel, catecholamines promote free fatty acid release from adipose tissue. The effects of
catecholamines on muscle appear to reflect α-adrenergic predominance, a change
mediated, in part, by the presence of increased free fatty acids.**

of in vitro studies in muscle and other tissues, β-mediated effects are
reduced by the presence of FFA (7,52). Thus, the increased concentration of FFA may modify the skeletal muscle response to catecholamines
so as to promote fatty acid uptake and oxidation and to restrain glycogenolysis and glucose use.

Another factor that may contribute to this change is the reduction in
insulin, because the presence of insulin favors β-adrenergic responses (2).
Similarly, local accumulation of metabolites or other factors also may
limit β-mediated phenomena. The fat phase of exercise thus features
metabolic responses in exercising muscle of a predominantly α-adrenergic character, heightened adrenal E secretion, and, possibly as well, a
slightly reduced level of sympathetic nervous system activity compared to
the previous phase. Thus, during the fat phase the decreasing insulin and
rising FFA concentrations, along with other factors, may contribute to
reduced β-adrenergic responsiveness in skeletal muscle.

Effect of training on sympathoadrenal responses to exercise

The sympathoadrenal system is affected by training. The decrease in
sympathetic neuronal function is demonstrable by a reduction in plasma
NE levels observed in subjects exercising at equivalent workloads before

and after a period of training (12,24,25,47,62) and by a decline in NE turnover in both resting and exercising animals (45). Because sympathetic activation by cold exposure also is lessened by exercise training at normal environmental temperatures (44), the limitations in sympathetic stimulation in these animals may reflect active central nervous system suppression of sympathetic activity, analogous to that postulated to occur during fasting. The plasma E response to exercise is similarly diminished by training (62), although adrenal medullary secretion in the conditioned state has not been studied as extensively as sympathetic nerve activity.

At present it is uncertain which is more important for a given adaptive response — the intermittent sympathoadrenal stimulation during exercise or the sustained reduction in activity between exercise periods. Training effects on the heart illustrate this latter consideration; cardiac hypertrophy more reflects catecholamine stimulation, whereas bradycardia more represents the withdrawal of sympathetic tone.

Summary

Because sympathoadrenal activity is continuously adjusted to meet the homeostatic needs of the organism, future research into this area of exercise biology must address the dynamic regulation of sympathetic nerves and adrenal medulla as well as changes in peripheral tissue responses to catecholamines.

Acknowledgments

This work has been supported in part by NIH grants AM 20378, AM 26455, HL 24084, and AG 00599.

References

1. Abramson, E.A., and Arky, R.A. Role of beta-adrenergic receptors in counterregulation to insulin-induced hypoglycemia. *Diabetes* **17**:141-146, 1968.

2. Alexander, W.D., and Oake, R.J. The effect of insulin on vascular reactivity to norepinephrine. *Diabetes* **26**:611-614, 1977.

3. Ballard, K., and Rosell, S. The unresponsiveness of lipid metabolism in canine mesenteric adipose tissue to biogenic amines and to sympathetic nerve stimulation. *Acta Physiol. Scand.* **77**:442-448, 1969.

4. Bihler, I., and Sawh, P.C. Effect of adrenaline on sugar transport in the perfused left atrium. *Can. J. Physiol. Pharmacol.* **54**:714-718, 1976.

5. Bralet, J., Beley, A., and Lallemant, A.M. Modifications du taux de renouvellement de la noradrenaline dans differents organes peripheriques du rat au cours de l'exposition et de l'acclimatation au froid. *Pflügers Arch.* **335**:186-197, 1972.

6. Bray, G.A., and Goodman, H.M. Effects of epinephrine on glucose transport and metabolism in adipose tissue of normal and hypothyroid rats. *J. Lipid Res.* **9**:714-719, 1968.

7. Burns, T.W., Langley, P.E., Terry, B.E., and Robinson, G.A. The role of free fatty acids in the regulation of lipolysis by human adipose tissue cells. *Metabolism* **27**:1755-1762, 1978.

8. Christensen, N.J. Abnormally high plasma catecholamines at rest and during exercise in ketotic juvenile diabetics. *Scand. J. Clin. Lab. Invest.* **26**:343-344, 1970.

9. Christensen, N.J., Christensen, S.E., Hansen, A.P., and Lundbaek, K. The effect of somatostatin on plasma noradrenaline and plasma adrenaline concentrations during exercise and hypoglycemia. *Metabolism* **24**:1267-1272, 1975.

10. Clancy, L.J., Critchley, J.A.J.H., Leitch, A.G., Kirby, B.J., Ungar, A., and Flenley, D.C. Arterial catecholamines in hypoxic exercise in man. *Clin. Sci. Molec. Med.* **49**:503-506, 1975.

11. Clark, M.G., and Patten, G.S. Adrenaline activation of phosphofructokinase in rat heart mediated by α-receptor mechanism independent of cyclic AMP. *Nature London* **292**:461-463, 1981.

12. Cousineau, D., Ferguson, R.J., de Champlain, J., Gauthier, P., Cote, P., and Bourassa, M. Catecholamines in coronary sinus during exercise in man before and after training. *J. Appl. Physiol. Respirat. Environ. Exercise Physiol.* **43**:801-806, 1977.

13. Cryer, P.E., Rizza, R.A., Haymond, M.W., and Gerich, J.E. Epinephrine and norepinephrine are cleared through β-adrenergic, but not α-adrenergic, mechanisms in man. *Metabolism* **29** (Suppl. 1):1114-1118, 1980.

14. Davies, C.T.M., Few, J., Foster, K.G., and Sargeant, A.J. Plasma catecholamine concentration during dynamic exercise involving different muscle groups. *Eur. J. Appl. Physiol.* **32**:195-206, 1974.

15. Exton, J.H. Mechanisms involved in α-adrenergic phenomena: Role of calcium ions in actions of catecholamines in liver and other tissues. *Am. J. Physiol.* **238** *(Endocrinol. Metab.* 1):E3-E12, 1980.

16. Exton, J.H., and Park, C.R. Control of gluconeogenesis in liver: II. Effects of glucagon, catecholamines, and adenosine 3',5'-monophosphate on gluconeogenesis in the perfused rat liver. *J. Biol. Chem.* **243**:4189-4196, 1968.

17. Galbo, H., Christensen, N.J., Mikines, K.J., Sonne, B., Hilsted, J., Hagen, C., and Fahrenkrug, J. The effect of fasting on the hormonal response to graded exercise. *J. Clin. Endocrinol. Metab.* **52**:1106-1112, 1981.

18. Galbo, H., Holst, J.J., and Christensen, N.J. Glucagon and plasma catecholamine responses to graded and prolonged exercise in man. *J. Appl. Physiol.* **38**:70-76, 1975.

19. Galbo, H., Holst, J.J., and Christensen, N.J. The effect of different diets

and of insulin on the hormonal response to prolonged exercise. *Acta Physiol. Scand.* **107**:19-32, 1979.

20. Galbo, H., Houston, M.E., Christensen, N.J., Holst, J.J., Neilsen, B., Nygaard, E., and Suzuki, J. The effect of water temperature on the hormonal response to prolonged swimming. *Acta Physiol. Scand.* **105**:326-337, 1979.

21. Gerich, J., Davis, J., Lorenzi, M., Rizza, R., Bohannon, N., Karam, J., Lewis, S., Kaplan, R., Schultz, T., and Cryer, P. Hormonal mechanisms of recovery from insulin-induced hypoglycemia in man. *Am. J. Physiol. Endocrinol. Metab. Gastrointest. Physiol.* **236**:E380-E385, 1979.

22. Gordon, R., Spector, S., Sjoerdsma, A., and Udenfriend, S. Increased synthesis of norepinephrine and epinephrine in the intact rat during exercise and exposure to cold. *J. Pharmacol. Exp. Ther.* **153**:440-447, 1966.

23. Gorski, J. Exercise-induced changes of reactivity of different types of muscle in glycogenolytic effect of adrenaline. *Pflügers Arch.* **373**:1-7, 1978.

24. Hartley, L.H., Mason, J.W., Hogan, R.P., Jones, L.G., Kotchen, T.A., Mougey, E.H., Wherry, F.E., Pennington, L.L., and Ricketts, P.T. Multiple hormonal responses to graded exercise in relation to physical training. *J. Appl. Physiol.* **33**:602-606, 1972.

25. Hartley, L.H., Mason, J.W., Hogan, R.P., Jones, L.G., Kotchen, T.A., Mougey, E.H., Wherry, F.E., Pennington, L.L., and Ricketts, P.T. Multiple hormonal responses to prolonged exercise in relation to physical training. *J. Appl. Physiol.* **33**:607-610, 1972.

26. Hesse, B., Kanstrup, I.-L., Christensen, N.J., Ingemann-Hansen, T., Hansen, J.F., Halkjaer-Kristensen, J., and Petersen, F.B. Reduced norepinephrine response to dynamic exercise in human subjects during O_2 breathing. *J. Appl. Physiol. Respirat. Environ. Exercise Physiol.* **51**:176-178, 1981.

27. Himms-Hagen, J. Effects of catecholamines on metabolism. In H. Blaschko and E. Muscholl (eds.), *Catecholamines.* Springer-Verlag, Berlin, 1972, pp. 363-462.

28. Issekutz, B., Jr. Energy mobilization in exercising dogs. *Diabetes* **28**(Suppl. 1):39-44, 1979.

29. Kneer, N.M., Bosch, A.L., Clark, M.G., and Lardy, H.A. Glucose inhibition of epinephrine stimulation of hepatic gluconeogenesis by blockade of the α-receptor function. *Proc. Natl. Acad. Sci. USA* **71**:4523-4527, 1974.

30. Kozlowski, S., Brzezinska, Z., Nazar, K., Kowalski, W., and Franczyk, M. Plasma catecholamines during sustained isometric exercise. *Clin. Sci. Molec. Med.* **45**:723-731, 1973.

31. Kusaka, M., and Ui, M. Activation of the Cori cycle by epinephrine. *Am. J. Physiol. Endocrinol. Metab. Gastrointest. Physiol.* **232**:E145-E155, 1977.

32. Kvetnansky, R., Sun, C.L., Lake, C.R., Thoa, N., Torda, T., and Kopin, I.J. Effect of handling and forced immobilization on rat plasma levels of

epinephrine, norepinephrine, and dopamine-β-hydroxylase. *Endocrinology* **103**:1868-1874, 1978.

33. Landsberg, L., and Young, J.B. Diet-induced changes in sympathoadrenal activity: Implications for thermogenesis. *Life Sci.* **28**:1801-1819, 1981.

34. Lawrence, J.C., Jr., and Larner, J. Evidence for α-adrenergic activation of phosphorylase and inactivation of glycogen synthase in rat adipocytes. *Molec. Pharmacol.* **13**:1060-1075, 1977.

35. Le Cam, A., and Freychet, P. Effect of catecholamines on amino acid transport in isolated rat hepatocytes. *Endocrinology* **102**:379-385, 1978.

36. Liang, C., and Hood, W.B., Jr. Afferent neural pathway in the regulation of cardiopulmonary responses to tissue hypermetabolism. *Circ. Res.* **38**:209-214, 1976.

37. Luzio, J.P., Jones, R.C., Siddle, K., and Hales, C.N. Dissociation of the effect of adrenalin on glucose uptake from that on adenosine cyclic 3',5'-monophosphate levels and on lipolysis in rat-isolated fat cells. *Biochim. Biophys. Acta* **362**:29-36, 1974.

38. Mason, J.W., Hartley, L.H., Kotchen, T.A., Mougey, E.H., Ricketts, P.T., and Jones, L.G. Plasma cortisol and norepinephrine responses in anticipation of muscular exercise. *Psychosom. Med.* **35**:406-414, 1973.

39. Nesher, R., Karl, I.E., and Kipnis, D.M. Epitrochlearis muscle: II. Metabolic effects of contraction and catecholamines. *Am. J. Physiol.* **239** (*Endocrinol. Metab.* **2**):E461-E467, 1980.

40. Newsholme, E.A. Sounding board. A possible metabolic basis for the control of body weight. *New Engl. J. Med.* **302**:400-405, 1980.

41. Niijima, A. Afferent impulse discharges from glucoreceptors in the liver of the guinea pig. *Ann. N.Y. Acad. Sci.* **157**:690-700, 1969.

42. Ninomiya, I., Nisimaru, N., and Irisawa, H. Sympathetic nerve activity to the spleen, kidney, and heart in response to baroreceptor input. *Am. J. Physiol.* **221**:1346-1351, 1971.

43. O'Dea, K., Esler, M., Leonard, P., Stockigt, J.R., and Nestel, P. Noradrenaline turnover during under- and over-eating in normal weight subjects. *Metabolism* **31**:896-899, 1982.

44. Ostman, I., and Sjostrand, N.O. Reduced urinary noradrenaline excretion during rest, exercise and cold stress in trained rats: A comparison between physically-trained rats, cold-acclimated rats and warm-acclimated rats. *Acta Physiol. Scand.* **95**:209-218, 1975.

45. Ostman, I., Sjostrand, N.O., and Swedin, G. Cardiac noradrenaline turnover and urinary catecholamine excretion in trained and untrained rats during rest and exercise. *Acta Physiol. Scand.* **86**:299-308, 1972.

46. Pequignot, J.M., Peyrin, L., and Peres, G. Catecholamine-fuel interrelationships during exercise in fasted men. *J. Appl. Physiol. Respirat. Environ. Exercise Physiol.* **48**:109-113, 1980.

47. Peronnet, F., Cleroux, J., Perrault, H., Cousineau, D., de Champlain, J., and Nadeau, R. Plasma norepinephrine response to exercise before and after training in humans. *J. Appl. Physiol. Respirat. Environ. Exercise Physiol.* **51**:812-815, 1981.

48. Popper, C.W., Chiueh, C.C., and Kopin, I.J. Plasma catecholamine concentrations in unanesthetized rats during sleep, wakefulness, immobilization and after decapitation. *J. Pharmacol. Exp. Ther.* **202**:144-148, 1977.

49. Richter, E.A., Galbo, H., and Christensen, N.J. Control of the exercise-induced muscular glycogenolysis by adrenal medullary hormones in rats. *J. Appl. Physiol. Respirat. Environ. Exercise Physiol.* **50**:21-26, 1981.

50. Rosell, S., and Belfrage, E. Blood circulation in adipose tissue. *Physiol. Rev.* **59**:1078-1104, 1979.

51. Rowe, J.W., Young, J.B., Minaker, K.L., Stevens, A.L., Pallotta, J., and Landsberg, L. Effect of insulin and glucose infusions on sympathetic nervous system activity in normal man. *Diabetes* **30**:219-225, 1981.

52. Saitoh, Y., Itaya, K., and Ui, M. Adrenergic α-receptor-mediated stimulation of the glucose utilization by isolated rat diaphragm. *Biochim. Biophys. Acta* **343**:492-499, 1974.

53. Schimmel, R.J. Roles of α- and β-adrenergic receptors in control of glucose oxidation in hamster epididymal adipocytes. *Biochim. Biophys. Acta* **428**:379-387, 1976.

54. Shaw, W.A.S., Issekutz, T.B., and Issekutz, B., Jr. Interrelationship of FFA and glycerol turnovers in resting and exercising dogs. *J. Appl. Physiol.* **39**:30-36, 1975.

55. Sonne, B., and Galbo, H. Simultaneous determinations of metabolic and hormonal responses, heart rate, temperature, and oxygen uptake in running rats. *Acta Physiol. Scand.* **109**:201-209, 1980.

56. Sun, C.L., Thoa, N.B., and Kopin, I.J. Comparison of the effects of 2-deoxyglucose and immobilization on plasma levels of catecholamines and corticosterone in awake rats. *Endocrinology* **105**:306-311, 1979.

57. Tamborlane, W.V., Sherwin, R.S., Koivisto, V., Hendler, R., Genel, M., and Felig, P. Normalization of the growth hormone and catecholamine response to exercise in juvenile-onset diabetic subjects treated with a portable insulin infusion pump. *Diabetes* **28**:785-788, 1979.

58. Vendsalu, A. Studies on adrenaline and noradrenaline in human plasma. *Acta Physiol. Scand.* **49**(Suppl. 173):57-69, 1960.

59. Wagner, J.A., Miles, D.S., and Horvath, S.M. Physiological adjustments of women to prolonged work during acute hypoxia. *J. Appl. Physiol. Respirat. Environ. Exercise Physiol.* **49**:367-373, 1980.

60. Walther, O.-E., Iriki, M., and Simon, E. Antagonistic changes of blood flow and sympathetic activity in different vascular beds following central thermal stimulation. *Pflügers Arch.* **319**:162-184, 1970.

61. Westfall, T.C. Local regulation of adrenergic neurotransmission. *Physiol. Rev.* **57**:659-728, 1977.

62. Winder, W.W., Hagberg, J.M., Hickson, R.C., Ehsani, A.A., and McLane, J.A. Time course of sympathoadrenal adaptation to endurance exercise training in man. *J. Appl. Physiol. Respirat. Environ. Exercise Physiol.* **45**:370-374, 1978.

63. Yajima, M., Hosokawa, T., and Ui, M. An involvement of α-adrenergic stimulation in exercise-induced hypoglycemia. *Eur. J. Pharmacol.* **42**:1-9, 1977.

64. Yamaguchi, N., de Champlain, J., and Nadeau, R. Regulation of norepinephrine release from cardiac sympathetic fibers in the dog by presynaptic α-and β-receptors. *Circ. Res.* **41**:108-117, 1977.

65. Young, J.B., and Landsberg, L. Sympathoadrenal activity in fasting pregnant rats: Dissociation of adrenal medullary and sympathetic nervous system responses. *J. Clin. Invest.* **64**:109-116, 1979.

66. Young, J.B., and Landsberg, L. Effect of concomitant fasting and cold exposure on sympathoadrenal activity in rats. *Am. J. Physiol.* **240** (*Endocrinol. Metabl.* **3**):E314-E319, 1981.

67. Young, J.B., and Landsberg, L. Adrenergic influence on peripheral hormone secretion. In: G. Kunos (ed.), *Adrenoceptors and catecholamine action,* Part B. John Wiley, New York, 1983, pp. 157-217.

Exercise and gastroenteropancreatic (GEP) function

Aaron I. Vinik and John R. Wesley
The University of Michigan Medical Center

Few studies have documented and reported genuinely beneficial or other effects of exercise on the functioning of the gastroenterpancreatic system. In a survey of the London Pacers Distance Running Club,[1] which consists of 57 members, 17 females and 40 males whose ages range from 16 through 67, were questioned about symptoms relating to the gastrointestinal tract. The distances run by the members ranged from 15-80 mi/wk. Heartburn occurred in only 10% of the runners and was possibly related to gastric acid hypersecretion, disturbances in gastric motility, or reflux caused by an incompetent lower esophageal sphincter. Abdominal cramps were found fairly commonly in about 25% of the runners. A desire to defecate occurred in at least ⅓ of the individuals each time they ran. Nausea or retching occurred in about 6%, generally associated with more tension and protracted exercise.

---

[1]Sullivan, S.N. The gastrointestinal symptoms of running (Letter to the Editor). *New Engl. J. Med.* **304**:915, 1981.

In members who went for what they considered an easy run, about ⅓ had an increase in appetite following the run, and ⅓ had a decrease in appetite, whereas the remaining third had no real change. However, for those who had what they considered to be a hard run, a marked reduction in appetite was experienced for ½ to 2½ hr following exercise.

Gastric emptying and acid secretion

The prevalence of peptic ulcer disease, unlike that of hardening artery disease, is progressively diminishing (16). While these data derive from epidemiological surveys, no known reason has been established. It is tempting to speculate that the decline is a mirror image of the increased prevalence of jogging, and that exercise is responsible for a reduction in the precipitating or causative factors. Hence, relevant questions are: (a) What are the effects of training on gastric acid secretion and gastric emptying; (b) do these differ with the intensity of exercise; (c) does the duration of exercise bear importance in relation to gastrointestinal secretion; and (d) is there a difference in the effect of exercise on the gastric emptying of liquid meals versus solid food?

People have been curious about the effects of exercise on gastric functions since Beaumont's time in 1838. He had noted that gastric digestion, by which he meant gastric emptying, was retarded by severe exercise but hastened by mild exercise. In a report by Fordtran and Saltin (13), the effects of 1 hr of exercise at 71% (64-78%) of maximal oxygen uptake, gastric emptying of a solution containing 13.3% glucose and 0.3% sodium chloride in four males and one female was unaffected by exercise. Gastric emptying of water was very slightly inhibited by the exercise. There was no difference in the amount of acid recovered from the stomach during rest compared to that during the exercise period (13).

Gastric emptying was shown to be much more rapid with water than with the saline or glucose solutions, but exercise had only a slight and inconsistent effect on the rate of gastric emptying. In contrast to these studies, Ramsbottom and Hunt (32) measured gastric emptying and secretion in six male subjects (18-20 yr old) exercising for 20 min on a bicycle ergometer. On the morning of the experiments, 12-hr fasted subjects had their stomachs washed out with 250 ml of tap water and 750 ml of a solution containing phenolphthalein marker; glucose at 37°C was instilled into the stomach. The subjects either sat still or pedaled for 20 min on the ergometer at workloads of between 140 and 750 kilopond-m/min (kpm). At the end of 20 min, the volume of gastric content recovered was measured and the dilution of the marker was used as an index of secretion. At less than 600 kpm/min, there was no effect on gastric emptying or on gastric acid secretion, but at greater than 600 kpm/min, emptying was decreased and acid secretion was reduced.

The two fittest subjects showed no effect of exercise on gastric emptying. A series of studies was undertaken (7) to determine what kind of solution should be administered to athletes to provide them with the caloric needs of protracted exercise. Effects of ingesting between 139 and 834 mmol of glucose ranging from 200 to 800 ml at temperatures ranging from 5 to 35°C were assessed on gastric emptying. Fifteen young men, 19-24 yr old, were 12-hr fasted; they ingested test solutions 5 min after the start of exercise on the cycle ergometer at workloads ranging from 42 to 90% of their aerobic power. After 20 min of exercise, gastric contents were aspirated through an indwelling gastric tube.

As the concentration of glucose solution increased, gastric emptying decreased. At high temperatures above 35°C, gastric emptying slowed, with the rate of emptying directly proportional to the volume ingested; the maximal rate of emptying was obtained at a volume of 600 ml. Exercise had no effect on gastric emptying until the work intensity exceeded 70% of $\dot{V}O_2$max. These data demonstrate the importance of minimizing the glucose content of solutions ingested in order to obtain an optimal rate of fluid replacement. With high-intensity exercise, even small amounts of carbohydrate delayed gastric emptying.

Markiewicz et al. (29) examined the effects of exercise at 15,120 ± 1,800 kpm for 20 min in subjects maintaining a sitting position on the bicycle ergometer. No change in basal acid secretion was noted, but a significant decrease occurred after 20 min of restitution postexercise.

Exercise and intestinal absorption

Water and electrolyte loss in sweat and depletion of glycogen may be the major factors that cause fatigue and impaired performance during severe exercise of long duration. Gastrointestinal absorption of fluid and electrolyte and of nutrients theoretically should supply the energy needs during exercise. Nutrient absorption by the gastrointestinal tract is, to a large part, determined by blood flow. In studies by Williams et al. (58), it was shown that carbohydrate absorption was markedly reduced when blood flow to the intestinal segment was reduced to 50% of the normal. It has been shown that intestinal blood flow (35) is only about 32-40% of the resting value at workloads of greater than 70% of maximal oxygen uptake. According to Fordtran and Saltin (13), 1 L of water containing about 400 g of glucose is absorbed during a 50-km cross-country ski race over a 3-hr period. In order to determine whether prolonged exercise altered gastrointestinal absorption of nutrients, Fordtran and Saltin (13) studied the effects of 1 hr of exercise at 71% $\dot{V}O_2$max in four males and one female. Intestinal absorption in both the jejunum and ileum was studied by a constant infusion of nutrients into the intestine. Exercise did not affect jejunal or ileal absorption of glucose, water, sodium, chloride, potassium, bicarbonate or of the passively transported substances xylose, ^{14}C-labeled urea, and tritiated water. Furthermore, infusions did not alter mesenteric blood flow during exercise or affect heart rate or blood lactic acid concentration. These results contrasted with previous studies which had shown that exercise at these levels did markedly reduce splanchnic blood flow in humans (35), and mesenteric blood flow as well as glucose and xylose absorption in the dog (48,58).

A further conflict arises between these studies and those of Williams et al. (58) which show that exercise in heat at 3-4.5 mph markedly reduced active glucose transport. Urinary excretion of orally ingested xylose was not influenced by exercise, suggesting that exercise did not affect passive absorption. However, Williams et al. (58) used indirect methods for assaying intestinal absorption — urinary excretion which could have been affected by variations in rate of gastric emptying, metabolism of the xylose, and renal clearance. Furthermore, the exercise was less intense but prolonged.

Exercise and gastrointestinal hormones

Since the turn of the century and the discovery of the first hormone, secretin (52), there has been an exponential growth in the discovery of new peptides. At least 30 peptides have been identified in the gastro-enteropancreatic axis. There are 18 clearly defined endocrine cell types in the gastrointestinal tract, but only 10 of the gastrointestinal-pancreatic hormones (GEP) have been found within specific cell types. Thus, a number of endocrine cells still require a hormone, and physiological functions of all but nine of the 30 peptides described have yet to be established. Many of the peptide hormones are present both in the gut and the nervous system such as substance P (54), somatostatin, gastrin, CCK, VIP, bombesin, neurotensin, enkephalin, corticotrophin, TRH and motilin and they most probably function not only as hormones but also as neurotransmitters. Table 1 lists those peptides with established physiological functions, the sites and the factors regulating their secretion, and their major biological actions.

The effects of exercise on gastrointestinal hormones has not been studied extensively. Brandsborg et al. (5) studied the effect of prolonged exercise on serum gastrin in patients with peptic ulcer, in vagotomized subjects, and in healthy subjects, all of whom showed a modest increase in serum gastrin which is mediated by the adrenergic β-receptor system. Similarly Berger et al. (2) showed that exercise induced a rise in plasma pancreatic polypeptide (PP) concentration which was blocked by propranolol, suggesting a β-receptor mechanism. Gastrin is produced by gastric antral G cells and G cells of the proximal duodenum and is released into the bloodstream and the gut lumen (9,11,22,49). The protein content of the food, antral distention, and vagal influences modulate

Table 1

Gastroenteropancreatic Hormones with Established Physiological Functions

Peptide	Distribution	Stimulus/inhibition	Action
CCK	Proximal small intestine	Fat, acid, amino acid	Contraction of gallbladder, stimulation of pancreatic enzyme-rich fluid
Gastrin	Antral G cells and G cells of proximal duodenum	Food; protein	Stimulation of gastric acid secretion
GIP	K cells of jejunal mucosa, duodenum, and ileum	Meals, glucose, and fat	Stimulates insulin, inhibits gastric acid and motility; small intestinal secretion
Glucagon	Pancreatic A cells	Hypoglycemia, amino acids	Glycogenolysis
GLI	L cells of distal ileum	Meals	Growth of intestine?
Insulin	B-cells of pancreas	Meals, glucose, amino acids	Increased cellular uptake of glucose
Motilin	EC cells of upper small intestine	Meals, fat. Acid in duodenum?	Initiation of interdigestive myoelectric complex
PP	PP (D$_2$) cells of pancreas	Vagal, cholinergic	Inhibition of pancreatic bicarbonate and enzyme secretion
Secretin	S cells of duodenum and proximal jejunum	Food, acid in duodenum	Stimulation of pancreatic bicarbonate secretion

gastrin secretion. Feedback regulation is mediated by antral acidification and by neural and hormonal regulatory mechanisms (44). The only established role of gastrin is to stimulate acid secretion (56,57). However, a trophic effect of gastrin on the gastrointestinal tract has been shown, but its role in this regard is controversial (19). There does not appear to be a consistent abnormality of gastrin secretion in patients with duodenal ulceration although an increased sensitivity to gastrin has been postulated (34). It does not seem that gastrin per se is noxious. High levels are found in patients with pernicious anemia and they suffer no ill effects. Thus, the increased secretion of gastrin with exercise would be of no consequence in the event that acid secretion is unaltered.

Exercise causes a rise in PP levels that is blocked by propranolol, suggesting a β-receptor mechanism (2). PP is a 36-amino acid polypeptide with a molecular weight of 4,200 daltons. It is found almost entirely in the pancreas in the D_2 cells of the islets, and to a lesser extent in the acinar portion of the gland (43). PP is released into the circulation in large quantities after ingestion of a meal which is thought to happen predominantly through a cholinergic mechanism (12).

The major action of PP is on pancreatic bicarbonate production and bile acid secretion with initial stimulation followed by inhibition, depending on the dose (30). PP has also been shown to inhibit pentagastrin-stimulated acid secretion (30). The only true physiological action of the hormone has been shown to be the inhibition of biliary and pancreatic secretion, and even then this action is weak (1,45). Insulin-induced hypoglycemia, CCK (38), pentagastrin, secretin (15), and bombesin (12) all stimulate the release of PP.

The inordinate PP sensitivity to cholinergic stimulation has suggested a usefulness for PP in the diagnosis of vagal integrity and also autonomic neuropathy in diabetes (25). PP responsiveness to adrenergic manipulation is six- to 10-fold greater in men than in women (47), which is possibly relevant to the greater incidence of autonomically mediated diseases in men compared to women. It would be thus of considerable interest to determine whether the exaggerated PP responsiveness to adrenergic stimulation in males is reduced after a period of training. In the study by Hilsted et al. (17), peripheral plasma concentrations of GEP hormones were measured during a 3-hr period of bicycle exercise at 40% maximal oxygen uptake in six normal men. Marked increases were found in circulating vasoactive intestinal polypeptide (1.8 ± .7 vs 22.3 ± 5.4 pmol/L at 3 hr), secretin (0.5 ± 0.5 vs 11.1 ± 2.7 pmol/L), pancreatic polypeptide (4.0 ± 1.5 vs 46.3 ± 11.5 pmol/L), and somatostatin (12.8 ± 1.2 vs 17.7 ± 0.6 pmol/L); whereas no change occurred in gastric inhibitory polypeptide (37.3 ± 5.9 vs 39.2 ± 9.8 pmol/L).

VIP is a 28-amino acid peptide with a molecular weight of 3,323 daltons. It has been isolated in both endocrine cells and nerves of gastrointestinal tract (36) and in the central nervous system (6,10). The change in VIP in plasma during exercise probably was a consequence of increased release of VIP from nerve fibers, because the antiserum used by the authors did not detect VIP in endocrine cells (6), but did recognize it in nerve fibers (6,21).

VIP has a number of actions in common with secretin, GIP, and glucagon because of the structural homology it shares with these peptides (37). Its widespread actions include inhibition of gastric acid secretion and stimulation of: insulin release; pancreatic water and bicarbonate secretion; hepatic glycogenolysis; intestinal fluid and electrolyte secretion; increases in intestinal mucosal cyclic AMP; the relaxation of smooth muscle; and an inotropic action on the heart. VIP most likely functions as a paracrine neurotransmitter substance rather than as a hormone (10,36,37). Effects of VIP that seem most relevant to exercise are the stimulation of glucagon secretion, lipolysis, and hepatic glycogenolysis with gluconeogenesis. Also, VIP-containing nerve fibers recently have been demonstrated in relation to the sweat glands and muscular resistance vessels in the cat (27), and these observations suggest speculations about the role of VIP in the circulatory and thermoregulatory adaptations to exercise.

Secretin is a highly basic peptide that contains 27 amino acids and has a molecular weight of 3,055 daltons (20). It is found in S cells throughout the small intestine, and its highest concentration is in the duodenum and proximal jejunum. The major stimulus to secretin release is HCL in the duodenum (39). The physiological actions of secretin appear to be its synergism with CCK in the stimulation of gallbladder contraction and the stimulation of a bicarbonate-rich pancreatic enzyme secretion (33). Because gastric acid secretion is equivocal during exercise, the changes in duodenal pH would hardly be responsible for the exercise-induced increase in blood secretin levels. What the role of secretin would be during exercise is difficult to comprehend, but increases during starvation, ketoacidosis, and a role in lipolysis have been found, and this hormone clearly merits further examination.

Somatostatin is a tetradecapeptide with a molecular weight of 1,640 daltons. It was originally isolated from the hypothalamus and subsequently found in large quantities in the gastrointestinal tract (40). In the gut it is present primarily in the D-cell of the pancreas and the gastric antrum (31). It has widespread inhibitory actions on peptide hormone secretion, and it also inhibits the release of growth hormone, TSH, gastrin, motilin, glucagon, and insulin (46). Somatostatin actions include the inhibition of gastric acid and pepsin secretion, a delay of gastric emptying, inhibition of gallbladder contraction, inhibition of bile and of pancreatic enzyme secretion (8). Somatostatin probably is released from the intestine (53) after the ingestion of a meal and during insulin-induced hypoglycemia (50,51). As somatostatin has been shown to delay the absorption of fat and a number of nutrients in the gastrointestinal tract, it may act as an important modulator of gastrointestinal nutrient transfer (42). The responses to exercise observed by Hilsted et al. (17) were similar to those reported in normal dogs and in humans after a fat-protein meal (41,50,51). Hilsted et al. (17) observed that glucagon concentration increased with exercise as had been previously observed by Galbo et al. (14), who studied the glucagon and catecholamine responses to graded and prolonged exercise in men. Eight men were studied during graded (47, 77, and 100% of $\dot{V}O_2$) and prolonged (76% of maximal $\dot{V}O_2$) treadmill running. During graded exercise, the glucagon concentration increased 35% after the heaviest load. During prolonged exercise, glucagon increased progressively to three times (226 ± 40 pg/ml) the resting value. Glucagon concentrations correlated significantly with norepinephrine and epinephrine concentrations during prolonged exercise, and with epinephrine during graded exercise.

The authors concluded that although increments in catecholamines might explain increased glucagon concentration during graded exercise, they cannot account completely for the rise of glucagon during prolonged exercise. During work of similar intensity, the muscle glycogen content has been shown to diminish gradually and the glucose uptake by the working muscles to increase progressively (55). As the blood glucose concentration was maintained throughout the prolonged exercise period, the authors speculate that a progressive rise in the hepatic glucose output via glucagon-stimulated gluconeogenesis (26) must have made the maintenance of blood glucose possible. Thus, it seems that the purpose of the increased glucagon secretion observed during prolonged work is possibly to maintain blood glucose homeostasis.

The secretion of glucagon is depressed by glucose both in vivo (4,28) and in vitro (18,23). It has been shown that vagal stimulation increases plasma glucagon concentrations (3); the authors proposed that glucagon regulatory centers in the brain stimulated release of pancreatic glucagon via parasympathetic stimulation (3). Furthermore, the low insulin concentrations found during prolonged work might inhibit the entry of glucose into the pancreatic α cell, thereby increasing glucagon secretion. These mechanisms might be functioning during work, as exercise-induced secretion diminished during glucose infusion in dogs (4,28). Pharmacological doses of glucagon have been shown to stimulate glycolysis in humans (26). A lipolytic effect of glucagon in physiological concentrations has not yet been established (24).

The only study to examine the effects of training on exercise-induced glucagon secretion has been that by Winder et al. (59). Six untrained subjects were asked to exercise for 30-50 min/day, 6 days/wk, for 9 wk. Glucagon and metabolic fuels were measured in response to 90 min of exercise at $58 \pm 2\%$ of the $\dot{V}O_2$max consumption. Before training, exercise induced a rise in glucagon concentration which reached a peak at 90 min and persisted for 1 hr after completion of the exercise. The maximal rise in circulating glucagon concentration with exercise had fallen significantly within 3 wk of training. After 9 wk of training, the rise that occurred was markedly attenuated; within 30 min of exercise the mean concentration had returned to basal. Whether this adaptation to exercise reflects a decreased need for hepatic glycogenolysis or enhanced sensitivity to glucagon is uncertain at present.

References

1. Adrian, T.E., Greenberg, G.R., and Bloom, S.R. *Actions of pancreatic polypeptide in man*. Churchill Livingstone, New York, 1981, pp. 206-212.

2. Berger, D., Floyd, J.C., Jr., Lampman, R.M., and Fajans, S.S. The effect of adrenergic receptor blockade on exercise-induced rise in pancreatic polypeptide in man. *J. Clin. Endocrinol. Metab.* **50**:33-39, 1980.

3. Bloom, S.R., Edwards, A.V., and Vaughan, N.J.A. The role of the autonomic innervation in the control of glucagon release during hypoglycemia in the calf. *J. Physiol.* **236**:611-623, 1974.

4. Böttger, I., Schlein, E.M., Faloona, G.R., Knochel, J.P., and Unger, R.H. The effect of exercise on glucagon secretion. *J. Clin. Endocrinol. Metab.* **35**:117-125, 1972.

5. Brandsborg, O., Christensen, N.J., Galbo, H., Brandsborg, M., and Løgreen, N.A. The effect of exercise, smoking and propranolol on serum gastrin in patients with duodenal ulcer and in vagotomized subjects. *Scand. J. Clin. Lab. Invest.* **38**:441-446, 1978.

6. Bryant, M.G., Bloom, S.R., Polak, J.M., Albuquerque, R.H., Modlin, I.M., and Pearse, P.G.E. Possible dual role for vasoactive intestinal peptide as gastrointestinal hormone and neurotransmitter substance. *Lancet* **I**:991-993, 1976.

7. Costil, D.K., and Saltin, B. Factors limiting gastric emptying during rest and exercise. *J. Appl. Physiol.* **37**:679-682, 1974.

8. Creutzfeldt, W., and Arnold, R. Somatostatin and the stomach: Exocrine and endocrine aspects. First International Somatostatin Symposium, Freilburg, Germany. *Metabolism* **27**(Suppl.):1309-1315, 1978.

9. Eckhauser, F.E., Vinik, A.I., McLeod, M., Porter-Fink, V., and Fiddian-Green, R.G. Secretin, a stimulus for duodenal and pancreatic gastrin release: Possible pathogenetic significance in Zollinger-Ellison syndrome. *J. Surg. Res.* **28**:356-366, 1980.

10. Fahrenkrug, T.V. Vasoactive intestinal polypeptide: Measurement, distribution and putative neurotransmitter function. *Digestion* **19**:149, 1979.

11. Fiddian-Green, R.G., Pittenger, G., Kothary, P., and Vinik, A.I. Role of calcium in the stimulus-secretion coupling of antral gastric release. *Endocrinology* (in press).

12 Floyd, J.C., Jr., and Vinik, A.I. *Pancreatic polypeptide*. Churchill Livingstone, New York, 1981, pp. 195-205.

13. Fordtran, J.S., and Saltin, B. Gastric emptying and intestinal absorption during prolonged severe exercise. *J. Appl. Physiol.* **23**:331-335, 1967.

14. Galbo, H.J., Holst, J., and Christensen, N.J. Glucagon and plasma catecholamine responses to grades and prolonged exercise in man. *J. Appl. Physiol.* **38**:70-76, 1975.

15. Glaser, B., Vinik, A.I., Sive, A.A., and Floyd, J.C., Jr. Plasma human pancreatic polypeptide responses to administered secretin. (Effects of surgical vagotomy, cholinergic blockade and chronic pancreatitis.) *J. Clin. Endocrinol. Metab.* **50**:1094-1099, 1980.

16. Grossman, M.I., and Elashoff, J.D. Trends in hospital admissions and death rates for peptic ulcer in the United States from 1970-1978. *Gastroenterology* **78**:280-285, 1980.

17. Hilsted, J., Galbo, H., Sonne, B., Schwartz, T., Fahrenkrug, J., Schaffalitzky de Muckadell, O.B., Lauritsen, K.B., and Tronier, B. Gastroenteropancreatic hormonal changes during exercise. *Am. J. Physiol.* **239**:G136-G140, 1980.

18. Iversen, J. Adrenergic receptors and the secretion of glucagon and insulin from the isolated, perfused canine pancreas. *J. Clin. Invest.* **52**:2102-2116, 1973.

19. Johnson, L.R. Regulation of gastrointestinal mucosal growth. *World J. Surg.* **3**:477-486, 1979.

20. Jorpes, J.E., and Mutt, V. *Secretin, cholecystokinin, pancreozymin and gastrin*. Springer-Verlag, New York, 1973.

21. Larsson, L.I., Fahrenkrug, J., Schaffalitzky de Muckadell, O.B., Sundler, F., Hakanson, R., and Rehfeld, J.F. Localization of vasoactive intestinal polypeptide (VIP) to central and peripheral neurons. *Proc. Natl. Acad. Sci. USA* **73**:3197-3200, 1976.

22. Larsson, L.I. *Peptides of the gastrin cell*. Academic, New York, 1979, p. 5.

23. Leclercq-Meyer, V., Brisson, G.R., and Malaisse, W.J. Effect of adrenaline and glucose on release of glucagon and insulin in vitro. *Nature* **231**:248-249, 1971.

24. Lefebvre, P.J., and Unger, R.H. *Glucagon*. Pergamon, London, 1972, pp. 213-244.

25. Levitt, N.S., Vinik, A.I., Sive, A.A., Van Tonder, S., and Lund, A. Impaired pancreatic polypeptide responses to insulin-induced hypoglycemia in diabetic autonomic neuropathy. *J. Clin. Endocrinol. Metab.* **50**:445-449, 1980.

26. Liljenquist, J.E., Bomboy, J.D., Lewis, S.B., Sinclair-Smith, E.C., Felts, P.W., Lacy, W.W., Crofford, O.B., and Liddle, G.W. Effects of glucagon

on lipolysis and ketogenesis in normal and diabetic men. *J. Clin. Invest.* **53**:190-197, 1974.

27. Lundberg, J.M. Enkephalin, substance P, VIP, somatostatin, gastrin, CCK and neurotensin in peripheral neurons. *Acta Physiol. Scand.* (Suppl.)**473**:14, 1979 (Abstr.).

28. Luyckx, A.S., and Lefebvre, P.J. Mechanisms involved in the exercise-induced increase in glucagon secretion in rats. *Diabetes* **23**:81-93, 1974.

29. Markiewicz, K., Cholewan, M., Goslin, L.L., and Chimura, J. Effect of physical exercise on gastric basal secretions in healthy men. *Acta Hepato-Gastroenterol.* **24**:377-380, 1977.

30. Parks, D., Gingerich, R., Jaffe, B.M., and Akande, B. Role of pancreatic polypeptide in canine gastric acid secretion. *Am. J. Physiol.* **236**:E488-E494, 1979.

31. Polak, J.M., Pearse, A.G.E., Grimelius, L., Bloom, S.R., and Arimura, A. Growth hormone release-inhibiting hormone in gastrointestinal and pancreatic D cells. *Lancet* **I**:1220-1222, 1975.

32. Ramsbottom, N., and Hunt, J.N. Effect of exercise on gastric emptying and gastric secretion. *Digestion* **10**:1-8, 1974.

33. Rayford, P.L., Miller, T.A., and Thompson, J.C. Secretin, cholecystokinin and newer gastrointestinal hormones. *New Engl. J. Med.* **294**:1093-1101, 1976.

34. Rehfeld, J.F. *Gastrointestinal hormones.* University Park Press, Baltimore, 1979, p. 291.

35. Rowell, L.B., Blackmon, J.R., and Bruce, R.A. Indocynanine green clearance and estimated hepatic blood flow during mild exercise to maximal exercise in upright man. *J. Clin. Invest.* **43**:1677-1690, 1964.

36. Said, S.I., and Mutt, V. Isolation from porcine intestinal wall of a vasoactive octacosapeptide related to secretin and glucagon. *Eur. J. Biochem.* **28**:199, 1972.

37. Said, S.I. *Vasoactive intestinal polypeptide (VIP) current status.* Univ. of Texas Press, Austin, 1975, p. 591.

38. Scarpello, J.H., Vinik, A.I., and Owyang, C. The intestinal phase of pancreatic polypeptide release. *Gastroenterology* (in press).

39. Schaffalitzky de Muckadell, O.B., Fahrenkrug, J., Watt-Boolsen, S., and Worning, H. Pancreatic response and plasma secretin concentration during infusion of low dose secretin in man. *Scand. J. Gastroenterol.* **13**:305-311, 1976.

40. Schally, A., Dupont, A., Arimura, A., Redding, T.W., Nishi, N., Linthicum, G.L., and Schlesinger, D.H. Isolation and structure of somatostatin from porcine hypothalami. *Biochemistry* **15**:509-514, 1976.

41. Schusdziarra, V., Harris, V., Arimura, A., and Unger, R.H. Evidence for a

role of splanchnic somatostatin in the homeostasis of ingested nutrients. *Endocrinology* **104**:1705-1708, 1979.

42. Schusdziarra, V., and Unger, R.H. *Physiology and pathophysiology of circulating somatostatin in dogs*. Churchill Livingstone, New York, 1981, pp. 366-370.

43. Schwartz, T.W. Pancreatic polypeptide and endocrine tumors of the pancreas. *Scand. J. Gastroenterol* **14**(Suppl. 53):93-100, 1979.

44. Soll, A.H., and Walsh, J.H. Regulation of gastric acid secretion. *Ann. Rev. Physiol.* **41**:35-53, 1979.

45. Taylor, I.L., Solomon, T.E., Walsh, J.H., and Grossman, M.I. Pancreatic polypeptide: Metabolism and effect on pancreatic secretion in dogs. *Am. J. Gastroenterol.* **76**:524-528, 1979.

46. Vale, W., Rivier, C., and Brown, M. Regulatory peptides of the hypothalamus. *Ann. Rev. Physiol.* **39**:473, 1977.

47. Valtysson, G., Vinik, A.I., Glaser, B., Zohglin, G., and Floyd, J.C., Jr. Sex difference in the sensitivity of the PP cell to autonomic nervous stimulation in man. Submitted to *J. Clin. Endocrinol. Metab.* Feb. 1982.

48. Varro, V., Blaho, G., Csernay, L., Jong, I., and Svarvas, F. Effect of decreased and local circulation on the absorptive capacity of a small intestine loop in the dog. *Am. J. Digest. Dis.* **10**:170-177, 1965.

49. Vinik, A.I. *Regulation of gastrin release from oriented sheets of human antral mucosa in vitro*. Churchill Livingstone, New York, 1978, pp. 156-157.

50. Vinik, A.I., Shapiro, B., Glaser, B., and Wagner, L. *Circulating somatostatin in primates*. Churchill Livingstone, New York, 1981, pp. 371-375.

51. Vinik, A.I., Levitt, N., Pimstone, B., and Wagner, L. Peripheral plasma somatostatin-like immunoreactive responses to insulin hypoglycemia and a mixed meal in healthy subjects and in noninsulin-dependent maturity onset diabetics. *J. Clin. Endocrinol. Metab.* **52**:330-337, 1981.

52. Vinik, A.I. The enterohormones—current status and review. *S. Afr. Med. J.* **48**:359-364, 1974.

53. Vinik, A.I., and Glaser, B. *Pancreatic endocrine tumors*. Grune and Stratton, New York, 1981, pp. 427-461.

54. Von Euler, U.S., and Pernow, B. *Substance P*. Proceedings of the Nobel Symposium. Raven Press, New York, 1977.

55. Wahren, J., Felig, P., Ahlborg, G., and Jorfeldt, L. Glucose metabolism during leg exercise in man. *J. Clin. Invest.* **50**:2715-2725, 1971.

56. Walsh, J.H., and Grossman, M.I. Circulating gastrin in peptic ulcer disease. *Mt. Sinai J. Med.* **40**:374-381, 1973.

57. Walsh, J.H., and Grossman, M.I. Gastrin. *New Engl. J. Med.* **292**:1324-1334, 1975.

58. Williams, J.H., Mager, M., and Jacobson, E.D. Relationship of mesenteric blood flow to intestinal absorption of carbohydrates. *J. Lab. Clin. Med.* **63**:853-863, 1964.

59. Winder, W.W., Hickson, R.C., Hagberg, J.M., Ehsani, A.A., and McLane, J.A. Training-induced changes in hormonal and metabolic responses to submaximal exercise. *J. Appl. Physiol.* **46**:766-771, 1979.

Effects of exercise and physical training on field utilization, insulin sensitivity, and insulin secretion

Philip Felig
Yale University School of Medicine

In this review we will discuss the changes in glucose disposal and turn-over that occur with short-term and prolonged exercise and the mechanisms involved in maintaining glucose homeostasis. Various changes that occur in the diabetic patient with regard to the utilization and production of glucose and other fuels will also be described. In addition, we will examine the effect of the postexercise recovery period on glucose utilization and insulin sensitivity. Finally, we will look at the effect of repeated exercise or physical training on insulin action as well as secretion. Although many investigators and numerous laboratories have contributed to the field of fuel homeostasis in exercise in normal subjects and diabetics (18), this review will deal primarily with work from the author's laboratory and in particular, collaborative studies with Dr. John Wahren and Dr. Gunvor Ahlborg at the Karolinska Institute, and Dr. Walter Zawalich at Yale University.

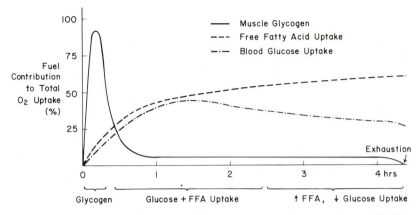

Figure 1—**Schematic representation of relative contributions of glycogen and blood-borne glucose and free fatty acids to overall fuel utilization during exercise.**

Overview of fuel utilization

Let us begin by considering the overall pattern of fuel utilization during exercise as it occurs in normal humans (Figure 1). The nature of the fuel utilized depends in part on the duration as well as the intensity of the exercise performed. Accordingly, we can identify three phases with regard to body fuel consumption. In the earliest phase of exercise, one is dependent on the breakdown of muscle glycogen. As exercise goes beyond the first 10 min or so there is increasing dependence on blood-borne glucose and fatty acids. Consequently, in exercise lasting longer than that performed by the sprinter, muscle glycogen is quantitatively less important whereas circulating glucose and free fatty acids contribute in approximately equal amounts. When exercise continues beyond 1-2 hr, we have a decline in the extent to which blood glucose is being utilized and an increasing dependence on free fatty acids (FFA). The level of FFA in the blood increases progressively with prolonged exercise (2). Availability of FFA thus becomes augmented at the time that the availability of glucose becomes reduced because of liver glycogen depletion (2). It is also recognized that although the quantitative importance of muscle glycogen is maximal in the first few minutes of exercise, there is an ongoing utilization of small amounts of glycogen throughout exercise. Consequently with prolonged exercise, as pointed out by Bergstrom and Hultman (6), exhaustion appears in association with depletion of muscle glycogen stores.

Glucose uptake and production

In normal humans, the effect of exercise on the utilization of glucose and the concentration of glucose in the blood depends on the duration and intensity of the exercise. With exercise lasting 40-90 minutes, there is a marked increase in glucose utilization in proportion to the intensity of the exercise performed (19). In this regard, it is noteworthy that resting muscle derives almost all of its fuel needs from the oxidation of free fatty acids (3). However, during exercise uptake of glucose by muscle will increase to values 7- to 40-fold of that which is observed in the resting state (19). Despite the marked increase in utilization of glucose with exercise, normal humans show little change in blood glucose concentration, or may demonstrate small increases with very intense exercise (19). This ability to maintain blood glucose homeostasis with the marked increase in glucose utilization underscores the existence of a finely integrated system for stimulating glucose production in response to exercise. In fact, overall glucose output from the liver increases as much as four-fold in response to intense exercise (19). These levels of glucose production are among the highest observed under any circumstances of physiology or pathophysiology.

The precise balance between glucose production and utilization which is maintained during periods of exercise lasting 40-90 min is, however, no longer preserved when exercise extends for periods of 2-3 hr or more. In such circumstances of prolonged exercise which would be comparable to a marathon run, a progressive decline in blood glucose concentration is observed (1,2). Recent studies have demonstrated that frank hypoglycemia (blood glucose below 45 mg/dl) is observed in as many as 30-40% of normal subjects during such prolonged exercise (9). The reason for this decline in blood glucose is a failure of glucose production by the liver to keep pace with the ongoing requirements for glucose by exercising muscle (6). This imbalance between glucose production and glucose utilization is a consequence of depleted liver glycogen stores and results in a decline in blood glucose (1).

An interesting question raised by the observations concerning the frequency of hypoglycemia in prolonged exercise is whether such hypoglycemia will impair exercise performance. To answer that question we examined the effect of administering glucose-containing solutions during exercise on exercise endurance. As shown in Figure 2, administration of glucose at 40 or 80 g/hr prevents the decline in blood glucose observed during cycle ergometer exercise at 60% of $\dot{V}O_2$max. On the other hand, as shown in Figure 3, the administration of glucose failed to have a consistent effect on endurance. These studies thus indicate that although hypoglycemia is not uncommon during prolonged exercise, its prevention fails to result in a consistent improvement of exercise performance.

Hormonal and neurogenic regulation
of glucose kinetics during exercise

As shown in Figure 4, exercise is associated with a multiplicity of hor-

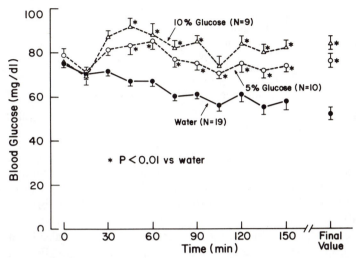

Figure 2 — The blood glucose response to cycle ergometer exercise performed at 60-65% of $\dot{V}O_2$max by normal subjects ingesting either water or glucose at rates of 40 g (5% glucose) or 80 g (10% glucose)/hr. From Felig et al. (9).

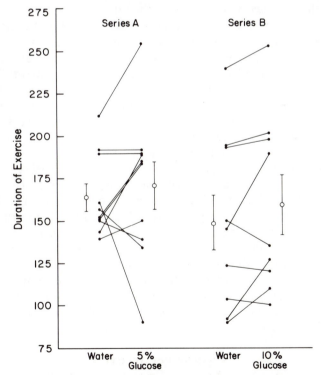

Figure 3 — Failure of glucose ingestion to cause a consistent increase in endurance during prolonged leg exercise. From Felig et al. (9).

↓ Insulin
↑ Glucagon
↑ Epinephrine
↑ Norepinephrine
↑ Cortisol
↑ Growth Hormone
↑ Splanchnic Sympathetic Nerve Discharge

Figure 4—Hormonal and neurogenic factors that influence glucose kinetics during exercise.

monal changes. It is notable that although glucose uptake is markedly increased during exercise, the concentration of plasma insulin declines (1,2,6,9,19). In fact, both in vivo and in vitro studies have demonstrated that only minimal amounts of insulin (concentrations of approximately 2 μU/ml) are required for muscle contraction to result in an increase in glucose uptake (4). Thus, muscle contraction per se acts as a local factor which stimulates glucose uptake independent of the changing hormonal milieu occurring in exercise. In fact, the overall hormonal milieu during exercise (low insulin and high concentrations of counterregulatory hormones) would be expected to reduce overall glucose utilization were it not for the contraction occurring in the muscle.

Although the hormonal pattern during exercise is not of itself expected to increase glucose utilization, it is in fact extremely important for increasing glucose production. Thus, hypoinsulinemia combined with elevated concentrations of glucagon, catecholamines, growth hormone and cortisol will markedly increase the rate of glycogenolysis and gluconeogenesis in the liver. The hormonal milieu is therefore a major factor in providing a signal to the liver that results in an increased glucose production in response to exercise.

It is of note that despite the multiple hormonal changes, no single aspect of this response is indispensible for increasing glucose production during exercise. Specifically, in circumstances in which a decrease in insulin is prevented (8), or an increase in glucagon is inhibited (7,8) there is nevertheless an increase in glucose production in response to exercise. Furthermore, in circumstances of both α- and β-adrenergic blockade in normal humans, glucose production is also increased during exercise (16). These various observations thus suggest that in addition to the hormonal mechanisms, neurogenic stimuli, perhaps in the form of increased outflow along the splanchnic and sympathetic nerves, may be of major importance in dictating the increased glucose production in response to prolonged exercise.

Postexercise recovery

In addition to the changes in glucose kinetics that occur during exercise, changes in glucose uptake and production persist during the recovery

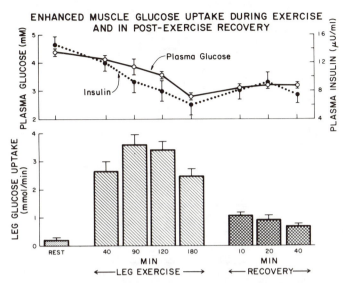

Figure 5 — Plasma insulin and glucose levels and glucose uptake by the legs before, during, and after prolonged leg exercise in normal subjects. Based on the data of Ahlborg and Felig (1).

period. After 2-3 hr of prolonged leg exercise, glucose utilization in previously exercising muscle remains three- to four-fold above basal levels for at least 40 min after cessation of exercise (1) (Figure 5). This increase in glucose uptake by previously exercising muscle is not observed in previously resting muscle and occurs in the face of plasma insulin levels that remain 50% below those observed in the resting state (1) (Figure 5). Thus, the recovery period after exercise constitutes a circumstance of increased insulin sensitivity as reflected by augmented glucose uptake with hypoinsulinemia (1). The importance of glycogen depletion in the previously exercising muscle as a major factor in enhancing this insulin sensitivity has recently been demonstrated by Garetto and colleagues (10). Whether changes in insulin receptors or postreceptor mechanisms mediate these changes in insulin sensitivity remains to be established. It is also noteworthy that when glucose is ingested during postexercise recovery, a relatively greater proportion of the ingested glucose load is utilized for uptake by muscle as compared to liver (14). Consequently, repletion of muscle glycogen would appear to take precedence over repletion of liver glycogen when carbohydrate is ingested in the recovery period.

Exercise in the diabetic

Exercise has long been recommended as part of the overall therapeutic regimen of the insulin-dependent as well as the insulin-independent

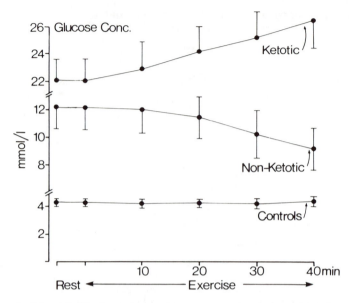

Figure 6 — The blood glucose response to exercise in poorly regulated and moderately regulated insulin-dependent diabetics. From Wahren et al. (14).

diabetic. It has, however, been recognized for more than 60 years that the response of the blood glucose to exercise will depend in part on the status of the diabetes prior to undertaking the exercise. Specifically, in the poorly regulated diabetic with hyperglycemia and ketonemia, exercise will cause an increase rather than a decrease in the blood glucose concentration (20) (Figure 6). On the other hand, even in the moderately well-regulated diabetic, exercise will decrease blood glucose concentration (Figure 6). These differences in response probably reflect the extent to which insulin is available at the time the exercise is initiated and its resultant effects on glucose kinetics.

Concerning glucose uptake by exercising muscle in the diabetic, it was already noted that minimal amounts of insulin (approximately 2 μU/ml) are required for muscle contraction to stimulate glucose utilization (4). Consequently, from a clinical standpoint, the diabetic who is sufficiently well to perform exercise (i.e., the diabetic who is not in overt diabetic ketoacidosis), will generally have sufficient insulin available for the exercise to stimulate glucose utilization. As shown in Figure 7, no diminution in glucose uptake by muscle during exercise was demonstrable in ketonemic or nonketonemic diabetics as compared to healthy controls.

If glucose utilization can be maintained even in poorly regulated diabetics, what is responsible for the increase in hyperglycemia? The rise in blood glucose is primarily a consequence of overstimulated glucose production. Thus, the diabetic who is insulin-deficient has an augmented

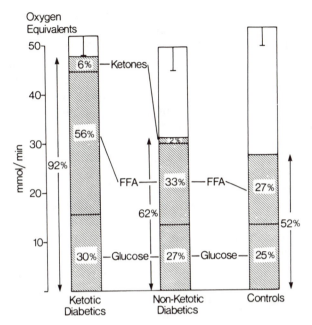

Figure 7—Influence of exercise on the uptake of glucose, free fatty acids, and ketones in normal and diabetic subjects. The "ketotic" diabetics had blood ketone acid levels of 3-4 mM but were not in frank diabetic ketoacidosis. From Wahren et al. (14).

rate of gluconeogenesis as well as ketogenesis in response to exercise (20). This increase in glucose production may not be a consequence of insulin deficiency per se, but may also be related to the excessive rise in counter-regulatory hormones which accompanies exercise in the poorly regulated diabetic (17). Poorly controlled diabetics demonstrate plasma concentrations of epinephrine, norepinephrine, and growth hormone that are greater than those observed in healthy controls or in well-regulated diabetics exercised at the same level of intensity (17).

The clinical implications of these findings are as follows: Exercise cannot be viewed as a substitute for but rather as an adjunct in the overall treatment of diabetes. Unless management of diabetes by means of insulin, diet, and/or oral agents results in at least moderate control of the diabetes, exercise cannot be expected to improve the clinical situation, but may in fact worsen blood glucose regulation.

Physical training

In recent years interest has been growing in the effects of physical training on glucose homeostasis and insulin sensitivity not only during exercise but in the resting state as well. Observations by Lohmann et al. (13)

have demonstrated that very well-trained athletes show low levels of plasma insulin in the resting state and in response to a glucose load. The ability to maintain normal glucose homeostasis in the face of low plasma insulin levels suggests an increase in insulin sensitivity. Inasmuch as insulin resistance is almost always present in Type II (insulin-independent) diabetes and may also be present in some patients with Type I (insulin-dependent) diabetes, the therapeutic usefulness of physical training in the management of diabetes has received attention. Detailed studies on the effects of physical training, however, reveal that it alters a multiplicity of aspects of glucose homeostasis which include muscle sensitivity to insulin, β-cell secretion of insulin, and insulin-inducible enzymes in liver.

Concerning muscle sensitivity to insulin, studies in normal subjects have demonstrated that a 6-week training program results in a 30-35% increase in the rate of insulin-mediated glucose uptake by muscle tissue (11). These changes in insulin sensitivity may be mediated by an increase in the number of insulin receptors, as studies have shown that athletes have augmented numbers of insulin receptors (12). These changes in muscle sensitivity to insulin have also been documented in the rat (5,15) and provide an explanation for the ability to maintain normal glucose homeostasis despite lower levels of plasma insulin in trained subjects.

In addition to the effects in muscle tissue, physical training also alters the responsiveness of the β-cells in the islets of Langerhans to the stimulatory effects of glucose on insulin secretion (21). As already noted, well-trained athletes demonstrate a diminished insulin response to glucose administration. In studies with perfused islets obtained from rats that underwent physical training for 3-6 weeks (running 2 miles or more per day), Zawalich et al. observed a diminished insulin response to the stimulatory effects of 10 mM glucose (21) (Figure 8). This decrease in glucose-mediated insulin secretion occurred in the absence of a change in β-cell sensitivity to glucose and is demonstrable in the absence of neurogenic or hormonal influences.

The third major site of glucose homeostasis that is influenced by physical training is the liver. In contrast to the increase in insulin sensitivity demonstrated by muscle, the liver from rats that have undergone physical training demonstrates evidence of an insulin-deficient and/or insulin-resistant state. In perfused livers obtained from rats that have undergone physical training, insulin was less effective in inhibiting glucose release by the liver (15). Furthermore, the activity of glucokinase, an insulin-inducible enzyme, was markedly reduced in livers obtained from exercise-trained rats (21). It is well-recognized that the activity of glucokinase is determined at least in part by the ambient insulin concentration and is reduced in circumstances of hypoinsulinemia such as starvation, diabetes, or carbohydrate restriction. Thus, the decrease in glucokinase observed after physical training suggests that the liver is re-

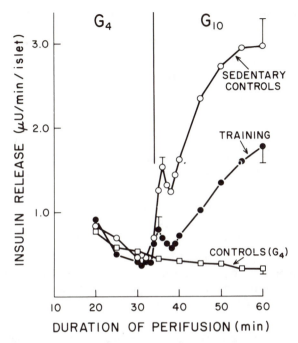

Figure 8 — Influence of physical training on the insulin response of perfused islets to basal glucose levels (4 mM) and physiological increments in glucose concentration (10 mM). Training resulted in a diminution in the insulin response to 10 mM glucose. From Zawalich et al. (21).

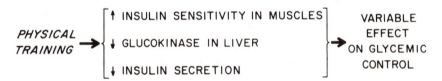

Figure 9 — Multiplicity of effects of physical training on muscle, liver, and islet cells. Because of this multiplicity of actions, the net effect on glucose tolerance in the diabetic is variable.

flecting the reduction in insulin secretion which characterizes physical training and does not demonstrate the enhanced insulin sensitivity observed in muscle tissue.

The multiple effects of physical training on muscle, liver, and islet cells indicate the complexity of the glucose response to physical training and its variable effect on glucose tolerance (Figure 9). A consistent effect of physical training in lowering plasma insulin levels and in increasing muscle sensitivity to insulin can be expected. On the other hand, because insulin secretion decreases and the liver will reflect the lack of insulin, an improvement in glucose tolerance may not be observed consistently. Thus, as in the case of acute exercise, the effects of physical training on overall blood glucose control in the diabetic will depend not only on physical training but also on other factors of management such as insulin administration, diet, and where appropriate, the use of oral hypoglycemic agents.

References

1. Ahlborg, G., and Felig, P. Lactate and glucose exchange across the forearm, legs and splanchnic bed during and after prolonged leg exercise. *J. Clin. Invest.* **69**:45, 1982.

2. Ahlborg, G., Felig, P., Hagenfeldt, L., and Wahren, J. Substrate turnover during prolonged exercise in man: Splanchnic and leg metabolism of glucose, free fatty acids and amino acids. *J. Clin. Invest.* **53**:1080, 1974.

3. Andres, R., Cader, G., and Zierler, K.L. The quantitatively minor role of carbohydrate in oxidative metabolism by skeletal muscle in intact man in the basal state. Measurements of oxygen and glucose uptake and carbon dioxide and lactate production in the forearm. *J. Clin. Invest.* **35**:671, 1956.

4. Berger, M., Hagg, S., and Ruderman, N.B. Glucose metabolism in perfused skeletal muscle: Interaction of insulin and exercise on glucose uptake. *Biochem. J.* **146**:231, 1975.

5. Berger, M., et al. Effect of physical training on glucose tolerance and on glucose metabolism of skeletal muscle in anaesthetized normal rats. *Diabetologia* **16**:179, 1979.

6. Bergstrom, J., and Hultman, E. A study of glycogen metabolism during exercise. *Scand. J. Lab. Clin. Invest.* **19**:218, 1967.

7. Bjorkman, O., Felig, P., Hagenfeldt, L., and Wahren, J. Influence of hypoglucagonemia on splanchnic glucose output during leg exercise in man. *Clin. Physiol.* **1**:43, 1981.

8. Felig, P., and Wahren, J. Role of insulin and glucagon in the regulation of hepatic glucose production during exercise. *Diabetes* **28**(Suppl. 1):71, 1979.

9. Felig, P., Ali Cherif, M.S., Minagawa, A., and Wahren, J. Hypoglycemia during prolonged exercise in normal man. *New Engl. J. Med.* **306**:895, 1982.

10. Garetto, L.D., Richter, E.A., and Ruderman, N.G. Increased insulin sensitivity of skeletal muscle following exercise. *Diabetes* **30**(Suppl. 1):63A, 1981.

11. Koivisto, V.A., DeFronzo, R., Hendler, R., and Felig, P. The difference in insulin sensitivity and metabolic response to acute exercise in trained and sedentary subjects. In: M. Berger, P. Christacopoulos, and J. Wahren (eds.), *Diabetes and exercise*, Hans Huber, Bern, 1982, pp. 122-132.

12. LeBlanc, J., et al. Effects of physical training and adipocity on glucose metabolism and ^{125}I-insulin binding. *J. Appl. Physiol.* **46**:235, 1979.

13. Lohmann, D., et al. Diminished insulin response in highly trained athletes. *Metabolism* **27**:521, 1978.

14. Maehlum, S., Felig, P., and Wahren, J. Splanchnic glucose and muscle glycogen after glucose feeding during post exercise recovery. *Am. J. Physiol.* **235**:E255, 1978.

15. Mondon, C.E., Dolkas, C.B., and Reaven, G.M. Site of enhanced insulin sensitivity in exercise-trained rats at rest. *Am. J. Physiol.* **239**:E169-E177, 1980.

16. Simonson, D., Sherwin, R., and DeFronzo, R. Adrenergic blockade alters glucose kinetics in diabetics during exercise. *Diabetes* **30**(Suppl. 1):43, 1981.

17. Tamborlane, W.V., Sherwin, R.S., Koivisto, V., Hendler, R., Genel, M., and Felig, P. Normalization of the growth hormone and catecholamine response to exercise in juvenile onset diabetics treated with a portable insulin infusion pump. *Diabetes* **28**:785, 1979.

18. Vranic, M., and Berger, M. Exercise and diabetes mellitus. *Diabetes* **28**:147, 1979.

19. Wahren, J., Felig, P., Ahlborg, G., and Jorfeldt, H. Glucose metabolism during leg exercise in man. *J. Clin. Invest.* **50**:2715, 1971.

20. Wahren, J., Hagenfeldt, L., and Felig, P. Splanchnic and leg exchange of glucose, amino acids and free fatty acids during exercise in diabetes mellitus. *J. Clin. Invest.* **55**:1382, 1975.

21. Zawalich, W., Maturo, S., and Felig, P. Influence of physical training on insulin release and glucose utilization by islet cells and liver glucokinase activity in the rat. *Am. J. Physiol.* **243**:E464, 1982.

Exercise, nutrition, puberty, and fertility: Delayed menarche and amenorrhea

Rose E. Frisch
Harvard Center for Population Studies

Too little fat or too much fat

Undernutrition delays sexual development in girls and boys (6,13) as in other mammals (19). Some factor other than chronological age therefore controls puberty. Undernutrition, chronic or acute, also causes the cessation of established reproductive ability in the human female (13) and male (23), as well as in other mammals.

Frisch and McArthur (13) found that the onset and maintenance of regular menstrual function in women are each dependent on the attainment and maintenance of a minimal weight for height, apparently representing a critical fat storage. Data from both nonanorectic and anorectic female patients showed that a loss of body weight in the range of 10-15% below normal weight for height, which represents a loss of about one-third of body fat, resulted in amenorrhea. Weight gain following refeeding restored cycles after varying intervals of time (27). These findings imply that a particular body composition of fat/lean, or fat/body weight may be an important determinant of menarche and of mature reproductive ability. Both the absolute and relative amounts of fat are important, since the lean mass and the fat must be in a particular absolute range as well as a relative range; that is, the individual must be big enough to reproduce (9). Metabolic rate was considered important because a food intake-lipostat-metabolic signal was hypothesized to explain Kennedy's elegant findings on weight and puberty in the rat (21,22).

Data of obese women show that excessive fatness also is associated with amenorrhea (20,32). Too much fat, or too little fat, therefore are both associated with disruption of sexual function in the human female (9).

The recent findings that aromatization of androgens to estrogens takes place in adipose tissue, in female breast fat and abdominal fat (30), in the omentum (34), and in the fatty marrow of the long bones (12) suggest that adipose tissue may be a significant extragonadal source of estrogen. Body weight, hence fatness, also influences the direction of estrogen metabolism to the most potent or least potent forms (4). The high percentage of fat, about 24% at menarche and about 26-28% (8) in the average (165 cm, 57 kg) US woman at the completion of her growth thus may influence reproductive ability directly.

Athletes, ballet dancers, and menstrual periodicity

The importance of a critical level of fat in relation to the lean body mass for successful reproduction suggested that high energy outputs, in addition to low nutritional intake, would affect female menstrual periodicity. Ballet dancers (18,40) and athletes who train seriously in fact have a high incidence of irregular cycles and amenorrhea, and girls who begin their training at young ages before menarche have a delayed age of menarche (16,17) as will be discussed in detail later.

Initial findings: Weight at puberty

The idea that relative fatness is important for female reproductive ability followed from our first findings that the events of the adolescent growth spurt, particularly menarche in girls, were each closely related to an average critical body weight (14). The mean weight at menarche for US girls was 47.8 ± 0.5 kg, at the mean height of 158.5 ± 0.5 cm and the mean age of 12.9 ± 0.1 yr. This mean age includes girls from Denver, who have a slightly later age of menarche than the rest of the population due to the slowing effect of altitude on growth rate (14).

Since individual girls have menarche at all different weights and heights, the notion of an average critical weight of 47 kg for early and late maturing girls at menarche was analyzed in terms of the components of body weight at menarche (15). Body composition was investigated because total body water (TW) and lean body weight (LBW, TW/0.72) are more closely correlated with metabolic rate than is body weight.

The greatest change in estimated body composition of both early and late maturing girls during the adolescent growth spurt was an 120% increase in body fat, compared to a 44% increase in lean body weight. There was thus a change in ratio of LBW to fat from 5:1 at initiation of the growth spurt to 3:1 at menarche (8,15).

The secular trend toward an earlier age of menarche

Even before analyzing the meaning of the critical weight for an individual girl, the idea that menarche is associated with a critical weight for a population explained simply many observations associated with early or late menarche. Observations of earlier menarche are associated with attaining the critical weight more quickly. The most important example is the secular trend toward an earlier menarche of about 3 or 4 months per decade in Europe and the US in the last 100 years. Our explanation, supported by historical data, was that children now are bigger sooner. Therefore, girls on the average reach 46-47 kg, the mean weight at menarche for the US and many European populations, more quickly (6). According to our hypothesis also, the secular trend should end when the weight of children of successive cohorts remains the same because of the attainment of maximum nutrition and child care, which now may have happened (3).

Conversely, a late menarche is associated with body weight growth that is slowed prenatally, postnatally, or both so that the average critical weight is reached at a later age; malnutrition delays menarche (6,10); twins have later menarche than singletons of the same population; and high altitude delays menarche (14).

Total body water as percentage of body weight, (TW/BWt%): An indicator of fatness

Total body water as a percentage of body weight (TW/BWt%) is a more important index than the absolute amount of total water because it is an index of fatness (5) (Table 1). Percentiles of total body water/body weight percentage, which are percentiles of fatness, were made at menarche and again for the same girls at age 18 yr (Figure 1), the age at which body composition was stabilized (13). From clinical data we found that 56.1% of total water/body weight, the 10th percentile at age 18 yrs, which is equivalent to about 22% fat of body weight, indicated a minimal weight for height necessary for the restoration and maintenance of menstrual cycles. For example, a 20-yr-old woman whose height is 160 cm (63 in.) should weigh at least 46.3 kg (102 lb) before menstrual cycles would be expected to resume (13) (Figure 1).

Table 1

Total Water/Body Weight Percentage[a] as an Index of Fatness: Comparison of Girl, Age 18, and Boy, Age 15, of Same Height and Weight

	Girl—18 yr	Boy—15 yr
Height (cm)	165.0	165.0
Weight (kg)	57.0	57.0
Total body water (TBW) (l)	29.5	36.0
Lean body weight (TBW/0.72) (kg)	41.0	50.0
Fat (kg)	16.0	7.0
$\dfrac{\text{Fat}}{\text{Body weight}}$ (%)	28.0	12.0
$\dfrac{\text{Total body water}}{\text{Body weight}}$ (%)	51.8	63.0

Fat/body wt % $= 100 - $ (TW/BWt%)/0.72.

[a]Estimated by equations in ref. 28.

Girls: TBW $= -10.313 + 0.252$ (Wt$_{kg}$) $+ 0.154$ (ht$_{cm}$), when ht ≥ 110.8 cm

Boys: TBW $= -21.993 + 0.406$ (Wt) $+ 0.209$ (ht), when ht ≥ 132.7 cm.

Reprinted from Frisch (11).

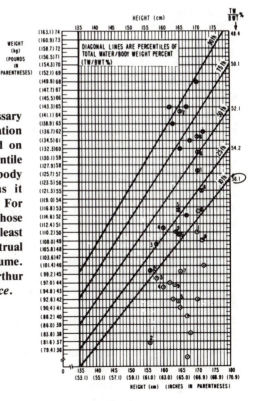

Figure 1 – Minimal weight necessary for a particular height for restoration of menstrual cycles is indicated on the weight scale by the 10th percentile diagonal line of total water/body weight percentage, 56.1%, as it crosses the vertical height line. For example, a 20-year-old woman whose height is 160 cm should weigh at least 46.3 kg (102 lb) before menstrual cycles would be expected to resume. Reprinted from Frisch and McArthur (13) with permission from *Science*.

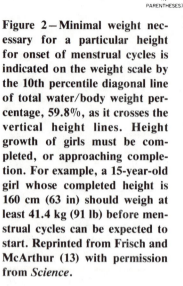

Figure 2 – Minimal weight necessary for a particular height for onset of menstrual cycles is indicated on the weight scale by the 10th percentile diagonal line of total water/body weight percentage, 59.8%, as it crosses the vertical height lines. Height growth of girls must be completed, or approaching completion. For example, a 15-year-old girl whose completed height is 160 cm (63 in) should weigh at least 41.4 kg (91 lb) before menstrual cycles can be expected to start. Reprinted from Frisch and McArthur (13) with permission from *Science*.

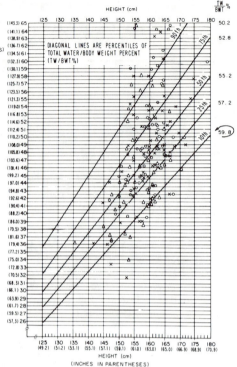

The weights at which menstrual cycles ceased or resumed in postmenarcheal patients ages 16 and older were about 10% heavier than the minimal weights for the same height observed at menarche (13) (Figure 2).

In accord with this finding, the data on body composition show that both early and late maturing girls gain an average of 4.5 kg of fat from menarche to age 18 yr. Almost all of this gain is achieved by age 16 yr, when mean fat is 15.7 ± 0.3 kg, 27% of body weight. At age 18 yr mean fat is 16.0 ± 0.3 kg, 28% of the mean body weight of 57.1 ± 0.6 kg. Reflecting this increase in fatness, the total water/body weight percentage decreases from 55.1 ± 0.2% at menarche (12.9 ± 0.1 yr in our sample) to 52.1 ± 0.2% (*SD* 3.0) at age 18 yr (8).

Because girls are less fat at menarche than when they achieve stable reproductive ability, the minimal weight for onset of menstrual cycles in cases of primary amenorrhea due to undernutrition is indicated by the 10th percentile of fractional body water at menarche, 59.8%, which is equivalent to about 17% of body weight as fat. For example, a 15-yr-old girl whose completed height is 160 cm (63 inches) should weigh at least 41.4 kg (91 lb) before menstrual cycles can be expected to begin (13) (Figure 2). The minimal weights indicated in Figure 2 also would be used

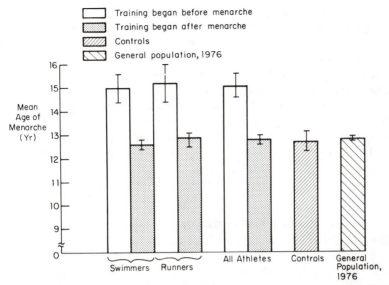

Figure 3 — Mean (± *SEM*) ages of menarche of swimmers, runners, and all athletes according to whether training began before or after menarche, compared to the mean menarcheal age of the controls and the general population, 1976. Reprinted from Frisch et al. (17) with permission of *J. Am. Med. Assoc.*

for girls who become amenorrheic as a result of weight loss shortly after menarche, as is often found in cases of anorexia nervosa in adolescent girls.

The absolute and relative increases in fatness from menarche to ages 16-18 yr coincides with the period of adolescent sterility (29). During this time there is still rapid growth of the uterus, the ovaries, and the oviducts (37).

Other factors, such as emotional stress, affect the maintenance or onset of menstrual cycles. Therefore, menstrual cycles may cease without weight loss and may not resume in some subjects even though the minimal weight for height has been achieved. Also, our standards apply as yet only to Caucasian US females and European females, since different races have different critical weights at menarche and it is not yet known whether the different critical weights represent the same critical body composition of fatness (13).

Fatness and reproductive efficiency

The weight changes associated with the cessation and restoration of menstrual cycles are in the range of 10-15% of body weight. Weight loss or weight gain of this magnitude is mainly loss or gain of fat (24). This suggested that a minimal level of stored, easily mobilized energy was necessary for ovulation and menstrual cycles in the human female (7,13).

The main function of the 16 kg of fat stored on average by early and late maturing girls by age 18 yr may be to provide easily mobilized energy for a pregnancy and for lactation; the 144,000 calories would be sufficient for a pregnancy, which requires about 50,000 calories over and above normal metabolic needs, and 3 months' lactation. Lactation requires about 1,000 calories a day (7).

Because infant survival is correlated with birth weight, and birth weight is correlated with the mother's prepregnancy weight, the regulation of female body size and body composition at menarche has obvious selective advantages for the species. In prehistoric times, when food supplies were scarce or fluctuated seasonally and lactation was a necessity, stored fat would have been important for successful reproduction (7,13).

Body weight changes and gonadotropin secretion

Endocrine studies of undernourished, nonanorectic subjects being refed showed that the mean initial serum follicle-stimulating hormone (FSH) concentration was within the limits of normal for young women of reproductive age, but the serum luteinizing (LH) concentration and the vaginal maturation score were low. As weight was regained, serum LH concentration increased and the vaginal maturation score rose. After weight gain to levels close to the normal range, spontaneous menses occurred but were anovulatory in 70% of the cases. Regular ovulatory cycles began with continued weight gain (27).

Boyer et al. (2) found that the type of LH secretory pattern, prepubertal or pubertal, was closely correlated with the extent of loss or gain of body weight. Comparison of total water/body weight percentage (TW/BWt%) with the normal values found at adolescence, menarche, and age 18 yr showed that a prepubertal body composition was correlated with a prepubertal LH secretory pattern, and a pubertal body composition was correlated with a pubertal LH secretion (9).

Vigersky et al. (39) concluded from hormonal data and temperature regulation of nonanorectic women with secondary amenorrhea that hypothalamic dysfunction may be caused by weight loss per se. Peak plasma LH hormone level response to LH-RH was delayed in these subjects and the delay was correlated with percentage below ideal body weight. Thermoregulation at 10 and 49°C was abnormal and correlated with the percentage below ideal body weight.

Delayed menarche and amenorrhea of dancers and athletes

Ballet dancers and athletes have a delayed age of menarche and a high incidence of irregular cycles and amenorrhea. Some dancers and athletes who began their training at age 9 or 10 years still had not had menarche at ages 18 to 20 years (16-18, 40). The delayed menarche, irregular cycles, and amenorrhea of the ballet dancers was correlated with excessive thinness (18).

However, the question arises: Does intense exercise cause delayed menarche and amenorrhea of athletes, or do late maturers choose to become athletes? To answer this question, menarche and changes in menstrual periodicity of 21 college swimmers and 17 runners, mean age 19.1 $\pm$ 0.2 yr were studied in relation to the age of training initiation, physical indices, and stress indices (16,17).

At the start of the study each athlete and control completed questionnaires on age of menarche, history of menstrual periodicity, and medical history. Athletes recorded duration and intensity of previous training and competition. Classifications of menstrual characteristics were: *primary amenorrhea*, "no menarche to date" (all athletes were 17 yr or older); *secondary amenorrhea*, a 6-month interval between cycles; *irregular*, cycles differing in length by 9 or more days. Age of menarche was recorded in yr and the month when known.

The athletes kept a log of menses, and a subset also kept a daily record of body temperature, taken with an oral basal temperature thermometer (Becton-Dickinson, 3 min) at bedtime, recording the time. Evening temperatures were used because temperature fluctuations are less at this time (17).

Covariance analysis of the age athletic training began and the age of menarche of all athletes showed that they were only weakly related: r_{xy} = -0.257. Therefore, the age of menarche and the age at which training began could be treated as independent variables (17).

The mean age of menarche of all the athletes, 13.9 $\pm$ 0.3 yr, was significantly later ($p < 0.001$) than that of the general population, 12.8 $\pm$ 0.05, in accord with other reports (26). However, the mean menarcheal age of the 18 athletes whose training began *before* menarche was 15.1 $\pm$ 0.5 yr, whereas the mean menarcheal age of the 20 athletes whose training began *after* their menarche was 12.8 $\pm$ 0.2 yr ($p < 0.001$). This latter mean age was similar to that of the college controls, 12.7 $\pm$ 0.4 yr, and the general population (Figure 3).

Both swimmers and runners showed this significant difference in menarcheal age according to when training began: Premenarcheal-trained swimmers averaged 15.0 $\pm$ 0.6 yr at menarche, whereas their postmenarcheal-trained teammates averaged 12.6 $\pm$ 0.2 yr ($p < 0.01$) at menarche. Similarly, the premenarcheal-trained runners averaged 15.2 $\pm$ 0.8 yr at menarche whereas the postmenarcheal-trained runners averaged 12.9 $\pm$ 0.4 yr at menarche.

For all premenarcheal-trained athletes, menarche was delayed 5 months (0.4 yr) for each year of training before menarche (Figure 4):

$$\text{Age of menarche} = 13.32 + 0.414 \, (\pm 0.162) \, \text{yr}_{tr}$$
$$p < 0.05; r = 0.527$$

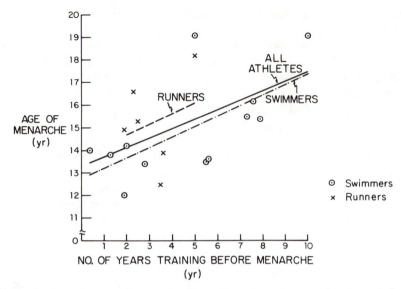

Figure 4 — Age of menarche as a function of number of years of training before menarche for 12 swimmers (⊙), six runners (x), and all athletes. For swimmers, menarche was delayed by 6 months (0.5 yr) for each year of training before menarche ($p < 0.05$). For all athletes, menarche was delayed by 5 months (0.4 yr) for each year of training ($p < 0.05$). The slope for the runners was not significantly different from zero. Reprinted from Frisch et al. (17) with permission of *J. Am. Med. Assoc.*

Differences in incidence of menstrual disturbances

At the start of the season, 61.1% of the 18 premenarcheal-trained athletes had irregular cycles, 22.4% were amenorrheic, and 16.7% had regular cycles. In contrast, 60.0% of the 20 postmenarcheal-trained athletes had regular cycles; 40.0% were irregular, and none were amenorrheic (Figure 5). During the athletic season both pre- and postmenarcheal-trained athletes had an increased incidence of oligomenorrhea and/or amenorrhea (Figure 5).

Physical indices

Five athletes, three of whom were amenorrheic and two oligomenorrheic, were below or very close to the minimal weight for their height found necessary for normal cycles in nonathletic women (13). The remaining athletes, however, were each above the minimal weight for her height (Figure 6). The runners were significantly ($p < 0.05$) leaner than their postmenarcheal-trained teammates. Ultrasound measurements of subcutaneous fat thickness of the mid-thigh, iliac crest pad, and abdomen (lateral to the umbilicus) of the athletes (Frisch, Birnholz, and

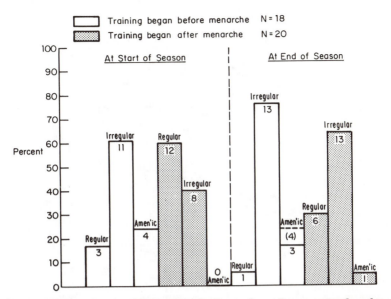

Figure 5 — Percentages of athletes with regular or irregular menstrual cycles, or amenorrhea at start and end of athletic season, according to whether training began before or after menarche. Dotted line (amenorrheic bar, end of season) includes one subject with primary amenorrhea who had cycles induced. Reprinted from Frisch et al. (17) with permission of *J. Am. Med. Assoc.*

Welbergen, unpublished data) showed that the top ranking athletes had little subcutaneous fat at these sites.

Endocrine studies

Six swimmers with secondary amenorrhea or oligomenorrhea averaged low-normal gonadotropins, prolactin, and estrogen. Progesterone concentration was consistent with levels observed in the follicular phase. Testosterone, free testosterone, and androstenedione were in the normal range, as were serum T_4, T_3, RT_3, and TSH (16). (Thyroid hormone assays were performed by Mark E. Molitch, M.D., Tufts New England Medical Center.) The average vaginal maturation score of the six swimmers was low, 52.1 ± 2.8 of a possible 100% (27).

Dietary record

A 7-day food diary showed that the 13 premenarcheal-trained athletes consumed significantly fewer daily calories, $1,773 \pm 156.3$, compared to the 11 postmenarcheal-trained athletes $2,288 \pm 144.8$, ($p < 0.05$). The premenarcheal group also ate significantly less protein, 71 ± 6.9 g, compared to 92 ± 7.1 g ($p < 0.05$); a lower percentage of calories from fat

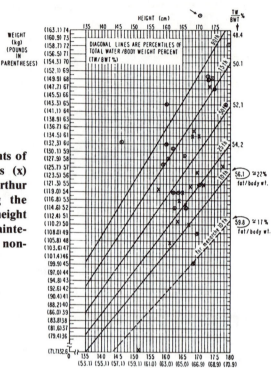

Figure 6—Heights and weights of swimmers (⊙) and runners (x) plotted on the Frisch-McArthur nomagram (13) indicating the minimal weight for a given height for menarche and the maintenance of regular cycles for non-athletc women.

($p < 0.05$), 32.8 ± 1.4 compared to 37.7 ± 1.2; less total fat, 65 ± 6.7 g, compared to 95 ± 6.2 g ($p < 0.01$); less saturated fat, 17.5 ± 2.1 g compared to 33.8 ± 2.5 g ($p < 0.001$); and less calcium, 856 ± 117 mg compared to 1,321 ± 147 mg ($p < 0.05$), than their postmenarcheal-trained teammates.

Conclusions from athlete study

Our findings from athletes classified by whether their training began before or after their menarche indicate that intense physical activity does in fact delay menarche, since the runners and swimmers who began their training before menarche attained menarche over 2 yr later than their teammates whose training began after menarche. Also, the average age of menarche of the postmenarcheal group did not differ from that of controls or the general population.

Irregular cycles and anovulatory cycles are expected for 1-3 yr after menarche. The greater incidence of irregularity and secondary amenorrhea among the premenarcheal-trained runners and swimmers, therefore, might be explained solely by their later average age of menarche. However, our data show that the intensive training directly increased the incidence of menstrual disturbances, since during the training season an increase in oligomenorrhea occurred not only among the premenarcheal-trained group, but also among the postmenarcheal-trained group.

The amenorrhea of swimmers who were below the threshold weight for height found necessary for regular cycles in nonathletic women may be explained in the same way as for nonathletic women (13) and dancers (18): too little fat in relation to the lean mass. The fact that a 2.3-kg (5-lb) weight increase above the threshold weight was followed by the reappearance of a cycle, and the loss of this weight was accompanied by a loss of the cycle in a swimmer, supports this explanation.

A raised lean/fat ratio may also be the explanation of the amenorrhea and oligomenorrhea of athletes who were of average or even above average weight for height, because their body weight undoubtedly represented a greater amount of muscle and less adipose tissue than the same weight for a nonathletic woman (1,26). Behnke et al. (1) found over three decades ago that physically fit male football players, who had been misclassified as overweight, in fact had little adipose tissue and a great deal of muscle. Pǎrízková (33) describes the change to increased muscularity in women athletes and also the reversion with inactivity, to less muscularity and an increase of adiposity. Also, a high proportion of athletes reported weight changes of more than 10% of their weight in the year preceding the study. Weight loss in this range (13,39) and rapid fluctuations in weight (32) are associated with menstrual disturbances.

Since human female adipose tissue in the breast, abdomen (30), omentum (34), and fatty marrow of the long bones (12) converts androgen to estrogen, adipose tissue is a significant extragonadal source of estrogen. Body weight, hence fatness, also affects the pathway of metabolism of estrogen to its most potent or least potent form (4). The amount of adipose tissue may thus directly affect hormonal regulation of short- or long-term feedback mechanisms controlling the menstrual cycle and ovulation (9,27).

Finally, the tension and stress of training and competition may increase the secretion of adrenal cortiscosteroids and catecholamines, which affects the hypothalamic control of gonadotropins (35,36). All these possibilities are consistent with the general explanation of dysfunction or failure of the hypothalamic pituitary axis (38). Because, as we and others found, a cessation of training (18,40), or a reduction in intensity of training, and/or increased nutrition (27) can result in the return of cycles, there is no reason to suspect long-term deleterious effects. However, long-range follow-up studies are needed to compare the menstrual and reproductive histories and lifespans of athletic and nonathletic women.

Nutrition and male reproduction

Undernutrition delays the onset of sexual maturation in boys, similar to the delaying effect of undernutrition on menarche (14). Undernutrition and weight loss in men also affects their reproductive ability. The sequence of effects, however, is different from that of the female. In men, loss of libido is the first effect of a decrease in caloric intake and subsequent weight loss. Continued caloric reduction and weight loss results in a loss of prostate fluid and decreased sperm motility and sperm longevity, in that order. Sperm production ceases when weight loss is in the range of 25% of normal body weight. Refeeding results in a restoration of function in the reverse order of loss (23). The effect of exercise on male reproductive ability has not been studied, as far as I know.

Summary and conclusions

We have proposed that adipose tissue itself may be a determinant of menarche and mature reproductive ability through: (a) the conversion of androgens to estrogen—a critical amount of estrogen may be necessary to prime the ovary (27); (b) body weight, hence fatness, influences the direction of estrogen metabolism to the most potent or least potent forms—extreme leanness may be related to the production of anti-estrogens, the catechol estrogens (4); and (c) changes in body fat composition are correlated with changes in sex hormone-binding globulin, thus regulating the availability of estradiol to the brain and other target tissues (31).

Clinically, the minimal weight for height findings have been found useful in cases of nutritional amenorrhea. Knuth et al. (25) point out that "dietary treatment of patients with amenorrhea and loss of weight may replace gonadotropin therapy for induction of ovulation in a significant proportion of patients with anovulatory infertility."

With the ever increasing number of serious women athletes and dancers, clinicians are seeing more cases of delayed menarche and amenorrhea due to regular intense exercise (16-18,40). These effects of undernutrition and exercise on menarche and the menstrual cycle are apparently reversible. In some subjects a 1 or 2 kg weight change will turn cycles on and off (17). However, nothing is known as yet about the mechanisms involved, or about the long-term effects on fertility.

Acknowledgments

The research on college athletes was supported by the Advanced Medical Research Foundation of Boston. I thank Dr. Mark Molitch, Tufts New England Medical Center, for the assays of the thyroid hormones, and

Dr. Seymour Reichlin, Tufts New England Medical Center, for helpful discussion. Thanks to Susan Morrison and Rosemary Moore for secretarial assistance with the manuscript.

References

1. Behnke, A.R., Feen, G.B., and Welham, W.C. The specific gravity of healthy men. Body weight:volume as an index of obesity. *J. Am. Med. Assoc.* **118**:495-498, 1942.

2. Boyer, R.M., Katz, J., Finkelstein, J.W., Kapen, S., Weiner, E.D., and Hellman, L. Anorexia nervosa: Immaturity of the 24-hour luteinizing hormone secretory pattern. *New Engl. J. Med.* **291**:861-865, 1974.

3. Damon, A. Larger body size and earlier menarche: The end may be in sight. *Soc. Biol.* **21**:8-11, 1974.

4. Fishman, J., Boyer, R.M., and Hellman, L. Influence of body weight on estradiol metabolism in young women. *J. Clin. Endocrinol. Metab.* **41**:989-991, 1975.

5. Friis-Hansen, B.J. Changes in body water compartments during growth. *Acta Paediatr. Stockholm Suppl.* **110**:1-67, 1956.

6. Frisch, R.E. Weight at menarche: Similarity for well-nourished and undernourished girls at differing ages, and evidence for historical constancy. *Pediatrics* **50**:445-450, 1972.

7. Frisch, R.E. Demographic implications of the biological determinants of female fecundity. *Soc. Biol.* **22**:17-22, 1975.

8. Frisch, R.E. Fatness of girls from menarche to age 18 years, with a nomogram. *Human Biol.* **48**:353-359, 1976.

9. Frisch, R.E. Food intake, fatness and reproductive ability. In: R. Vigersky (ed.), *Anorexia nervosa*, Raven, New York, 1977, pp. 149-161.

10. Frisch, R.E. Population, food intake and fertility. *Science* **199**:22-30, 1978.

11. Frisch, R.E. What's below the surface? *New Engl. J. Med.* **305**:1019-1020, 1981.

12. Frisch, R.E., Canick, J.A., and Tulchinsky, D. Human fatty marrow aromatizes androgen to estrogen. *J. Clin. Endocrinol. Metab.* **51**:394-396, 1980.

13. Frisch, R.E., and McArthur, J.W. Menstrual cycles: Fatness as a determinant of minimum weight for height necessary for their maintenance or onset. *Science* **185**:149-151, 1974.

14. Frisch, R.E., and Revelle, R. Height and weight at menarche and a hypothesis of menarche. *Arch. Dis. Childhood* **46**:659-701, 1971.

15. Frisch, R.E., Revelle, R., and Cook, S. Components of weight at menarche and the initiation of the adolescent growth spurt in girls: Estimated total water, lean body weight and fat. *Human Biol.* **45**:469-483, 1973.

16. Frisch, R.E., von Gotz-Welbergen, A., McArthur, J.W., Albright, T., Witschi, J., Bullen, B., Birnholz, J., Reed, R.B., and Hermann, H. Annual Meeting, Endocrine Society, Program Abstract 147, June 1981, Cincinnati, p. 119.

17. Frisch, R.E., von Gotz-Welbergen, A., McArthur, J.W., Albright, T., Witschi, J., Bullen, B., Birnholz, J., Reed, R.B., and Hermann, H. Delayed menarche and amenorrhea of college athletes in relation to age of onset of training. *J. Am. Med. Assoc.* **246**:1559-1563, 1981.

18. Frisch, R.E., Wyshak, G., and Vincent L. Delayed menarche and amenorrhea of ballet dancers. *New Engl. J. Med.* **303**:1125-1126, 1980.

19. Hammond, J. (ed.) *Progress in the physiology of farm animals*, vol. 2, Butterworths, London, 1955.

20. Hartz, A.J., Barboriak, P.N., Wong, A., Katayama, K.P., and Rimm, A.A. The association of obesity with infertility and related menstrual abnormalities in women. *Int. J. Obesity* **3**:57-73, 1979.

21. Kennedy, G.C. Interactions between feeding behavior and hormones during growth. *Ann. N.Y. Acad. Sci.* **157**:1049-1061, 1969.

22. Kennedy, G.C., and Mitra, J. Body weight and food intake as initiation factors for puberty in the rat. *J. Physiol. London* **166**:408-418, 1963.

23. Keys, A., Brozek, J., Herschel, A., Mickelson, O., and Taylor, H.L. *The biology of human starvation*, vols. 1 and 2, University of Minnesota Press, Minneapolis, 1950.

24. Kleiber, M. *The fire of life*, John Wiley, New York, 1961.

25. Knuth, U.A., Hill, M.G.R., and Jacobs, H.S. Amenorrhea and loss of weight. *Br. J. Obstet. Gynecol.* **84**:801-807, 1977.

26. Malina, R.M., Spirduso, W.W., Tate, C., and Baylor, A.M. Age at menarche and selected menstrual characteristics in athletes at different competitive levels and in different sports. *Med. Sci. Sports* **10**:218-222, 1978.

27. McArthur, J.W., O'Loughlin, K.M., Beitins, I.Z., Johnson, L., and Alonso, C. Endocrine studies during the refeeding of young women with nutritional amenorrhea and infertility. *Mayo Clin. Proc.* **51**:607-615, 1976.

28. Mellits, E.D., and Cheek, D. The assessment of body water and fatness from infancy to adulthood. In: J. Brozek (ed.), *Physical growth and body composition*. Soc. Res. Child Dev. monograph **35**:12-26, 1970.

29. Montagu, A. *The reproductive development of the female: A study in the comparative physiology of the adolescent organism*, 3rd ed., PSG Publishing, Littleton, MA, 1979.

30. Nimrod, A., and Ryan, K.J. Aromatization of androgens by human abdominal and breast fat tissue. *J. Clin. Endocrinol. Metab.* **40**:367-372, 1975.

31. Nisker, J.A., Hammond, G.L., and Siiteri, P.K. More on fatness and reproduction. *New Engl. J. Med.* **303**:1125, 1981.

32. Nodate, Y. Estrogen metabolism. *Sanfujinka No. Jissai* **18**:219-229, 1969.

33. Parízková, J. Physical activity and body composition. In: J. Brozek (ed.), *Human body composition: Approaches and applications*, Pergamon, Oxford, vol. 7, 1965, pp. 161-176.

34. Perel, E., and Killinger, D.W. The interconversion and aromatization of androgens by human adipose tissue. *J. Steroid Chem.* **10**:623-626, 1979.

35. Reichlin, S. Neuroendocrinology. In: R.H. Williams (ed.), *Textbook of endocrinology*. 6th edn., Wm. Saunders, Philadelphia, 1981.

36. Renold, A.E., Quigley, T.B., Kennard, H.E. et al. Reaction of the adrenal cortex to physical and emotional stress in college oarsmen. *New Engl. J. Med.* **244**:754-757, 1951.

37. Scammon, R.E. The measurement of body in childhood. J.A. Harris, C.M. Jackson, D.G. Paterson, and R.E. Scammon (eds.), *The measurement of man*, University of Minnesota Press, Minneapolis, 1930, pp. 174-215.

38. Thorn, G.W. Disturbances of menstruation. In: G.W. Thorn, R.D. Adams, E. Braunwald et al. (eds.), *Harrison's principles of internal medicine*, 8th edn., McGraw-Hill, New York, 1977, pp. 241-245.

39. Vigersky, R.A., Andersen, A.E., Thompson, R.H., and Loriaux, D.L. Hypothalamic dysfunction in secondary amenorrhea associated with simple weight loss. *New Engl. J. Med.* **297**:1141-1145, 1977.

40. Warren, M.P. The effects of exercise on pubertal progression and reproductive function in girls. *J. Clin. Endocrinol. Metab.* **51**:1050-1057, 1980.

Exercise-related disturbances in the menstrual cycle

Arend Bonen
Dalhousie University

In the past 20 years sports participation by women has increased dramatically, as have the intensity of, and the time devoted to, training. Several early reports have linked participation in sports with increased irregularity in the menstrual cycle (see 22). This report will focus on (a) the incidence of menstrual cycle disturbances in athletic populations based on survey data, (b) the endocrine events that have been observed in athletes with menstrual cycle irregularities, and (c) the exercise-induced alterations in reproductive hormones.

Menstrual cycle disturbances in athletes

The incidence of menstrual cycle disorders in athletes can range anywhere from 7-100% depending on how menstrual cycle disturbances are categorized (15,19,24,58,68,73). When only oligo/amenorrhea is considered, the figures range from 7 to 43% and if other disturbances are included, such as shortened or lengthened menstrual cycles, the figures can increase to as much as 100%.

The large range in these data are attributable to many factors. First, the grouping of different types of athletic populations will mask the true incidence of menstrual cycle disorders in specific groups, because it is quite clear that in activities involving long, demanding training hours there is a greater incidence of menstrual cycle irregularity (68). Second, the age of the respondents in the surveys is also a factor, as it is well known that younger women have a greater incidence of menstrual cycle disturbances (18). This situation also suggests that younger athletes will be a more susceptible population if training does provoke these disturbances. Third, in more recent reports the incidence of irregularities has increased (7,19,68) and may be a result of broader categorization of menstrual cycle disturbances (68). However, these findings probably also reflect the fact that more women are training more frequently, for longer periods of time each day, and at a greater intensity. Consequently, the normal menstrual cycle is markedly altered in many groups of athletes.

Shangold (52) has expressed the view that exercise participation per se is not the cause of oligo/amenorrhea, because participants in the New York City marathon experiencing menstrual cycle irregularities during training had also experienced these prior to training. Although it is not unusual to expect that such individuals may be a higher risk group when they begin to train, evidence suggests that menstrual cycle disorders are also experienced by women who have a normal gynecological history prior to training. Specifically, in the survey data reported by Speroff and Redwine (58) most women who became amenorrheic experienced normal cycles before training, as did those in the studies by Baker et al. (7). In a prospective study it has been shown that women with normal menstrual cycles will experience menstrual cycle changes with the onset of a training program, and these changes generally become more prevalent as training mileage increases (12). Clearly, then, pretraining menstrual irregularities need not necessarily have been present to provoke disturbances in the menstrual cycle during training.

From the surveys to date one discriminator among young individuals appears to be the total energy expenditure during training, so that the highest incidence of menstrual cycle disturbances occur in those subjects who train the most (68). In young runners (19.5 yr) who accumulate less than 20 miles/week, the incidence of amenorrhea was 7.9%. As soon as these training distances increased to 20 miles/week there was a pronounced increase incidence of amenorrhea to 20%. Thereafter this figure increased proportionately with increasing training mileage so that for women who ran approximately 80 miles/week the incidence was 43% (24).

In older runners, such a direct relationship is not evident (7,19). In runners (> 30 miles/week) and joggers (5-30 miles/week) the incidence of amenorrhea was 32-33% and only 4% in age-matched control subjects

(19). Similarly, Baker et al. (7) found amenorrhea to be present in 26.6 and 37.5% of high mileage (> 41 miles/week) and lower mileage (< 40 miles/week) runners. The lower incidence of amenorrhea in these latter two investigations seems to be attributable to the age of the subjects, 29-30 yr (7,19), when compared to the population (19.5 yr) studied by Feicht et al. (24). Most studies support the view that the incidence of amenorrhea is greatest in younger athletes (7,58), even when they run less than older subjects (7). It has been proposed that athletic amenorrhea may also be related to a later onset of menarche in such subjects (7), though this is not always the case (58).

For some time now Frisch (cf. 28) has proposed that secondary amenorrhea is attributable to a marked decline in body fat in athletes. Trussel (63) has raised very serious questions about the statistical basis used to arrive at Frisch's hypothesis. This controversy obviously needs to be resolved and the hypothesis should also be tested, as neither has been done.

Recently Speroff and Redwine (58) have implicated absolute weight and weight loss as a critical factor in the onset of amenorrhea after women had begun to train. Amenorrhea occurred more frequently in women who weigh less than 120 lb. A higher incidence of amenorrhea also occurred in relation to the amount of weight lost during training. Yet a large proportion of women do *not* become amenorrheic with moderate training or with considerable weight loss.

In the study by Baker et al. (7) differences in weight and height did not differ between amenorrheic and normally cycling runners, though body fat was somewhat lower ($p < 0.05$) in the amenorrheic group (14.1 ± 1.2%) than in the normal group (17.7 ± 0.8%). The data may therefore be interpreted to suggest that those who are predisposed to becoming amenorrheic are more susceptible when they have a large weight loss.

At present, there are no physiological data relating changes in body fat in women to changes in menstrual cycle hormones. In premenarcheal girls, however, changes in lean body mass rather than total body fat appear to be more closely associated with hormonal changes prior to puberty (47). In college-age women an acute fast (24 hr) reduces the concentrations of LH by 24% (unpublished data).

Dale et al. (19) have shown that parity is also related to amenorrhea in runners. They reported incidences of 51% for nulliparous runners and 21% for women who had been pregnant. Similar incidences of amenorrhea also occurred in the report of Baker et al. (7) for parous (25%) and nulliparous subjects (46.6%). However, these results appear to be related to the women's age rather than the maturity of the hypothalamic-pituitary-ovarian axis, since the parous women were significantly older (33 ± 2 yr) compared to the nulliparous group (27 ± 2 yr) (7).

Most investigations have focused on amenorrhea as the sole index of menstrual cycle disturbances associated with training, which unfortunately merely reflects investigative convenience. Menstrual cycle histories can be obtained by recall or having subjects maintain their own menstrual records. Subsequent analyses therefore permit only a crude categorization of menstrual cycles as being normal or abnormal. Thus, abnormality is difficult to partition beyond oligo/amenorrhea in the absence of any endocrine and/or clinical evaluations. Yet disturbances in the menstrual cycle must have an underlying endocrine basis, because the events of the normal human menstrual cycle are carefully regulated by the complex interaction of gonadotropin and ovarian hormones. In several studies menstrual cycles have been categorized as normal based on their length alone, but when these cycles were partitioned into follicular and luteal phases, based on the day of the LH surge, an abnormally short luteal phase was present (9,53). This finding suggests that the incidences of exercise-related menstrual cycle disturbances reported to date are very conservative; except for the studies of Shangold et al. (53) and Bonen et al. (9), such disturbances have not been based on the subjects' endocrine profiles. Consequently, endocrine disturbances less obvious than amenorrhea will not be detected, and will quite erroneously be termed normal. No doubt this error has already occurred in many of the survey studies.

Endocrine basis of the menstrual cycle disturbances in athletes

The ovarian cycle is divided into three distinct phases: (a) the follicular phase when the influence of LH and FSH permit the growth and maturation of the follicle, (b) ovulation when the follicle is luteinized and the ovum is expelled from the follicle, and (c) the luteal phase when the follicles enlarge and are now called the corpus luteum, an endocrine organ secreting progesterone under the influence of low levels of LH.

None of these events occur haphazardly but each appears to be regulated by the secretory patterns of LH and FSH, which also result in a cyclical pattern of the ovarian hormones 17β-estradiol (E_2) and progesterone (P). These patterns are summarized chronologically and schematically with the development of the follicle and the corpus luteum (Figure 1).

Except for the one study from our laboratory (9), there are no other reports in which hormonal patterns of athletic subjects have been monitored on a daily basis. The reasons for this situation are quite practical. It is difficult to design prospective studies with athletes because (a) not all will develop problems with their menstrual cycles, (b) the studies need to be long-term, involving daily blood sampling for at least one menstrual cycle (preferably more), and (c) prospective studies that encompass the monitoring of cycles during control, training, and detrain-

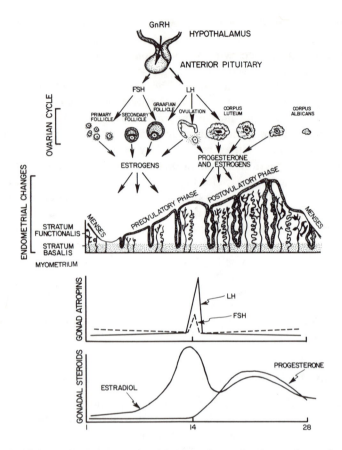

Figure 1—Schematic representation of the major endocrine and associated morphological events during the human menstrual cycle.

ing periods require 18-24 months to complete, with daily blood sampling for a minimum of three complete menstrual cycles over a 2-yr period. Obviously, many subjects find it difficult to commit themselves for such extended periods, let alone participate in a 2-yr experiment. It is therefore hardly surprising that the few studies available consist of extremely small samples (9,53); conversely, larger groups have been studied with the result that blood sampling has been intermittent (7,19). This second approach is severely limited because the cyclic nature of the hormones (Figure 1) makes it impossible to adjust the data to the same point in the menstrual cycle. Therefore, comparisons between subjects or between groups are not valid as any difference may reflect only different sampling periods within the menstrual cycle.

The endocrine basis of athletic amenorrhea has not been described thoroughly. Baker et al. (7) have monitored hormone concentrations, based on only one or two blood samples, in amenorrheic runners. In comparison to runners with normal menstrual cycles, LH concentrations were greater and E_2 concentrations were lower in the amenorrheic group. No differences occurred in the other hormones monitored, dehydroepiandrosterone, androstenedione, testosterone, E_2, cortisol, dehydroepiandrosterone sulfate, FSH, LH, and prolactin. Because patterns of these hormones are not at all constant in amenorrheic women (71), failure to detect statistical significance between the two groups may merely reflect the inadequacy of the infrequent sampling procedure. Specifically, wide fluctuations have been observed in LH, FSH, E_2, P, androstenedione, testosterone, and estrone in amenorrheic women over a 30-day period involving daily sampling (71), so that the expected interindividual difference for any of these hormones obtained on a single occasion will be large, with some subjects experiencing high concentrations on that day and others having low concentrations. Consequently, statistical significance may be difficult to attain, especially when group numbers are also small. More meaningful data can therefore be obtained with daily sampling procedures.

We (9) investigated the menstrual cycle patterns in swimmers because they spend many hours training at high rate of energy expenditure. From our initial group of volunteers, we studied four girls who had been training regularly for the past year, 2-3 hr/day, 6 days/week. Their training histories ranged from 3-6 years. They were compared with four other teenagers, matched for gynecological age, and with a group of parous adult women. In all groups blood samples were obtained daily and analyzed for LH, FSH, E_2, P, 17α-hydroxyprogesterone (17α-OHP), and prolactin (HPr).

The follicular and luteal phase lengths were determined from the hormone data and the onset of menstrual flow in two consecutive menstrual cycles. Specifically, the follicular phase is the duration from the first day of menstruation until the day a pronounced LH peak is observed, and the luteal phase duration is the remaining number of days until the next onset of menstruation.

The menstrual cycle of the four swimmers (20.0 $\pm$ 1.8 days, mean $\pm SD$) was shorter than that of the adult women (28.5 $\pm$ 3.4 days) and that of the control group (28.3 $\pm$ 6.4 days) ($p < 0.05$) (Figure 2). Because differences in the length of the follicular phases among the three groups were not statistically significant ($p > 0.05$), the swimmers' abbreviated menstrual cycle was attributed to the severely shortened time between the LH surge and the onset of menses. The luteal phase was only 4.5 $\pm$ 0.6 days for the swimmers compared to 7.8 $\pm$ 3.0 days for the control group ($p < 0.05$) and 13.4 $\pm$ 1.7 days for the adults ($p < 0.05$). The difference in luteal phase duration between control and adult groups was also significant ($p < 0.05$).

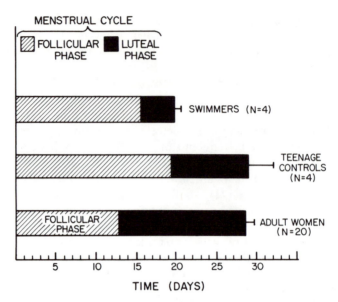

Figure 2—Comparisons of menstrual cycle durations and follicular and luteal phase durations in teenage swimmers, teenage controls and parous adult women ($\overline{X} \pm SEM$) (data from Bonen et al. [9]).

The LH patterns of all groups before the LH peak were normal, but the concentrations of LH (follicular phase) were greater in the swimmers than in the control group ($p < 0.05$) and the adult women ($p < 0.05$). LH differences among the groups on the day of the LH peak and during the early luteal phase were not significant ($p > 0.05$). Also, differences between the adult group and the control group were not significant at any time throughout the menstrual cycle ($p > 0.05$).

The characteristic FSH peak was not observed in the swimmers (Figure 3). In addition, FSH concentrations showed little change throughout the cycle and were lower during the follicular and luteal phases than in the other two groups ($p < 0.05$). No differences were observed between the control group and the adult women ($p > 0.05$).

In the swimmers the FSH-LH ratio was significantly reduced through-out the menstrual cycle compared to the concentrations observed for the control group and the adult women (Figure 4). This low FSH-LH ratio is attributable to the concomitant suppression of FSH and the elevation of LH during the swimmers' menstrual cycle. There was no difference in the FSH-LH ratio between the teenage control group and the adult women ($p > 0.05$).

E_2 concentrations in the swimmers and women were similar during the midfollicular phase and increased in both groups before the LH peak. Maximal E_2 concentrations were noted in the swimmers on the day

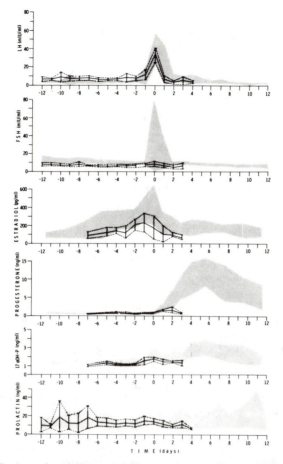

Figure 3—Hormonal profiles of teenage swimmers throughout an entire menstrual cycle ($\overline{X} \pm SD$). Data are centered on the day of the LH peak (O). Follicular and luteal phase days are preceded by − and + symbols, respectively. Grey shaded area represents data ($\overline{X} \pm SD$) of parous adults (data from Bonen et al. [9], republished with permission).

before the LH peak, whereas maximal E_2 concentrations were found on the day of the LH peak in the adult women. On the day of the LH peak and during the luteal phase, the E_2 concentrations were significantly lower in the swimmers than in the adult women ($p < 0.05$).

The P concentrations during the follicular phase were higher in the swimmers than in the adults ($0.05 > p < 0.10$), and the lowest concentrations occurred in the control group. The characteristic increments in P concentrations on the day of the LH peak and during the luteal phase were significantly lower ($p < 0.05$) than the increments observed on those occasions in the adult women (Figure 3) and the control group.

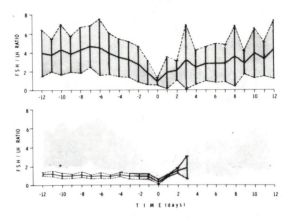

Figure 4—Comparison of FSH/LH ratio during the menstrual cycle in parous adult women and in teenage swimmers ($\bar{X} \pm SD$). Grey shaded area represents the adult data from the upper panel (data from Bonen et al. [9], republished with permission).

The 17α-OHP concentrations during the follicular phase were similar in the swimmers and the adults (Figure 3). In the swimmers a small increase occurred on day -1, but this was less pronounced than a similar increase in the adult women. By day $+2$ through day $+4$ a decrease was already appparent in the swimmers ($p < 0.05$).

Differences in HPr concentrations between the swimmers and the adults were not significant ($p > 0.05$) during the follicular phase and the day of the LH peak. In the luteal phase a slight difference was apparent ($0.05 > p < 0.10$).

The results of our study (9) cannot be attributed to the age of the subjects alone. Admittedly they were young, but the patterns of their hormonal profiles were very dissimilar to those of the matched nonathletic control group. In these subjects the profiles were similar to those of the adults. Recently we also had the opportunity to monitor again the entire menstrual cycle of one of the subjects 5 yr after she had participated in the original study. She was still training each day and still experiencing a short luteal phase and deficient corpus luteum as judged from very low P concentrations in the luteal phase (Figure 5) (31).

The deficient progesterone production in the swimmers has also been observed in a marathon runner (53). Blood samples obtained in the luteal phase revealed a 50% decrease in progesterone during training periods (32, 21, 16 miles/week during three training cycles), compared to three control cycles (2, 2, 0 miles/week during control cycles). In addition, with the reduction of P concentrations the duration of the luteal phase was also reduced, and this occurred in direct proportion to the weekly training mileage of the subject ($r = 0.81$; luteal phase length days = 13.3

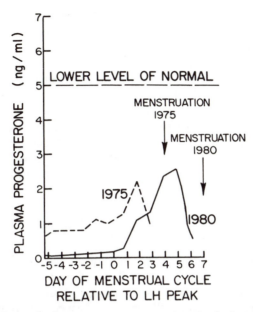

Figure 5—Comparison of progesterone concentrations in the luteal phase in the same swimmer in 1975 and 1980. The subject was still training in 1980 (data from Jacobson and Bonen [31]).

− 0.11 × weekly mileage). Thus, for every additional 10 miles/week of running, the luteal phase length was reduced by about one day.

In the study of Dale et al. (19) luteal phase P concentrations were also about 50% lower in runners (>30 miles/week) than in the controls and joggers (5-30 miles/week). In addition, the FSH and LH levels were also reduced in the runners (19). In ballet dancers secondary amenorrhea has been observed with concomitant decrements in LH and FSH to premenarcheal levels (67).

These studies (9,19,53,67) indicate clearly that there is a definite endocrine basis to the training-related disturbances in the menstrual cycle of many athletes. Although amenorrhea represents the most severe disturbance, we (9) and others (53) have noted that a milder disturbance appears to manifest itself as a shortening of the luteal phase. This phenomenon is not detectable by simply recording the duration and frequency of menstrual periods but requires monitoring of the athletes' hormonal profiles.

Possible mechanisms underlying
the menstrual cycle disturbances in athletes

At present we can only speculate about the etiology of the exercise-provoked menstrual cycle disturbances in athletes (9). In the case of our swimmers (9) they present an almost classic picture of the short luteal phase first described by Strott et al. (59), and later by others (27,32,55, 56,62,69,70,72). In adult women such short luteal phases are now recognized as representing one type of infertility, that of a subnormal corpus luteum that cannot sustain an adequate progesterone production. Hence, the associated morphological structures acquired during the follicular phase are not supported by the appropriate endocrine environment, with the result that premature menstruation ensues (23,32,56,59, 62). It has been proposed that short luteal phases are provoked by an altered pituitary hormone environment during the follicular phase (59). Thus, a fundamental understanding of the influence of FSH and LH on folliculogenesis is important.

Pituitary hormone influence on folliculogenesis

Follicular development is regulated by the presence of the pituitary hormones LH and FSH. Each is required for unique purposes and therefore acts on different cells within the follicle. Mitosis of the follicular cells of the primordial follicle produces layers of granulosa cells. Outside the primary follicle the thecal cells are then formed. LH binds to the thecal cells and FSH binds to the granulosa cells.

The available data suggest that LH and FSH must interact cooperatively to ensure the production of E_2 in the follicular phase. In order for this to occur a two-cell model has been proposed, linking the function of the thecal and granulosa cells (5). Under the influence of LH, steroidgenesis is stimulated in the thecal cells of the follicle. However, aromatization of these androgens (primarily testosterone and androstenedione) is severely limited in these thecal cells (23,25,40,64). Located in close proximity to the thecal cells are the granulosa cells. These cells are stimulated by FSH to produce E_2. However, these granulosa cells have only a limited capacity to synthesize androgens (26, 46,64) from C_{21}-precursors, presumably because of a lack of 17α-hydroxylase and/or $C_{17,20}$-lyase enzymes (5). The two-cell model postulates that the androgens from the thecal cells diffuse through the basement membrane into the granulosa cells, where the FSH-stimulated aromatization of androgens is possible (4,5). Because nonaromatizable androgens (5α-dihydrotestosterone and androsterone) can facilitate the FSH-induction of aromatizing enzymes, androgens appear to serve not only as a substrate but they may also act synergistically with FSH to stimulate their own aromatization (4). This E_2 production, under the influence of FSH and androgens, appears to be significant to maintain appropriate follicular growth, characterized by proliferation of granulosa cells and the accumulation of follicular fluid (29).

It is presumed that the increased E_2 in the circulation (derived from the augmented follicular E_2 production) reduces the FSH secretion from the anterior pituitary, resulting in reduced concentrations of circulating FSH (74). Despite this reduced FSH availability the E_2-producing follicle will actually concentrate FSH (44), presumably due to more highly developed vasculature (76), and thus E_2 production is maintained (47).

In the follicles that cannot concentrate FSH, high levels of androstenedione ($\simeq 700$ ng/ml) and low levels of E_2 (150 ng/ml) are present compared to the FSH-sensitive follicles. These have an androstenedione content of ($\simeq 250$ ng/ml) (42,43) and an E_2 content of 3,500 ng/ml (6,43). It is tempting to speculate that the high androgen content promotes atresia observed in the majority of follicles (13).

FSH is therefore particularly critical for enabling the follicle to mature normally. In combination with E_2, these two hormones appear to be responsible for preparing the maturing follicle to respond fully to the LH surge (45,75).

In recent years the role of prolactin has assumed increasing importance in considerations of normal folliculogenesis. In women with secondary amenorrhea approximately 20% experience hyperprolactemia (48) and bromocriptine treatment restores fertility in most (30). In women with a short luteal phase, hyperprolactemia may or may not be present (62).

The exact mechanism of prolactin action is unknown. Normally, follicular fluid prolactin concentrations are comparable to those in the circulation until just before ovulation when the levels decrease sharply. A disturbance at this point may therefore impair normal luteinization, and subsequently corpus luteum functioning.

The modes of action of prolactin-impaired menstrual cycle dysfunction are diffuse. The effects of this hormone may be mediated at the levels of the hypothalamus, the pituitary, and the ovary. At the pituitary level prolactin may suppress the responsiveness to luteinizing hormone-releasing hormone (LHRH) but more importantly, prolactin acts primarily on the hypothalamus to cause a decrease in LH-RH secretion (57). Prolactin inhibits progesterone synthesis and interferes with FSH-stimulated synthesis of estrogen in the granulosa cells. This interference is accomplished by reducing the aromatase activity that is normally stimulated by FSH to facilitate aromatization of androstenedione and testosterone to estrogen (21). These distinct effects of prolactin may therefore create a deficient steroid and/or gonadotropin milieu that impairs normal folliculogenesis.

Pituitary hormones and the short luteal phase

The cause of the short luteal phase is still speculative. However, Strott et al. (59) and others (20,55) have proposed that subnormal P production in the menstrual cycles with a short luteal phase is attributable to the endocrine events in the follicular phase, namely the deficiency of FSH and an imbalance in the FSH/LH ratio. These deficiencies are clearly present in our swimmers (9). Elegant support for this hypothesis has recently been provided in vivo with rhesus monkeys. In these primates selective FSH suppression by porcine follicular fluid in the peri-ovulatory phase resulted in markedly reduced P concentrations in the luteal phase (77,78). Thus, the presence of normal gonadotropin levels for the developing follicle are critical once the thecal cells have been acquired.

Short luteal phase menstrual cycles seem to have multiple etiologies (62) and therefore follicular phase deficiencies of FSH may not be the only explanation for a defective corpus luteum. Improper induction of luteinization by the midcycle LH surge (i.e., LH peak too low or duration too short) will yield a defective corpus luteum, even if normal follicular growth has been present. Alternatively, low tonic concentrations of LH in the luteal phase may diminish P production (52). Indeed, several reports have found low levels of LH (19,67) that seem to be caused by an impaired release of LH (41).

Altered luteal phase LH concentrations may have a role in deficient corpus luteum functioning in athletes. In the study by Shangold et al. (53) a reduced P concentration was observed when training occurred in the follicular and luteal phases (20 miles/week). This schedule was then maintained for another 4 months (Shangold, personal communication). In the following cycle (control) running occurred only during the follicular phase, not during the luteal phase. With the latter protocol normal luteal phase P concentrations were restored, which implies that training during the follicular phase need not impair corpus luteum functioning and that it is the endocrine events during the luteal phase that suppress P production. The observed increase in LH during the luteal phase of the control cycle may have been significant to permit an adequate stimulation of the corpus luteum's P production, and the very high P concentrations may possibly also represent corpus luteum hypersensitivity to LH. Unfortunately, the absence of follicular phase gonadotropin data in that study precludes any definitive conclusions about the relative importance of follicular and luteal phase gonadotropin events in athletes.

The incidence of short luteal phases in nonathletes is unknown as menstrual cycles may be of normal duration (55), and are not necessarily related to previous histories of menstrual cycle irregularities (59). Younger women may, however, be more susceptible (59). Two common characteristics of cycles with short luteal phases are (a) low concentrations of FSH in the follicular phase and (b) low concentrations of P in the luteal phase (9,50,55,59,62). In young girls a slow rise of FSH preceded the reduced P production of the luteal phase (3). In other studies, slightly elevated (50) or low-to-normal (55,59) LH values have been reported. Low E_2 concentrations in the follicular (20) and luteal phases (55) and 17αOH-P (46) and testosterone (3) in the follicular phase have also been reported. These studies suggest that short luteal phases are provoked by alterations in the pattern(s) of pituitary hormone release or in the feedback control of pituitary gonadotropins by steroids of ovarian and/or adrenal origin.

Exercise and pituitary hormones

Whether exercise can alter the concentrations of pituitary gonadotropins has not yet been clearly demonstrated. We have not observed a change in FSH or LH during a single bout of exercise. Jurkowski et al. (33) also have reported that these gonadotropins were not altered by acute exercise in the follicular and luteal phases of the menstrual cycle. However, inappropriate statistical analyses (multiple paired t-test [33]), seem to account for the lack of significance in the follicular phase LH concentrations. Yet these concentrations clearly appear to be increasing. Reanalyses of these data indicated that this increment was statistically significant (Jurkowski, personal communication).

It may not be possible to extrapolate results from untrained subjects to trained subjects. We have attempted to study the effects of bicycle ergometer training on young women. Unfortunately, this provoked severe menstrual cycle irregularities (see Bonen et al. [11] for details). Posttraining retesting at the same absolute workload provoked a slight but significant reduction in FSH (Table 1). The inability to control the posttraining testing in the same phase of the menstrual cycle make these results difficult to compare with the pretraining data. Yet this FSH reduction with exercise is in the direction observed for this hormone in trained swimmers at rest (Figure 3). This raises the possibility that the pituitary or hypothalamic function(s) change with training, but whether this change ultimately provokes a short luteal phase is unknown.

Several recent studies support the concept that the hypothalamic-pituitary axis sensitivity is dissimilar in trained and untrained women. Brisson et al. (14) have shown that moderate exercise (75% VO_2max) provokes marked increments in prolactin of 40 and 80% at min 15 and 30 of exercise, respectively, in women who were accustomed to strenuous exercise. In women unaccustomed to such exercise no significant prolactic alterations occurred. TRH-stimulated prolactin responses in the mid-follicular phase are also increased after training (12). These complementary results indicate that repeated training bouts can interfere with the normal hypothalamic-pituitary-ovarian axis. However, prolactin levels in trained athletes are not altered at rest (7,9,53).

The menstrual cycle dysfunction in our swimmers (9,31) is likely attributable to the depressed FSH concentrations throughout the follicular phase. In such an environment, E_2 formation and the consequent follicular growth and maturation are presumably subnormal. The result then is a corpus luteum that is hypofunctional as judged by the low P

Table 1

Serum Concentrations of Menstrual Cycle Hormones 15 min Prior to Exercise and at the End of 30 min of Exercise, Before (74.5 ± 3.5% $\dot{V}O_2max$) and After Training (68.3 ± 3.0% $\dot{V}O_2max$)[a]

Hormone		Pre-training			Post-training		
		Pre-exercise	Post-exercise	%Δ	Pre-exercise	Post-exercise	%Δ
P (ng/ml)	X ± SEM	1.2 ± 0.5	1.5 ± 0.5[b]	+40.5 ± 10.6	0.5 ± 0.3	0.6 ± 0.4	−0.4 ± 4.2
E$_2$ (pg/ml)	X ± SEM	148.6 ± 44.7	167.5 ± 52.7[b]	5.1 ± 8.4	89.5 ± 17.9	74.3 ± 11.8[d]	−8.4 ± 9.0[d]
LH (mIU/ml)	X ± SEM	9.0 ± 4.7	5.8 ± 1.9	−8.0 ± 9.7	4.1 ± 0.8	3.2 ± 0.6	−14.7 ± 7.3
FSH (mIU/ml)	X ± SEM	6.0 ± 0.3	6.1 ± 0.4	+2.1 ± 6.5	6.0 ± 0.3	5.3 ± 0.3[c]	−11.1 ± 2.8
FSH/LH	X ± SEM	1.5 ± 0.3	1.6 ± 0.3	+11.1 ± 7.6	1.8 ± 0.3	1.6 ± 0.3	+14.7 ± 9.7

Note. Data from Bonen et al. (11). Reprinted with permission.

[a] n = 9 exercise sessions. Data were obtained from seven subjects, two subjects participated in two sessions at different intensities on different days

[b] $p < 0.05$, pre-exercise vs. post-exercise

[c] $p < 0.10$, pre-exercise vs. post-exercise

[d] $n = 8$

%Δ = 100 (post. ex. − pre-ex.)/pre-ex

concentration in the luteal phase. Prolactin alterations would not appear to be implicated as these did not differ in the adults and swimmers. However, the high variability of this assay in our study precludes a definitive conclusion as to the role of this hormone.

The cause of FSH suppression is unknown. However, the increased concentration of androgens has been implicated in several studies (3,20,66). This factor may be important in exercising athletes in whom these steroids are markedly increased during exercise (54,60).

Alterations in release of adrenal and ovarian steroids

The regulation of FSH and LH secretion is very complex and an elaboration is beyond the scope of this paper (for review see 51). The positive feedback of E_2 on LH and FSH release prior to ovulation is well known. Indeed, Knobil et al. (35) have suggested that the normal menstrual cycle periodicity of estrogens, and not necessarily the hypothalamic-gonadotropin-releasing hormones, regulate pituitary gonadotropin-secretory patterns. Their experiments suggest that it is the alteration in the patterns of estradiol that is recognized by the pituitary and that regulates the FSH and LH secretions. Thus the menstrual cycle probably is not directed by the alterations in GnRH per se, though this hormone does seem to have a permissive and obligatory function in conjunction with estradiol (35).

It may be a reasonable supposition that one factor is the presence of the steroid hormones that provokes alterations in the levels of FSH and LH in women with irregular menstrual cycles. Indeed, in menstrual cycles with short luteal phases Dodson et al. (20) have attributed the depressed release of FSH to slightly elevated concentration of progesterone in the follicular phase. Also, implantation of progesterone-containing capsules in the follicular phase reduces the FSH concentration in rhesus monkeys (49). Other steroids may also be implicated in the regulation of gonadotropin secretion. It is known that some anabolic steroids will induce premature menstruations via their antigonadotropin actions (i.e., suppression of LH and FSH (8,17).

An important factor to consider, then, are the possible effects of negative feedback regulation of ovarian and/or adrenal steroids on the pituitary to alter gonadotropin secretion. Such considerations may be important in the female athlete because exercise can dramatically increase the concentration of ovarian and adrenal steroids (11,33; unpublished data).

Gonadal steroids unquestionably provide a feedback mechanism that regulates LH and FSH secretion, as evident from the marked rise in LH and FSH that follows bilateral gonadectomy in most species (51). These effects, however, may be provoked in part by inhibin rather than the steroids per se, though inhibin has not yet been detected in peripheral circulation. Also, inhibin-like activity in serum is similar in athletes with short luteal phases compared to normally menstruating nonathletes (unpublished data). It is possible therefore that the combined interactive effects of steroids may be an important consideration, rather than any one single hormone.

Low doses of testosterone suppress LH release, though not the pituitary content of LH (61) in female rats. Dihydrotestosterone (DHT) inhibits FSH release, but not LH release, to stimulating doses of GnRH. In particular, the ratio of DHT to E_2 determines the FSH response. Testosterone proprionate suppresses the stimulating effects of E_2 on both LH and FSH (36). These data thus suggest that pituitary sensitivity to GnRH by steroids depends on the availability of other steroids. The pituitary response to GnRH also appears to be modulated by the relative presence of various steroids and the time sequence of exposure to these steroids (36).

In humans the roles of steroids on gonadotropin release have not been well identified for obvious experimental limitations. The available evidence consists of associations between elevated androgen and reduced gonadotropin concentrations.

The levels of androgens such as testosterone, dihydrotestosterone, and androstenedione all demonstrate cyclical variations during the menstrual cycle with the highest concentrations in the peri-ovulatory phase and the lowest values in the early follicular and late luteal phases. Dehydroepiandrosterone apparently varies randomly (65).

In adolescent girls elevated androgen levels (i.e., testosterone and androstenedione) are common in anovulatory cycles (3). In a subsequent study it was shown that testosterone and androstenedione are elevated early (days 6-9) and late (days 20-23) in anovulatory cycles (66). The adrenal steroid dehydroepiandrosterone is similar in ovulatory and anovulatory cycles (66). These data strongly suggest that testosterone and androstenedione may be responsible for anovulatory cycles since in rats increased ovarian androgen production inhibits follicular maturation (39). In addition, clinical conditions such as polycystic ovarian syndrome and congenital adrenal hyperplasia which increase androgen production also lead to anovulation and loss of normal cycles.

Direct evidence for the effects of androgens on gonadotropins in humans is derived from studies involving administration of anabolic steroids. In males, such treatment (methandrostenolane [dianabol], 20-35 mg/day for 14 days) provokes significant reductions in LH and FSH (17). In women, some anabolic steroids administered 2 days after ovulation reduced the luteal phase length by 4 days and lowered circulating concentrations of LH, FSH, and progesterone (8). This concomitant reduction in the ovarian steroid and the gonadotropins suggests that the anabolic steroids impair the normal pituitary functioning by reducing the output of the gonadotropins.

If, in athletes, LH and FSH are altered in a similar manner, an increased presence of steroids would be expected. Interestingly, in most athletes studied to date the concentration of adrenal and/or ovarian steroids is elevated at rest (7,9,19). Specifically, we have observed high levels of progesterone but not estradiol in the follicular phase (9), and Dale et al. (19) found high levels of testosterone in the luteal phase. No doubt other steroids are also elevated. These increases possibly represent changes in adrenal and/or ovarian production of these steroids (1,2) or a reduction in the aromatization of testosterone to estradiol in adipose and muscle tissue where such peripheral conversion occurs (37,38). It is unknown whether such alterations may be induced by heavy training programs.

Exercise and steroid hormones

Some evidence suggests that single bouts of exercise have pronounced effects on the circulating concentrations of various steroids. During a swim training practice serum androgens increase 19.5% in female swimmers (60), and after 30 min of running testosterone increases more during the follicular phase than in the luteal phase (54). We have shown that 30 min of acute exercise (60-85% $\dot{V}O_2$max) increases circulating progesterone 40-44% in the luteal phase and during menstruation. Estradiol changed about +21% in the luteal phase but decreased during menstruation (−17.0%). It also appeared that exercise intensities needed to exceed 60% $\dot{V}O_2$max to observe the increments in these steroids in the luteal phase (11).

In several studies it has been found that P concentrations increased only during the luteal phase, not in the follicular phase (10,33) and suggests indirectly that in untrained subjects, the adrenal contribution to P is negligible. Recent data from our laboratory also suggest that fasting eliminates the P responses during exercise. E_2 increased only with exhaustive exercise in the follicular phase, whereas progressive increments in this hormone occurred in the luteal phase as exercise intensity increased (33).

Both our study (11) and that of Jurkowski et al. (33) demonstrate quite clearly that steroid concentrations will increase with exercise, though care must be taken as to which phase of the cycle is studied. It is unlikely, however, that the steroidal changes represent ovarian secretion, as Keizer et al. (34) have shown a dramatic decline in the metabolic clearance rate of E_2 during exercise. They have also shown that this decrease will persist for at least 30 min after exercise (Keizer, personal communications). However, this finding does not imply that the observed increments are not physiologically significant. Repeated, daily exercise-induced changes in these hormones may have a profound long-term effect on the menstrual cycle regularity, though this is not yet known.

It is possible that the abnormal reduction in menstrual cycle lengths observed in our trained swimmers (9) was attributable to repeated androgen increments during training. The large increment in steroid concentrations commonly observed during exercise should not be ignored, especially because the interactive and/or synergistic effects of one or more steroids on gonadotropin secretion may impair pituitary sensitivity to GnRH as shown in rats (36).

Future studies with human subjects are exceedingly difficult and it would seem worthwhile to develop an animal model from which more definitive data can be obtained at present. The only animal study to date suggests that ovarian hypofunction is a consequence of training. Decrements in marker enzymes of steroidgenesis (Δ^5-3β-hydroxysteroid dehydrogenase) and steroid hydroxylation (glucose-6-phosphate dehydrogenase), and in ovarian weight, along with increments in cholesterol and ascorbic acid, all point to an exercise-induced malfunction (16).

In summary, chronic exercise can provoke menstrual cycle irregularities, the causes of which are unknown. Relatively little endocrine data are available and therefore much remains to be done.

References

1. Abraham, G.E. Ovarian and adrenal contribution to peripheral androgens during the menstrual cycle. *J. Clin. Endocrinol. Metab.* **39**:340-346, 1974.

2. Abraham, G.E., and Chakmakjian, Z.H. Serum steroid levels during the menstrual cycle in a bilaterally adrenalectomized woman. *J. Clin. Endocrinol. Metab.* **37**:581-587, 1973.

3. Apter, D., Viinikka, L., and Vhiko, R. Hormonal patterns of adolescent menstrual cycles. *J. Clin. Endocrinol. Metab.* **47**:944-954, 1978.

4. Armstrong, D.T. Regulation of follicular steroid biosynthesis. In: R.I. Tozzini, G. Reeve, and R.L. Pineda (eds.), *Endocrine physiopathology of the ovary*, Elsevier/North Holland, Amsterdam, 1980, pp. 165-178.

5. Armstrong, D.T., and Dorrington, J.H. In: J.A. Thomas and R.L. Singhal (eds.), *Advances in sex hormone research*, University Park Press, Baltimore, MD, 1977, pp. 217-258.

6. Baird, D.J., and Fraser, I.S. Concentration of oestrone and oestradiol in follicular fluid and ovarian venous blood of women. *Clin. Endocrinol.* **4**:259-266, 1975.

7. Baker, E.R., Mathur, R.S., Kirk, R.F., and Williamson, H.O. Female runners and secondary amenorrhea: Correlation with age, parity, mileage, and plasma hormonal and sex-hormone-binding globulin concentrations. *Fertil. Steril.* **36**:183-187, 1981.

8. Bolch, O.H., and Warren, J.C. Induction of premature menstruation with anabolic steroids. *Am. J. Obstet. Gynecol.* **117**:121-125, 1973.

9. Bonen, A., Belcastro, A.N., Ling, W.Y., and Simpson, A.A. Profiles of selected hormones during menstrual cycles of teenage athletes. *J. Appl. Physiol. Respirat. Environ. Exercise Physiol.* **50**:545-551, 1981.

10. Bonen, A., Haynes, F., Watson-Wright, W., Sopper, M., Pierce, G., and Graham, T.E. Substrate and hormonal responses to exercise in the follicular and luteal phases of fasted and glucose-loaded women. *Can. J. Appl. Sport Sci.* (abstract) **6**:149, 1981.

11. Bonen, A., Ling, W.Y., MacIntyre, K.P., Neil, R., McGrail, J.C., and Belcastro, A.N. Effects of exercise on the serum concentrations of FSH, LH, progesterone and estradiol. *Eur. J. Appl. Physiol. Occup. Physiol.* **42**:15-23, 1979.

12. Boyden, T.W., Pamenter, R.W., Grosso, D., Stanforth, P., Rotkis, T., and Wilmore, J. Prolactin responses, menstrual cycles and body composition of women runners. Endocrine Society Meeting, Cincinnati, June 1981.

13. Brailly, S., Gougeon, A., Bomsel-Helmreich, O., and Papiernik, E. Androgens and progestins in the human ovarian follicle: Differences in the evolution of preovulatory, healthy non-ovulatory, and atretic follicles. *J. Clin. Endocrinol. Metab.* **53**:128-134, 1981.

14. Brisson, G.R., Volle, M.A., Decarufel, D., Desharnais, M., and Tanaka, M. Exercise-induced dissociation of the blood prolactin response in young women according to their sports habits. *Hormone Metab. Res.* **12**:201-205, 1980.

15. Chalupa, M. Some results gained by a gynecologist during a follow-up of female top-sportswomen. *Czech. Gynekol.* **43**:268-270, 1973.

16. Chandra, A.M., Patra, P.B., Chatterjee, P., and Deb, C. Effect of long-term treadmill running on gonadal activity in female rats. *Endokrinologie* **72**:299-303, 1978.

17. Clerico, A., Ferdeghini, M., Palombo, F.C., Leoncini, R., del Chicca, M.G., Sardano, G., and Mariani, G. Effect of anabolic treatment on the serum levels of gonadotropins, testosterone, prolactin, thyroid hormones, and myoglobin of male athletes under physical training. *J. Nucl. Med. Allied Sci.* **25**:79-88, 1981.

18. Collet, M.E., Wertenberger, G.E., and Fiske, V.M. The effect of age upon the pattern of the menstrual cycle. *Fertil. Steril.* **5**:437-445, 1954.

19. Dale, E., Gerlach, D.H., and Wilhite, A.L. Menstrual dysfunction in distance runners. *Obstet. Gynecol.* **54**:47-53, 1979.

20. Dodson, K.S., MacNaughton, M.C., and Coutts, J.R.T. Infertility in women with apparently ovulatory cycles. I. Comparison of their plasma sex steroid and gonadotropin profiles with those in the normal cycle. *Br. J. Obstet. Gynaecol.* **82**:615-624, 1975.

21. Dorrington, J., and Gore-Langton, R.E. Prolactin inhibits oestrogen synthesis in the ovary. *Nature* **290**:600-602, 1981.

22. Erdelyi, G. Effects of exercise on the menstrual cycle. *Phys. Sports Med.* **4**:79-81, 1976.

23. Erickson, G.F., and Ryan, K.J. Stimulation of testosterone production in isolated rabbit thecal tissue by LH/FSH, dibutyryl cyclic AMP, FGF, and PGE_2. *Endocrinology* **99**:452-458, 1976.

24. Feicht, C.B., Johnson, T.S., Martin, B.J., Sparks, K.E., and Wagner, W.W. Secondary amenorrhea in athletes. *Lancet* **2**:1145-1146, 1978.

25. Fortune, J.E., and Armstrong, D.T. Hormonal control of 17^β-estradiol biosynthesis in proestrous rat follicles: Estradiol production by isolated theca versus granulosa. *Endocrinology* **102**:227-235, 1978.

26. Fowler, R.G., Fox, N.L., Edwards, R.G., Walters, D.E., and Steptoe, P.C. Steroidgenesis by cultured granulosa cells aspirated from human follicles using pregnenolone and androgens as precursors. *J. Endocrinol.* **77**:171-183, 1978.

27. Friedrich, E., Keller, E., and Schindler, A.E. Corticoid treatment of the short luteal phase: A case report. In: V.H.T. James, M. Serio, and G. Giusti (eds.), *The endocrine function of the human ovary*, Academic, New York, 1976, pp. 387-392.

28. Frisch, R.E. Nutrition, fatness, puberty and fertility. *Compr. Therapy* **7**:15-23, 1981.

29. Goldenberg, R.L., Vaitukaitis, J.L., and Ross, G.T. Estrogen and follicle stimulation hormone interactions on follicular growth in rats. *Endocrinology* **90**:1492-1498, 1972.

30. Horrobin, D.F. Prolactin: Role in health and disease. *Drugs* **17**:409-417, 1979.

31. Jacobson, W., and Bonen, A. Persistence of a short luteal phase in a young athlete after 5 years. *Can. J. Appl. Sport Sci.* (abstract) **6**:155, 1981.

32. Jones, G.S. The luteal phase defect. *Fertil. Steril.* **27**:351-356, 1976.

33. Jurkowski, J.E., Jones, N.L., Walker, W.C., Younglai, E.V., and Sutton, J.R. Ovarian hormonal responses to exercise. *J. Appl. Physiol. Respirat. Environ. Exercise Physiol.* **44**:109-114, 1978.

34. Keizer, H.A., Poortman, J., and Bunnik, G.S. Influence of physical exercise on sex hormone metabolism. *J. Appl. Physiol. Respirat. Environ. Exercise Physiol.* **48**:765-769, 1980.

35. Knobil, E., Plant, T.M., Wildt, L., Belchetz, P.E., and Marshall, G. Control of the rhesus monkey menstrual cycle: Permissive role of hypothalamic gonadotropin releasing hormone. *Science* **207**:1371-1373, 1980.

36. Kulkarni, P.N., Simpson, A.A., and Moger, W.H. Modulation of pituitary responsiveness to LHRH by androgens in ovariectomized female rats. *Can. J. Physiol. Pharmacol.* **55**:188-192, 1977.

37. Longcope, C.L., Pratt, J.H., Schneider, S.H., and Fineberg, S.E. The in vivo metabolism of androgens by muscle and adipose tissue of normal men. *Steroids* **28**:521-533, 1976.

38. Longcope, C.L., Pratt, J.H., Schneider, S.H., and Fineberg, S.E. Aromatization of androgens by muscle and adipose tissue in vito. *J. Clin. Endocrinol. Metab.* **46**:146-152, 1978.

39. Louvet, J.P., Harman, S.M., Schreiber, J.R., and Ross, F.T. Evidence for a role of androgens in follicular maturation. *Endocrinology* **97**:366-372, 1975.

40. Makris, A., and Ryan, K.J. Progesterone, androstenedione, testosterone, estrone, and estradiol synthesis in hamster ovarian follicle cells. *Endocrinology* **96**:694-701, 1975.

41. MacArthur, J.W., Bullen, B.A., Beitins, I.Z., Panago, M., Badger, T.M., and Klibanski, A. Hypothalamic amenorrhea in runners of normal body composition. *Endocrin. Res. Comm.* **7**:13-25, 1980.

42. McNatty, K.P., and Baird, D.T. Relationship between follicle stimulating hormone, androstenedione and oestradiol in human follicular fluid. *J. Endocrinol.* 527-531, 1978.

43. McNatty, K.P., Baird, D.T., Bolton, A., Chambers, P., Corker, C.S., and McLean, H. Concentrations of estrogens and androgens in human ovarian venous plasma and follicular fluid throughout the menstrual cycle. *J. Endocrinol.* **71**:77-85, 1976.

44. McNatty, K.P., Hunter, W.M., McNeilly, A.S., and Sawers, R.S. Changes in the concentration of pituitary and steroid hormones in the follicular fluid of human Graffian follicles throughout the menstrual cycle. *J. Endocrinol.* **64**:555-571, 1975.

45. McNatty, K.P., and Sawers, R.S. Relationship between the endocrine environment within the Graffian follicle and the subsequent rate of progesterone secretion by human granulosa cells in vitro. *J. Endocrinol.* **66**:391-400, 1975.

46. Moon, Y.S., Tsung, B.K., Simpson, C., and Armstrong, D.T. 17β-estradiol biosynthesis in cultured granulosa thecal cells of human ovarian follicles: Stimulation by follicle stimulating hormone. *J. Clin. Endocrinol. Metab.* **47**:263-267, 1978.

47. Parra, A., Cervantes, C., Sanchez, M., Fletes, L., Garcia-Balnes, G., Argote, R.M., Sojo, I., Carranco, A., Arias, R., and Cortes-Gallegos, V. The relationship of plasma gonadotropins and steroid concentration to body growth in girls. *Acta Endocrinol.*-**98**:161-170, 1981.

48. Pepperell, R.J. Prolactin and reproduction. *Fertil. Steril.* **35**:267-274, 1981.

49. Resko, J.A., Ellinwood, W.E., and Knobil, E. Differential effects of progesterone on secretion of gonadotropic hormones in the rhesus monkey. *Am. J. Physiol.* **240**:E489-E492, 1981.

50. Ross, G.T., and Hillier, S.G. Luteal maturation and luteal phase defect. *Clin. Obstet. Gynaecol.* **5**:391-409, 1978.

51. Savoy-Moore, R.T., and Schwartz, N.B. Differential control of FSH and LH secretion. In: R.O. Greep (ed.), *Reproductive physiology III. International review of physiology*, vol. 22, University Park Press, Baltimore, MD, 1980, pp. 203-248.

52. Shangold, M.M. Do women sports lead to menstrual problems? *Contemp. Obstet. Gynecol.* **17**:53-62, 1981.

53. Shangold, M., Freeman, R., Thyson, B., and Gatz, M. The relationship between long-distance running, plasma progesterone and luteal phase length. *Fertil. Steril.* **31**:130-133, 1979.

54. Shangold, M., Gatz, M.L., and Thysen, B. Acute effects of exercise on plasma concentrations of prolactin and testosterone in recreational women runners. *Fertil. Steril.* **35**:699-702, 1981.

55. Sherman, B.M., and Korenman, S.G. Measurement of plasma LH, FSH, estradiol and progesterone in disorders of the human menstrual cycle. The inadequate luteal phase. *J. Clin. Endocrinol. Metab.* **39**:145-149, 1974.

56. Sherman, B.M., and Korenman, S.G. Measurement of serum LH, FSH, estradiol and progesterone in disorders of the human menstrual cycle. The inadequate luteal phase. *J. Clin. Endocrinol. Metab.* **39**145-149, 1974.

57. Smith, S.M. Role of prolactin in regulatory gonadotropin. Secretion and gonad function in female rats. *Fed. Proc.* **39**:2571-2576, 1980.

58. Speroff, L., and Redwine, D.B. Exercise and menstrual function. *Phys. Sports Med.* **5**(8):42-52, 1980.

59. Strott, C.A., Cargille, C.M., Ross, G.T., and Lipsett, M.B. The short luteal phase. *J. Clin. Endocrinol. Metab.* **30**:246-251, 1970.

60. Sutton, F.R., Coleman, M.J., Casey, J., and Lazarus, L. Androgen responses during physical exercise. *Br. Med. J.* **1**:520-523, 1973.

61. Tang, L. Effect of serum sex steroids on pituitary LH response to LHRH and LH synthesis. *Am. J. Physiol.* **238**:E458-E462, 1980.

62. Taubert, H.D. Luteal phase insufficiency. In: P.J. Keller (ed.), *Contributions to gynecology and obstetrics: Female infertility*, New York, 1978, pp. 79-111.

63. Trussel, J. Statistical flaws in evidence for the Frisch hypothesis that fatness triggers menarche. *Human Biol.* **52**:711-720, 1980.

64. Tsang, B.K., Moon, Y.S., Simpson, C.W., and Armstrong, D.T. Androgen biosynthesis in human ovarian follicles: Cellular source, gonadotropic control, and adenosine 3$_{/}$,5$_{/}$-monophosphate mediation. *J. Clin. Endocrinol. Metab.* **48**:153-158, 1979.

65. Vermeulen, A., and Verdonck, L. Plasma androgen levels during the menstrual cycle. *Am. J. Obstet. Gynecol.* **125**:491-494, 1976.

66. Vihko, R., and Apter, D. The role of androgens in adolescent cycles. *J. Steroid Biochem.* **12**:369-373, 1980.

67. Warren, M.P. The effects of exercise on pubertal progression and reproductive function in girls. *J. Clin. Endocrinol. Metab.* **51**:1150-1157, 1980.

68. Webb, J.L., Millan, D.L., and Stoltz, C.J. Gynecological survey of American female athletes competing at the Montreal Olympic Games. *J. Sport Med. Phys. Fitness* **19**:405-412, 1979.

69. Wentz, A.C. Physiological and clinical considerations in luteal phase defects. *Clin. Obstet. Gynecol.* **22**:169-185, 1979.

70. Wentz, A.C. Body weight and amenorrhea. *Obstet. Gynecol.* **56**:482-487, 1980.

71. Wu, C.H., and Mikhail, G. Plasma hormone profile in anovulation. *Fertil. Steril.* **31**:258-266, 1979.

72. Yoshida, T., Hattori, Y., Suzuki, H., and Noda, K. Gonadotropin in follicular phase in women with luteal phase defect. *Tohoku J. Exp. Med.* **129**:135-138, 1979.

73. Zaharieva, E. Survey of sports women at the Tokyo Olympics. *J. Sports Med. Phys. Fitness* **5**:215-219, 1965.

74. Zeleznik, A. Premature elevation of systemic estradiol reduces serum levels of follicle stimulating hormone and lengthens the follicular phase of the menstrual cycle in rhesus monkeys. *Endocrinology* **109**:352-355, 1981.

75. Zeleznik, A.J., Midgley, A.R., and Reichert, L.E., Jr. Granulosa cell maturation in the rat: Increased binding of human chorionic gonadotropin following treatment with follicle stimulating hormone in vivo. *Endocrinology* **95**:818-825, 1974.

76. Zeleznik, A.J., Schuler, H.M., and Reichert, Jr. Gonadotropin binding sites on the rhesus monkey ovary: Role of the vasculature in the selective distribution of human chorionic gonadotropin to the preovulatory follicle. *Endocrinology* **109**:356-362, 1981.

77. Zerega, di, G.S., and Hodgen, G.D. Luteal phase dysfunction infertility: A sequel to aberrant folliculogenesis. *Fertil. Steril.* **35**:489-499, 1981.

78. Zerega, di, G.S., Turner, C.K., Stouffer, R.L., Anderson, L.D., Channing, C.P., and Hodgen, G.D. Suppression of follicle-stimulating-hormone-dependent folliculogenesis during the primate ovarian cycle. *J. Clin. Endocrinol. Metab.* **52**:451-456, 1981.

Motor psychophysics: Correlations between brain cell activity and motor performance

Edward V. Evarts
National Institute of Mental Health

The term "psychophysics" is used in reference to a branch of science that relates the physical properties of a stimulus to the sensations the stimulus evokes. Psychophysical studies can be carried out both in human subjects and subhuman primates, with studies in subhuman primates allowing the neural mechanisms underlying stimulus-detection to be investigated by recording single nerve cells in various way-stations of the brain. The work of Mountcastle (9) provided the basic paradigm in which data from human subjects were related to data obtained from neurophysiological-behavioral investigations in the monkey. The term "motor psychophysics" as used in this report refers to a field in which motor function is examined using the same basic paradigm that Mountcastle originally introduced.

The studies to be summarized here have examined the activity of brain cells in monkeys during performance of precisely controlled, skilled movements. In such studies it has been found that afferent feedback automatically controls output of both sensory and motor cortexes, especially under conditions in which the movements to be performed are precise and of low amplitude. While closed-loop feedback control systems operate for movements of low amplitude, open-loop control systems come into play to optimize performance of large, high-velocity movements. Thus, afferent input is especially important in controlling small movements but is relatively less important in controlling large movements.

Data illustrating the features just summarized have been obtained in (a) the pyramidal tract neurons (PTNs) from precentral motor cortex, (b) PTNs located in the postcentral sensory cortex, (c) corticorubral neurons (CRNs) located in motor cortex, and (d) red nucleus neurons (RNNs). Prior to considering these classes of neurons, however, it will be useful to contrast motor cortex PTNs with spinal cord motoneurons (MNs). Several major similarities between motor cortex PTNs and spinal cord MNs were discovered early: Their electrical stimulation caused muscular contraction and their destruction led to paralysis. But it soon became apparent that the paralysis following motor cortex lesions was partial rather than complete, and that electrical stimulation of areas of the cerebral cortex beyond motor cortex also elicited movement. These facts indicated that, although sharing certain properties with spinal cord MNs, motor cortex PTNs differed in several important respects.

With the introduction of techniques for recording motor cortex PTN activity during voluntary movement (3), several additional differences have become apparent. One of the most striking of these differences is the presence of continuous tonic activity in most motor cortex PTNs even during periods of complete muscular quiescence. It is perhaps paradoxical that this *difference* between motor cortex PTNs and spinal cord MNs is associated at the same time with a *similarity*. Just as there is a "size principle" in spinal cord MNs whereby smaller MNs tend to be tonically active at low levels of muscular contraction and larger MNs are active phasically during intense exertion, so is there a relationship between axonal conduction velocity and tonic vs phasic activity in PTNs: Smaller PTNs are tonically active even during absence of any discoverable muscular contraction, whereas many larger PTNs are silent in the absence of overt muscular activity (2), exhibiting discharge only when muscles become active. A second major difference between PTNs and MNs is seen in the fact that a very large proportion of motor cortex PTNs related to a given movement exhibit intense modulation for movements involving activity of a relatively small fraction of the corresponding motoneurons. Indeed, just as a very large part of the motor cortex is focused on those muscles important to precisely controlled movements, it is also the case that a very large proportion of PTNs within an area of cortex controlling a given movement is focused on that fraction of the motoneuron pool that is recruited early and that is of critical importance in precise, fine control. Here then, one sees both parallels and differences between PTNs and MNs. Finally, in contrasting PTNs and MNs one should note a most fundamental difference: A given MN sends its axon to muscle fibers of one and only one muscle, whereas a given PTN sends its axon to motoneuron pools of a number of different muscles as well as to other cortical areas and to subcortical motor control centers. In many ways, the PTN has certain properties resembling those of the "command neuron" (8) with an axon that diverges to the set of elements whose coordinated activity is necessary for a particular movement. This fact has been demonstrated unequivocally by the results of recent investigations in which HRP was injected intraaxonally into a single pyramidal tract axon. That procedure helped identify the axon terminals' widespread ramification to motoneuron nuclei of several different muscles on both sides of the spinal cord.

PTNs in postcentral sensory cortex

As originally used, the terms motor cortex and sensory cortex seemed to imply the existence of areas with sharply differing functions. However, the studies of Woolsey (10) showed that such sharp distinctions were unwarranted: Responses to afferent inputs were found in motor cortex and electrical stimulation of sensory cortex elicited movement even after total extirpation of the precentral gyrus. These observations, taken together with the fact that almost one-half of the PTNs in cerebral cortex are located in the parietal lobe (areas 3a, 3b, 1, 2, and 5), make it clear that the motor cortex is sensory as well as motor and that the sensory cortex is motor cortex as well as sensory. It was indeed for this reason that Woolsey introduced the term MsI for the precentral motor area and SmI for the postcentral sensory area.

Recent experiments in our laboratory have been carried out to identify and characterize the properties of PTNs in the postcentral gyrus (4,5). In these studies, antidromically identified PTNs in motor cortex and sensory cortex were contrasted according to three features: (a) timing with respect to onset of motor activity, (b) discharge frequencies as a function of muscular activity level, and (c) responses to afferent input. It was found that postcentral PTNs receive central inputs prior to movement as well as inputs from the periphery once receptors have been activated in the course of movement. Indeed, the onset of activity in area 3a occurred even earlier than that in area 4 prior to voluntary movement. The fact that the discharge of postcentral PTNs occurs in advance of muscular contraction means that outputs from the postcentral gyrus to the spinal cord can play a role in motor control well in advance of muscular contraction. It remains for further studies to obtain additional data contrasting the targets and functional roles of these pre- and postcentral PTNs.

Finally it should be emphasized that the postcentral gyrus itself is far from homogeneous, and that certain areas (3a and 2) in receipt of input from deep receptors seem to differ in many significant respects from those regions receiving inputs from cutaneous receptors.

Contrasting properties of motor cortex PTNs and corticorubral neurons

The studies of Jones and Wise (7) have now clarified the laminar position of the output elements in the cerebral cortex and have shown that all of the major classes of neurons projecting to lower motor control centers are located in the fifth layer. These include corticostriatal neurons, corticorubral neurons, corticobulbar neurons, cortico-olivary neurons, and certain additional classes as well. Just as a better understanding of the functional significance of motor cortex PTN output can be derived from contrasting pre- and postcentral PTNs, so can it be useful to contrast PTNs in motor cortex with other motor cortex output neurons.

In a recent study (6), activity of motor cortex PTNs and neighboring neurons identified antidromically by electrical stimulation of the red nucleus was recorded in the same monkey. There were major differences between PTNs and corticorubral neurons (CRNs) with respect to their time of discharge in relation to onset of movement: 90% of the PTNs related to the monkey's movement (a supination-pronation movement) exhibited changes in discharge frequency prior to the onset of muscular contraction and only 10% exhibited such changes after the movement. In contrast, only 26% of the related CRNs exhibited changes prior to muscular contraction, with the remaining 74% of the CRNs exhibiting changes only after movement onset.

A second way in which PTNs and CRNs differed was in their relation to force. The PTNs related to a particular movement commonly exhibited changes in discharge frequency with different force levels, whereas this was not true for CRNs. Finally, the sensory responsiveness of motor cortex PTNs was strikingly greater than that of CRNs. These differences between activity patterns in PTNs and CRNs point to the importance of identifying the neurons recorded in motor cortex according to the regions to which their axons project.

Contrasts between motor cortex and red nucleus

Some striking differences also exist between motor cortex PTNs and red nucleus neurons (RNNs); these differences parallel the differences already mentioned between motor cortex PTNs and CRNs. RNNs as a class discharge relatively later than motor cortex PTNs, and for large movements the discharge of RNNs commonly begins only after muscular contraction has already started. But while failing to discharge prior to large movements, RNNs often discharge in advance of small movements where the end-point of the movement is very close to the point of movement initiation. In speculating as to the significance of this finding, one must know the loci to which axons of the RNNs in question project. It seems likely that many of the RNNs whose activity we recorded were in the parvocellular part of the red nucleus. Appelberg (1) has shown that in addition to their well known projection to the inferior olive the axons of neurons in the parvocellular part of the red nucleus project to a bulbar nucleus that controls dynamic γ-motoneurons. On the basis of Appelberg's observation one may put forward the hypothesis that the RNNs whose activity we have recorded may have a role in controlling dynamic γ-motoneurons that come into play during those phases of movement especially dependent on afferent feedback. It seems possible that the early phases of large displacements are, relatively speaking, carried out "open-loop" whereas the terminal phases of large displacements as well as the entire course of the very small movements (already near their terminal point when they start) are much more dependent on closed-loop mechanisms.

A number of previous studies by other investigators have indicated that reflex responses to peripheral inputs are indeed less effective in the early phases of high-velocity movements and more effective later in the course of movements. In psychophysical studies carried out with human subjects, these differences between effects of afferent input in the early as compared to the later phases of movement are also apparent if one compares the effects of afferent input delivered early in the course of large, compared to small, movements. This finding further supports the view that afferent inputs produce more significant effects when they occur in the course of fine, small, low-velocity, compared to larger, high-velocity movements.

References

1. Appelberg, B. Selective central control of dynamic gamma motoneurons utilised for the functional classification of gamma cells. In: A. Taylor and A. Prochazka (eds.), *Muscle receptors and movement*, McMillan, London, 1981, pp. 97-108.

2. Evarts, E.V. Relation of discharge frequency to conduction velocity in pyramidal tract neurons. *J. Neurophysiol.* **28**:216-228, 1965.

3. Evarts, E.V. A technique for recording activity of subcortical neurons in moving animals. *Electroenceph. Clin. Neurophysiol.* **24**:83-86, 1968.

4. Evarts, E.V., and Fromm, C. Transcortical reflexes and servo control of movement. *Can. J. Physiol. Pharmacol.* **59**:757-775, 1981.

5. Fromm, C., and Evarts, E.V. Pyramidal tract neurons in somatosensory cortex: Central and peripheral inputs during voluntary movement. *Brain Research* **238**:186-191, 1982.

6. Fromm, C., Evarts, E.V., Kröller, J., and Shinoda, Y. Activity of motor cortex and red nucleus neurons during voluntary movement. In: O. Pompieano and C. Ajmone Marsan (eds.), *Brian mechanisms and perceptual awareness*, Raven, New York, 1981, pp. 269-294.

7. Jones, E.G., and Wise, S.P. Size, laminar and columnar distribution of efferent cells in the sensory-motor cortex of monkeys. *J. Compr. Neurol.* **175**:391-398, 1977.

8. Kennedy, D., Evoy, W.H., and Hanawalt, J.T. Release of coordinated behavior in crayfish by single central neurons. *Science* **154**:917-919, 1966.

9. Mountcastle, V.B. The problem of sensing and the neural coding of sensory events. In: G.C. Quarton, T. Melnuchuk, and F.O. Schmitt (eds.), *The neurosciences: A study program*, The Rockefeller University Press, New York, 1967, pp. 393-407.

10. Woolsey, C.N. Organization of somatic sensory and motor areas of the cerebral cortex. In: H.F. Harlow and C.N. Woolsey (eds.), *Biological and biochemical bases of behavior*, University of Wisconsin Press, Madison, 1958, pp. 68-81.

Nigrostriatal dopaminergic function in aging, exercise, and movement initiation

Waneen Wyrick Spirduso
The University of Texas at Austin

Old but physically trained humans can initiate a motor response to a visual or auditory stimulus significantly faster than their age-matched sedentary peers. This is typically seen in tests of reactive capacity, in which both simple and choice reaction times in physically active older men (12,54,60,63) and women[1] (26) are faster than those of their nonactive counterparts. Similarly, in an animal model the reactive capacity of old rats (720 days) that had initiated a daily running program at 350 days of age was also significantly faster at the conclusion of 2 and 6 months of training than that of their sedentary controls (64). Although some findings have not supported the hypothesis that physically trained older subjects react more quickly to a stimulus than sedentary ones, an analysis of the experimental designs and procedures of all relevant studies generally supports the relationship (61).

---

[1]Hart, B.A. Fractionated reflex and response times in women by activity and age. Unpublished dissertation, University of Massachusetts, 1980.

Peripheral mechanisms

The chronic effect of training on central nervous system (CNS) function has not received the attention in the past 50 years that it probably will receive in the next 50 years. A massive literature exists with regard to muscle disuse consequent to physical restraint, tenotomy, or denervation, but research focused on CNS response to training is sparse. Except for a few pioneering observations such as the one by Brown (10) on the effect of an assumed high physical fitness level on patellar tendon reflex amplitudes, and others by Tipton and Karpovitch (69), Francis and Tipton (19), and Reid (47) on the effects of increases in muscular strength on patellar reflex latency, little research has been reported on the topic. Ten years passed before the subject was again addressed by Clarkson (11), who found no influence of a self-reported life style of physical activity on fractionated patellar tendon reflex latencies.

Just as neurons have profound transneuronal trophic effects on post-synaptically associated neuronal structures (43) and on the muscle fibers they innervate, muscular contraction has a trophic influence on its innervating neuron and associated interneurons (16). It may be possible that postsynaptic muscle fiber transfers chemical(s) to the presynaptic terminals (3,5). In fact, Frank (20, p. 367) has suggested that "some substance continuously released from each muscle fiber influences the facilitation properties of its own synaptic terminals." Gutman and Hanzlikova (25) were convinced that the greatest effect of aging on the motor system is the decline in neurosecretory trophic exchange, a function highly influenced by the degree of neural activity and by spontaneous transmitter release. Neurosecretory trophic exchanges occur in all neurons, and supraspinal exchanges could very well be involved in a complex chain of activation that incorporates muscular contraction.

Although peripheral factors such as changes in the morphology and electrical properties of populations of motor units must be recognized, these factors can't account for the magnitude of the loss in behavioral reactivity of the aged. Peripheral factors also don't explain very well the effect that whole body exercise such as running seems to have on the capacity to react quickly with one unexercised digit. For studies in which simple and choice reaction times produced by lower limb activation, such as kicking a target, were studied in conjunction with an aerobic running program, the onset of electromyographic premotor bursts was used to measure reaction latency, effectively excluding training-related contributions of changes in muscle fiber characteristics to the response. Exercise must affect CNS function in a way that is more general than would be anticipated from the neuromotor specificity of training principle. Training must act, by some mechanism not yet totally clear, to tune the nervous system at several levels and in many different ways so that it maintains its integrity throughout a substantial portion of the last few decades of life.

The dependence of motor control on neurotransmitter systems, in conjunction with the observation that neurotransmitter systems may become imbalanced with aging (50) but are also strongly affected by neuroendocrine responses, suggests that neurotransmitter systems might be influenced by chronic exercise and thus serve as a mechanism by which reactive capacity is maintained. While recognizing the substantial limitations inherent in limiting oneself to a single neurotransmitter for study, we nevertheless turned our attention to the nigrostriatal dopaminergic neurotransmitter system. This system is severely affected by aging, contributes substantially to motor control, and is susceptible to neuroendocrine influences.

Decreases in nigrostriatal dopamine with age

The effects of age on brain neurotransmitters are seen most dramatically in the catecholamine systems (18), in which the nigrostriatal dopamine system has been the target of extensive study. Several markers of dopamine integrity have been shown to decline with age: dopamine uptake (17,29,50,57), turnover (43), and dopamine receptor binding (25,33,41). Decreases in dopamine receptors in aged animals are implied by the decreased binding of dopamine antagonists to striatal membranes in rabbits (37,38), rats (23,24,38), and mice (51,52). It has also been suggested (46) that cells postsynaptic to the nigrostriatal pathway may be impaired at an earlier age than those in the nigrostriatal pathway itself. Even compensatory mechanisms, such as postsynaptic supersensitivity that occurs in response to decreased presynaptic output, may be compromised by age (46).

Dopamine-related enzyme systems are also affected by aging. Striatal tyrosine hydroxylase, the rate-limiting enzyme of dopamine synthesis, substantially declines, with losses as great as 35% in the Wistar rat neostriatum (39-41). Both of the catecholamine synthetic enzymes decrease with age, whereas the catabolic enzyme monamine oxidase (Type A vs B) increases with age (14,48). The substantial age-related losses in enzymes affecting dopamine initiate a progressive imbalance between dopaminergic, cholinergic, and gabaergic tone, as the extrapyramidal enzymes choline acetyltransferase and glutamic decarboxylase do not decline at similar rates (35,41). Furthermore, aging may not only selectively affect the nigrostriatal system, but may also selectively affect specific DA receptor subtypes, such as DA-1 and DA-2, which may be associated with different DA pathways (R.E. Wilcox, personal communication). These receptor subtypes may deteriorate at different rates and may also have different functions in movement control. What is the role of the nigrostriatal dopaminergic system in movement initiation?

Nigrostriatal dopamine and movement initiation

The relationship between nigrostriatal DA depletion and motor dysfunction has been hypothesized for years, largely on the basis of the observation that decreased DA levels and nigrostriatal cell deterioration in humans precede the decomposition of movement that occurs in aging and in Parkinson's disease (29). Furthermore, the symptoms of Parkinson's disease — slowness of movement, muscular rigidity, and tremor — are more likely to occur in older individuals (4). More direct analyses of dopaminergic function and movement initiation can be made by using the animal model of Parkinson's disease. In this model, nigrostriatal lesions are produced unilaterally and bilaterally by a neurotoxic drug, 6-hydroxydopamine (6-OHDA). Injection of 6-OHDA, both in substantia nigra or pathways leading from the substantia nigra to the striatum, has been shown to induce a profound decrease in motor behavior. Injections of 6-OHDA in both nigrostriatal pathways bilaterally cause destruction of ascending nigrostriatal DA pathways, mimicking the type of destruction seen in Parkinson's diseased patients and resulting in profound akinesia (slowness to initiate movement), bradykinesia (slow movement), and poverty of movement (absence of movement). The unilateral destruction of ascending nigrostriatal DA pathways appears to be strongly associated with a unilateral motor bias (71-73) (Figure 1); an imbalance of DA activity in the two sides occurs and the animal turns in tight and frequent circles. Turns are toward the lesioned side when the motor bias is facilitated by the nonlesioned, more active contralateral striatum. Movement is away from the lesioned side when the motor bias is induced by supersensitivity of the denervated ipsilateral striatum.

Direction of turning can also be manipulated by drugs that mimic DA and/or DA blockers (antagonists). Pycock and Marsden (46) suggested that drug-induced circling is a two-component mechanism resulting from activation of both striatal and limbic areas. Apomorphine, for example, when injected intraperitoneally into a unilaterally lesioned animal with partial DA depletion of one nigrostriatum, stimulates the "supersensitive" postsynaptic membranes in the striatum. Greater activity of the lesioned side leads to greater contralateral motor activation and body turning toward the lesioned side (Figure 2).

Many studies exist documenting the observation that the nigrostriatal DA system is in some way involved in the performance and acquisition of goal-directed movement, but not in reflex behavior. Neuroleptic drugs (antagonists of postsynaptic dopamine receptors and thus blockers of DA) impair operantly conditioned avoidance behavior in rats, but not the more reflexive behavior of escape (62). Thus, unilateral disruption of the nigrostriatal DA system by 6-OHDA lesions impaired acquired skilled movement in the limb contralateral to the lesion but not stereo-

Figure 1—Left and right nigrostriatal
pathways in an animal lesioned in right
substantia nigra (SN). Destruction of
the inhibitory substantia nigra cells results in a release of inhibition and consequently an imbalanced outflow from
the pallidum, internal portion of the
thalamus, and the cortex. The hatch
marks symbolize DA destruction and
the dashed lines reflect resultant abnormal output.

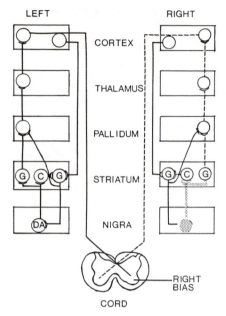

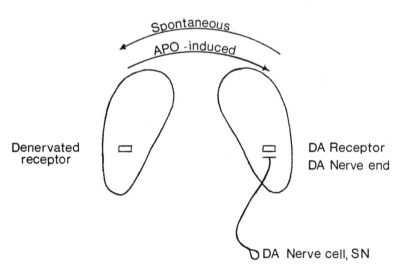

Figure 2—Differential directions of spontaneous and apomorphine (APO)-
induced turning. Spontaneous turning occurs toward the side of the lesion and
contralateral to the intact DA system. The more "active" DA system is the intact
system. Apomorphine-induced turning is contralateral to the lesion. APO stimulates the remaining DA receptors of the denervated side. Because they have developed a supersensitivity to DA and DA agonists such as APO, this side now is
more "active" with respect to the intact side; consequently the animal turns contralateral to the supersensitive, more active side (71).

typed movements such as grasping, grooming, and food-holding (55).

Although many indirect lines of evidence point to a dependence of reactive capacity on nigrostriatal DA integrity, the relationship is not resolved. The apparent age-related decrease in movement initiation speed seen in older individuals and Parkinson's patients may be related indirectly, rather than causally, to decreases in DA level. Indeed, evidence for DA involvement from most animal models has been generally based on relatively slow motor tasks such as pressing a bar or avoiding a shuttle box (31). A better way to understand the contribution that the nigrostriatal DA system makes to movement initiation is to isolate the initiation of the response from the execution of it.

The separation of the onset of response from the response itself can be accomplished using premotor latency to the onset of electromyogram (EMG) as distinguished from the duration of activity in the EMGs of human subjects, but biochemical assays of the nigrostriatum contralateral to the response are not possible in humans. Conversely, implantation of EMG electrodes in the muscles of operantly conditioned animals is an invasive and cumbersome procedure. To address these problems, we have recently developed in our laboratories[2] (75) a behavioral movement initiation task that enables us to isolate initiation from execution and duration of response and reduces the movement duration time to approximately 10 msec, whereas the initiation latency of the response requires at least 120 msec, in the fastest animal. The rat holds a lever in a depressed position and releases it as quickly as possible when a buzzer (conditioned stimulus, CS) or shock (unconditioned stimulus, UCS) is initiated. This provides reaction latencies from 120 to 1,000 msec, depending on the CS-UCS interval. In order to assess the DA function we have used the measurements of cerebral DA receptor binding and affinity in the caudate nuclei.

In an initial experiment in our laboratories (75), the caudate nuclei of two strains of rat known to differ in behavioral response speed were assayed for DA binding affinity and receptor density. The rats in the CR-CD/F strain were fast and successful at the task, whereas the Zivic-Miller (ZM) rats were significantly slower; 57% of the ZM rats were unable to reach criterion performance levels. Figure 3 shows that DA receptor binding affinity (K_D values) may be the more important correlate of movement initiation of the two DA parameters, whereas DA receptor density (Bmax) may serve as a compensatory mechanism. The binding affinity was highest (low K_D) in the fast-reacting strain (CR-CD/F) but low and similar in the slow successful and the unsuccessful ZM-CDs. Conversely, increases may occur in the receptor density (Bmax) of the

---

[2]Wolf, M.D. Strain differences in nigrostriatal function and the initiation of movement. Unpublished dissertation, University of Texas at Austin, 1979.

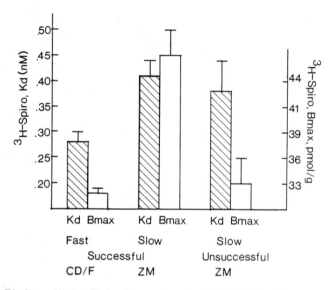

Figure 3 — Binding affinity (K$_D$) and receptor density (Bmax) in the two strains of rat which differed in the latency to initiate a shock avoidance task; fast, successful CR-CD/F rats (left); slow, successful ZM rats (center); and culled ZM rats (right). Left ordinate indicates the unit values of K$_D$ (nM) whereas the right ordinate indicates unit values of Bmax (pmol/g).

slow but successful rats within a strain that compensate for the lower binding affinity. Although the binding affinity of both ZM-CD groups was low, the receptor density was significantly higher in the successful group. This study prompted a series of experiments to confirm the relationship between DA and movement initiation speed in a movement initiation task that challenged the reactive capacity of the animal.

Within-strain DA binding and reactive capacity

Finding a relationship between binding affinity and speed of response within the same strain would present a stronger case for the relationship than does such a relationship between two different strains. Twenty young male Fisher 344 rats (120 days) were conditioned in five computerized reactive capacity chambers using a shaping protocol modified from Wolf et al. (75) for eight sessions of 50 trials each. A [³H]spiroperidol binding assay was completed on the two caudate nuclei of each of the six fastest and six slowest animals based on the percentage avoidance and latency scores obtained using the 500-msec UC-UCS interval during the seventh and eighth days of conditioning (64). Binding affinity was significantly greater in the fast group compared to the slow group ($t = 3.66$, $p = < .01$; see Figure 4). Thus, the relationship be-

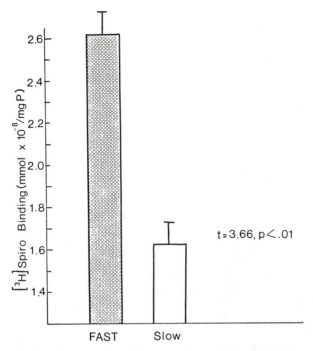

Figure 4 — Spiroperidol binding with the DA receptors in the striatum of the six fastest rats compared with the six slowest rats in a group of 20 Fisher 344 rats.

tween DA binding and movement initiation seen between two strains was also seen within a strain.

Nigrostriatal lesions

In order to induce selective unilateral degeneration of the nigrostriatal pathway and thus curtail DA transmission ipsilateral to the injection site, we conducted a series of experiments in which 6-OHDA was injected unilaterally into the brain and the movement initiation by the rat's paw was examined. The extent of nigrostriatal DA system degeneration was first assessed by examination of stereotypic circling (73) in response to intraperitoneal injections of apomorphine, a dopamine agonist. Ten Long-Evans male rats (150 days) were trained in the movement initiation task (50 trials on each of 7 days) 2 months following unilateral 6-OHDA lesioning. On the last 3 days of the testing, the unilaterally lesioned animals ($n = 5$) generally chose to use the ipsilateral paw, but were still slower than controls ($n = 15$) and shams ($n = 5$). When tested on the movement initiation task with the paw contralateral to the lesion or with the paw ipsilateral to the lesion, on separate days, the behavioral indices of unilateral DA depletion (turning direction and intensity) predicted ac-

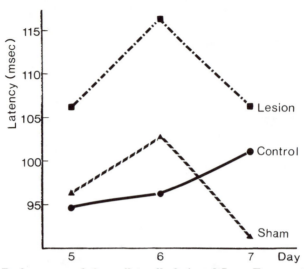

Figure 5 — Performance of the unilaterally lesioned Long-Evans rats (5), compared to a sham group (n = 5) and a control group (n = 15) in the shock-avoidance task. Ordinate values are length of time in msec from onset of an auditory cue (buzzer) to the release of the lever.

curately the superiority of one paw's movement initiation over the other (Table 1).

In another experiment, 16 Long-Evans male rats were lesioned unilaterally, with behavioral testing conducted 2 months postlesion (65). Once again, paws ipsilateral to the lesion were preferentially used and the contralateral paw performance was inversely related to nigrostriatal DA uptake (r = -74). Depletions as small as 22% resulted in substantial delays in movement initiation (Figure 6), demonstrating the high sensitivity of our movement initiation task. Animals exhibiting 50% or greater DA uptake deficit failed to reach performance criterion.

In the third experiment, Long-Evans male rats (120 days) were shaped on the movement initiation task for 7 days, after which the lesion group (n = 10) received unilateral microinjections of 6-OHDA in the medial forebrain bundle of the substantia nigra, the sham group (n = 5) received a vehicle injection, and the normal group (n = 10) received no treatment. Seven days later all groups were retested on the capacity to respond directly to the shock, as in an escape paradigm, or to the buzzer (CS) as in an avoidance behavior. The lesion group was substantially slower than the other two not only in response to unconditional shock (escape response; see Figure 7) but also in response to the buzzer (avoidance response; see Figure 8). Several of the lesion group animals could not perform the task successfully with either paw, and those that could always used the paw ipsilateral to the lesion.

Table 1

**Concordance Among Lesion Side and Predicted,
and Observed Paw Superiority**

Lesion	Turning		Predicted	Observed	
(6-OHDA)	Intensity[a]	Direction[b]	superiority[c]	superiority	Concordance[d]
L1	1.27	Contra	Left	Left	+
L2	0.8	Ipsi	Right	Right	+
L3	4.0	Contra	Left	Left	+
L4	4.0	Contra	Left	Neither	−
L5	4.0	Contra	Left	Left	+
Sham					
S1	.2	Either	Either	Neither	+
S2	.2	Either	Either	Neither	+
S3	.2	Either	Either	Neither	+
S4	.2	Either	Either	Right	+
S5	.2	Either	Either	Right	+

[a]Turning intensity = number of 180° turns made in 1 min.

[b]Direction of turning with respect to the lesioned side.

[c]Predicted superiority of one paw response in lever release compared to the other. All lesions were left striatal lesions; consequently, on the basis of observed apomorphine-induced turning contralateral to the lesion, left paw superiority would be predicted. Paw superiority was defined as one paw being significantly faster than the other.

[d]Concordance: A + indicates paw superiority was in the direction of that predicted by asymmetrical turning.

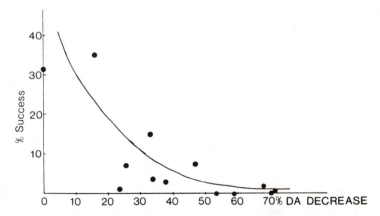

Figure 6 — Comparison of percentage success in the avoidance reactivity task and extent of DA depletion. DA decrease is expressed as the percentage decrease in DA of the lesioned caudate relative to the nonlesioned side.

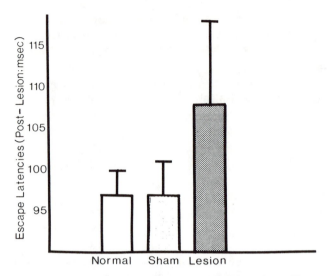

Figure 7 — Escape latencies of sham, normal, and lesioned Long-Evans rats (120 days of age). Latencies, in msec, are the length of time from the onset of shock to the release of the lever.

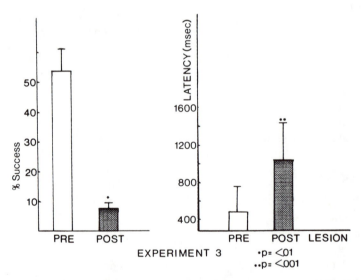

Figure 8 — Percentage success and latencies of Long-Evans rats (120 days) pre- and post-6-OHDA unilateral lesion. Percentage success = percentage of trials in which the lever was successfully released during the delay provided between onset of stimulus (buzzer) and onset of shock. Latencies are length of time from onset of buzzer to release of lever for those trials in which the release was within the CS-UCS interval.

Exercise and nigrostriatal dopaminergic function

The results of the previous three experiments clearly revealed a strong relationship between the nigrostriatal DA system and initiation of fast movement. An obvious implication, then, is that the behavioral deficits seen in movement initiation in old animals may be, at least in part, the result of a deteriorating nigrostriatal dopaminergic system. If trained, old animals and humans have the capacity to initiate movement faster than sedentary animals, could this be attributed to a possible trophic effect of training that retarded the deterioration of the nigrostriatal DA system? Four possibilities are entertained by which a training effect might influence this system, and consequently, brain function: (a) a direct increase in DA turnover and DA levels in brain, (b) prevention of high blood glucose levels in the brain and the subsequent suppression of DA neuronal firing, (c) a decrease in circulating corticosteroids, which damage brain cells, and (d) continued stimulation of DA neurons by training-induced increases in endorphins.

Brown and Van Huss (9) reported that whole brain levels of norepinephrine (NE) were higher in rats that had trained; Brown et al. (8) found that NE levels increased in the cerebrum and 5-HT concentrations increased in the midbrain in rats after an 8-week exposure to exercise. Increased concentrations of neurotransmitters could be a significant factor in maintaining normal behavioral functioning in older animals.

Saller and Chiodo (49) reported that increased levels of glucose suppressed the basal firing of DA neurons in the zona compacta of the substantia nigra. They suggested that glucose-induced increases in insulin might directly stimulate cerebral insulin receptors and alter the metabolism of nigrostriatal DA neurons, or affect indirectly the metabolism of other neurotransmitters that interact with DA, such as GABA, glycine, or serotonin.

Cerebral blood glucose utilization decreases with age, particularly in the sensory motor cortex, caudate nucleus, and globus pallidus (58). Decreases in utilization, coupled with increased insulin resistance that occurs with aging, could lead to increased levels of circulating glucose which would in turn act to suppress DA firing. Exercise, conversely, might partially reverse this process by enhancing insulin sensitivity (7,34,42,59,70,74).

Exercise may provide a trophic effect on DA neurons by decreasing circulating corticosteroids which in turn may lower blood glucose, reduce neuronal destruction of brain cells by glucocorticoids, and increase the trophic neural stimulation provided by the positive feedback produced by increased production of ACTH. Finch (17) proposed a neuroendocrine theory of aging in which a cascade of neuroendocrine imbalances leads to an impaired performance and inability to cope with metabolic challenges. Landfield (33) suggested even more specifically that adrenal corticosteroids (primarily glucocorticoids) are a major factor in aging of the brain (1), whereas high levels of ACTH serve a trophic function in the maintenance of brain cells (32). Brain morphology of adrenalectomized rats with low corticosteroids and high levels of ACTH (produced by the pituitary in response to lowered corticosteroids in the blood), was similar to that of the young group. In addition, morphological markers of old rats injected with a neuropeptide analog of ACTH was not different from those of the young rat brains.

Exercise stimulates the release of ACTH (21,67) and training results in a decreased response of both ACTH and corticosteroids (67) and to a lowered sympathetic response to work tasks (67). If the adaptation to exercise resulting in reduced endocrine response occurs at the adrenal cortex, it could lead to an increase of the ACTH/corticosteroid ratio, which might postpone the neurological deterioration proposed by Landfield.

Another way exercise might influence nigrostriatal function and therefore reactivity is by stimulating dopamine turnover through the release of endorphins. Substantia nigra cell dopaminergic nerve endings have a large population of opiate receptors (44,45). When these receptors are activated by opiates, dopamine turnover in the striatum of both the rat (2,13,22,66) and mouse (36,53,56), is increased, but functional increases in dopamine appear only in the mouse. Wood et al. (76), however, found that endorphin injected intraventricularly in rats produced dose-dependent elevations in dopamine metabolites.

Two differentiated endorphin pools have been identified, one in peripheral blood coming from the pituitary (15,68), and one directly synthesized by peptidergic neurons of the brain (28,67). The effects of exercise on these pools and the interaction of hormonally influenced peripheral pools on the centrally mediated pools are unknown.

Plasma levels of endorphins have been shown to be elevated in marathon runners at rest, 60 miles into, and after a 100-mile race (6). Norepinephrine and DOPAC (3-4 dihydroxyphenylacetic acid) were also elevated, whereas dopamine levels were unaffected. Fraioli et al. (21) found large increases in endorphins and ACTH at maximal effort, and at 15 and 30 min. after treadmill running in eight male athletes.

Brown et al. (8) suggested that changes in exercise-induced cortical norepinephrine and 5-HT concentrations occurred in 75-day-old and adult male rats (9), so it seemed reasonable to hypothesize that chronic exercise might also change DA receptor binding. Gilliam et al.[3] have found preliminary evidence that [3H]spiroperidol receptor binding in the

---

[3]Gilliam, P., Spirduso, W., Wilcox, R., Martin, T., and Farrar, R. Effects of interval and distance training on [3H]spiroperidol binding in the caudate nucleus of Sprague-Dawley rats. Unpublished data, Spring 1982.

caudate nucleus of young Sprague-Dawley rats that have experienced 8 weeks of aerobic training or interval training was significantly higher than in sedentary rats. It is probable that these training effects will be even more substantial when examined in old rats in whom 20-30% depletion of DA is commonly observed. In these age groups, exercised animals may retain a greater number of nigrostriatal DA neurons due to a greater amount of neuroendocrine stimulation. This condition in turn would cause enhanced performance of any behavior for which the nigrostriatal system is an essential component.

Acknowledgment

Appreciation is extended to R.P. Farrar, R.E. Wilcox, and Timothy Schallert for their scholarly interaction and generous conceptual contributions and critique in the preparation of this manuscript. Gratitude is also extended to Priscilla Gilliam, Dana Vaughn, and Meg Upchurch for their assistance in the data collection and analysis of the studies reported from our laboratories.

References

1. Adelman, R.C. An age dependent modification of enzyme regulation. *J. Biol. Chem.* **245**:1032-1035, 1970.

2. Ahtee, L., and Kaaraninen, I. The effect of narcotic analgesics on the homovanillic acid content of rat nucleus caudatus. *Eur. J. Pharmacol.* **22**:206-208, 1973.

3. Atwood, H.L., and Bittner, G.D. Matching of excitatory and inhibitory inputs to crustacean muscle fibers. *J. Neurophysiol.* **34**:157-170, 1971.

4. Bernheimer, W., Birkmayer, O., Hornykiewicz, O., Jellinger, K., and Seitelberger, F. Brain dopamine and the syndrome of Parkinson and Huntington. Clinical, morphological and neurochemical correlations. *J. Neurol. Sci.* **20**:415-455, 1973.

5. Bittner, G.D. Differentiation of nerve terminals in the crayfish opener muscle and its functional significance. *J. Gen. Physiol.* **51**:731-758, 1968.

6. Bortz, W.M., Angwin, P., Mefford, I.N., Boarder, M.R., Noyce, N., and Barchas, J.D. Catecholamines, dopamine, and endorphin levels during extreme exercise. *New Engl. J. Med.* **305**:466-467, 1981.

7. Bjorntorp, P., Faklen, M., Grimby, G., Gustafson, A., Holm, J., Renstrom, P., and Schersten, T. Carbohydrate and lipid metabolism in middle-aged physically well-trained men. *Metabolism* **21**:1037-1044, 1972.

8. Brown, B.S., Payne, T., Kim, C., Moore, G., Krebs, P., and Martin, W. Chronic response of rat brain norepinephrine and serotonin levels to en-

durance training. *J. Appl. Physiol. Respir. Environ. Exercise Physiol.* **46**:19-23, 1979.

9. Brown, B.S., and Van Huss, W. Exercise and rat brain catecholamines. *J. Appl. Physiol.* **34**:664-669, 1973.

10. Brown, L.T. The influence of exercise in muscle tonus as exhibited by the knee jerk. *Am. J. Physiol.* **72**:241-247, 1925.

11. Clarkson, P.M. The relationship of age and level of physical activity with the fractionated components of patellar reflex-time. *J. Gerontol.* **33**:650-656, 1978.

12. Clarkson, P.M., and Kroll, W.P. Practice effects on fractionated response time related to age and activity level. *J. Motor Behav.* **10**:275-286, 1978.

13. Costa, E., Cheney, D.L., Racagni, G., and Zsilla, G. An analysis at synaptic level of the morphine action in striatum and N accumbens: Dopamine and acetylcholine interactions. *Life Sci.* **17**:1-8, 1975.

14. Coté, L.J., and Kremzer, L.T. Changes in neurotransmitter systems with increasing age in human brain. *Trans. Am. Soc. Neurochem.*, 5th Ann. Meeting, 1974, p. 83.

15. Cox, B.M., Ohheim, K.E., Teschmacher, H., and Goldstein, A. A peptidelike substance from pituitary that acts like morphine. 2. Purification and properties. *Life Sci.* **16**:1777-1782, 1975.

16. Eccles, J.C. Trophic influences in the mammalian central nervous system. In: M. Rockstein (ed.), *Development and aging in the nervous system.* Academic, New York, 1973.

17. Finch, C.E. The regulation of physiological changes during mammalian aging. *Q. Rev. Biol.* **51**:49-83, 1976.

18. Finch, C.E. Neuroendocrine and autonomic aspects of aging. In: C.E. Finch and L. Hayflick (eds.), *Handbook of the biology of aging*, Van Nostrand Reinhold, New York, 1977.

19. Francis, P.R., and Tipton, C.M. Influence of a weight training program on quadriceps reflex time. *Med. Sci. Sport* **1**:91-94, 1969.

20. Frank, E. Matching facilitation at the neuromuscular junction of the lobster: A possible case for influence of muscle on nerve. *J. Physiol.* **233**:635-658, 1973.

21. Fraioli, F., Moretti, C., Pavolucci, D., Alicicco, E., Crescenzi, F., and Fortunio, G. Physical exercise stimulates marked concomitant release of β-endorphin and adrenocorticotropic hormone (ACTH) in peripheral blood in man. *Experientia* **36**:987-989, 1980.

22. Gauchy, C., Agid, Y., Glowinski, J., and Cheramy, A. Acute effects of morphine on dopamine synthesis and release and tyrosine metabolism in the rat striatum. *Eur. J. Pharmacol.* **22**:311-319, 1973.

23. Govoni, S., Loddo, P., Spano, P.F., and Trabucchi, M. Dopamine receptor

sensitivity in brain and retina of rats during aging. *Brain Res.* **138**:565-570, 1977.

24. Govoni, S., Spano, P.E., and Trabucci, M. [^{3}H]Haloperidol and [^{3}H]spiroperidol binding in rat striatum during aging. *J. Pharm. Pharmacol.* **30**:448-449, 1978.

25. Gutman, E., and Hanzlikova, V. Age changes in the neuromuscular system. *Scientechnica*, Bristol, 1972, pp. 82-83.

26. Hart, B.A. The effect of age and habitual activity on the fractionated components of resisted and unresisted response time. *Med. Sci. Sports Exercise* **13**:78, 1981.

27. Hornykiewicz, O. The mechanisms of action of L-DOPA in Parkinson's disease. *Life Sci.* **15**:1249-1260, 1974.

28. Hughes, J. Isolation of an endogenous compound from the brain with pharmacological properties similar to morphine. *Brain Res.* **88**:295-308, 1975.

29. Jones, V., and Finch, C.E. Aging and dopamine uptake by subcellular fractions of the C57BL/6J male mouse brain. *Brain Res.* **91**:197-215, 1975.

30. Joseph, J.A., Berger, R.E., Engel, B.T., and Roth, G.S. Age-related changes in the nigrostriatum: A behavioral and biochemical analysis. *J. Gerontol.* **33**:643-649, 1978.

31. Kempf, E., Greilsamer, J., Mack, G., and Mandel, P. Correlation of behavioral differences in 3 strains of mice with differences in brain amines. *Nature* **247**:483-485.

32. Landfield, P.W. An endocrine hypothesis of brain aging and studies on brain-endocrine correlations and monosynaptic neurophysiology during aging. In: C. Finch, D. Potter, and A. Kenny (eds.), *Proceedings of the 2nd Tarbox Parkinson's Disease Foundation Symposium: Aging and Neuroendocrine Regulation*, Plenum, New York, 1979, pp. 179-199.

33. Landfield, P.W., Waymire, J.C., and Lynch, G. Hippocampal aging and adrenocorticoids: Quantitative correlations. *Science* **202**:1098-1102, 1978.

34. LeBlanc, J., Nadeau, A., Boulay, M., and Rousseau-Migneron, S. Effects of physical training and adiposity on glucose metabolism and ^{125}I-insulin binding. *J. Appl. Physiol.* **46**:235-239, 1979.

35. Lloyd, K., Dreksler, S., and Bird, E.D. Alterations in ^{3}H-GABA binding in Huntington's chorea. *Life Sci.* **21**:747-754, 1977.

36. Loh, H.H., Hitzemann, R.J., and Way, E.L. Effect of acute morphine administration on the metabolism of brain catecholamines. *Life Sci.* **12**:33-41, 1973.

37. Makman, M.H., Ahn, H.S., Thal, L.J., Dvorkin, B., Horowitz, S.G., Sharpless, N.S., and Rosenfeld, M. In: C.E. Finch, D.E. Potter, and A.D. Kenny (eds.), *Aging and neuroendocrine relationships*, Plenum, New York, 1978.

38. Makman, M.H., Ahn, H.S., Thal, L.J., Sharpless, N.S., Dvorkin, B., Horowitz, S.G., and Rosenfeld, M. Aging and monoamine receptors in brain. *Fed. Proc.* **38**:1922-1926, 1979.

39. McGeer, E.G., Fibiger, H.C., McGeer, P.L., and Wickson, V. Aging and brain enzymes. *Exp. Gerontol.* **6**:391-396, 1971.

40. McGeer, E.G., McGeer, P.L., and Wada, J.A. Distribution of tyrosine hydroxylase in human and animal brain. *J. Neurochem.* **18**:1647-1658, 1971.

41. McGeer, P.L., and McGeer, E.G. Enzymes associated with the metabolisms of catecholamines, acetylcholine and gaba in human controls and patients with Parkinson's disease and Huntington's chorea. *J. Neurochem.* **26**:65-76, 1976.

42. Mondon, C.E., Dolkas, C.B., and Reaven, G.M. Site of enhanced insulin sensitivity in exercise trained rats at rest. *Am. J. Physiol.* **239**:E169-E177, 1980.

43. Mufson, E.J., and Stein, D.G. Degeneration in the spinal cord of old rats. *Exp. Neurol.* **70**:179-186, 1980.

44. Pollard, H., Llorens, C., and Schwartz, J.C. Enkephalin receptors on dopaminergic neurons in rat striatum. *Nature London* **268**:745-747, 1977.

45. Pollard, H., Llorens, C., Schwartz, J., Gros, C., and Dray, F. Localization of opiate receptors and enkephalins in the rat striatum in relationship with the nigrostriatal dopaminergic system: Lesion studies. *Brain Res.* **151**:392-398, 1978.

46. Pycock, C.J., and Marsden, C.D. The rotating rodent: A two component system? *Eur. J. Pharmacol.* **47**:167-175, 1978.

47. Reid, J.G. Static strength increase and its effect upon triceps surae reflex time. *Res. Q.* **38**:691-697.

48. Robinson, D.S., Nies, A., Davis, J.N., Bunney, W.E., David, J.M., Colburn, R.W., Bourne, H.R., Shaw, D.M., and Coppen, A.J. Aging, monamines, and monamine oxidase levels. *Lancet* **1**:290-291, 1972.

49. Saller, C.F., and Chiodo, L.A. Glucose suppresses basal firing and haloperidol-induced increases in the firing rate of central dopaminergic neurons. *Science* **210**:1269-1271, 1980.

50. Samorajski, T. Central neurotransmitter substances and aging: A review. *J. Am. Geriatr. Soc.* **25**:337-347, 1977.

51. Severson, J.A., and Finch, C.E. Presentation at the Ann. Meeting of the Gerontol. Soc., 1978.

52. Severson, J.A., and Finch, C.E. Reduced dopaminergic binding during aging in the rodent striatum. *Brain Res.* **192**:147-162, 1980.

53. Sharmon, D.F. Changes in the metabolism of 3,4-dihydroxyphenylethylamine (dopamine) in the striatum of the mouse induced by drugs. *Br. J. Pharmacol.* **28**:153-163, 1966.

54. Sherwood, D.E., and Selder, D.J. Cardiorespiratory health, reaction time, and aging. *Med. Sci. Sports* **11**:186-189, 1979.

55. Siegfried, B., and Bureš, J. Handedness in rats: Blockade of reaching behavior by unilateral 6-OHDA injections into substantia nigra and caudate nucleus. *Physiol. Psychol.* **8**:360-368, 1980.

56. Smith, C.B., Sheldon, M.T., Bednarczyk, J.H., and Villarreal, J.E. Morphine-induced increases in the incorporation of ^{14}C-tyrosine into ^{14}C-dopamine and ^{14}C-norepinephrine in the mouse brain: Antagonism by naloxone and tolerance. *J. Pharmacol. Exp. Ther.* **1980**:547-557, 1972.

57. Smith, R.C., Strong, J.R., Leelavathi, D.E., and Rolsten, C. Aging produces greater behavioral effects of dopamine agonists in rodents. *Soc. Neurosci. Abstr.*, 1977.

58. Sokoloff, L. Effects of normal aging on cerebral circulation and energy metabolism. In: F. Hoffmeister and C. Muller (eds.), *Brain function in old age*, Springer-Verlag, New York, 1979.

59. Soman, V.R., Koivisto, V.A., Grantham, P., and Felig, P. Increased insulin binding to monocytes after acute exercise in normal man. *J. Clin. Endocr. Metab.* **47**:216-219, 1978.

60. Spirduso, W.W. Reaction and movement time as a function of age and physical activity level. *J. Gerontol.* **30**:435-440, 1975.

61. Spirduso, W.W. Physical fitness in relation to motor aging. In: J.A. Mortimer, F.J. Pizzorola, and G.J. Maletta (eds.), *Adv. Neurogerontol: The Aging Motor System*, 1982, 120-151.

62. Spirduso, W.W., Abraham, L.D., and Wolf, M.D. Effects of chlorpromazine on escape and avoidance responses: A closer look. *Pharmacol. Biochem. Behav.* **14**:433-438, 1981.

63. Spirduso, W.W., and Clifford, P. Neuromuscular speed and consistency of performance as a function of age, physical activity levels, and type of physical activity. *J. Gerontol.* **33**:26-30, 1978.

64. Spirduso, W.W., and Farrar, R.P. Effects of aerobic training on reactive capacity: An animal model. *J. Gerontol.* **36**:654-662, 1981.

65. Spirduso, W.W., Wilcox, R.E., Schallert, T.J., Gilliam, P., Vaughn, D., and Upchurch, M. Rapid avoidance behavior deficits and movement initation in rats after 6-OHDA microinjections in substantia nigra. *Soc. Neurosci. Abstr.*, 1981.

66. Sugrve, M.F. The effects of acutely administered analgesics on the turnover of noradrenaline and dopamine in various regions of the rat brain. *Br. J. Pharmacol.* **52**:159-165, 1974.

67. Terjung, R.L. Endocrine systems. In: R.H. Strauss (ed.), *Sports medicine and physiology*, W.B. Saunders, Philadelphia, 1979.

68. Teschemacher, H., Opheim, K.R., Cox, B.M., and Goldstein, A. A peptide-like solution. *Life Sci.* **16**:1771-1775, 1975.

69. Tipton, C.M., and Karpovich, P.V. Exercise and the patellar reflex. *J. Appl. Physiol.* **21**:15-18, 1966.

70. Tremblay, A., LeBlanc, J., Nadeau, A., and Richard, D. Effect of nutrition and training on glucose tolerance and plasma insulin in human subjects. *Med. Sci. Sports Exercise* **13**:84, 1981.

71. Understedt, U. Post-synaptic supersensitivity after 6-OHDA induced degeneration of the nigrostriatal dopamine system in the rat brain. *Acta Physiol. Scand.* **82**:69-93 (Suppl. 367), 1971.

72. Understedt, U. In: T. Malinfors and H. Thoenen (eds.), *6-Hydroxydopamine and catecholamine neurons.* North Holland, Amsterdam, 1971, p. 315.

73. Ungerstedt, U., and Arbuthnott, G. Quantitative recording of rotational behavior in rats after 6-hydroxydopamine lesions of the nigrostriatal dopamine system. *Brain Res.* **24**:485-493, 1970.

74. Wirth, A., Holm, G., and Bjorntorp, P. Effect of physical training on insulin uptake by the perfused rat liver. *Med. Sci. Sports Exercise* **13**:83, 1981.

75. Wolf, M.D., Wilcox, R.E., Riffee, W.H., and Abraham, L.D. Strain differences in dopamine receptor function and the initiation of movement. *Pharmacol. Biochem. Behav.* **13**:5-7, 1980.

76. Wood, P.L., Stotland, M., Richard, J.W., and Rackham, A. Action of mu, kappa, sigma, delta, and agonist antagonist opiates on striatal dopamine function. *J. Pharmacol. Exp. Ther.* **215**:697-703, 1980.

The neuroendocrine effects of exercise

Katarina T. Borer and Pamela Raymond
The University of Michigan

Linda A. Dokas
Medical College of Ohio

The endocrine concomitants of exercise

Physical activity elicits a wide variety of endocrine responses in animals including humans. Some are concomitant with exercise and thus transient, whereas others are protracted beyond the termination of exercise or even delayed. Most of the acute endocrine changes serve the bioenergetic and homostatic needs of exercise: mobilization of metabolic fuels, conservation of body fluids and sodium, and increased delivery of oxygen to muscles.

Acute endocrine responses to exercise generally mirror the time course of bioenergetic needs and fluid-electrolyte changes induced by exercise, and seldom last much beyond the end of physical activity (25,29,30,42, 52,61,64,73). When animals and humans engage repeatedly, over substantial portions of their lifespan, in prolonged physical activities that occupy a large portion of their day, they undergo changes in endocrine function of a different nature. For instance, prolonged exposure to physical activity often changes the magnitude of acute endocrine responses to exercise. Thus, acute insulin (6,7,8,32,33,35,48), growth hormone (68), glucagon (33), catecholamine (5,33), cortisol (52), and pancreatic polypeptide (34) responses to exercise are blunted. Further, in response to prolonged exposure to physical activity, acute β-endorphin (18,23,24), LH (26,58), testosterone (58) and thyroxine (2,22,40,41,71), responses to exercise are potentiated, the direction of circulating progesterone response is reversed (10,63), and increased prolactin release is elicited (20,56). Such changes in endocrine function often are attributed to metabolic adaptations to prolonged physical activity (38) which increase the efficiency of fuel mobilization or of conservation of fluids and electrolytes.

In addition, repeated exposure to prolonged physical activity leads to alterations in the magnitude and pattern of release of several hormones at rest. Some examples of such protracted and pervasive endocrine changes are the reduced release of insulin in response to carbohydrate challenge (4,6,7,32,35,44), increased release and metabolism of thyroxine (2,3,40,41,76), increases in circulating LH in the follicular phase, and decreases in circulating gonadotropins in the luteal phase of the female menstrual cycle (9), increases in circulating androgens (58,67), decreases in serum progesterone (63), and increased serum concentrations of GH (67).

The mechanisms by which prolonged, repeated physical activity induces alteration in endocrine function at rest are incompletely understood. Thus, a reduction in body fat content associated with the regime of endurance physical activities, and attendant changes in adipocyte sensitivity to lipogenetic (53,60) and antilipolytic (54) actions of insulin have been singled out as the most probable causes of reduced insulin response to carbohydrate challenge (44,59). Similarly, reduction in body fatness below some threshold value has been proposed as the cause of altered pituitary gonadotropin release and amenorrhea in dancers or long-distance runners (1,28,31,50,74) by analogy to anorexia nervosa in which the degree of body fatness determines the nature or prepubertal pattern of gonadotropin release (19).

Little attention has been given to date to the possibility that repeated and prolonged physical activity may directly alter neuroendocrine functioning. Recent research with several species of laboratory animals, however, has made this hypothesis plausible.

Studies relating the timing of spontaneous physical activity and of ultradian secretory pulses of several anterior pituitary and pineal hormones have shown that their periodicities are linked. For instance, there is close association between the timing of spontaneous locomotion and pulses of luteinizing hormone release in sheep (57). When one removes light as the entrainer of circadian rhythms by placing rodents in continuous darkness or by blinding them, individual behavioral and endocrine rhythms manifest their endogenous "free-running" rhythmicity. Under such circumstances, the rhythm of spontaneous running activity has the same periodicity and phase as the rhythms of diurnal ACTH (69), corticosterone (36,37), and melatonin release (70). In addition, the free-running estrous-cycle rhythm in hamsters is exactly four times the length of the free-running physical activity rhythm (66). Also, the rhythms of running activity and photosensitivity display identity in period length and phase. Thus, the time of onset of running activity and the time of onset of the 12-hr photosensitive period in the hamster coincide (65) and shift in parallel in response to changes in day length (27,65,75). Such a close functional relationship between the rhythms of physical activity on one hand, and endocrine or photosensitivity rhythms on the other, prompts the hypothesis that long-distance running and professional dancing induce protracted changes in endocrine function not as a reaction to changes in somatic variables such as reduced body fatness, but through alteration, over prolonged periods of time, in pattern and timing of hormone secretion. We will outline the evidence, generated in a freely running hamster as a model, supporting the hypothesis that physical activity can alter neuroendocrine functioning.

Hamster as the long-distance runner

Mature hamsters will run between 11 and 16 km each night if they are provided with a horizontal activity disc, and slightly shorter distances if they are exposed to a rotating drum. They generate such high volumes of activity by running at a moderate speed of 25 m/min for about 45 min without interruption. They pause only for about 2-3 min and engage in between 10 and 20 running bouts each night (11).

There is no good homeostatic explanation for hamsters' propensity for generating such high levels of physical activity. Physical activity is not used as a means of maintenance of energy balance, since hamsters and other rodents increase the volume of running in proportion to the magnitude of weight loss, and decrease the volume of running whenever they gain weight or body fat (12). Thus, spontaneous physical activity compromises survival in the energy-deprived rodent and does not counteract accumulation of fat in an obese one (12).

These observations as well as a recent finding that the blockade of endogenous opiate receptors reduces the volume of voluntary running in hamsters (55) suggest that prolonged running activity on spinning or rotating activity devices is inherently rewarding to hamsters and other small rodents. Voluntary activity in the hamster produces biochemical changes in the muscle indicative of endurance training as indicated by the results of experiment 1.

Experiment 1: Increased oxidative capacity
of muscles in freely running hamsters

Materials and methods

Eleven female golden hamsters (*Mesocricetus auratus* Waterhouse) were assigned to exercising ($n = 6$) and sedentary ($n = 5$) groups and were generally maintained as previously described (11). On day 28 of exercise, animals were killed by decapitation 2 hr after the onset of light and exsanguinated. The right quadriceps muscle was quickly removed, weighed, minced, and homogenized on ice in 10 volumes of homogenizing medium (175 mM KCl, 2 mM EDTA pH 7.4) with Polytron homogenizer (Brinkman Instruments). The capacity of whole muscle homogenates to oxidize pyruvate and malate was determined by procedure of Hooker and Baldwin (39).

Oxygen uptake of muscle homogenates in the absence of pyruvate-malate substrate was subtracted from the measurements obtained in the presence of substrates. An aliquot of muscle homogenate was used for determination of protein concentration (49).

Results

Hamsters weighed 93.3 ± 0.6 g at the start of the experiment. After 28 days, exercising hamsters weighed 134.5 ± 3.1 g and sedentary hamsters 106 ± 3.5 g ($p < 0.05$). Exercising hamsters ran about 21,874 RPDs or an equivalent of 9-12 km each night.

Voluntary running significantly increased net oxygen consumption of muscle homogenates whether the values are expressed per unit of wet muscle weight (exercising: 3446.3 ± 362.2 vs 2070.3 ± 387.4 μL O_2/hr/g wet weight in sedentary, $p < 0.05$), or per unit protein weight (24.1 ± 2.5 in exercising or 14.8 ± 3.2 μL O_2/hr/mg protein in sedentary, $p < 0.05$).

Conclusions

Voluntary running on a horizontal activity disc can be classified as a form of prolonged physical activity done repeatedly over significant portions of an animal's lifespan. In terms of distance traveled and metabolic adaptations for increased oxygen uptake by muscle, this activity resembles long-distance running or similar endurance events in humans.

Voluntary running accelerates growth in mature hamsters

Within one week of exposure to voluntary running on horizontal discs or in rotating drums (11), hamsters display a significant increase in the rate of weight gain, provided they are given unlimited supplies of food. Increased weight gain in exercising hamsters reflects increased lean body mass, reduced body fat content (to about 50% of sedentary control after 4 weeks of exercise) (14,72), and increased skeletal growth (17).

Evidence for exercise-induced neuroendocrine facilitation of growth in hamsters

Growth is controlled by a complex neuroendocrine mechanism that involves several different neurotransmitters within the hypothalamus and the limbic structures of the brain (51). Growth also depends on nutrient adequacy and abundance and involves cellular proliferation rather than hypertrophy alone.

We have performed several experiments designed to determine the relative contribution of nutrition, facilitated GH secretion, and cellular proliferation in exercise-induced growth.

Experiment 2: The role of nutrition in acceleration of growth by exercise

The question asked was whether exercise would facilitate somatic growth if the stimulus of exercise and nutrient adequacy for execution of growth were dissociated in time. The experiment (15) involved four groups of mature female hamsters of equivalent age and weight at the outset and assigned to exercise (EX) or sedentary conditions (SED) with ad libitum supply of food, and to exercise (RESTEX) and sedentary conditions (RESTSED) with restricted access to food. RESTEX hamsters were limited to the quantity of food (approximately 11 g/day) eaten by sedentary hamsters. RESTSED hamsters were limited to approximately one-half of that amount in order to match the weight loss seen in RESTEX animals.

Measurements were made of food intake, body weight, and linear growth during the 4 weeks of exercise and 4 weeks of retirement from exercise. After 4 weeks, the treatment variables nutrition and exercise were reversed in the RESTEX group. RESTEX hamsters, which were to that point exposed to exercise stimulus and inadequate nutrition, were now exposed to ad libitum supplies of food and denied exercise. EX hamsters were retired from activity, and RESTSED hamsters were given ad libitum access to food at the same time.

Results of this experiment are summarized in Figure 1. RESTEX hamsters, which exhibited a volume of voluntary activity similar to EX hamsters, lost weight during exercise and food restriction (Figure 1, left) and displayed subnormal linear growth (Figure 1, right). The same was true of RESTSED hamsters. In contrast, ad libitum-fed exercising hamsters, which increased their energy uptake by about 30%, displayed significant ponderal and linear growth during the 4 weeks of exercise.

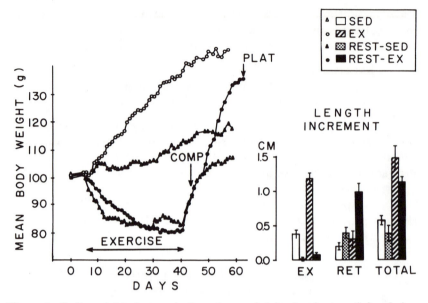

Figure 1 — Left: weight changes in hamsters maintained sedentary (triangles) or exposed to 35 days of exercise (circles) with ad libitum (open symbols) or restricted access to food (solid symbols). Food-restricted exercising hamsters were limited to the amount of food consumed by nondeprived sedentary hamsters. Food-restricted sedentary hamsters were given enough food to match weight changes in restricted exercising hamsters. Right: linear growth of whole body of ad libitum-fed sedentary (open bar) and exercising (cross hatched bar) hamsters and of food-restricted sedentary (stippled bar) and exercising hamsters (solid bar) during exercise (left), during 18 days of retirement (center), and during combined periods of exercise and retirement. Vertical lines designate 1 *SEM*. Reproduced from ref. 15 with permission of the publisher.

Following the reversal of treatment variables, RESTEX hamsters displayed striking delayed ponderal and skeletal growth (Figure 1). During the retirement from exercise, the rate of weight gain and skeletal growth of RESTEX hamsters significantly exceeded the somatic growth rate of continuously well nourished EX hamsters. During the brief retirement period, RESTEX hamsters carried out nearly the same amount of ponderal and skeletal growth as did the well nourished EX hamsters during the periods of exercise and retirement combined.

What was the cause of the intense catch-up growth in hamsters stimulated by exercise to grow, but prevented from doing so by inadequate nutrition? Either exercise produced a neuroendocrine facilitation of somatic growth that lasted until a given amount of growth had taken place, or exercise induced cellular proliferation in undernourished hamsters, and manifest hypertrophy of these new cells took place after adequate nutrition was made available. Experiment 3 addressed the second of the two alternatives.

Experiment 3: The relative contributions of exercise and nutrition to cellular proliferation in bone and muscle

Evidence for cellular proliferation was sought in the bone by microscopic examination of the width of distal femoral epiphyseal growth zone (EGZ) in the hamster knee and by quantification of the number of labeled nuclei in the EGZ of animals injected with ^{3}H-thymidine. Evidence for cellular proliferation in the muscle was sought by quantitative determination of muscle DNA and of ^{3}H-labeled, newly synthesized DNA.

Materials and methods

Ninety-eight mature female golden hamsters were obtained and maintained as previously described. They were assigned to four treatment groups: EX ($n = 14$), SED ($n = 21$), RESTEX ($n = 39$), and RESTSED ($n = 24$), in which the variables of exercise and nutrition were applied as described in experiment 1. The duration of exposure to exercise was 28 days. Unlike experiment 1, some exercising animals were sacrificed on the last day of exercise (8 EX, 6 RESTEX) whereas others were sacrificed during the first 5 days of retirement (33 RESTEX), or after 4 weeks of retirement (6 EX), by which time their rate of growth had returned to sedentary norm. After the examination of results, the data obtained from RESTEX hamsters killed on the last day of exercise while food-restricted, or killed during retirement and 3-5 days of ad libitum realimentation did not differ, and they were therefore pooled for ease of presentation. Likewise, there was no difference between the data from EX hamsters after 4 weeks of retirement whose rate of weight gain had returned to low sedentary level, and SED hamsters, and they were also pooled.

In order to determine cellular growth in the distal femoral EGZ, hamsters received an intraperitoneal injection of 2 μCi/g of ^{3}H-thymidine (50-80 Ci/mM, New England Nuclear, Boston, MA) 3 hr before sacrifice by overdose of sodium pentobarbital. The femur was dissected, fixed overnight to several days in 10% formalin, and subjected to decalcification (48 hr in 15 ml of Decal, Scientific Products), paraffin embedding, 10-micron sectioning, and autoradiography. The width of the distal femoral EGZ measured in micrometer units and in cell numbers as well as the number of labeled nuclei were used as indices of cellular proliferation in the bone.

Autoradiography of the mounted bone sections was done by the procedure of Kopriwa and Leblond (43). Slides were dipped in Kodak NTB-3 nuclear track emulsion in the darkroom (emulsion at 40°C). Effective exposure time was 6 weeks at 4°C in the dark. Slides were developed at 15°C with Dektol developer and fixed with Kodak fixer, stained with eosin and hematoxylin, dehydrated through graded alcohols, and coverslipped for microscopic examination.

DNA synthesis in the muscle was measured by modification of Schneider's procedures (62). Following the injection of ^{3}H-thymidine, the quadriceps was dissected, weighed, and homogenized in 10 volumes of water as described in experiment 1.

Homogenate (0.1 ml) was spotted onto a Whatman No. 2 filter paper disc and allowed to dry. Paper was extracted in two 20-ml washes of 10% trichloracidic acid (TCA) on ice for 10 min. TCA was removed with two 10-min washes with 20 ml of 4:1 ether-absolute ethanol mix. Discs were washed in ether, combusted in Beckman TRI-CARB tissue oxidizer and counted in 10 ml of Monophase-40 scintillant in a Beckman β-spectrometer.

Quantitative colorimetric determination of DNA was done with 2 ml of muscle homogenate. Cells were lysed and DNA was precipitated with sequential washes (followed by 10-min centrifugation at 1,500 × g) with: 0.5 ml of 50% TCA, 2 ml of 10% TCA (3 times), 2 ml of 95% ethanol (2 times), and ether. The pellet was incubated in 2 ml of 1 N KOH overnight at 37°C. An aliquot (0.1 ml) was removed for protein determination (49). The solution was neutralized and DNA and protein were precipitated with 0.4 ml of 6 N HCl and 2 ml of 5% TCA, and centrifuged. The RNA-containing supernatant was discarded. DNA was suspended in 1.3 ml water and 1.3 ml of 10% TCA by heating to 90°C for 15 min. The supernatant was saved, and the procedure was repeated with 1 ml of 5% TCA. The two supernatants were pooled and used in the diphenylamine (DP) test for DNA (21). One g of DP was dissolved in 100 ml of glacial acetic acid and 2.75 ml of sulfuric acid. Two ml of DP reagent was added to 1 ml of DNA solution and to standard tubes containing between 25 and 100 μg of calf-thymus DNA in 1 ml of 5% TCA. Samples were boiled in a water bath 10 min, cooled, and their absorbance was read at 600 nm in a Beckman spectrophotometer.

Results

Acceleration of growth by exercise in EX hamsters and disappearance of this effect 4 weeks after the retirement from exercise are shown in Figure 2 for animals from experiment 3. Figure 2 also illustrates absence of growth during food restriction with appearance of catch-up growth in RESTEX hamsters, and weight recovery in RESTSED hamsters, during the ad libitum realimentation. Mean activity levels of EX and RESTEX hamsters were 28,660 and 35,682 RPD, respectively.

Table 1 summarizes the data on cellular proliferation in the bone. Exercise had a significant growth-promoting effect on each of the three in-

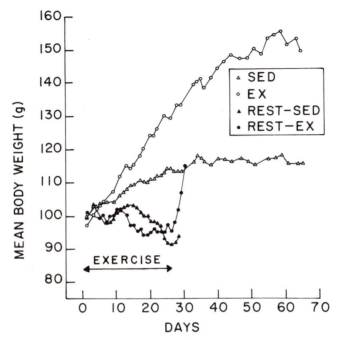

Figure 2 — Mean weight changes in ad libitum-fed exercising (EX, *n* = 14) and sedentary (SED, *n* = 21) hamsters and food-restricted exercising (RESTEX, *n* = 39) and sedentary (RESTSED, *n* = 24) hamsters from experiment 3. Duration of exercise was 28 days.

dices of cellular bone growth: the number of radioactive nuclei and the width of the EGZ expressed in numbers of cells or in micrometer units. By contrast, food restriction had a significant growth-inhibitory influence on the three indices of cell growth as was previously shown to be the case in undernourished rats (45,46). In addition, exercise was significantly more effective in facilitating ^{3}H-thymidine uptake into the dividing bone nuclei in the ad libitum-fed than in the food-restricted hamsters.

Table 2 summarizes data on the synthesis of new DNA in the quadriceps muscle. When the new radioactive DNA and total DNA per unit wet weight are considered, exercise is shown to have a significant stimulatory effect on DNA without a modifying influence of nutrition. If however, one normalizes exercise-induced variance in muscle protein concentration, undernutrition appears to block increases in muscle DNA due to exercise.

Conclusions

When undernutrition blocks acceleration of growth by exercise (Figures 1 and 2), cellular proliferation in exercising bone and DNA accumulation

Table 1

Indices of Cellular Proliferation in the Distal Femoral Epiphysical Growth Zone (EGZ) of Female Hamsters as a Function of Exercise and Nutrition

| | Ad libitum-fed | | Food-restricted | | Significance |
	Exercising ($n = 8$)	Sedentary ($n = 14$)	Exercising ($n = 21$)	Sedentary ($n = 9$)	($p < 0.05$)
Number of labeled nuclei in EGZ	62.5 ± 6.3[a]	21.7 ± 3.6	20.3 ± 3.7	12.1 ± 2.1	E[b],N[c],E × N[d]
Width of EGZ (number of cells)	18.1 ± 0.8	14.2 ± 0.3	16.3 ± 0.4	11.1 ± 0.6	E,N
Width of EGZ (micrometers)	194.2 ± 18.7	157.0 ± 3.3	181.8 ± 17.0	102.3 ± 6.5	E,N

[a]Mean ± SEM.
[b]E = significant effect of exercise, 2 × 2 analysis of variance.
[c]N = significant effect of nutrition.
[d]E × N = significant interaction between nutrition and exercise.

Table 2

Indices of Nuclear Proliferation in the Quadriceps Muscle as a Function of Exercise and Nutrition

	Ad libitum-fed		Food-restricted		Significance
	Exercising (n = 7)	Sedentary (n = 27)	Exercising (n = 39)	Sedentary (n = 24)	(p < 0.05)
dpm in DNA/mg DNA	50588 ± 5051[a]	29952 ± 2905	73060 ± 6500	32943 ± 2904	E[b]
µg DNA/g wet weight	694.1 ± 75.0	466.4 ± 19.2	573.5 ± 25.7	437.4 ± 12.6	E
mg protein/g wet weight	135.6 ± 14.3	203.3 ± 17.0	187.9 ± 6.7	200.7 ± 8.5	
µg DNA/mg protein	5.75 ± 0.85	2.60 ± 0.31	2.91 ± 0.16	2.28 ± 0.12	E,N[c],E×N[d]

[a] Mean ± SEM.
[b] E = significant effect of exercise, 2 × 2 analysis of variance.
[c] N = significant effect of nutrition.
[d] E × N = significant interaction between nutrition and exercise.

in exercising muscle are likewise blocked or reduced. It is, therefore, improbable that the exercise-induced delayed catch-up growth reacts to signals generated by nuclear and cellular proliferation in exercised muscle and bone. Instead, it is more likely that compensatory growth results from exercise-induced changes in the neuroendocrine mechanism controlling secretion of growth hormone.

Voluntary running leads to protracted facilitation of growth hormone secretion in mature hamsters

In order to test the hypothesis that repeated exposure to numerous long bouts of running activity leads to protracted facilitation of growth hormone secretion in hamsters, we have measured the concentrations of this hormone in ad libitum-fed and sedentary hamsters several hours after cessation of nocturnal running activity, as well as in RESTEX hamsters whose somatic growth has been blocked by inadequate nutrition.

Experiment 4: Facilitation of growth hormone release by exercise in hamsters

Materials and methods

The experimental design was comparable to that described in experiments 2 and 3. Four groups of hamsters (EX, SED, RESTEX, and RESTSED) were exposed to variables of exercise or sedentary condition and of unlimited or restricted nutrition in a 2 × 2 design. Animals were exposed to appropriate nutritional and exercise variables and then killed by decapitation during the third hour after the onset of light and several hours after cessation of running (Figure 3). Trunk blood was collected in chilled tubes and allowed to clot. Serum was separated by centrifugation (1,500 × g) and stored at 20°C for subsequent GH hormone analyses.

A double antibody homologous radioimmunoassay for hamster GH was used as described previously (16). Within the four experimental groups, the timing of killing and presence of food were varied to provide answers to the following two questions:

- Does exercise facilitate GH secretion regardless of whether the nutritional regime allows somatic growth? To obtain this answer blood was collected from EX ($n = 13$), SED ($n = 23$), RESTEX ($n = 11$), and RESTSED ($n = 12$) hamsters on the 28th day of exposure to exercise. Experiments 2 and 3 have shown that food restriction prevents exercising hamsters from carrying out accelerated somatic growth. Experiment 4 was designed to clarify whether exercise facilitated GH release regardless of the rate of somatic growth.

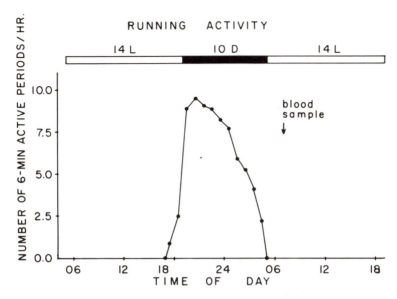

Figure 3 — The timing of blood collection for GH determination and of spontaneous running activity in six female hamsters maintained under lighting conditions (14L:10D) approximating those in experiment 4 (12L:12D). Volume of running activity was measured as number of hourly 6-min periods of unbroken activity throughout the day (27,75).

- Does exercise induce delayed facilitation of GH release during realimentation of undernourished hamsters? In order to obtain this answer, blood was collected from retired RESTEX ($n = 11$) and from RESTSED ($n = 11$) hamsters during the third day of ad libitum realimentation (15).

Results

The results of experiment 4 are presented in Table 3. Exercise was associated with a significant increase in serum GH concentration regardless of the adequacy of nutrients for the execution of growth. Serum GH concentration was increased not only in rapidly growing, well nourished EX hamsters, but also in exercising, growth-arrested RESTEX hamsters.

Furthermore, increased serum GH concentration persisted into the period of retirement from exercise. Three to 5 days after they have been denied exercise and given unlimited supplies of food, RESTEX hamsters continue to display high serum concentrations of GH.

Conclusions

Exercise has a facilitative influence on GH release in adult hamsters. In-

Table 3

Serum Growth Hormone Concentration (ng/ml)

as a Function of Exposure to Exercise and Variable Abundance of Food

	Ad libitum-fed		Food-restricted		Significance
	Exercising	Sedentary	Exercising	Sedentary	($p < 0.05$)
Day 28 of exercise	64.2 ± 18.6[a]	17.3 ± 3.2	104.1 ± 39.4	14.5 ± 2.6	E[b]
Day 3 of retirement			158.5 ± 51.6	22.5 ± 7.2	E[c]

[a]Mean ± SEM.
[b]E = significant effect of exercise, 2 × 2 analysis of variance.
[c]E = significant effect of exercise, student's t-test. Due to nonhomogenous distribution of growth hormone values, statistical analyses were performed on logarithmic transformation of the data.

creased GH release is seen several hours after cessation of physical activity. It persists in spite of caloric blockade of somatic growth and it can persist several days following the termination of exercise. These observations suggest that voluntary activity has a facilitative effect on the neuroendocrine controls of GH secretion, and that this effect does not require increased energy intake or other conditions supporting rapid somatic growth.

Voluntary running facilitates reproductive function in mature hamsters

Besides its effects on facilitation of GH secretion and acceleration of somatic growth, voluntary running in hamsters appears to reinstate estrous cycles in animals that have been rendered anestrous by 12 weeks of exposure to a nonstimulatory photoperiod (8L:16D;13). In four out of seven hamsters, exercise immediately counteracted the inhibitory effects of photoperiod and reinstated nearly all estrous cycles during the 4 weeks of activity. In three out of seven animals, estrous cycles were reinstated by exercise after a delay of 1-3 weeks. By contrast, all but one sedentary hamster, maintained in nonstimulatory photoperiod, failed to display any estrous cyclicity. The mechanisms by which prolonged and repeated physical activity reinstates reproductive function in hamsters remains to be elucidated but probably involves alterations in the neuroendocrine control over pituitary gonadotropic hormone release.

Putative biological roles for the neuroendocrine effects of exercise in hamsters

We have shown that hamsters voluntarily engage in large amounts of daily physical activity when provided with a suitable activity device. We have also shown that such physical activity produces at least two different kinds of changes in neuroendocrine function. Are these phenomena artifacts of laboratory environment or do they reflect a biological role for exercise in hamster growth and reproduction?

Although no quantitative data on amount of physical activity in hamsters in their natural environment was available to us, it is unlikely that any environmental circumstances would impel a hamster to run as much as 11-15 km per night. A horizontal disc appears to facilitate unusually high levels of physical activity in hamsters (11). As such, it exaggerates the neuroendocrine effects that exercise may exert on the biology of hamsters, and that are, under natural circumstances, likely to be more subtle.

In the natural environment, exercise may play a key role in the timing of growth and reproduction in seasonal breeders by mediating the effects of changing day length. Seasonal increases in day length increase the volume of physical activity in hamsters (27,75), thereby facilitating somatic growth. Increases in day length also shift the phases of rhythms of running and photosensitivity to start at the end of daytime (27,65,75), thereby exposing hamsters' reproductive axis to stimulation by light. The speed with which voluntary running reinstated estrous cyclicity in reproductively quiescent hamsters suggests a direct influence of exercise on the reproductive function. High amounts of physical activity in seasonal breeders may stimulate secretion of pituitary gonadotropins to insure advantageous seasonal timing of reproductive function. On the other hand, high volumes of physical activity in seasonal migrants may suppress reproduction through direct influence over the appropriate neuroendocrine mechanism (47). Thus, contemporary alterations in reproductive function in physically active women may activate a link between physical activity and neuroendocrine function which served a different biological role in humans' evolutionary past.

Acknowledgments

This research was supported in part by the grants from the Weight Watchers' Foundation and from The National Science Foundation (PCM 78-07626 and PCM 81-04375). I thank Jayne Blemly and Kathleen O'Connor for skilled technical assistance, and Timothy P. White and John Villanacci for performing the oxygen consumption determinations on muscle homogenates.

References

1. Baker, E.R., Mathur, R.S., Kirk, R.F., and Williamson, H.D. Female runners and secondary amenorrhea. Correlation with age, parity, mileage, and plasma hormonal and sex-hormone-binding globulin concentrations. *Fertil. Steril.* **36**:183-187, 1981.

2. Balsam, A., and Leppo, L.E. Stimulation of the peripheral metabolism of L-thyroxine and 3,5,3,-L-triiodothyronine in the physically trained rat. *Endocrinology* **95**:299-302, 1974.

3. Balsam, A., and Leppo, L.E. Effect of physical training on the metabolism of thyroid hormones in man. *J. Appl. Physiol.* **38**:212-215, 1975.

4. Berger, D., Floyd, J.C., Jr., Lampman, R.M., and Fajans, S.S. The effect of adrenergic receptor blockade on the exercise-induced rise in pancreatic polypeptide in man. *J. Clin. Endocr. Metab.* **50**:33-39, 1980.

5. Bernet, F., and Denimal, J. Evolution de la réponse adrénosympathique a l'exercise au cours de l'entraînement chez le rat. *Eur. J. Appl. Physiol.* **33**:57-70, 1974.

6. Björntorp, P., Berchtold, P., Grimby, G., Lindholm, B., Sanne, H., Tibblin, G., and Wilhelmsen, L. Effects of physical training on glucose tolerance, plasma insulin and lipids on body composition in men after myocardial infarction. *Acta Med. Scand.* **192**:439-443, 1972.

7. Björntorp, P., DeJounge, K., Sjöström, L., and Sullivan, L. The effect of physical training on insulin production in obesity. *Metabolism* **19**:631-638, 1970.

8. Björntorp, P., Fahlen, M., Grimby, G., Gustafson, A., Holm, J., Renström, P., and Scherstén, T. Carbohydrate and lipid metabolism in middle-aged physically well-trained man. *Metabolism* **21**:1037-1044, 1972.

9. Bonen, A., Belcastro, A.N., Ling, W.Y., and Simpson, A.A. Profiles of selected hormones during menstrual cycles of teenage athletes. *J. Appl. Physiol.* **50**:545-557, 1981.

10. Bonen, A., Ling, W.Y., MacIntyre, K.P., Neil, R., McGrail, J.C., and Belcastro, A.N. Effects of exercise on the serum concentrations of FSH, LH, progesterone, and estradiol. *Eur. J. Appl. Physiol.* **42**:15-23, 1979.

11. Borer, K.T. Characteristics of growth-inducing exercise. *Physiol. Behav.* **24**:713-720, 1980.

12. Borer, K.T. The nonhomeostatic motivation to run in the golden hamster. In: A.R. Morrison and P.L. Strick, (eds.), *Changing concepts of the nervous system*, Academic, New York, 1982.

13. Borer, K.T., Campbell, C.S., Tabor, J., Jorgenson, K., Vandarian, S., and Gordon, L. Exercise reverses photoperiodic anestrous in golden hamsters. *Biol. Reprod.* (in press).

14. Borer, K.T., Hallfrisch, J., Tsai, A.C., Hallfrisch, C., and Kuhns, L.R. The effects of exercise and dietary protein on somatic growth, body composition, and serum cholesterol in adult hamsters. *J. Nutr.* **109**:222-228, 1979.

15. Borer, K.T., and Kelch, R.P. Increased serum growth hormone and somatic growth in exercising adult hamsters. *Am. J. Physiol.* **234**:E611-E616, 1978.

16. Borer, K.T., Kelch, R.P., and Hayashida, T. Hamster growth hormone. Species specificity and physiological changes in blood and pituitary concentrations as measured by a homologous radioimmunoassay. *Neuroendocrinology* **35**:349-358, 1982.

17. Borer, K.T., and Kuhns, L.R. Radiographic evidence for acceleration of skeletal growth in adult hamsters by exercise. *Growth* **41**:1-13, 1977.

18. Bortz, W.M., II, Angwin, P., Mefford, I.N., Boarder, M.R., Noyce, N., and Barchas, J.D. Catecholamines, dopamine and endorphin levels during extreme exercise. *New Engl. J. Med.* **305**:466-467, 1981.

19. Boyar, R.M., Katz, J., Finkelstein, J.W., Kapen, S., Weiner, J., Weitzman, E.D., and Hellman, L. Anorexia nervosa: Immaturity of the 24-hour luteinizing hormone secretory pattern. *New Engl. J. Med.* **291**:861-865, 1974.

20. Brisson, G.R., Volle, M.A., DeCarufel, P., Desharnais, M., and Tanaka, M.

Exercise induced dissociation of the blood prolactin response in young women according to their sports habits. *Hormone Metab. Res.* **12**:201-205, 1980.

21. Burton, K. Determination of DNA concentration with diphenylamine. *Methods Enzymol.* **12b**:163-166, 1968.

22. Caralis, D.G., Edwards, L., and Davis, P.T. Serum total and free thyroxine and triiodothyronine during dynamic muscular exercise in man. *Am. J. Physiol.* **233**:E115-E118, 1977.

23. Carr, D.B., Bullen, B.A., Skrinar, G.S., Arnold, M.A., Rosenblatt, M., Beitins, I.Z., Marin, J.B., and McArthur, J.W. Physical conditioning facilitates the exercise-induced secretion of β-endorphin and β-lipotropin in women. *New Engl. J. Med.* **305**:560-563, 1981.

24. Colt, E.W.D., Wardlaw, S.L., and Frantz, A.G. The effect of running on plasma endorphin. *Life Sci.* **28**:1637-1640, 1981.

25. Convertino, V.A., Brock, P.J., Keil, L.C., Bernauer, E.M., and Greenleaf, J.G. Exercise training-induced hypervolemia: Role of plasma albumin, renin, and vasopressin. *J. Appl. Physiol.* **48**:665-669, 1980.

26. Dessypris, A., Kuoppasalmi, K., and Adlercreutz, H. Plasma cortisol, testosterone, androstenedione and luteinizing hormone, in a non-competitive marathon run. *J. Steroid Biochem.* **1**:33-37, 1976.

27. Ellis, G.B., and Turek, F.W. Changes in locomotor activity associated with the photoperiodic response of the testes in male golden hamsters. *J. Compr. Physiol.* **132**:277-284, 1979.

28. Feicht, C.B., Johnson, T.S., Martin, B.J., Sparkes, K.B., and Wagner, W.W. Secondary amenorrhea in athletes. *Lancet* **2**:1145-1146, 1978.

29. Follenius, M., and Brandenberger, G. Influence de l'exercise musculaire sur l'evolution de la cortisolemie et de la glycemie chez l'homme. *Eur. J. Appl. Physiol.* **33**:23-33, 1974.

30. Frenkl, R., Csalay, L., and Csakvary, G. A study of the stress reaction elicited by muscular exertion in trained and untrained men. *Acta Physiol. Acad. Sci. Hungary* **36**:365-370, 1969.

31. Frisch, R.E., Wyshak, G., and Vincent, L. Delayed menarche and amenorrhea in ballet dancers. *New Engl. J. Med.* **303**:17-19, 1980.

32. Galbo, H., Hedeskov, C.J., Capito, K., and Vinten, J. The effect of physical training on insulin secretion of rat pancreatic islets. *Acta Physiol. Scand.* **111**:75-79, 1980.

33. Galbo, H., Richter, E.A., Holst, J.J., and Christensen, N.J. Diminished hormonal responses to exercise in trained rats. *J. Appl. Physiol.* **46**:953-958, 1977.

34. Gingerich, R.L., Hickson, R.C., Hagberg, J.M., and Winder, W.W. Effect of endurance exercise training on plasma pancreatic polypeptide concentration during exercise. *Metab. Clin. Exp.* **28**:1179-1182, 1979.

35. Hartley, L.H., Mason, J.W., Hogan, R.P., Jones, L.G., Kotchen, T.A., Mougey, E.H., Wherry, F.E., Pennington, L.L., and Ricketts, P.T. Multiple hormonal responses to prolonged exercise in relation to physical training. *J. Appl. Physiol.* **33**:607-610, 1972.

36. Honma, K., and Hiroshige, T. Internal synchronization among several circadian rhythms in rats under constant light. *Am. J. Physiol.* **235**:R243-R249, 1978.

37. Honma, K., Watanabe, I.K., and Hiroshige, T. Effects of parachlorophenylalanine and 5.6-dihydroxytryptamine on the free-running rhythms of locomotor activity and plasma corticosterone in the rat exposed to continuous light. *Brain Res.* **169**:531-544, 1979.

38. Holloszy, J.O., and Booth, F.W. Biochemical adaptations to endurance exercise in muscle. *Ann. Rev. Physiol.* **38**:273-291, 1976.

39. Hooker, A.M., and Baldwin, K.M. Substrate oxidation specificity in different types of mammalian muscle. *Am. J. Physiol.* **236**:C66-C89, 1979.

40. Irvine, C.H.G. Thyroxine secretion rate in the horse in various physiological states. *J. Endocrinol.* **39**:313-320, 1967.

41. Irvine, C.H.G. Effect of exercise on thyroxine degradation in athletes and non-athletes. *J. Clin. Endocrinol.* **28**:942-947, 1968.

42. Kachadorian, W.A., and Johnson, R.E. Renal responses to various rates of exercise. *J. Appl. Physiol.* **28**:748-752, 1970.

43. Kopriwa, B.M., and Leblond, C.P. Improvements in the coating technique of radioautography. *J. Histochem. Cytochem.* **10**:269-284, 1962.

44. Le Blanc, J., Nadeau, A., Boulay, M., and Rousseau-Migneron, S. Effects of physical training and adiposity on glucose metabolism and ^{125}I-insulin binding. *J. Appl. Physiol.* **46**:235-239, 1979.

45. Lee, M. Skeletal growth and body size of rats during protein-energy malnutrition and during rehabilitation. *Nutr. Rep. Int.* **13**:527-533, 1976.

46. Lee, M., and Myers, G.S. The effect of protein-energy malnutrition on appositional bone growth in the rat. *Experientia* **35**:824-825, 1979.

47. Lessman, C.A., and Herman, W.S. Flight enhances juvenile hormone inactivation in *Danaus plexippus plexippus L.* (Lepidoptera. Danaidae). *Experientia* **37**:599-601, 1981.

48. Lohman, D., Liebold, F., Heilmann, W., Singer, H., and Pohl, A. Diminished insulin response in highly trained athletes. *Metab. Clin. Exp.* **27**:521-524, 1978.

49. Lowry, D.H., Rosebrough, N.J., Farr, A.L., and Randall, R.J. Protein measurement with the Folin phenol reagent. *J. Biol. Chem.* **193**:265-275, 1951.

50. Malina, R.M., Spirduso, W.W., Tate, C., and Baylor, A.M. Age at menarche and selected menstrual characteristics in athletes at different levels and in different sports. *Med. Sci. Sports* **10**:218-222, 1978.

51. Martin, J.B. Brain regulation of growth hormone secretion. In: L. Martin and W.F. Ganong (eds.), *Frontiers in neuroendocrinology*, vol. 4, Raven, New York, 1976, pp. 129-168.

52. Newmark, S.R., Himathongham, T., Martin, R.P., Cooper, K.H., and Rose, L.H. Adrenocortial response to marathon running. *J. Clin. Endocr. Metab.* **40**:845-849, 1975.

53. Olefsky, J.M. Mechanisms of decreased insulin responses of large adipocytes. *Endocrinology* **100**:1169-1177, 1979.

54. Olefsky, J.M. Insensitivity of large adipocytes to the antilipolytic effects of insulin. *J. Lipid Res.* **18**:459-464, 1977.

55. Potter, C.D., Borer, K.T., and Katz, R.J. Opiate receptor blockade reduces voluntary running but not self-stimulation in hamsters. *Pharmacol. Biochem. Behav.* **18**:217-223, 1983.

56. Prior, J.C., Jensen, L., Yuen, B.H., Higgins, H. and Brownlee, L. Prolactin changes with exercise vary with breast motion-analysis of running versus cycling. *Fertil. Steril.* **36**:268, 1981.

57. Rasmussen, D.D., and Malven, P.V. Relationship between rhythmic motor activity and plasma luteinizing hormone in ovariectomized sheep. *Neuroendocrinology* **32**:364-369, 1981.

58. Remes, K., Kuoppasalmi, K., and Adlercreutz, H. Effect of long-term physical training on plasma testosterone, androstenedione, luteinizing hormone and sex-hormone-binding globulin capacity. *Scand. J. Clin. Lab. Invest.* **39**:743-749, 1979.

59. Richard, D., and LeBlanc, J. Effects of physical training and food restriction on insulin secretion and glucose tolerance in male and female rats. *Am. J. Clin. Nutr.* **33**:2588-2595, 1980.

60. Richardson, D.K., and Czech, M.P. Primary role of decreased fatty acid synthesis in insulin resistance of large adipocytes. *Am. J. Physiol.* **234**:E182-E189, 1978.

61. Rose, L.I., Friedman, H.S., Beering, S.C., and Cooper, R.H. Plasma cortisol changes following a mile run in conditioned subjects. *J. Clin. Endocrinol.* **31**:339-341, 1970.

62. Schneider, W.C. Determination of nucleic acids in tissues by pentose analysis. *Methods Enzymol.* **3**:680-684, 1957.

63. Shangold, M., Freeman, R., Thysen, B., and Gatz, M. The relationship between long-distance running, plasma progesterone and luteal phase length. *Fertil. Steril.* **31**:130-133, 1979.

64. Skika, W., Boning, D., Deck, K., Kulpmann, W., and Meurer, K. Reduced aldosterone and sodium excretion in endurance-trained athletes before and during immersion. *Eur. J. Appl. Physiol. Occup. Physiol.* **42**:255-261, 1979.

65. Stetson, M.H., Elliott, J.A., and Menaker, M. Photoperiodic regulation of hamster testis: Circadian sensitivity to the effects of light. *Biol. Reprod.* **13**:329-339, 1973.

66. Stetson, M.H., and Watson-Whitmyre, M. Nucleus suprachiasmaticus: The biological clock in the hamster? *Science* **191**:197-199, 1976.

67. Sutton, J.R., Coleman, M.J., Casey, J., and Lazarus, L. Androgen responses during physical exercise. *Biol. Med. J.* **1**:520-522, 1973.

68. Sutton, J., and Lazarus, L. Effect of adrenergic blocking agents on growth hormone responses to physical exercise. *Hormone Metab. Res.* **6**:428-429, 1974.

69. Szafarczyk, A., Ixart, G., Malaval, F., Nougier-Soule, J., and Assenmacher, I. Correlation entre les rhythmes circadiens de l'ACTH et de la corticosterone plasmatiques, et de l'activite motrice, evoluant en "libre cours" apres enucleation oculaire chez le rat. *C.R. Acad. Sci. Paris* **290**:587-592, 1980.

70. Tamarkin, L., Reppert, S.M., Klein, D.C., Pratt, B., and Goldman, B.D. Studies of the daily pattern of pineal melatonin in the Syrian hamster. *Endocrinology* **107**:1525-1529, 1980.

71. Terjung, R.L., and Winder, W.W. Exercise and thyroid function. *Med. Sci. Sports* **7**:20-28, 1975.

72. Tsai, A.C., Bach, J., and Borer, K.T. Somatic, endocrine, and serum lipid changes during detraining in adult hamsters. *J. Clin. Nutr.* **34**:373-376, 1981.

73. Wade, C.E., Dressendorfer, R.H., O'Brien, J.C., and Claybaugh, J.R. Renal function, aldosterone, and vasopressin excretion following repeated long-distance running. *J. Appl. Physiol.* **50**:709-712, 1981.

74. Warren, M.P. The effects of exercise on pubertal progression and reproductive function in girls. *J. Clin. Endocr. Metab.* **51**:1150-1157.

75. Widmaier, E.P., and Campbell, C.S. Interaction of estradiol and photoperiod on activity patterns in the female hamster. *Physiol. Behav.* **24**:923-930, 1980.

76. Winder, W.W., and Heninger, R.W. Effect of exercise on tissue levels of thyroid hormones in the rat. *Am. J. Physiol.* **221**:1139-1143, 1971.

Perspective of exercise biology:
A look to the future

Ronald L. Terjung
State University of New York at Syracuse

In this final paper of the proceedings I would like to focus on a number of issues raised. Rather than reiterate all of the specific unanswered questions brought to our attention by these excellent presentations, I would like to present one perspective of exercise biology within which the myriad issues and diversity of approaches can be placed conveniently. Some specific observations, however, will be used for illustration. It will become obvious that some rather arbitrary distinctions have been made. This has been done in part as a matter of necessity, in part for convenience, and certainly in the hope of stimulating further consideration.

Extensive interest has been displayed in understanding the multitude of responses to exercise. At this point, it is relatively unimportant to discriminate between different exercise conditions. The requisite condition is simply *muscle contractile activity* and the attendant changes in other systems required for its initiation and continuance. Thus, we might consider an action requiring fine motor control, the integrated response during locomotion, an intense effort requiring extensive force development typified, for example, by weight lifting, a powerful ballistic action common to many sports activities, or simply sustained dynamic large muscle activity such as cycling or running. If these forms of muscle use are performed on a fairly regular basis, changes often occur which lead to an altered state or function. The end product is described as "conditioned," "adapted," or "trained." Evidence of alterations or conditioning often are manifest by inherent physiological, biochemical, and morphological changes apparent without any exercise stimulus. However, most alterations established by training become especially evident during the exercise effort itself.

The responses associated with the exercise effort can be somewhat arbitrarily grouped into three categories: obligatory, supportive, and associated. Factors that precede and cause muscle contraction head the list of obligatory factors. Initiation of a volitional effort brings about an efficient processing of information and execution of a motor task with precision and economy of resources. As we have seen, much of the recent characterization of the distinctions among types of motor units has permitted an expanded understanding of neuromuscular function, especially with regard to locomotion.

Immediately upon the initiation of muscle contraction ATP utilization increases and vascular adjustments occur within muscle that attempt to enhance oxygen supply to the contracting fibers. A number of factors have been implicated in causing the initial decrease in resistance at the onset of muscle contraction. These include increased K^+ and hypertonicity in the interstitial fluid, direct myogenic response of the arteriole caused by the developing muscle tension, and even an intrinsic neural response initiated by depolarization of the motor nerve. However, despite considerable research attention, there still is no resolution as to the cellular factors responsible for the sustained reduction in free-flow vascular resistance during prolonged muscle contractile activity. Nonetheless, it is generally agreed that the sustained vascular response is coupled to metabolic events in the muscle, because oxygen supply is generally well matched to the oxygen demand.

In this context, it is instructive to recall the differences in skeletal muscle fiber types. It has been recognized for a long time that blood flows are different between high-oxidative slow-twitch muscles, such as the soleus, and relatively low-oxidative fast-twitch muscles, such as the cat gastrocnemius (6). A more general relationship between muscle blood flow and the tissue's oxidative capacity and peak oxygen consumption has been shown by Maxwell et al. (13). Interestingly, this high correlation could not necessarily be predicted by muscle capillarization, because the cap/fiber ratio is rather similar for the different muscle fiber types. This general relationship between the oxidative capacity of an entire muscle and its blood flow, however, does not represent the fine resolution of blood flow distribution with the muscle, as most muscles are composed of a mixture of fiber types (1). The extreme is seen in many fast-twitch muscles that contain about equal proportions of high-oxidative red and low-oxidative white fibers. In rodents, for example, the difference in oxidative capacity between these two fiber types is approximately four-fold (2).

In recent work by Mackie and Terjung (12), peak blood flows observed in the different fiber type sections of the rat were found to be quite different (Figure 1). An in situ preparation was used and blood flows were determined using 15-μ microspheres. Peak flows were assessed by increasing the frequency of muscle contractile activity from 7½ to 120 tetanic contractions/min. It appears that peak flow in the low-oxidative white gastrocnemius section was achieved at even the lowest contraction condition, suggesting that contractile efforts above 7½ tetani/min might be performed in a relatively ischemic environment. This expectation has been confirmed recently (Dudley and Terjung, unpublished observations), because at contraction rates of 15 tetani/min and higher the white gastrocnemius section cannot maintain an energy balance and suffers a decline in ATP levels. In contrast, the high-oxidative fast-twitch red gastrocnemius enjoys an impressively rich blood flow (Figure 1) and an ability to maintain ATP levels through 45 tetani/min. The peak blood flow observed in the slow-twitch red soleus is intermediate between that of the two fast-twitch fibers. Interestingly, these differences in observed peak blood flows are roughly similar to their differences in mitochondrial content.

Because the FTW motor units seem to be recruited only during the more intense work efforts (4,17), the data reinforce the expectation that the FTW motor units have relatively little chance of maintaining a prolonged contractile effort supported via oxidative metabolism. Further, the existence of these low-oxidative fibers in most mammalian skeletal muscle suggests a caution may be needed in interpreting the results of some blood flow control studies. A given stimulation intensity (e.g., 3 Hz) is likely to cause a flow-restricted metabolic response in the FTW fiber, but not in the FTR fiber. How this metabolic response could, in turn, affect the vascular function of neighboring high-oxidative fibers remains to be established. Certainly this added dimension is not needed for the already complex muscle microvascular system so nicely characterized for us.

The second category of responses found during exercise that I have termed supportive contains those responses to exercise not necessarily essential to the performance of the specific motor task itself; they serve to sustain or even enhance the performance during a continued effort. For example, we can cite the coordinated responses illustrated by cardiovascular adjustments and altered circulating substrates during dynamic, whole-body exercise. Here a general cascade of sympathoadrenal influences appears essential. However, a distinction between

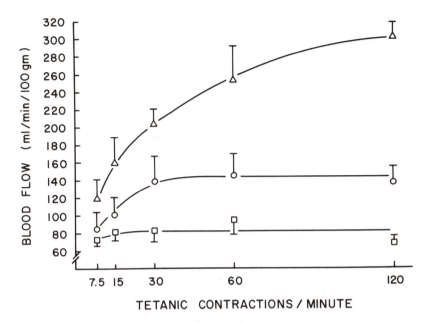

Figure 1 — Blood flows to the three fiber types of the rat during tetanic contraction. (□) white gastrocnemius, (○) soleus, (△) red gastrocnemius. Taken from the work of Mackie and Terjung (12) with permission.

local tissue sympathetic influences and the generalized adrenal stress response has been emphasized. Thus, in future work, simple determinations of circulating catecholamine levels are unlikely to be helpful in assessing complex and often subtle influences during exercise.

The third category of associative responses encompasses the wide variety that occurs during exercise, but as yet do not have a recognized function or may even have a deleterious influence. Clearly this category is rather volatile, because as our understanding of basic physiology increases, the significance of certain responses will become appreciated. We have seen that a wide variety of endocrine changes are elicited by exercise, with many remaining poorly understood. For example, attempts to identify the physiological significance of changes in gastroenteropancreatic hormones induced during exercise certainly represent one area that will receive extensive attention in the future. In fact, work in this general area of gastroenteropancreatic hormones is so incomplete that considerable confusion will probably prevail before extensive understanding is achieved. Other responses associated with exercise may actually have deleterious influences. For example, the ketotic diabetic patient's condition may be worsened by prolonged exercise. In another case, again in a diabetic, the exercise-induced greater absorption of insulin from the site of injection can cause a hypoglycemic crisis.

Training responses can also be categorized along similar lines as those used for the exercise responses. Exercise performed on a routine basis over an extended period of time brings about a division between chronological age and physiological age. This is most easily demonstrated in work capacity. The decline in work capacity that normally occurs during aging is significantly diminished by life-long participation in exercise programs. This influence of training probably has its foundation in a wide variety of fundamental processes; for example, we have seen that alterations in connective tissue metabolism offer one system for which fruitful research on the influence of exercise may be expected. Further, we have seen a relationship between mental acuity in eliciting a motor response and habitual physical activity in elderly people. This suggests that in addition to the adage "practice makes perfect," we might also say "practice keeps perfect."

Another issue dealt with in considerable detail involves the process of muscle enlargement during functional overload. The development of a technique that counts all fibers of a muscle confirms previous fears that attempting to make quantitative estimates of fiber numbers from single cross-sectional counts is inappropriate. Unfortunately, the complexity of muscle architecture, as amply illustrated by Gans (7), obligates the use of this tedious measurement technique. Most evidence now indicates that muscle enlargement induced by chronic overload caused by muscle ablation is accomplished by hypertrophy of muscle fibers and not hyperplasia. Further, the appearance of bizarre fibers containing bifurcations, characterized as "splitting" or branching, seems to be an inherent characteristic of skeletal muscle morphology. Their increased frequency has not been established in long-term, steady-state enlarged muscle. Nonetheless, it is clear that different stimuli have been used to produce muscle enlargement. Not all experimental procedures have been assessed with the total fiber count procedure, however, so we can expect the future will produce a number of studies attempting to provide definitive hypertrophy vs hyperplasia answers for all muscle enlargement models currently used. Another implication of muscle overload is the relatively acute response of possible muscle fiber injury, leucocyte infiltration, and increased activity of muscle hydrolytic enzymes (see 20).

We have also seen that stretched muscle, even in cultured cells, leads to cellular responses consistent with anabolic processes. Further, this response is dependent on muscle fiber membrane events specifically related to Na^+-K^+ ATPase. Although this stretch response would seem to have immediate utility in developing muscle for fiber orientation and elongation, its applicability as a factor influencing mature skeletal muscle remains a distinct possibility. Thus, the intriguing response so far characterized in cultured myotubes could have far-reaching implications for muscle biology.

We have also seen that fundamental neuroendocrine relationships may be altered by chronic physical activity. One such response has been characterized in the hamster. Although the specific effect of an enhanced rate of somatic growth may not be a general phenomena in all species, the change in neural endocrine function that it represents may be indicative of other systems, for example, the gonadotrophins.

Additional training responses are those especially evident during exercise itself and serve to support or enhance the exercise performance. These may be as poorly understood as the local vascular response in trained working muscle which may result in a lower blood flow requirement, but a greater oxygen extraction (see 9), or as actively studied as the enhanced oxidation of fatty acids with the attendant slowing of muscle glycogenolysis during moderately intense prolonged exercise (9).

It is apparent that a number of training responses have yet to be assigned a significant role. An example is pancreatic polypeptide, for which the increase during exercise is less after training (8). Again, as increased knowledge is gained about the functions of pancreatic polypeptide, its physiological significance during exercise can be assessed. It is also clear that the summated responses of routine, relatively intense physical activity may be, in a sense, maladaptive. We have seen that serious physical training can delay menarche, create menstrual irregularities, and enhance the frequency of amenorrhea. The long-term consequences of these changes, if any, are unknown, and whether they are a direct result of hormonal changes with each exercise bout, a secondary response to generalized stress, or altered nutrition also remains to be determined. Depending on one's perspective, the changes can be maladaptive. The maladaptive aspects of this example, however, can be short-lived, as cessation of intense training seems to remove the effect.

Exploring the responses that lead to a training effect can greatly enhance our understanding of fundamental processes in biology. These responses may actually have little to do with muscle itself; the training response explored by Oscai and co-workers (14) is a good illustration (Figure 2). Based on earlier work demonstrating a circulating triglyceride (TG) lowering effect of exercise in hyperlipidemic individuals (10), Oscai sought to characterize the time course of its response. I have taken the data from their study to show that with only 4 days of physical activity the initially elevated fasting TG levels were normalized. Further, the training response was lost in only 4 days of inactivity. This rapid time course of the training response may surprise those of us with a mental image that training processes should require extended time periods to develop. This short time course simply reflects the lability of the control system brought into play. More importantly, an identification of the factor or factors responsible for this effect could provide an understanding of the metabolic defect yielding the increased TG levels in the first place.

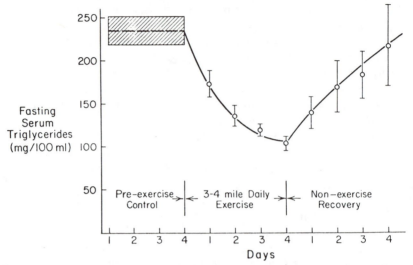

Figure 2 — Influence of exercise on fasting serum triglyceride levels in hyperlipidemic patients. Drawn from the data of Oscai et al. (14).

Even though working muscle exhibits an enhanced uptake of circulating TG (11,19), the changes responsible for the TG lowering effect shown here probably occur in the liver and are related to TG and lipoprotein synthesis (16). Additional examples of how training responses may be useful in assessing fundamental physiological processes have been apparent in these presentations. Thus, future work related to the dynamics of insulin binding and target cell response, neuroendocrine control, muscle mutability, and aging should provide insight.

I would like to present one final example for your consideration. Dr. Faulkner has pointed out the need to assess the control systems operating in the exercise and training responses. The importance of these analyses cannot be overemphasized, as they build upon the quantitative relationships between the variables brought into play to maintain homeostasis. Unfortunately, relatively few analyses are possible because we lack much information about the underlying processes. This is particularly true about training responses. For example, very little quantitative data are available describing, in any comprehensive manner, the influence of exercise duration and intensity on training responses.

Consider the situation of the increased mitochondrial content in trained muscle. The cellular process responsible for this increase is thought to be due to an increase in the synthesis of mitochondrial protein (3). However, the factor(s) responsible for inducing the change in synthesis is unknown. Further, any characterization of this cellular signal must be able to account for the observed training changes. At this point we simply know that repeated exercise bouts (apparently the longer the

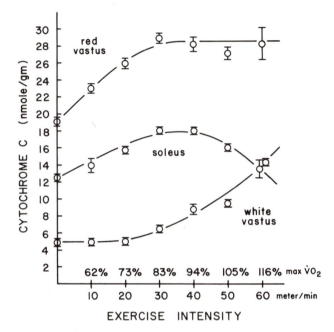

Figure 3 — Influence of training running intensity on the cytochrome c concentration in the three skeletal muscle fiber types of rats. Taken from the work of Dudley et al. (4) with permission.

better [5,18]) elevate oxidative capacity. It therefore seems essential to characterize the induced response with respect to the demands placed on the muscle. At present we must describe the controlled variables in terms of the exercise effort, using both exercise intensity and exercise bout duration. In recent work, Dudley and co-workers (4) sought to characterize the influence of exercise intensity, independent of the influence of exercise bout duration, on the induced increase in mitochondria in each of the fiber types by measuring the cristae component cytochrome c. This task was accomplished by training three or four groups of rats at each of these six running intensities for increasing durations necessary to describe a time-independent response. At each intensity, the induced change in cytochrome c concentration caused by exercise duration generally followed a first-order process. The peak asymptotic response for each running intensity was then used in Figure 3. Thus, this characterization of intensity is relatively free from exercise duration influences.

A number of interesting observations can be noted from these data. First, as should be expected the process of motor unit recruitment is important. A saturation response is observed in the FTR fiber type. Exercise intensity affected cytochrome c concentration up until approximately 30-40 m/min. This corresponds to an exercise intensity approaching

80-85% of the rat's VO_2max (15). Furthermore, increasing the running intensity induced no further changes in oxidative capacity. This response may simply reflect the influences of motor unit recruitment. For example, a progressive recruitment of the FTR motors in this red vastus section may have occurred until a saturation developed at approximately 30-40 m/min. If this interpretation is correct, then the more intense exercise efforts required by faster treadmill speeds might only be achieved by additional recruitment of the FTW motor units, an expectation supported by the response shown in the white vastus section at the bottom of Figure 3. Note that the cytochrome c concentration did not change during the easy exercise programs at 10 and 20 m/min, but increased disproportionally at the more intense running speeds. Again, this finding may be interpreted as a result of the progressive recruitment of these FTW fibers. Thus, as was so apparent from the presentation by Dr. Edgerton, the influence of fiber recruitment cannot be ignored when assessing the training responses in muscle. This fact obligates us to evaluate the response in each fiber type.

Second, the inducing signal within the muscle seems to be very different between fiber types and probably is modified by the inherent metabolic characteristics of the cell. For example, the relative increase in cytochrome c content was approximately 50% in the fast-red fiber, but nearly 200% in the FTW fiber during the most intense training program. This means that FTW muscle fiber's response, for example, in increasing the synthesis of cytochrome c, had to be far greater than that in the FTR fiber. Further, this relatively smaller response in the FTR fiber may be altogether reasonable if the training stimulus is at all influenced by the inherent metabolic characteristic (e.g., the oxidative capacity) found in the cell at the onset of training.

Additional characterization of the training stimulus is illustrated in Figure 4. It is apparent that whatever the cellular signal may be, it is lost or becomes ineffective as exercise bout duration is lengthened. In the case of the FTW fiber, running durations longer than approximately 60 min/day were ineffective in further altering cytochrome c levels. More importantly, it is clear that the influence of exercise duration and exercise intensity interact. Note that as exercise intensity caused an increased cytochrome c level, the run time necessary to achieve the peak asymptotic response was shortened. For example, the peak cytochrome c level was achieved with approximately 10 min running/day in the 60-m/min program, with approximately 15-20 min/day in the 50-m/min program and with approximately 30-60 min/day in the 40-m/min program. Thus, as exercise intensity increases, the events during the early stages of the exercise effort become more important. It is unlikely that progressive recruitment of more muscle mass within the FTW section could account for this effect, as simple recruitment should produce a family of curves with dif-

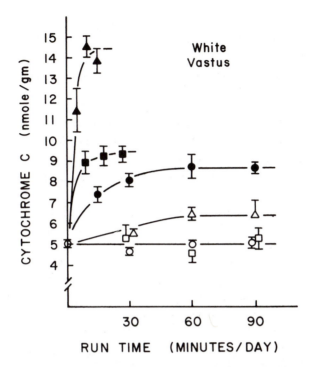

Figure 4— Influence of daily training duration on the cytochrome c concentration of fast-twitch white muscle of the rat when running: (○) 10-m/min, (□) 20-m/min, (△) 30-m/min, (•) 40-m/min, (■) 50-m/min or (▲) 60-m/min. Taken from the work of Dudley et al. (4) with permission.

ferent asymptotic values but with similar rate constants of change. Although this characterization of the exercise intensity and duration influences is, at present, limited to the overtly controlled factors of treadmill speed and exercise bout duration, the use of a well defined, easily measured response of mitochondrial change provides a useful system in which cellular events responsive to muscle use can be assessed as potential adaptive stimuli.

It seems clear, from the extent and diversity of information presented at the symposium, that in pursuing those future issues in exercise biology, we must: choose the proper model, characterize unambiguously, seek to assess control processes, and integrate from diversified approaches.

References

1. Ariano, M.A., Armstrong, R.B., and Edgerton, V.R. Hindlimb muscle fiber populations of five mammals. *J. Histochem. Cytochem.* **21**:51-55, 1973.

2. Baldwin, K.M., Klinkerfuss, G.H., Terjung, R.L., Molé, P.A., and Holloszy, J.O. Respiratory capacity of white, red and intermediate muscle: Adaptive response to exercise. *Am. J. Physiol.* **222**:373-378, 1972.

3. Booth, F.W., and Holloszy, J.O. Cytochrome c turnover in rat skeletal muscles. *J. Biol. Chem.* **252**:416-419, 1977.

4. Dudley, G.A., Abraham, W.M., and Terjung, R.L. The influence of exercise intensity and duration on biochemical adaptations in skeletal muscle. *J. Appl. Physiol. Respirat. Environ. Exercise Physiol.* **53**:844-850, 1982.

5. Fitts, R.H., Booth, F.W., Winder, W.W., and Holloszy, J.O. Skeletal muscle respiratory capacity, endurance, and glycogen utilization. *Am. J. Physiol.* **228**:1029-1033, 1975.

6. Folkow, B., and Halicka, H.D. A comparison between "red" and "white" muscle with respect to blood supply, capillary surface area and oxygen uptake during rest and exercise. *Microvasc. Res.* **1**:1-14, 1968.

7. Gans, C. Fiber architecture and muscle function. *Exp. Sport Sci. Rev.* **10**:160-207, 1982.

8. Gingerich, R.L., Hickson, R.C., Hagberg, J.M., and Winder, W.W. Effect of endurance exercise training on plasma pancreatic polypeptide concentration during exercise. *Metabolism* **28**:1179-1182, 1979.

9. Holloszy, J.O., and Booth, F.W. Biochemical adaptations to endurance exercise in muscle. *Ann. Rev. Physiol.* **38**:273-291, 1976.

10. Holloszy, J.O., Skinner, J.S., Toro, G., and Cureton, T.K. Effects of a six month program of endurance exercise on the serum lipids of middle-aged men. *Am. J. Cardiol.* **14**:753-760, 1964.

11. Mackie, B.G., Dudley, G.A., Kaciuba-Uscilko, H., and Terjung, R.L. Uptake of chylomicron triglycerides by contracting skeletal muscle in rats. *J. Appl. Physiol. Respirat. Environ. Exercise Physiol.* **49**:851-855, 1980.

12. Mackie, B.G., and Terjung, R.L. Muscle blood flow to different skeletal muscle fiber types during contraction. *Am. J. Physiol.* **245**:(*Heart Circ. Physiol.* **14**): H000-H000, 1983.

13. Maxwell, L.C., White, T.P., and Faulkner, J.A. Oxidative capacity, blood flow and capillarity of skeletal muscles. *J. Appl. Physiol. Respirat. Environ. Exercise Physiol.* **49**:627-633, 1980.

14. Oscai, L.B., Patterson, J.A., Bogard, D.L., Beck, R.J., and Rothermel, B.L. Normalization of serum triglycerides and lipoprotein electrophoretic patterns by exercise. *Am. J. Cardiol.* **30**:775-780, 1972.

15. Shepherd, R.E., and Gollnick, P.D. Oxygen uptake of rats at different work intensities. *Pfluegers Arch.* **362**:219-222, 1976.

16. Simonelli, C., and Eaton, R.P. Reduced triglyceride secretion: A metabolic consequence of chronic exercise. *Am. J. Physiol.* **234**:(*Endocrinol. Metab. Gastrointest. Physiol.* **3**):E221-E227, 1978.

17. Sullivan, T.E., and Armstrong, R.B. Rat locomotory muscle fiber activity during trotting and galloping. *J. Appl. Physiol. Respirat. Environ. Exercise Physiol.* **44**:358-363, 1978.

18. Terjung, R.L. Muscle fiber involvement during training of different intensities and durations. *Am. J. Physiol.* **230**:946-950, 1976.

19. Terjung, R.L., Budohoski, L., Nazar, K., Kobryn, A., and Kaciuba-Uscilko, H. Chylomicron triglyceride metabolism in resting and exercising fed dogs. *J. Appl. Physiol. Respirat. Environ. Exercise Physiol.* **52**:815-820, 1982.

20. Vihko, V., Salminen, A., and Rantamäki, J. Exhaustive exercise, endurance training, and acid hydrolase activity in skeletal muscle. *J. Appl. Physiol. Respirat. Environ. Exercise Physiol.* **47**:43-50, 1979.